HANDBOOK OF BEHAVIORAL ECONOMICS

Volume B · 1986

BEHAVIORAL MACROECONOMICS

To Leah and Lois

HANDBOOK OF BEHAVIORAL ECONOMICS

BEHAVIORAL MACROECONOMICS

Editors: **BENJAMIN GILAD**
STANLEY KAISH
Rutgers University
Newark, New Jersey

VOLUME B · 1986

JAI PRESS INC.

Greenwich, Connecticut   *London, England*

Library of Congress Cataloging-in-Publication Data

Handbook of behavioral economics.

Includes bibliographies.
Contents: v. A. Behavioral microeconomics—
v. B. Behavioral macroeconomics.
1. Economics—Psychological aspects—Handbooks,
manuals, etc. I. Gilad, Benjamin.   II. Kaish,
Stanley, 1931-
HB74.P8H36   1986   330'.01'9   86-10315
ISBN 0-89232-539-9 (Set)
ISBN 0-89232-700-6 (V. A)
ISBN 0-89232-701-4 (V. B)

Copyright © 1986 JAI PRESS INC.
36 Sherwood Place
Greenwich, Connecticut 06830

JAI PRESS INC.
3 Henrietta Street
London WC2E 8LU
England

ISBN: 0–89232–701–4
ISBN: 0–89232–539–9 (set)

Library of Congress Catalog Card Number: 86-10315

Manufactured in the United States of America

CONTENTS

VOLUME B (BEHAVIORAL MACROECONOMICS)

CONTENTS

PART III: THE THEORY OF THE FIRM

Section A: Entrepreneurial and Managerial Behavior

Section B: Intra-Firm Considerations in Productivity

Section C: Extra-Firm Considerations in Productivity

Section D: Industrial Organization

CONTENTS

LIST OF CONTRIBUTORS

Paul Andreassen

Department of Psychology
Harvard University

Bruce J. Caldwell

Department of Economics
University of North Carolina
at Greensboro

Richard M. Coughlin

Department of Sociology
University of New Mexico

William T. Dickens

Department of Economics
University of California,
Berkeley

Randall K. Filer

Department of Economics
Hunter College
The City University of
New York

Robert Forsythe

Department of Economics
University of Iowa

Roger S. Frantz

Department of Economics
San Diego State University

William Gerin

Department of Psychology
Columbia University

Benjamin Gilad

Department of Business
Administration
Rutgers University, Newark

Sebastian Green

The London Business School

Amyra Grossbard-Shechtman

Department of Economics
San Diego State University

Donald C. Hood

Department of Psychology
Columbia University

F. Thomas Juster

Director of the Institute
for Social Research
University of Michigan

Stanley Kaish

Department of Economics
Rutgers University, Newark

Philip A. Klein

Department of Economics
Pennsylvania State University

Howard Kunreuther

Department of Decision Sciences
The Wharton School
University of Pennsylvania

Harvey Leibenstein

Department of Economics
Harvard University

Alan Lewis

School of Humanities and
Social Sciences
University of Bath

Schlomo Maital

Faculty of Industrial Engineering
Technion – Israel Institute of
Technology
Haifa

John J. McGonagle, Jr.

Vice President
Helicon Group
Allentown, Pennsylvania

James N. Morgan

Senior Research Scientist
Institute for Social Research
University of Michigan

Stanley Schachter

Department of Psychology
Columbia University

Julian Simon

College of Business and
Management
University of Maryland

Martin Spechler

Department of Economics
University of Indiana

Burkhard Strümpel

Professor of Economics
Free University of Berlin
Berlin, West Germany

John F. Tomer

Economics and Finance
Department
Manhattan College

W. Fred van Raaij

Department of Economics
Erasmus University
Rotterdam, The Netherlands

Karl-Erik Wärneryd

Stockholm School of Economics

Sidney G. Winter

School of Management
Yale University

E. Yuchtman-Yaar

Professor of Sociology
University of Tel Aviv

PREFACE

The impressive development of classical economic analysis over the past 200 years has been accomplished with the use of extremely simple assumptions about the behavior of the human actors on the economic scene. The consumer maximizes his or her utility; the business firm, its profit. Today we know that powerful results can be obtained from analysis using these assumptions, but we also know something about the limits of those results for explaining the actualities of the economic world.

The limits show up, for example, in the current confusions and uncertainties of macroeconomists about government policies for combating underemployment and inflation. For lack of empirically founded theories of how economic actors actually make decisions in the face of uncertainty and complexity—where the assumptions of global rationality are no longer even approximately valid—neoclassical economics provides us with little help in understanding business cycles or the longer movements of economic development.

At the level of the business firm and the consumer, classical theory gives few hints as to how real human beings make real decisions in a world that rarely provides them with the data and computational resources that would be required to apply, literally, the theory of the textbooks. We need empirically valid theories of how business organizations operate, of how investment decisions are actually made, of how the levels of salaries and wages are determined, and of the growth and sizes of business firms.

In sum, we need to augment and amend the existing body of classical and neoclassical economic theory to achieve a more realistic picture of economic processes as well as a more accurate understanding of the equilibrium toward which these processes move.

Behavioral economics is the name we give to the research enterprise that seeks to meet these needs. It is no new thing. Alfred Marshall of *Industry and Trade* could well have labeled himself a behavioralist. And, of course, behavioral economics can claim John R. Commons, Thorstein Veblen, Joseph Schumpeter, George Katona, and many other distinguished economists of past and recent generations.

But behavioral economics, with its emphasis on the factual complexities of our world, has not always appeared as attractive as the axiomatized certainties of marginal analysis and subjective expected utility. Classical and behavioral economics have stood apart, eying each other nervously and suspiciously. They have put off the synthesis that we shall need to fully grasp the economic world around us.

I am encouraged, at the present time, by what I perceive as a strong ground swell of interest in behavioral economics and in closing the gap between behavioral and classical theory. With enough patience and diligence in exploring the empirical realities of economic processes, and enough ingenuity in modeling these processes, we will be able, in time, to return economics to the real world. I welcome this volume as a survey of the work that is carrying us in that direction.

Herbert A. Simon
Carnegie-Mellon University

INTRODUCTION*

Economists have known about psychology since Adam Smith's day. Indeed, it is possible that they were more aware of it then than now. From Ricardo on, the mainstream has gradually moved away from Smith's broad view of the full human experience to its present ascetic state where the bare bones of rationalism dominate and very little human flesh is to be seen covering them. For the past hundred years or so some economists have been warning other economists that they had better make provision to include psychology in their field or it would be in trouble. By and large, although the warnings were acknowledged, they were ignored when it came to the serious work of economics. Veblen's place in the history of thought is as an iconoclast; Mitchell is accused of empiricism without theory; J. M. Clark is better known for his work on the accelerator theory than on behavioralism. Rather than becoming more behavioral, mainstream economics opted for the positivistic point of view that the reality of the assumptions doesn't matter—only the results.

The trouble is, the results are turning bad too. Even while economic science is attempting to establish hegemony over child rearing, crime and punishment, mating and dating, and the political process, it is still no closer to accurately predicting business-cycle turning points than it

---

*Portions of this introduction are reproduced, by permission, from our article in *The Journal of Behavioral Economics* (Winter, 1984).

was a generation ago. Economists are in danger of moving to a situation where the only people who take them seriously are other economists, and even that may be in doubt.[1] There is nothing wrong with straining reader credulity about the irrelevancy of behavioral assumptions when the results are good. However, we may not have this luxury when the public's need for results isn't being met. Faith has its bounds.

Modern behavioral economics doubtless owes its revival to the ever-growing dissatisfaction with the direction economics is taking and to the recent work that offers a viable alternative. In this volume we combine the work of some of the veterans of the behavioral wars, such as Simon, Leibenstein, Winter, and the associates of George Katona, with that of the young Turks in the field who are seizing on the insights of Amos Tversky and Daniel Kahneman and carrying the battle to all subjects in economics. The theme that ties behavioral economists together is a shared set of *objections* to the mainstream tradition of economic theorizing. Among these objections are (1) a rejection of positivism as *the* methodological foundation for economic research, (2) a refusal to accept the use of deductive reasoning as a sufficient basis for a (social) science, and (3) a marked dislike of static analysis of equilibrium *outcomes* rather than disequilibrium processes. But their most important criticism of mainstream theory is (4) an objection to the *simplistic* economic model of rational agents exhibiting optimizing behavior.

As alternate points of focus, some behavioralists seek substitutes for conscious utility maximization (e.g., satisficing, heuristics, routines);[2] some examine the difference between optimizing behavior that individual members of an organization may exhibit for their own good and the less than optimal decisions this produces for the organization they belong to (the economic unit);[3] some have no objection to the utility maximization assumption but advocate a behaviorally modified objective function that reflects dissonance and framing biases found in the laboratory.[4] All agree that the neoclassical model of perfect information availability, optimal information processing, and the utility maximization that results is in severe need of overhaul.

It is often claimed that a common cause stated in a rejectionist mode is not sufficient to define a new field. Does this apply to behavioral economics? We think not for two reasons. First, behavioral economics is not a field in economics as much as a way of looking at the traditional fields in economics. Second, while shared objections bind us together, behavioral economics is indeed defined by a *positive* common denominator.

Evidence that behavioral economics is not a field in itself is found in the diversity of the fields of specialization represented in this book. James Morgan, Thomas Juster, and their associates at the Michigan Institute of Social Research engage in behavioral macroeconomics; Harvey Leibenstein, John Tomer, and Randall Filer do behavioral microeconomics; Stanley Schachter and his team of psychologists at Columbia University study what might be termed behavioral finance; Sidney Winter offers a behavioral theory of the firm; while Amyra Grossbard-Shechtman's research is in behavioral labor economics and Howard Kunreuther and his Wharton group are interested in behavioral public finance. In our opinion the best label for behavioral economics is to call it *an approach to doing economic research*—an approach that conforms to the following broad behavioral postulates (the positive platform):[5]

1. Economic theory must be consistent with the accumulated body of knowledge in the behavioral disciplines, including psychology, sociology, anthropology, organization theory, and decision sciences. This requirement is at the root of the behavioral economics studies attempting to improve the *assumptive realism* of economic theory (e.g., Simon [1978, 1979]).
2. Economic theory should concentrate on and be able to explain real observed behavior. This shift in emphasis to what actually happens rather than the logical conditions necessary for things to happen unites behavioral economists in a quest for a stronger descriptive base to economics. The survey-based research of Katona (1980) and his successors is a manifestation of this postulate.[6]
3. Economic theory should be empirically verifiable with field, laboratory, survey, and other microdata-generating techniques being acceptable means of verification. The recent rise in the popularity of experimental economics is certainly consistent with the "behaviorification" of economics.

Given these three postulates, it is not surprising to find Keynesians, post-Keynesians, institutionalists, Austrians, and some basically neoclassical economists with open minds engaged in behavioral economics research. Some critics may view this diversity as a weakness. We believe the contrary to be the case. The underlying strength of this new approach to economic theorizing is contained in its independent flowering in various places. Baumol observed in his 1981 presidential address to the American Economic Association that: "No uprising by a tiny band of rebels can hope to change an established order, and when the time for rebellion is ripe it seems to break out simultaneously and independently in a variety of disconnected centers, each offering its own program for the future" (Baumol, 1982, p. 1).

Baumol, of course, was referring to the new industrial organization theory of contestable markets, but his definition of a revolution is certainly just as appropriate for behavioral economics. Pursuing his point further, Baumol suggests that a true revolution should offer a novel look at a given phenomenon, provide a unifying analytical structure, and offer useful insights for empirical work and public policy.

Judging by the ideas presented in this book and by the work presently being carried out in Europe and the United States, behavioral economics fulfills all three conditions for a genuine uprising. It looks at micro and macro behavior in a novel way through its use of new empirical techniques and findings taken from a variety of disciplines. The emerging picture of economic man is definitely that of a less than fully rational, organizationally rooted creature who is systematically biased, often misinformed, always a role player, and who frequently violates the rationality postulates of consistent ordering and transitivity. When aggregated into groups he carries his psychology with him, making organizational behavior no more rational than that seen among individuals. But most important for economics, his behavior can still be modeled and these models tested empirically. Finally, in terms of usefulness for policy formulation, once we deal with real behavior with its foundation of real motives, real aspirations, and empirically determined dynamics, we have a better chance of judging whether public policy achieves the positive goals its proponents intended.

POLICY IMPLICATIONS AND NORMATIVE BEHAVIORAL ECONOMICS

One of the issues brought to the focus of attention by several works in this volume is the implication of behavioral research to normative economics. Several studies suggest a new rationale for government intervention in the economy, given the failure of markets to promote a classical optimization due to individual judgment bias. The long-run efficiency produced by the standard competitive model rests on the assumption of Pareto optimal allocation of resources, which in turn assumes agents who maximize expected utility. If maximization and full information are questioned, the normative criterion of orthodox economics is in doubt. As Nelson and Winter (1982, p. 356) say, "The normative properties associated with competitive equilibrium become meaningless, just as that equilibrium is meaningless as a description of behavior." Do the advances in behavioral economics therefore open the door for promiscuous intervention due to market failure? Not necessarily.

As early as 1945, Hayek's famous essay, "The Use of Knowledge in Society," contended that the most important function of the market system is "the utilization of knowledge which is not given to anyone in its totality." Thus the market is especially important in its function as a mechanism of coordination *because* people are imperfect, possess less than complete knowledge, and make biased choices based on unstable preferences. The assumption of full rationality, so essential to standard welfare theory, is crucial for the defense of the standard *competitive model* but not for the real world market system. Several contemporary economists have advanced the notion of markets as instruments (or processes) of economic experimentation and entrepreneurial discovery, with the related criterion of success being higher coordination (Kirzner, 1973) or Schumpeterian evolution (Nelson and Winter, 1982). As Hayek pointed out, the market in orthodox theory is just a computational device for the mathematical solution to the social allocation problem, *assuming full information* in preferences and the availability of resources to satisfy them. This is quite different from the view of markets as social instruments for "mobilizing all the bits of knowledge scattered throughout the economy" (Kirzner, 1973, p. 214). In short, conclusions regarding market failure and the need for governmental intervention are not the inevitable implication of behavioral economics research, but are the inevitable result of using the concept of market equilibrium as found in standard welfare theory.

Despite the disagreement on the implication of behavioral economics for normative economics, the usefulness of behavioral economics research to policy makers is unquestionable. There is little doubt, following the studies by Dickens, Juster, Kunreuther, Strumpel, and many others, that the *effectiveness* of public policy can be enormously enhanced by introducing behavioral considerations. The response of the constituents, as well as the effect of framing on the choice of policy options, are among the issues policy design must face. Without behavioral considerations even the best intentions underlying a policy may lead down that famous paved pathway to perdition.

With this volume we hope to provide economists with the starting steps in the long and tortuous journey to make economics more relevant and economic policy more effective. This is an ambitious—perhaps even pretentious—goal. But it is most worthwhile.

B. Gilad and S. Kaish
Newark, New Jersey, 1985

NOTES

1. See Filippello (1985) for a bleak assessment of economics from the business economist's point of view and Ulmer (1984) and Eichner (1983) for a view from within academia.

2. See Simon (1955, 1959, 1979), Kahneman and Tversky (1982, 1984), and Nelson and Winter (1982), as well as Heiner's (1983) interesting article.

3. See Leibenstein (1976).

4. See Akerlof and Dickens (1982); Gilad, Loeb, and Kaish (forthcoming); Cohen and Axelrod (1984); Spechler (1982–1983); and Kunreuther et al. (1978, 1983).

5. We are grateful to Alfred Eichner for his insights on this issue during a recent conversation.

6. As Philip Klein observed, by this postulate institutionalists such as Mitchell [were] behavioral economists long before the term was coined (see also Klein, 1983). We might add that several other schools such as post-Keynesian also have a more behaviorally oriented approach to economics.

REFERENCES

Akerlof, George A. and William T. Dickens, "The Economic Consequence of Cognitive Dissonance," *American Economic Review*, 72 (June 1982), 307-319.

Baumol, William J., "Contestable Markets: An Uprising in the Theory of Industry Structure," *American Economic Review*, 72 (March 1982), 1-13.

Cohen, Michael D. and Robert Axelrod, "Coping with Complexity: The Adaptive Value of Changing Utility," *American Economic Review*, 74 (March 1984), 30-42.

Eichner, Alfred S., "Why Economics is Not Yet a Science," *Journal of Economic Issues*, XVII (June 1983), 507-520.

Filippello, Nicholas A., "Presidential Address: Where Do Business Economists Go From Here," *Business Economics*, 20, no. 1 (January 1985).

Gilad, Benjamin, Peter D. Loeb and Stanley Kaish, "Cognitive Dissonance and Utility Maximization: A General Framework." *Journal of Economic Behavior and Organization*, forthcoming.

Hayek, Frederick A., "The Use of Knowledge in Society," *American Economic Review*, 35 (1945), 519-530.

Heiner, Ronald A., "The Origin of Predictable Behavior," *American Economic Review*, 73 (September 1983), pp. 560-595.

Kahneman, Daniel and Amos Tversky, "The Psychology of Preferences," *Scientific American*, 246 (January 1982), 162-173.

Kahneman, Daniel and Amos Tversky, "Choices, Values and Frames," *American Psychologist*, 39 (1984), 1-10.

Katona, George, *Essays on Behavioral Economics*. Ann Arbor: Survey Research Center, The University of Michigan, 1980.

Kirzner, Israel M., *Competition and Entrepreneurship*. Chicago: The University of Chicago Press, 1973.

Klein, Philip A., "The Neglected Institutionalism of Wesley Clair Mitchell: The Theoretical Basis for Business Cycle Indicators," *Journal of Economic Issues*, XVII (December 1983), 867-899.

Kunreuther, H., R. Ginsberg, L. Miller, et al., *Disaster Insurance Protection: Public Policy Lessons*. New York: Wiley and Sons, 1978.

Kunreuther, H., W. Sanderson and R. A. Vetschera, "A Behavioral Model of the Adoption of Protective Activities." Decision Sciences Department Working Paper No. 83-03-03, The Wharton School, University of Pennsylvania, 1983.

Leibenstein, Harvey, *Beyond Economic Man*. Cambridge, MA: Harvard University Press, 1976.

Nelson, Richard and Sidney Winter, *An Evolutionary Theory of Economic Change*. Cambridge, MA: Harvard University Press, 1982.

Simon, Herbert A., "A Behavioral Theory of Rational Choice," *Quarterly Journal of Economics*, 69, (February 1955), 99-118.

Simon, Herbert A., *Administrative Behavior*, 2nd ed. New York: Macmillan, 1959.

Simon, Herbert A., "Rationality as Process and as Product of Thought," *American Economic Review*, 68, (May 1978), 1-16.

Simon, Herbert A., "Rational Decision Making in Business Organizations," *American Economic Review*, 69, (September 1979), 493-513.

Spechler, Martin C., "Taste Variability is Indisputable," *Forum for Social Economics* (Fall/Winter, 1982-1983).

Ulmer, Melville J., "Economics in Decline," *Commentary* (November 1984), 42-46.

PART I

AGGREGATE VARIABLES

INTRODUCTION TO PART I:
AGGREGATE VARIABLES

Just as the rationality assumptions of economic man are what primarily upset behavioral microeconomists, there is little doubt that the rational expectations assumptions of the new classical economics is the *bête noire* of behavioral macroeconomics. In this part, two of the three papers on macroeconomics take dead aim at the rational expectations school of thought.

Klein considers the advent of rational expectations to be a retrogressive step for the profession on both positive and normative grounds. Keynesian economics, he argues, with its stress on expectations and uncertainty, is behavioral in nature. Furthermore, its behavioral assumptions were in large measure testable. Several generations of graduate students have measured the consumption function, for example. This behavioralism represented a step forward from the more narrow strictures of neoclassical formalism. Then along came Lucas and his followers to suggest once again strict rationality and market-clearing equilibria. It is these latter concepts that Klein characterizes as the reinvented square wheel. He argues that Keynes and Katona pointed economic theory in the right direction. The mechanistic properties of monetarism and new classical economics mark them as a diversion that would best be abandoned.

Klein's normative objections revolve around the new classical economics' set of priorities. He says that by espousing the idea that nothing be undertaken in the way of discretionary policy, the new classical econom-

3

ics implicity sets lowered inflation ahead of lowered unemployment in its list of priorities. True to his Keynesian preferences, Klein would have it the other way.

Kaish focuses on the factors underlying the business cycle. As a frame of reference he contrasts Mitchell's vision of the cycle as an inherent endogenous element of capitalistic societies with the Lucas view that the economy is stable and the cycle results from faulty signals given out by inappropriate monetary and fiscal policy. In the view of the new classical economics, information processing is perfect but the information received by economic actors is itself flawed. The Mitchell perception is that neither the information nor the decision-making process has any claim to infallibility. Kaish considers the possibility that the excesses found during business expansions are the result of faulty management decision-making by reviewing recent research on cognitive dissonance, heuristics, and prospect theory. He concludes that there is enough evidence that we characteristically employ "irrational" decision-making mental processes to cast serious doubt on rationality postulates in either a micro or macro world.

The Juster paper demonstrates the importance of knowing the intimate details of the construction of the macroeconomic data with which you work. In this case it is the National Income and Product Accounts and Flow of Funds data on saving. After disaggregating; correcting for statistical discrepancies; classifying as contractual or voluntary, asset, or liability; and comparing and contrasting the parts, Juster is able to offer clear answers to several questions that have concerned macroeconomists. His data tell us whether people save more when faced with inflation, as Katona contended, or accelerate their spending before prices rise further, as conventional economics would suggest. He addresses the question raised by Feldstein and debated ever since of whether or not social security cuts down on personal saving. His data also provide new insight into the important supply-side question of the responsiveness of saving to interest-rate changes. In each instance, Juster's findings support behavioral reasoning and are at odds with the neoclassical view of rational behavior.

Less behavioral work has been done in macroeconomic than in microeconomic areas. The reason may lie in the objections behavioral economists have to the underlying postulates of economics about rationality and economic man—both microeconomic by nature. However, macroeconomic policies can have a far more immediate and relevant impact on our lives. Efforts to explore the microfoundations of macroeconomics are therefore important, and it is doubly important, given the critical nature of the policy measures, that the microfoundations be right.

REINVENTING THE SQUARE WHEEL:

A BEHAVIORAL ASSESSMENT

OF INFLATION

Philip A. Klein

In recent years it has become common to describe macroeconomics as being in disarray. The combination of high inflation and unemployment during much of the 1970s in most market-oriented economies could not easily be explained by conventional Keynesian theory alone. This theory had been the most widely accepted explanation of how aggregate income, output, and employment are determined. This paper focuses on the relationship between current "neoclassical" explanations of inflation, which buttress the case for nonintervention by government, and the original classical explanation leading to the same policy conclusion. The role of rationality in both is considered and related to the phenomenon of "inflationary psychology," frequently cited as a major cause of the intractability of the inflation problem in the modern world. The attitude of behavioral economics to rationality as it applies to the inflation problem is stressed throughout.

I. "RATIONALITY" AS AN ASSUMED CHARACTERISTIC OF BEHAVIOR IN ECONOMICS

Pick up any basic economic theory book and one discovers that households, in the process of maximizing utility, and business firms, in the process of maximizing profits, are both assumed to act "rationally."

Viewed from the perspective of behavioralism, the notion of rationality in economics has always verged on circularity. This has been true at least since Jeremy Bentham declared that "nature has placed mankind under the governance of two sovereign masters, pain and pleasure. It is for them alone to point out what we ought do, as well to determine what we shall do" (Bentham, 1823). There is in Bentham's work no sure way to differentiate an individual's pain from his pleasure except to observe what the individual does and to assume that what is done implies avoiding pain and seeking pleasure. Rationality in conventional price theory has invariably been assumed at the outset to be a fact, and subsequent behavior is interpreted as though that fact were true. For example, in his widely used book on price theory, which appeared shortly after World War II, George Stigler (1947) noted, "It is said that an individual may have the facts concerning his desires and their means of satisfaction, and yet irrationally fail to act in such away as to maximize his satisfactions." He offers several illustrations but dismisses all as not worth really bothering about. In the end he dismisses the possibility of irrationality.

It is impossible to this day to find a discussion of the actions of economic agents that does not in similar fashion assume that they are rational. "To say the the consumer behaves rationally means that the consumer calculates deliberately, chooses consistently, and maximizes utility" (Watson and Holman, 1977, p. 67). As for imperfections in knowledge, "the gap between expectations and fulfillment are ... set aside in the theory of consumer behavior ... for the sake of simplicity" (Watson and Holman, 1977, p. 67). "Rational behavior is nothing more than action well-suited to achieve your goals.... Everyone behaves irrationally to some extent.... In view of the prevalence of irrationality, how can rationality be postulated in economics? ... Since it is the aggregate behavior of a great number of individuals that determines social results, the cumulative effect of even a limited degree of rationality tends to dominate over the unsystematic irrational elements" (Hirshleifer, 1976).

A slightly different approach, but one that comes to the same conclusion nonetheless, is the following: "Given the consumer's tastes, we assume he is rational.... In other words, he tries to maximize his utility" (Mansfield, 1970). But maximum utility is, by definition, nothing more than what it is the consumer in fact maximizes.

Finally, we consider the view of Lionel Robbins. In his *An Essay on the Nature and Significance of Economic Science* (1946) he developed the essential propositions in terms of which much of economics as a positive science has been developed in the last forty years. Robbins indeed wrestled with what rationality might mean and concluded that it did not mean "ethically appropriate"—he was always careful to see to it that economics remained *wertfrei*, to use Max Weber's word. Individuals did pursue their own values, presumably, he argued, in a way that was consistent to that individual. Individuals pursued their own objectives in purposive ways.

These illustrations serve to corroborate the contention that the assumption of rationality in human conduct has long been a pillar of mainstream economic analysis, especially micro theory. What are the implications of such an assumption? The question could scarcely be answered more eloquently or definitively than in the following statement:

> In the social sciences we are suffering from a curious mental derangement. We have become aware that the orthodox doctrines of economics, politics, and law rest upon a tacit assumption that man's behavior is dominated by rational calculation. We have learned further that this is an assumption contrary to fact. But we find it hard to avoid the old mistake, not to speak of using the new knowledge. In our prefaces and introductory chapters some of us repudiate hedonism and profess volitional psychology or behaviorism. Others among us assert that economics at least can have no legitimate relations with psychology in any of its warring forms. In the body of our books, however, we lapse into reasonings about behavior that apply only to creatures essentially reasonable.

This remarkable statement (which, we shall see a bit further on, can be applied to some of the newest theoretical propositions proffered to the economics profession) was written by Wesley Clair Mitchell (1918; reprinted in Page, 1968), a founder of American institutionalism (and a critic, therefore, of the behavioral assumptions of the classical and neoclassical economic theory), long before Robbins reformulated the propositions in the form in which, as we have seen, they remain imbedded more or less intact in modern economic theory. The passage originally appeared in 1918.

This paper will argue that the dubious assumptions about human rationality traditionally incorporated in mainstream micro theory are rather carefully eschewed by Keynesian macro theory. But they have recently been reincorporated in the "new classical theory," which, we are constantly told, has arisen to fill the "void" left by the "collapse" of Keynesian theory.[1] That Keynesian explanations are less than adequate for all modern macro problems Keynes himself would no doubt have been the first to suggest. But the treatment of rationality in modern theory is but one example of how progress and retrogression become confused in the history of economic thought.

II.   TESTING THE ASSUMPTION OF RATIONALITY

In mainstream micro theory, rational agents are assumed to have perfect knowledge. Perfect knowledge has two elements: first, the assumption that economic agents always know their own objectives perfectly and choose the most appropriate economic means at their disposal to attain them and second, the assumption that they have complete understanding of all existing information that might have a bearing on their decision.

For Lionel Robbins (1946), "perfect knowledge" was an assumption that turned out in the last analysis to be a convenience that in fact gets the economist closer to understanding the real world.[2]

Heterodox economists have long criticized both parts of this assumption, as the above quotation from Mitchell suggests.[3] It can be argued that George Katona, who devoted his life to testing the assumptions of economic analysis in light of the principles of behavioral psychology, was largely following in the footsteps of Mitchell. Institutional economists have long argued that the economy is not merely a passive receptacle into which economic agents pour their exogenously determined "wants." Micro theory to this day finds it surpassingly convenient to assume that "consumer tastes are given." yet, in a passage that any behavioral psychologist would have applauded, Ruth P. Mack (1952, p. 213) some years ago commented:

> In twentieth-century America, virtually everything that influences what a person is and how he got that way—a process of constant interaction between the evolving individual and his social field—influences what and when and how much he buys and saves.... Currently his buying is a function of what is, what he has, the recent history of his purchases, what others have, what he expects, what he hopes, the habits that he has established and very nearly anything else. The dynamics of consumption is in our society coextensive with the dynamics of personality.

In much the same vein Katona (1980, p. 13) once noted that contrary to the views of mainstream economists, behavioral economists had found that instead of the careful surveying of all the alternatives so as to maximize utility or profits, economic behavior frequently takes the form of "doing what has been done in the past." Today, as we shall see, surveys of entrepreneurs and consumers are an integral part of assessing the impact of behavior on economic performance.

Here precisely is the issue posed for microeconomics by behavioral psychology. Mainstream economics assumes away concern with the determinants of individual consumption patterns and indeed turns its back on the dynamics of personality, preferring instead to "freeze" personality in an endless series of *ceteris paribus* states, none of which need confront the impact of real factors on economic decision making. The factors include those involving the interaction of the economy itself and consumers. The truth then is that neither the consumer nor the economy is "sovereign." They influence each other profoundly, and to note that it is human and societal interaction that is sovereign is to open issues of want creation and resource manipulation that mainstream economists have never been comfortable contemplating, much less confronting.[4] Conventional welfare economics has, for example, almost always simply finessed the question.[5]

III. KATONA AND THE SQUARE WHEEL

In micro theory the previous discussion would be said to question the assumption that consumer tastes are given. For macro theory, which is of major concern here, the discussion calls into question the circular implications of welfare economics as evaluated with the surpassingly convenient use of the notion of Pareto optimality. Tastes are given and economic agents act rationally, in the sense that they do what they do because that is what they most want to do (otherwise they would have done something else). It follows then that the value implications of emergent resource allocation are that the system has efficiently maximized human welfare (given the tastes, technology, and resources available to the community). Has it? What factors might impede this conveniently arrived-at conclusion?

This is the stuff of which many critiques of mainstream analysis have been fashioned. Marxists and radicals have developed explanations around exploitation and the sheer imposition of the welfare objectives of the powerful on the powerless. Institutional economists have developed an analysis less dogmatically tied to previously selected class or other social mechanisms. Their misgivings are strengthened by consideration of the second aspect of the perfect-knowledge assumption. It is questionable whether consumers can in any meaningful a priori sense be said to know their wants. There is equal doubt about their complete knowledge of the extent of the means of attaining their wants, however they are determined. Classical and neoclassical theory routinely assumed perfect knowledge, defined to mean that the consumer or business firm knows all the alternatives before choosing the line of action the theory applies to the system being examined. For heterodox economists the major difficulty with this assumption was never that there are physical limitations to the ability of any economic agent to know all these options. (A caveat to the effect that resources are not entirely mobile, for example, is often encountered, but the possibilities of limitations imposed by this on the ideal quality of emergent resource allocation are rarely pursued very far.)

The deliberate feeding of misinformation to economic agents by those whose self-interest is thereby enhanced is a far more serious limitation, but it is virtually left out of mainstream analysis. Institutional economists are troubled, as are radicals, by the ambiguity of the implications for emergent value of the resources allocation that is achieved by pluralistic economies presumably devoted to democratic principles. They are equally concerned about the impact of concentrated power and purposeful manipulation of the many by the powerful on what the economy in fact achieves, rather than what it professes to achieve. In short, if rationality in mainstream microeconomic theory is the square wheel that heterodox economists have always argued it is, it was invented by classical and neoclassical economists because of its convenience and because it made the value implications of the theory so much more amenable to simple treatment. The more realistic perspective toward motivation and the subsequent actions of economic agents proferred by behavioral psychologists were largely ignored. One who devoted his life to suggesting that this particular wheel was indeed square was George Katona. If there is a single thread to the work and perspective of Katona it is that human behavior can never simply be taken as given in scientific analysis. That there is much appeal in the approach to human behavior taken by mainstream economic analysis is attested to by the tenacity with which its assumptions have survived. Katona took a far more direct approach: if you want to know what motivates consumers or business firms, there are ways to find out. One way is to ask them, and the Survey Research Center at the University of Michigan has been doing just that since 1946. A second way, of course, is to observe them, and presumably the observations of experts can reveal things about human motivation that might not be apparent even to the agents. This has, of course, been the approach of behavioral and experimental psychologists, but it has also often been the approach of political scientists, sociologists, and cultural anthropologists—in short, of most social scientists with the exception of mainstream economists.[6] (Use of the "qualitative indicators" in forecasting economic activity will be considered briefly below.)

In all this, Katona and his associates argued that human behavior is far more complicated than the simplistic assumptions of mainstream theory suggested. Katona was, in short, offering economists the possibility of following in the footsteps of other social scientists and was suggesting that the introduction of modern behavioral psychology into the body of conventional economic theory (primarily but not exclusively the micro theory we have been discussing thus far) could bring that theory closer to what a long line of heterodox economists (Veblen, Mitchell, and others from an earlier day; Ayres, Galbraith, Myrdal, and the institutional or evolutionary economists of today) have always argued is essential if theory is appropriately to confront the problems economic policy must face.[7] Katona thus knew that a round wheel can achieve its purposes more effectively in economic analysis as elsewhere.

IV.   RATIONALITY AND THE WHEELS OF MACROECONOMICS

Whatever else one may say of the macroeconomics introduced by John Maynard Keynes, it does not require the simple psychological assumptions of the mainstream micro theory we have been discussing. If one considers conventional Keynesian theory, it is readily apparent that the outcome of the analysis is heavily couched in terms of the nature of the psychological influences on economic agents.[8] The consumption function in general and the marginal propensity to consume in particular represent assumptions about consumer behavior based on observations, tested (presumably) by at least crude empirical methods by Keynes in the process of formulating them, and refined by a whole host of post-Keynesian economists, all of whom in varying degrees based their notions on empirical observations. The work of Duesenberry (1949), Modigliani and Brumberg (1954), Farrell (1965), Friedman (1957), and others has raised questions about the precise nature of consumer behavior,[9] but it would be fair to say that the overall nature of the consumption-income relationship, as promulgated by Keynes, has withstood the test of time. The inclusion of credit, expectations, and other factors has not changed its role.

Two other pieces of the Keynesian system, the liquidity preference function and the marginal efficiency of investment, are critical to the outcome of Keynesian analysis, and they too essentially imbed psychological assumptions in the theory. Unlike the consumption function, they have become controversial (again). One impact they have always had is to render the outcome of economic activity dependent on the view of the psychological perspective and motivation of economic agents at any given time. In the theory these were explicitly variable, unlike the unvarying assumptions of mainstream micro theory. It may be true, as some have charged, that having introduced expectations explicitly into his system, Keynes then made simplifying assumptions. But he is certainly clear enough (see Chap. 22 of his *General Theory* [1936], for example) in stating that the change in investment from period to period is far more likely to be brought about by changes in expectations than by changes in interest rates alone.

Let us make this assertion more concrete by introducing a simple and conventional diagrammatic exposition of the determination of investment in conventional Keynesian analysis (but with an unconventional twist). In Figure 1 we may suppose, for example, that the economy is overheating and this is an attempt to pursue restrictive monetary policy, causing the interest rate to rise from r to r'. There is in principle nothing

Figure 1. Expectations and monetary policy in a Keynesian world: a
behaviorial possibility.

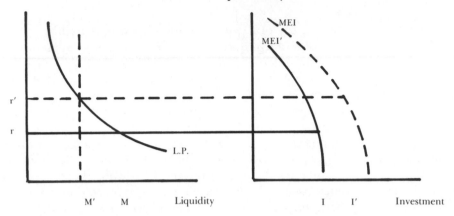

to prevent investors' expectations from becoming more optimistic at the
same time, so that rather than reducing them, investors attempt to increase investments from I to I'. One can argue the reverse quite as
easily—that an easy monetary policy could be offset by more pessimistic
expectations (indeed, the collapse in the marginal efficiency of investment is the classic Keynesian explanation of a major cyclical downturn).
While it may make sense to argue that, in general, factors furthering
pessimism would affect both investors and potential lenders simultaneously, there is also in principle no reason why interventionist monetary
policy could not be offset by contrary shifts in expectations. Far from
vitiating interventionist policy, however, such a possibility suggests that
stabilization policy might succeed in mitigating rather than exacerbating
instability. Unless one makes assumptions about stable velocity (as orthodox monetarists do) the brunt of Keynes' analysis would seem to
suggest that expectations play a central role in the operation of the macro
economy. No simple assumptions about how economic agents behave
can eliminate this source of uncertainty in the outcome of the interrelationships at work in the macro economy. Expectations, however, surely
play a role in persistent "underemployment equilibrium."

The upshot of these reflections, therefore, is that however much
Keynes himself may have simplified his own analysis, the psychological
underpinnings of Keynesian macroeconomics would appear from the
outset to have been somewhat closer to both empirical testability and
reality than those of mainstream microeconomics. At the very least they
were situated in macro theory in a way that made the theory itself amenable to alteration as further (empirical) research might suggest. Behavioral psychologists could conceivably be consulted, economic agents

could be tested and/or observed, experiments could be designed, and so on—all pointing toward improving both the realism and the relevance of macro theory. Such efforts could well be viewed as *wertfrei*, to return to the Robbins perspective, in the sense that understanding more about how expectations are formed and how they affect the interplay of macroeconomic variables could be achieved independently of one's views about the efficacy of interventionist policy.

In the heyday of post-Keynesian influence concerning our ability to comprehend economic problems and develop sound public policy, Paul Samuelson (1964, p. 361) was fond of talking about what he called the "grand neoclassical synthesis"—the "mastery of the modern analysis of income determination genuinely validates the basic classical pricing principles." The success, in short, of macroeconomic analysis (hence policy) was going to revalidate classical microeconomic analysis along with its mechanistic view of human nature. Twenty years have turned the direction of influence around 180 degrees. It is the "rediscovery" of presumed new profundities in the perspective of microeconomics that has threatened to transform macroeconomics.

V. INFLATION AND THE CRISIS IN MACROECONOMICS

It is commonplace today, as was noted at the outset, to argue that it was the inflation of the 1970s along with rising unemployment that produced the current crisis in macroeconomics. To note that Keynesian theory, circa 1936, might not be adequate to confront all subsequent macroeconomic problems, any more than Smithian and Marshallian theory can adequately confront contemporary modern micro problems, is to say nothing very profound. Indeed, heterodox economists have been railing against the inadequacies of microeconomics at least since Veblen. Despite the contributions of Chamberlin, Robinson, Fellner, and others to micro theory (not to mention the long list of empirical investigations into the ways in which the economy diverged from the competitive paradigm), microeconomics has been remarkably impervious to erosion from all these influences. It is odd, therefore, in view of the generally more realistic psychological basis from which macroeconomics began, that it has recently been seemingly *more* vulnerable. It is not odd, of course, if one considers the purposes of the attack on macroeconomics.

George Katona (1951, p. 257) once observed that inflation has been around now for two thousand years. He noted that the most common explanation of inflation in earlier times was that the money supply increased more than the real output of the economy, forcing up general price levels. Notes Katona:

> It was known centuries ago and has been repeatedly demonstrated in the twentieth century that these theories alone do not suffice. There have been periods of increasing money supply, and periods of decreasing supply of goods, in which prices did not rise. Moreover, the extent of price increases was usually not proportional to the size of the gap between the supply of money and goods. That there was no correspondence between the alleged cause and its effect has been amply demonstrated, for instance, in studies of the German hyper-inflation of the twenties (1951, pp. 258–259).

Katona, not widely known for his views on the causes of inflation, could expect to get considerable argument here from Milton Friedman, et al, not widely known for any other explanations of inflation. The difference, in part, is that Katona is not through with his explanation. He goes on to note that discrepancies between the change in money and the change in prices are explained by how people behave. People, for example, sometimes don't choose to spend money (i.e., velocity is not necessarily stable).

Katona suggests that a "purely economic" explanation of inflation is therefore modified by psychological factors. He goes on to note, however, that one can turn the process around and begin with a purely psychological explanation of inflation. Such an explanation of inflation would explain it in terms of mass hysteria:

> Certain opinions and beliefs may get hold of people, because of rumors, for instance, which may be wholly or partly unfounded. Correctness of the opinions is not essential; people's disposition to believe them alone matters. If people in general are anxiety-ridden, they may embrace beliefs that are not well-founded and may act according to them. Runs on banks may originate in that way, as well as mistrust in the value of money. . . . Widespread fear that the value of money will decline is then identified as the real cause of inflation. If it is prevalent, even slight economic causes, such as a small increase in the money supply, may bring about vast price effects, or if the fear is absent, even a large increase in the money circulation may have no effect on prices (1951, p. 259).

Katona is of course discovering what today we call "inflationary psychology." He concludes that neither the purely economic nor the purely psychological explanation is satisfactory. The purely psychological theory of inflation surely eschews the rationality we have seen embedded in much economic theory, and it captures well the phenomena of self-fulfilling prophecies with which the operation of modern market-oriented economies has long been replete. But clearly, "real" economic variables can intrude on these psychological mechanisms and condition the way in which subjective and objective influences on economic inter-relationships unfold.

VI. MONETARISM AND INFLATION

Katona's approach differs from the monetarist approach, which revolves largely around a single mechanistic relationship. "Changes in the behavior of the money stock have been closely associated with changes in economic activity, money income, and prices. The relationships have been stable, and the direction of change has often been from monetary changes to economic activity" (Friedman and Schwartz, 1963, p. 676).

There is scarcely any need now to present either the monetarist position or the evidence both for and against it that the economics profession has been debating for a quarter of a century. Suffice it to note that the question of the direction of causality has not been easily laid to rest. The implications for the central argument of the "long and variable lags" that continue to evidence themselves have made statistical evidence difficult to marshall convincingly (perhaps on either side); and the continued persistence of periods of time when the economy and the money supply move in spectacularly unmonetarist directions (e.g., 1982) has continued to raise doubts.

The implications of all this for the policy debates in macroeconomics are mixed. No longer can anyone claim "money doesn't matter," if ever indeed that was the case; it is difficult to claim today that "only money matters." Failures in monetary policy suggest a need for improvements in forecasting and analysis rather than no intervention, just as medical failures suggest the need for further research rather than no medical intervention at all.

For our purposes, the overriding fact about monetarism is that its most vigorous assault on behavioral psychology is only indirect—to claim it need not be considered. The "simple monetary rule," so beloved of true monetarists, suggests only that the psychological condition of economic agents is, in the final analysis, irrelevant. In the long run (provided we are not, as Keynes suggested, all dead) we shall be forced to reduce spending to noninflationary rates, *regardless* of the virulence of presumed inflationary psychology, if only the monetary authorities hold to "the rule."

Nonmonetarists have trouble with this, partly because of technical matters (Is velocity stable, or predictable if not stable? Is the pain of disinflation irreducible and/or unavoidable? Is the cure permanent or merely temporary—that is, cyclical?). All these questions reopen (if it was ever closed) the possibility that psychological factors must after all be incorporated into any lasting, efficacious, equitable, and feasible attack on inflation. But monetarism need take no position on behavioralism. There is not, in short, anything in monetarism to suggest that a behavioral approach to economic problems is necessarily wrong—just unnecessary. People might, in fact, behave precisely as Katona, in his "purely psychological explanation," suggests except that their inability to get money would thwart them in their erstwhile efforts to inflate the economy. Monetarism short-circuits a consideration of behavior.

In the final analysis, then, monetarism simply sidesteps the debate between mainstream economists and heterodox economists about the impact of behavior on economic activity and the appropriateness of the conventional behavioral assumptions heterodox economists have long criticized.

VII.   THE RATIONAL-EXPECTATIONS REVERSION[10]

Distressing as behavioralists might find the treatment of the psychological underpinnings of economic activity as viewed by monetarists, the views of the new group known as the rational-expectations school would appear to be infinitely more upsetting.[11] They manage to confront the question of human behavior frontally and to conclude that none of the worries of heterodox economists are justified. Indeed, they manage the heroic feat of making the treatment of human behavior in macroeconomics as sterile as it has always been in microeconomies. In this, all the implicit advances in the treatment of human behavior made possible through the Keynesian framework are, in effect, undone. The wheel has truly been reinvented in its original square form. A well-known recent macroeconomics text summarizes the rational-expectations position succinctly:

> The notion of rational expectations itself assumes that individuals use information efficiently and do not make systematic mistakes in their expectations. . . . One other assumption is made by those we identify as belonging to the school. It is that markets always clear, and that economic agents set wages and prices (given their information) so as to achieve full employment, maximize profits, and maximize economic welfare (Dornbusch and Fischer; 1981, p. 583; 1984, p. 566).[12]

We are back in the world of Jean Batiste Say. There is no involuntary unemployment, economic objectives are recognized by noting what economic agents in fact do, and optimal economic welfare is not only self-fulfilling but automatically recognizable through casual observation.

What about inflation? That is presumably a creation of wrong-headed intervention, however well meaning, by the monetary or fiscal authorities. Economic agents use all the information available to them at any given time. In its extreme form, one might argue that therefore a credible announcement to the effect that the money-supply growth rate was to be lowered, when added to the arsenal of available information, ought to suffice to end inflation.

Pushed to its logical extreme, the rational-expectations school makes the failure to eliminate inflation a failure of the general will to do so (and in this sense comes to a conclusion close to that of the monetarists). Monetarists blame macro failures on wrongly conceived interventionist monetary policies. Rational-expectations believers presumably must fall back on unannounced and inappropriate policies (monetary or other), having declared that announced policies will be discounted *ex ante*.

Behavioralists need not necessarily dismiss out of hand the psychological implications of the rational-expectations argument. An analogy may make the point. It might be argued that in planning a trip from Boston to New York City a driver might well take the announced speed limit of fifty-five miles per hour into account in assessing his total driving time (he might conclude that he would average no more than five miles over the speed limit) and that therefore the only speed limit that might alter his plans would be an unannounced limit, as for construction, where the limit is posted as thirty miles per hour and he would exceed it only by his usual five miles. While the announced limit might be "discounted," it does not follow that changing announced policies cannot alter macro behavior in directions sought by policy setters. Reducing the speed limit, it can be argued, has led to fuel efficiencies and reduced accident rates. Further change in the speed limit might alter the realization of these objectives further. The analogy can, of course, be pushed too far. The Keynesians have always laid great stress on the volatility of expectations, rather than assuming constant reactions to policies, whether announced or not. This does not necessarily vitiate the policies or the effort to set policy, nor does it necessarily suggest that no policy at all (or a simple announced policy) is preferable to a flexible policy stance. All it suggests is that reactions to policies, announced or unannounced, and however "most appropriate" a given policy change may be viewed, can be variable over time. Doing the best one can may still produce results that vary in their effectiveness from time to time in any case. Interventionists no doubt would argue in this way.

George Katona (1972, p. 555) once noted that "what contributes to the formation of any expectations about any variable is not restricted to what has happened to the same variable in the past.... The reasons for changes in expectations can be determined after the fact, but a change in expectations cannot be predicted from earlier objective developments."

Katona would presumably agree with the Keynesian emphasis on the volatility of expectations. Changing an announced policy might produce a change in expectations and therefore behavior, just as there might be changes in behavior without a change in announced policy.

The leading exponent of rational expectations is, of course, Robert E. Lucas, Jr. In the final analyis Lucas has led the way toward a return to viewing the macro economy largely from the perspective taken in the pre-Keynesian days. There is an implicit, and often explicit, belief that the market economy, left to its own devices, would perform more adequately than when intruded upon. He has declared that "the central theoretical problem of macroeconomics is to find out how "real output fluctuations are triggered by unanticipated monetary-fiscal shocks" (Lucas, 1981, p. 180). This effectively circumvents the Keynesian suggestion that output fluctuations might originate spontaneously (or at least in the absence of government intrusion) in the interrelationships that constitute the private sector. Lucas has declared that much (not all) of the unemployment that occurred in the Great Depression could be explained by rigidities in the wage-price adjustment process. "For the post-World War II period . . . the assertion that lags in price-wage expectations are sufficient to account for *all* observed labor-market rigidity remains valid" (Lucas, 1981, p. 61). (Despite all this, Lucas insists he is not saying the depression was not caused by aggregate-demand shifts.)

This means that the difference between the Keynesian perspective and the Lucas perspective could be interpreted as temporal. Keynes certainly left the impression that his "underemployment equilibrium" was a genuine equilibrium in the sense that it might remain for long periods of time (at least until aggregate demand changed). Lucas suggests that unemployment is a matter of lags in adjustment and therefore would disappear automatically in due course, in which case the underemployment equilibrium is not stable.

The case for intervention could be made on grounds that it might increase the speed of adjustment even if underemployment equilibrium disappeared on its own. Rational-expectations adherents believe this is not the case, however, and that, moreover, the situation might well be exacerbated by intervention, which is in any case not necessary.

The Lucas methodology may be illustrated by the way in which he constructs a model of the business cycle. "In contrast to conventional macroeconomic models, the model studied below has three distinguishing characteristics: prices and quantities at each point in time are determined by competitive equilibrium; the expectations of agents are rational, given the information available to them; information is imperfect, not only in the sense that the future is unknown, but also in the sense that no agent is perfectly informed as to the current state of the economy" (Lucas, 1981, pp. 179–180). The model developed on the basis of these assumptions is mathematically sophisticated and econometrically complex. The assumption that fluctuations are the result of monetary-fiscal shocks produces (assuming lags in information and an accelerator) procyclical price movements and nominal interest rates and procyclical fluctuations in the percent of output devoted to investment. Lucas concludes that one need not introduce "market failures" to account for business cycles, only monetary or fiscal shocks, and the implication that the simple monetary rule combined with a balanced budget constitutes the ideal stabilization objective for public policy is, therefore, strong.

Underlying rational expectations is a fundamental belief in the efficiency of private markets. This colors the attitude toward inflation. The implications of the rational-expectations approach for controlling inflation are, predictably, that efforts to offset unemployment by permitting inflation will in the end be self-defeating.

It appears that a policy designed to sustain an inflation can temporarily reduce unemployment, but unless the higher rate of increase in prices can be permanently maintained, a subsequent attempt to return to the original rate of inflation will result in an offset to the initial employment gains (Lucas, 1981, pp. 19–58, especially p. 34).

One must be impressed with the internal logic, along with the facile econometric manipulation and the precision, achieved in such analysis. One must also be struck by the reintroduction into macroeconomic analysis of the essence of the simplifying psychological assumptions that accompanied classical microeconomics and that Keynesian and post-Keynesian macroeconomics has explicitly attempted to make more realistic. Except for the assumption that Lucas's Economic Man lacks perfect knowledge, he differs little from the Economic Man introduced in the microeconomics from whence came the competitive model Lucas utilizes.

Moreover, if dropping the assumption of perfect knowledge is regarded as a move toward realism in defining rationality, in comparison with the microeconomic definition considered earlier, it is offset by the explicit assumption of efficiency in the use of information. Classical assumptions probably ruled out what Leibenstein (1950) once termed the "bandwagon effect," along with the Veblenian notion of conspicuous consumption. Neither suggests that consumers are always "efficient" agents. Clearly, the new classical "rational" expectations are similarly expectations in which economic agents react optimally to all available information and are not influenced by the myriad interactive factors that behavioral economics has always suggested can be crucial. In the rational-expectations world, individual agents react to changes in technology or taste or price, but the validity of the fallacy of composition and the concomitant possibility that *all* agents reacting to changes occurring may be different than *each* reacting individually to the same exogenous changes is not faced.

These factors appear to be crucial in the attempt to confront inflationary psychology. A consideration of inflation or inflationary psychology in Lucas's world is reduced to a consideration of how interventionism might produce or aggravate inflationary psychology. Were inflation to arise in the private sector, and were it ignored by the monetary authorities, market forces would presumably deal with it. How long such a process might take, and how much pain might be caused in the meantime, we cannot say. The model leaves us to conclude only that interventionist efforts to ameliorate such pain would be doomed mostly to exacerbate rather than mitigate the situation.

What the rational-expectations school has done, in sum, is to consider the impact of volatile expectations, which figure so prominently in conventional Keynesian and post-Keynesian macro analysis. It has recast them so as to argue that the psychological assumptions of pre-Keynesian theory are far more appropriate than heterodox economists have maintained. By combining rational expectations with competitive equilibrium (i.e., market clearing) the new approach to macroeconomics resembles that taken in conventional microeconomics and makes the charges Ruth Mack (quoted earlier) leveled at the behavioralism of microeconomics apply almost as well to this type of macroeconomics.

We cannot leave a discussion of rational expectations without a final comment on the policy implications. If its proponents are correct that economic agents use information efficiently and so have discounted all announced policies, why should the policy officials be exempt from similar rational expectations? In this case game theory of the sort introduced by Von Neumann and Morgenstern (1947) and applied to economic bargaining situations so cleverly by Siegel and Fouraker (1960) could be introduced into macro-policy debates. Present policy makers, *knowing* that announced policies will be discounted, can take this into account in announcing the policies they select. Depending on how "rational" rational expectations are assumed to be, this process of reactive realization can be adumbrated for any number of rounds, and anti-inflation policy could be reintroduced.

In the final analysis, of course, the impact of the rational-expectations approach is to return policy making virtually to the conditions it was in before economists argued that macro problems required concentration on more than the mere summing of micro units.

Lucas (1981, p. 235) in fact says this explicitly.

> What could be more natural then, than to view the task of aggregative economics as that of discovering which policies will lead to a more desirable situation, and then advocating their adoption? This was the promise of Keynesian economics, and... now... the scientific emptiness of this promise is more evident.

In this sense the rational-expectation approach contributes to the reversal of Samuelson's grand neoclassical synthesis referred to earlier. It has not been the efficacy of interventionist macro policy that has brought mainstream microeconomics back to a pivotal position, but the assumption that the micro units in the final analysis cope most effectively with macro problems. This conclusion renders interventionist macro policy either pernicious or futile. How one reacts to all this will depend in large part on how one reacts to the behavioral implications of the rational-expectations approach.

VIII. JUDGING THE IMPACT OF EXPECTATIONS

In sum, monetarists, the rational-expectations school, and conventional microeconomics all have one critical factor in common: their psychological or behavioral descriptions of economic agents are not the subject of either explicit observation or experimentation; they are customarily simply assumed. The logic of the analysis in all three cases depends heavily on the validity of the particular behavioral assumptions made. Macroeconomic analysis in the Keynesian tradition, on the other hand, includes the expectations of economic agents, particularly entrepreneurs, explicitly. Without information on the character of expectations—best attained by observation of their nature at any given time—forecasting macroeconomic aggregates including the inflation rate cannot very easily be done.

It is, indeed, precisely because expectations are critical to any realistic explanation of how agents make decisions and because by nature expectations are subject to volatility and influence from many factors— exogenous, endogenous, and interactive—that forecasting economic activity is difficult. How difficult is not easy to say, but Keynesians would argue that it is not so difficult that all interventions via discretionary policies must necessarily be eschewed because they exacerbate economic conditions.

Monetarists argue there is a direct link between money and economic activity—that the rate of change in the money supply, therefore, will eventually affect the rate of inflation. Expectations do not presumably affect the critical relationship. Rational-expectations theory assumes that agents use information efficiently and that only surprises affect behavior. Neither group suggests investigation of behavior. Empirical study of human behavior is no more required than it was in the neoclassical economist's assumption of rationality and perfect knowledge. In the macroeconomic system introduced by Keynes, however, expectations are critical, although how they affect the operation of the economy at any given time would need explicit and continuous study. In Keynesian terminology, for example, we have noted that the shape, position, and stability of the marginal efficiency of investment is always a critical factor in the stability and growth of the system. But the determinants of the marginal efficiency of investment indeed change, and so the phenomenon of changing expectations needs explicit attention continuously if one is to keep up with where the economy is heading and how strongly.

The so-called qualitative indicators—surveys of consumer buying intentions and entrepreneurs' attitudes toward the factors that affect their investment decisions—are today very popular as indicators of business-cycle fluctuations. This is particularly true in Europe, where the quantitative indicators of cyclical fluctuations long followed in the United States are just beginning to be readily available and of reasonably high quality. But surveys are also very popular in the United States. The Dun and Bradstreet survey of entrepreneurial profit expectations has been a fixture for many years. The Survey Research Center at the University of Michigan has been surveying consumer buying intentions for many years as well, and there are others.

These surveys can be helpful in assessing the expectations that are utilized in Keynesian or neo-Keynesian models of anticipated aggregate performance. It is perhaps interesting to speculate on whether survey results shed light on the accuracy of the rational-expectations group's behavioral assumptions. If monetarists tend to ignore behavior, the rational-expectations group advocates, as noted, *assume* behavior in their approach rather than regarding it as a subject to be tested or monitored itself. This is nowhere clearer than in the analysis of inflation and inflationary trends.

By now quite a lot is known about how economic agents adjust to inflationary expectations and, indeed, how inflationary expectations of future inflation will induce people to spend more now instead of later. This is an example, of course, of the self-fulfilling prophesies with which economics abounds. Subjective views alter objective reality in the direction of the subjective views. If people see prices rising, they may assume that they will rise further, which is what in fact happened, for example, in 1978 in the case of house and automobile purchases. This suggests that price increases generate fear of inflation and produce spending spurts, which in turn exacerbate inflationary forces.[13] This is not the only possible reaction to rising prices. It is possible to argue that rising prices create uncertainty. Zaltman and Wallendorf (1984, p. 86) suggest, for example, "When people are highly uncertain about their future economic situation, they will postpone expenditures on durables and will attempt to increase their level of saving." There is some evidence that this may have been the situation in the early 1980s. Certainly it is a way to link inflation to subsequent recession. When classical economists confronted consumer behavior, they coped with the assumption of "perfect knowledge."

Macro analysis in the Keynesian tradition spawned a large literature concerning the nature of the consumption function, factors that might produce discontinuities or shifts in the functions, and so on. Despite the overall stability in consumer behavior in the system, there is room for varying expectations and, therefore, varying impact on inflation and other cyclical indicators. The new macroeconomics would dispense with the explicit study of consumer behavior.

Surveys of entrepreneurs can be as useful as those of consumers in assessing the impact of expectations on aggregate performance. There have now been a good number of efforts to survey entrepreneurial expectations in general and to dissect their attitudes toward inflation in particular. The entreprenurial surveys, for example, reported monthly by the European Economic Commission (EEC), include a question asking entrepreneurs whether "selling price expectations in the months ahead are 'up,' 'unchanged,' or 'down.' " This is, of course, not the same as asking directly about inflation in general, but it bears on the question of how notions of inflation are formed and forecast because it casts light on an underlying factor—where attitudes toward price changes come from. Geoffrey H. Moore and I (1985, Chap. 5) analyzed the turning points in the "net balances" for the entrepreneurial replies—that is, the percent of the entrepreneurs who thought prices would rise less the percent who thought they would fall. These percentages, when examined on a month-to-month basis, are conceptually equivalent to examining the change in, say, the consumer price index. We can compare the turning points in the entrepreneurs' view of expected price changes with the actual price changes experienced by the economy. We were able to make this comparison in the case of Germany, France, and Italy. In all three cases we found that the turns in the expected price changes followed the turns in the actual price changes—on the average by six months in the case of Germany and France and five months in the case of Italy.

What this suggests, of course, is in line with what we have found to be true of many types of survey questions. The respondents extrapolate the past—in this case, they think prices will change in whatever way corresponds to their movement in the recent past. Entrepreneurs here appear on the average to expect the price changes that, in actuality, they experienced six months earlier. While expectations are critical variables, in the case of selling prices the influence appears to run from actual price changes to expected price changes, not the other way around.[14]

The role of expectations shows up in much of the analyses of surveys such as the EEC survey or similar surveys taken in the United Kingdom and the United States. Production expectations, for example, turn pessimistic before business cycle peaks in West Germany and the United Kingdom, but they do not turn before actual production starts to decline. In short, expectations about real economic variables appear to be influenced mostly by the behavior observed in the variable. The fact that the expectations change no doubt makes the declines less tractable.

This does not dispose, however, of the influence of expectations on the stability of variables—including inflation. There are many survey questions that suggest that entrepreneurs' attitudes or expectations are in line with quantitative variables. Shortly after entrepreneurs report that their new orders have turned up or down, for example, the quantitative data on new orders show the same movement. An increase in new orders by entrepreneurs partly reflects the entrepreneurs' response to the liquidation of inventories that typically precede a pickup in orders and partly reflects entrepreneurs' expectations that sales will increase, which typically succeeds the increase in orders. In contraction the sequence is reversed. In this way expectations about economic developments parallel the interrelations involved in the unfolding of cycles as described by Burns and Mitchell in their definition of cycles—one phase merges into the next. And as phases merge and one is succeeded by the next, there are a whole series of behavioral responses by, in this case, entrepreneurs that can be followed. Expectational responses need not be the same in every cyclical episode—indeed, the complex of factors influencing the attitudes of entrepreneurs, consumers, or other economic agents might well be the result of a complex of factors that can shift in subtle ways. This shift of factors makes the link between survey efforts and the ongoing forecasting of inflation and other factors critical. It can be combined with theoretical models that take explicit notice of the role of expectations. It meets resistance in those approaches that either ignore behavioral factors or assume them to be constant.

To say that qualitative indicators are useful, therefore, in monitoring the behavior of economic agents is to say, in Keynesian terms, that they shed light on the changing character of the marginal efficiency of investment, or the liquidity preference function, or perhaps the consumption function. These are, in the final analysis, behavioral variables that must be fleshed out on a continuous basis. It is in this sense that mainstream macroeconomic analysis is amenable to empirical investigation about the impact of behavior on a continuing basis.

IX. INFLATION AND THE PURPOSE OF ECONOMIC ACTIVITY

One of the not-so-subtle changes introduced by the new classical economists in recent years has been a shift in the relative importance of various macroeconomic objectives. Monetarists, supply-siders, and the rational-expectations school all appear to believe that an ideal goal for public policy ought to be to get the inflation rate down to zero. Their tolerance for unemployment is considerably larger. Even allowing for the ambiguity over how much unemployment is cyclical rather than structural or seasonal or frictional, it is clear that no one suggests that getting cyclical unemployment down to a couple of percentage points is a necessary goal for macro policy.

In 1948 Paul Samuelson, however, in the first edition of his Principles text, took precisely this attitude toward inflation (not unemployment).

> An increase in prices is usually associated with an increase in employment. In mild inflation the wheels of industry are well lubricated and total output goes up. Private investment is brisk, and jobs plentiful. Thus a little inflation is usually to be preferred to a little deflation (p. 282).

This attitude was far from unusual. It wasn't that galloping inflation (to use the term then popular to distinguish rampant from mild inflations) was unknown. It was just that tolerance for inflation was greater and tolerance for unemployment, lower. The subsequent introduction of the notion of a "natural rate of unemployment" provided a good rationalization for suggesting that unemployment rates can be targeted as unrealistically low.

It is probably not unreasonable to argue that getting the inflation down to zero is no more and no less difficult than getting the cyclical component of the unemployment rate down to zero. (Frictional unemployment could be reduced by improved information channels, and structural unemployment could be similarly reduced by the introduction of appropriate long-run policies.) If getting either rate down to zero seems a remote possibility, reducing both seems essential. In so doing there seems little to be gained by laying more importance on the inflation rate reduction than on the unemployment rate reduction.

Could the "natural rate of unemployment" be a convenient new classical rationalization for permitting millions to remain unemployed more or less indefinitely? Were we to revert to the 1948 Samuelson perspective, we could suggest that there is a "natural rate of inflation" below which it is unwise to attempt to push with macro policy. Were we to do this, it would have no big advantage over the view of the new classicists. They forget that economic theory and policy are best viewed as in the service of economic agents, including the unemployed. Inflation is an indication of difficulties showing up in one major measure of economic activity. As such, a choice between a little inflation or a little unemployment ought to be tilted toward the human rather than the measuring-rod variable. Economies, designed for serving human ends, ought, after all, to place higher priorities on their human participants than on the measures of activity, of which prices are but one. Obviously, high inflation is intolerable, but why should the inflation standards be higher than the employment standards in an economy designed to serve human beings? So viewed, we can see how the new classicists end up, all of them, tolerating performance in the economy which leaves many disadvantaged or failing to participate, rather than permitting the introduction of standards of performance established by the participants by means of some presumably democratic process of choice.

X. CONCLUSIONS

One need not claim that any particular post-Keynesian model is definitive in order to note that a Keynesian approach has the singular virtue of permitting the inclusion of changing human behavior over time and in differing circumstances. Its view of human behavior is also amenable to empirical investigation.

We have argued here that neoclassical economic theory (especially micro theory) largely ignored the question of whether its assumptions about human behavior were true. This is scarcely a new charge. Conventional theory to this day would argue that the insights of the theory are useful despite the unvarying and unrealistic nature of the behavioral assumptions made. Opinion about this might vary, but one question that could be investigated is whether other approaches that include more realistic behavioral assumptions could be developed that shed as much or more light on the problems being investigated.

Monetarists argue that behavior is ultimately overwhelmed by the press of inevitable and unavoidable objective factors at work in the economy. Believers in rational expectations assume information is used efficiently and that shocks are all that can change the behavior by real magnitudes.

This is a proposition that appears to be testable, but there does not seem to be a penchant for that kind of investigation among followers of the rational-expectations school. Rather they argue, like classical theorists, that much that is interesting and useful can be learned about the real world by operating within the fairly rigid assumptions of their models. Without even questioning that insights have been made, we may legitimately ask whether more could be learned, or learned faster, about how the economy generates inflation, for example, were more realistic behavioral assumptions made. George Katona (1975, pp. 6–7) once wrote:

> Traditional economics might be more accurately described as 'economics with mechanistic psychology' rather than as 'economics without psychology.' But the latter is equally appropriate if by 'psychology' is meant the scientific discipline as we know it today and not a priori psychological assumptions. Psychology is an empirical discipline. It acknowledges one source of evidence only, namely, controlled observation. It aims at the establishment of relationships between specific conditions and specific forms of behavior, rather than general laws of human nature. Because of the pliability and modifiability of behavior, psychology is skeptical about broad generalizations that posit invariable relationships.

It has been our purpose here to suggest that this description of "traditional economics," by which Katona obviously meant microeconomics, represents a description as well of the "new classical theory"—of which Keynesian macroeconomics was far less guilty. Controlled observations could indeed be made of the psychological assumptions lying back of the consumption function, the liquidity preference function, and, most particularly, the marginal efficiency of investment. Much of the work done in macroeconomic theory in the Keynesian tradition in the past half century has taken the form of controlled observation designed to shed light on the nature of these functions—their shape, position, and so on. This is precisely what both monetarism and rational expectations have turned their figurative backs on.

It is the singular achievement of these "new classicists" that the behavioral flexibility and amenability to empirical analysis, which had long been two of the strengths of macroeconomic theory, has been excised in preference to the relative aridity of behavioral assumptions patterned on those of mainstream microeconomic theory. Behavioralists can conclude only that we have made progress by going backwards. We have reinvented the square wheel.

ACKNOWLEDGMENT

I would like to thank Benjamin Gilad, Ruth P. Mack, and Monroe Newman for their helpful comments on an earlier draft.

NOTES

1. For example, "Currently the field of macroeconomics is involved in sifting through the dust after the collapse of the Keynesian system to determine whether only parts of the system are worth saving or whether the system itself will rise again like the phoenix" (Boyes, 1984, p. iv).

2. "Perfect foresight [is one of the number of assumptions] which it is sometimes convenient to postulate.... The purpose of these assumptions is...to enable us to study, in isolation, tendencies which, in the world of reality, operate only in conjunction with many others and then...to turn back to apply the knowledge thus gained to the explanations of more complicated situations" (Robbins, 1946, p. 94).

3. I made a similar point myself some years ago, writing, "We have noted a rather long list of economists—Veblen, Knight, Duesenberry, Leibenstein, Galbraith, and Lancaster, among others—who have made significant contributions to our thinking about demand. However, despite their efforts...the basic presentation of demand from Marshall's eighth edition to Samuelson's eighth edition has undergone virtually no fundmental change" (Klein, 1973, p. 231).

4. Heterodox economists have, of course considered such matters of central concern for many years. Many years ago Clarence Ayres (1944, p. 84) noted, "If anything is known in the field of the social sciences today, it is that 'wants' are not primary. They are not inborn physical mechanisms and they are certainly not spiritual attributes. They are social habits." This is, of course, precisely what, in part, John Kenneth Galbraith (1967, chap. XIX) was alluding to when he coined the phrase "the revised sequence." He was noting that many economic agents have an interest in what consumer wants are and instead of regarding them as "sovereign," they mobilize the mechanisms of society to affect, if indeed not to determine, wants.

5. For example, "we will assume in the present study that individual values are taken as data and are not capable of being altered by the nature of the decision process itself." This is, of course the standard view of economic theory (though the unreality of this assumption has been asserted by such writers as Veblen, J. M. Clark, and Knight). "...If individual values can themselves be affected by the method of social choice, it becomes much more difficult to learn what is meant by one method's being preferable to another ..."(Arrow, 1963).

6. For a consideration of this view of the relationship of economic methodology to that of other social sciences, see Klein (1980, pp. 871–893).

7. Modern heterodox economists have, for close to twenty years, been applying their perspective to economic analysis in the pages of the *Journal of Economic Issues.*

8. Indeed, Keynes' *General Theory* (1936) is peppered with passages referring to the explicit consideration of psychological variables and to the concern for the factors that nowadays are often the subject of surveys. (See "Expectation as Determining Output and Employment" (Chap. 5), "The Propensity to Consumer: The Subjective Factors" (Chap. 9), "The State of Longterm Expectations" (Chap. 12), and "Psychological and Business Incentives to Liquidity" (Chap. 15), to take examples only from chapter titles.)

9. One of the ironies of recent economic debate is that Friedman is quite willing to contemplate complicating the theory of consumption by introducing expectations and so making consumption a function of more than merely current income, but he appears unwilling to permit expectations to play a similar role in investment, preferring the "simple monetary rule" to a theory recognizing that changing entrepreneurial expectations may influence investment decisions as much as or more than changes in the cost of investment as reflected in interest-rate changes. (See the subsequent discussion of monetarism.)

10. There is diversity in all schools of thought, including rational expectations. We concentrate here on what appears to be central to the group.

11. In addition to the works cited in the discussion below, the reader may consult the *Journal of Money, Credit and Banking*, November 1980, Part II, which is devoted to the papers presented at a seminar sponsored by the American Enterprise Institute and dealing with rational expectations.

12. In the 1984 edition the authors substitute *utility* for *welfare*, and the argument is somewhat prolix.

13. The house and automobile buying spurt was discussed by F. Thomas Juster in "An Expectational View of Consumer Spending Prospects," *Journal of Economic Psychology*, Vol. 1, June 1981, pp. 87–103. It is in line with the traditional view of reaction to inflation discussed, for example, in George Katona's "The Psychology of Inflation" (1976, pp. 9–19). Our discussion here draws upon Zaltman and Wallendorf, *The Economics of Consumption*, Chapter 4.

14. This is in line with the view, however, known as adaptive expectations rather than rational expectations.

REFERENCES

Arrow, Kenneth, J., *Social Choice and Individual Values*, 2nd ed. New York: John Wiley & Sons, 1963.

Ayres, Clarence E., *The Theory of Economic Progress*. Chapel Hill, NC: University of North Carolina Press, 1944.

Bentham, Jeremy, *An Introduction to the Principles of Morals and Legislation*, 1823. (Reprinted in Alfred N. Page, *Utility Theory*. New York: John Wiley & Sons, 1968, p. 3.)

Boyes, William J., *Macroeconomics, The Dynamics of Theory and Policy*. Cincinnati, OH: South Western Publishing Company, 1984.

Burns, Arthur F. and Wesley C. Mitchell, *Measuring Business Cycles*. New York: National Bureau of Economic Research, 1947.

Dornbusch, Rudiger, and Stanley Fischer, *Macroeconomics*, 2nd ed. New York: McGraw-Hill 1981 (3rd ed., 1984).

Duesenberry, James S., *Income, Savings, and the Theory of Consumer Behavior*. Cambridge, MA: Harvard University Press, 1949.

Farrell, M. J., "The New Theories of the Consumption Function," *Economic Journal*, 1959. (Reprinted in R. A. Gordon and L. R. Klein, *Readings in Business Cycles*, American Economics Association, Richard D. Irwin, Inc., 1965.

Friedman, Milton, *A Theory of the Consumption Function*. New York: National Bureau of Economic Research, Inc.; Princeton, NJ: Princeton University Press, 1957.

Friedman, Milton, and Anna Schwartz, *A Monetary History of the United States*. New York: National Bureau of Economic Research, Inc.; Princeton, NJ: Princeton University Press, 1963.

Galbraith, John Kenneth, *The New Industrial State*. Boston: Houghton Mifflin, 1967.

Hirshleifer, Jack, *Price Theory and Its Applications*. Englewood Cliffs, NJ: Prentice-Hall, 1976.

Katona, George, *Essays on Behavioral Economics*. Ann Arbor, MI: Survey Research Center, 1980.

Katona, George, *Psychological Analysis of Economic Behavior*, New York, McGraw-Hill Book Company, 1951.

Katona, George, "The Psychology of Inflation," in R. Curtin, ed., *Surveys of Consumers*

1974–1975: Contributions to Behavioral Economics. Ann Arbor, MI: Institute for Research, 1976.

Katona, George, *Psychological Economics.* New York: Elsevier, 1975.

Katona, George, "Theory of Expectations," in B. Strumpel, J.N. Morgan, and E. Zahn, eds., *Essays in Honor of George Katona.* San Francisco: Jossey-Bass, 1972, p. 555.

Keynes, John Maynard, *The General Theory of Employment, Interest, and Money.* New York: Harcourt Brace and Company, 1936.

Klein, Philip A., "Confronting Power in Economics: A Pragmatic Evaluation," *Journal of Economic Issues*, XIV, no. 4 (December 1980), pp. 871–896.

Klein, Philip A., "Demand Theory and the Economist's Propensity to Assume," *Journal of Economic Issues*, VII, no. 2 (June 1973), pp. 209–239.

Klein, Philip A., and Geoffrey H. More, *Monitoring Business Cycles in Market-Oriented Countries.* Cambridge, MA: National Bureau of Economic Research, Ballinger Press, 1985.

Leibenstein, Harvey, "Bandwagon, Snob, and Veblen Effects in the Theory of Consumers' Demand," *Quarterly Journal of Economics*, 14 (May 1950): 183–207.

Lucas, Robert E., Jr., *Studies in Business Cycle Theory.* Cambridge, MA: The MIT Press, 1981.

Mack, Ruth P., "Economics of Consumption," in Bernard Haley, ed., *A Survey of Contemporary Economics*, Vol. 2. Homewood, IL: Richard D. Irwin, 1952.

Mansfield, Edwin, *Macroeconomics, Theory and Applications.* New York: W. W. Norton, 1970.

Mitchell, Wesley Clair, "Bentham's Felicific Calculus," *Political Science Quarterly*, XXXIII (June 1918), 161–183. (Reprinted in Alfred N. Page, *Utility Theory.* New York: John Wiley & Sons, 1968.)

Modigliani, Franco, and Richard Brumberg, "Utility Analysis and the Consumption Function: An Interpretation of Cross Section Data," in *Post-Keynesian Economics.* New Brunswick, NJ: Rutgers University Press, 1954.

Robbins, Lionel, *The Nature and Significance of Economic Science.* London: Macmillan, 1946.

Samuelson, Paul A., *Economics*, 1st ed. New York: McGraw-Hill, 1948 (6th ed., 1964).

Siegel, Sidney, and Lawrence E. Fouraker, *Bargaining and Group Decision Making.* New York: McGraw-Hill, 1960.

Stigler, George J., *The Theory of Price.* New York: Macmillan, 1947.

Strumpel, Burkhard, James N. Morgan, and Ernest Zahn, eds., "Human Behavior in Economic Affairs," *Essays in Honor of George Katona.* San Francisco: Jossey-Bass, 1972.

Von Neumann, J., and O. Morgenstern, *Theory of Games and Economic Behavior*, 2nd ed. Princeton, NJ: Princeton University Press, 1947.

Watson, Donald S., and Mary A. Holman, *Price Theory and Its Uses*, 4th ed. Boston: Houghton Mifflin, 1977, p. 67.

Zaltman, G., and M. Wallendorf, *The Economics of Consumption*, 2nd ed., 1984.

BEHAVIORAL ECONOMICS IN THE THEORY OF THE BUSINESS CYCLE

Stanley Kaish

A mathematician's mood exercises no influence upon his solution of an algebraic equation; but it does affect his opinion about the advisability of buying the bonds offered him.

—*Wesley C. Mitchell*

The business cycle seems to be one of the enduring constants of economic life. Despite repeated reports of its demise—most recently during the 1960s—recession and expansion and recession again follow one another inexorably. They not only do so in the United States but in profit-based economies all over the world, and have for hundreds of years. The cycle resists the best efforts of policy makers whose programs are intended to promote stability, of businessmen's staffs hired to anticipate and deal with cyclical turning points, and of individual investors who scan the papers and buy the services of "experts" in hope of profits. Despite all these efforts, cyclical turns come and go, and in their wake the economic landscape is left littered with billions in lost assets.

The economic literature has suffered no scarcity of explanations of the cyclical phenomenon. There are overinvestment theories (Hayek, Mises, Machlup); underconsumption theories (Malthus, Marx, Hobson); money-expansion theories (Friedman, Hawtrey, Bruner); inventory-adjustment theories (Abramowitz, Metzler); multiplier, accelerator the-

31

ories (Hicks, Harrod-Domar, Samuelson); agricultural theories (Jevons, Moore); political machinations theories (Nordhaus, Macrae) and so on.[1] For the most part, these theories deal with the roles different institutions such as banks, corporations, and government play and problems that arise when the timing of the activities of one sets up a course of action in another that is ultimately unsustainable. The analyses tend to be aggregative and the processes, once under way, mechanical and inevitable.

Little learning takes place, and such adaptation as does occur is retrospective rather than prospective, leaving tomorrow's actors prepared for yesterday's script. Scant attention is paid to what might be called behavioral issues. Decisions are made by institutions and not individual people within them. This dehumanizing of the institutions, we will see, is a serious omission. The position taken in this paper is that the business cycle is caused by faulty decisions, and that faulty decisions are made by people, not institutions. Unless we understand the biases built into people's decision making, we are unlikely to grasp the nature of the cyclical phenomenon.

Wesley Mitchell (1941) saw prosperity ending as a result of excesses in production, hiring, borrowing, and related activities. As decisions to expand impinge on capacity limits of the labor force, bank lending ability, and capital stock during a business expansion, materials prices, wages, and interest rates encroach on selling prices, thereby reducing profit. The reduction in profit thereby makes future investment appear less attractive and sets off a wave of diminishing demand. Higher interest rates reduce the capitalized value of collateral on loans, discouraging further lending and, indeed, inducing foreclosure on some loans that are outstanding. Full employment brings poorly suited workers into the economy and reduces productivity at the margin to such an extent that it becomes unprofitable to hire further. All these developments spread from the capital goods and raw materials industries to the consumer sector, diffusing throughout the economy and creating a general slowing that worsens into recession. Thus businessmen's decisions to expand production, borrow, and hire beyond sustainable levels create the downturn.[2]

One result of a downturn caused by wrong decisions is to make other, otherwise sound, decisions also wrong. During the recession year of 1982, failing businesses left nearly $16 billion in liabilities. During August of that year alone more than 300 major firms with liabilities of $3 billion went out of business. Most of these represented business decisions made wrong by the general downturn in business activity.[3]

Why were so many incorrect business decisions made in the face of the widely known and easily available facts concerning the business cycle? After all, the index of leading indicators is constructed and widely pub-

lished by the Department of Commerce. Each month this figure is reported in the financial press. As if that wasn't enough, *Business Week* now
publishes a weekly index of leading indicators.[4] It is well known to economic historians that business expansions during the postwar period
have averaged only about four years in length each to be followed by a
year of contraction. Avid newspaper readers cannot avoid the news when
the index of leading indicators gives a convincing signal of economic
reversal. Those who believe that "this time is different" should be aware
of what several studies of economic indicators have confirmed: that while
particular series included in the official list of leading indicators have
been modified from time to time, the underlying economic relationships
have held constant over the years. Average work week, stock prices, and
new orders received led general business activity 50 years ago and they
lead it today. The behavioral question is why, in spite of the availability
of this information and its documented usefulness, businessmen are
surprised when business conditions change. Why is it that the best decision makers in the country, who modern theory maintains are able to
incorporate all knowable information into their decisions, do not behave
as if they knew that markets periodically languish and that when they
do, sales, jobs, capital, and, of course, sleep will be lost?

I. INFORMATION IN THE BUSINESS CYCLE

Two possibilities concerning faulty decision making suggest themselves.
Either (1) inadequate or inaccurate information is being processed in
the best way possible to produce the bad result, or else (2) accurate and
adequate information is being improperly processed. The first proposition is consistent with the rational-expectations view of the economy.
The second is consistent with the behavioral viewpoint and will be discussed at length in this paper. In the rational-expectations model, the
economy is in continuous market-clearing equilibrium. All systematically
generated information is known and regularly discounted by adjustments in prices, interest, and other nominal values. Real values, however,
do not respond to systematically occurring events. They adjust to secular
changes in production capacity, unexpected policy changes, and random
events occurring in the system. The result of this is the well-known
conclusion that announced public policy efforts designed to alter real
levels of employment or output through aggregate demand manipulation will fail, because they will be anticipated and countered by offsetting
supply adjustments.

Given the assumption that adjustments are rapid and equilibrium
maintained, it is hard to find an explanation of the business cycle in

rational-expectations theory. Lucas (1980) has drawn on the Arrow-Debreu general equilibrium model to suggest one possible explanation. He suggests that different parts (islands) of the economy receive different information and that the adjustments are made in terms of local, rather than global, awareness. Each economic unit has better information concerning its own activities than of others. When a single seller perceives an increase in demand leading to higher prices of his product, he doesn't know if the increase in price is occurring everywhere in the economy, as the result of a general inflation, or if it is a microeconomic shift in demand for his product alone. If it is the former, his rational response would be an increase in price; if the latter, an increase in output. Lucas suggests businessmen may mistakenly interpret the demand bulge produced by expansionary monetary policy as an increase in relative prices. As a result, they mistakenly expand output, thereby creating a business boom. It is only later on that they learn that their interpretation of the demand rise was in error, and the subsequent downward adjustment of output creates the broadly experienced business contraction.

This information-misperception theory of the business cycle is criticized on two major lines: first, as we have pointed out, there is abundant public information available in the form of newspapers and government reports that decision makers could access costlessly, or certainly at a cost modest enough to make it worth doing; and second, the duration of business-cycle phases, four years for an average expansion, suggests that there must be almost *invincible ignorance* on the part of the islanders for the expansion to result solely from their failure to recognize a generalized inflation rather than a microeconomic shift in demand. The facts suggest that there is more than enough time for an error in perception to be clarified (see Okun, 1980). Therefore, given the unlikelihood of the misperception theory being a reasonable model of cyclical behavior, we turn away from the idea that humans are perfect processors of imperfect information to the other possibility: humans as imperfect processors of information, perfect or otherwise.

II. THE ROLE OF PSYCHOLOGY IN BUSINESS-CYCLE THEORY

Once we turn to the idea of business cycle as the result of individual decisions made by business managers, labor leaders, and bankers instead of an impersonal convergence of disequilibrium forces, a world of new approaches opens up. Psychologists have been just as fascinated with decision making under conditions of uncertainty as have economists and have studied the topic at great length in the laboratory. Their findings on how people deal with risk and uncertainty in their daily lives differ greatly from the axiomatic assumption of economics that orderings of preference are consistent, transitive, and subject to well-behaving utility functions. Instead the psychologists have found all manner of anomalies: purposeful avoidance of useful information; choice reversal; intransitivity; escalating commitments to demonstrably poor choices; and a variety of simplification processes that obviate analysis altogether. In this article, three psychological mechanisms will be examined in the context of decision making in a business-cycle environment: cognitive dissonance, prospect theory, and cognitive simplification. It seems demonstrably clear to this writer that the rational-expectations explanation of perfect analysis of imperfect information is a less convincing rationale for faulty decision making than is imperfect analysis of comparatively perfect information, once these mechanisms are taken into consideration. Hopefully, the reader too will be convinced.

III. COGNITIVE DISSONANCE

Consider the following quotation from Lavington, in which he likens businessmen to skaters on a pond:

> Indeed, the confidence of each skater in his own safety is likely to be reinforced rather than diminished by the presence of numbers of his fellows....The rational judgment that the greater their numbers the greater will be the risk is likely to be submerged by the mere contagion of confidence which persuades him that the greater the numbers the more safely he himself may venture (Haberler, 1958, p. 147).

When investment behavior resembles the behavior of the skaters on the pond, the scene is set for an economic downturn. Schumpeter, Mitchell, and Keynes would all agree on that. The interesting point is that the statement reflects a behavior that we all recognize as ironically accurate and yet one we also know is essentially irrational. Why is that so?

We can look to the theory of cognitive dissonance to get one insight into this seemingly irrational, or at least inconsistent, behavior. Cognitive dissonance is a theory of motivation that, simply put, states that people are uncomfortable in the fact of inconsistent beliefs. If having cognition A implies having cognition B, a dissonant relationship exists when the person has cognition A and the obverse or opposite of cognition B (see Wicklund and Brehm, 1976; Festinger, 1957). This dissonant set of cognitions creates tension in the person. Since tension is unpleasant the individual acts to reduce it by restoring cognitive consonance, or consistency among cognitions. The outcome of this action is what an observer

frequently sees as irrational behavior. Dissonance reduction is achieved
by (1) denying or blocking out one of the dissonant cognitions, (2) bolstering or selectively letting in information that would make the cognitions seem less dissonant, and (3) action that removes one of the dissonant
elements from the immediate environment.

In the skating anecdote we have the dissonant cognitions that the ice
is probably unsafe and yet everyone (including myself) is on it. The more
skaters go on, the less safe it is, and yet the more safe public opinion
seems to say it is. Dissonance reduction can take the form of (1) not
considering seriously anyone's suggestion that the ice might not be safe,
(2) stressing in one's own thoughts how cold it has been recently and
how solidly frozen the ice must be, or (3) leaving the ice and warning
others to do so. The theory states that the avenue least likely to be taken,
or at least taken last, is the one most subject to resistance. This is usually
a step requiring overt action instead of merely a mental process. Hence
it is likely that one will remain on the ice longer than is prudent as a
result of employing rationalizations 1 and 2. Finally, if the overcrowding
becomes too obviously dangerous, overt action aimed at tension reduction will be taken and the ice abandoned. Or, of course, everyone may
fall in.

Since Lavington's example was offered as an allegory, and investment
decisions rather than skating decisions were being described, we should
extend the dissonance-reducing behavior in that direction. Information
avoidance takes many forms. It may consist of ignoring the warnings of
the Henry Kaufmans and Elliot Janeways of the world and instead fixing
attention on the more optimistic economic and trade opinions. Or it may
be more subtle. In his 1913 book (reissued in 1941), Mitchell offers this
description of creditor behavior during the business expansion:

> The effect of these definite changes in the business situation is heightened by the
> prevailing sense of confidence. On the same facts submitted by an applicant for
> discounts bankers will pass a more favorable verdict; the credit men of wholesale
> houses have less critical eyes for the orders sent in by retail dealers; and manufac-
> turers are more easily induced to make up goods to be paid for after delivery (p. 65).

Investment commitments continue despite signs that might disquiet a
"rational" businessman. With each commitment, the need to allow in
bolstering information and screen out dissonant information arises, since
commitment and responsibility are a precondition of dissonance arousal.
Meanwhile, as the expansion phase of the business cycle progresses, the
objective facts continue to deteriorate and the probability of the next
period turning out profitably declines. As the commitment becomes
more and more estranged from the surrounding economic climate

needed to support it, one of two outcomes may occur. There can be type 3 dissonance reduction. That is, once discounting dissonant beliefs no longer offers the least resistant road to tension reduction, overt action will take place. New investment will be stopped, production slowed, borrowing curtailed, cost-cutting programs implemented. Consonance will be restored, not by making the beliefs fit the facts but by making the facts match the conditions. The second possible outcome, of course, is that businesses will fail. At this point, dissonance reduction will take the form of the businessmen concerned reading about how many other major firms also failed, believing how, except for bad luck or an unreasonable creditor, their businesses might have survived and how no one could have foreseen the downturn.

Cognitive dissonance, then, accounts for a lag between information and response to it. It forces a wedge into the decision-making process much as transaction costs do. At low levels of dissonance, selective exposure filters out dissonant information, but when the dissonance grows too large, the blocking of information reverses itself and the initial decision is revised in line with the external evidence.

Staw, in a series of studies (see, Staw, 1981; Fox and Staw, 1979) has found most irrational behavior among managers. When projects for which they are responsible show signs of failing, rather than retrenching they are more likely to escalate their commitment. He suggests that "prime candidates for escalation include resource allocation or investment decisions that are identified by an entering and exit value, life choices that are linked together with the label of a career and policy decisions for which administrators are held accountable by others in an organization or by the general public" (Staw, 1981, p. 585). This sounds like a clinical case study of cognitive dissonance. Furthermore, such escalation commitments during the peaking of the business cycle contribute to the excesses that are so much a part of Mitchell's theory and that are difficult to explain in a rational-expectations framework.

The differences in behavior suggested by cognitive dissonance on the one hand and standard economic assumptions on the other are striking. In the standard theory, reaction to information is immediate. Cognitive dissonance induces delays. In the standard theory, the search for information is continuous. Cognitive dissonance blocks out information. In the standard theory, adjustments are made entirely in light of marginal considerations. Under cognitive dissonance, *sunk costs play an important role in decision making*, because once commitment has been given to a course of action, abandonment of that course is the most resistant form of dissonance reduction—witness the phenomenon of escalating commitment in the face of evidence that a project is failing.

IV. PROSPECT THEORY

The microeconomic theory of business decision making stresses evaluation of all possible results, their probability of occurrence, and a calculation of expected value. Given a monotonic utility function, these are ordered and the highest one chosen. While some anomalous results such as risk taking and insurance buying by the same decision maker were explainable by the assumption of a nonlinear utility function (see, e.g., Friedman and Savage, 1948), choice by subjective expected utility (SEU) does produce a reliable and practical guide. Its reliability lies in its compliance with two axioms of ordinal utility theory: dominance and invariance. Dominance requires that if choice A is as good as choice B in every respect and better than B in at least one, A should be preferred to B. Invariance requires that the way the choices are described, that is, the way the outcomes are "framed," should not determine the preference ranking among choices.

The empirical work of Amos Tversky and Daniel Kahneman (1979, 1981) has demonstrated that neither axiom can be relied on. They have demonstrated that preference depends more on how the choices are framed to the decision maker than on the underlying probabilities and outcomes. Review articles by Schoemaker (1982), Grether and Plott (1979), and Slovic and Lichtenstein (1983) suggest that preference reversal is not simply a laboratory-created curiosity but, according to Slovic and Lichtenstein (1983), "one of a broad class of findings that demonstrate violations of preference models due to the strong dependence of choice and preference upon information processing considerations" (p. 597) Slovic and Lichtenstein go on to note that "the most striking result of these studies is the persistence of preference reversals in the face of determined efforts to minimize or eliminate them" (p. 599).

Tversky and Kahneman (1979) explain preference reversal and the framing phenomenon with the help of prospect theory, an alternative to the more widely accepted SEU model. Prospect theory posits that (1) the utility function is nonlinear, taking the form of a stylized S; (2) what matters in decision making is not the final position but changes from a reference point; and most significantly, (3) the utility of each uncertain outcome is not weighted by the probability of its occurrence, as in SEU theory, but by a "decision weight which is a monotonic function of p but is not a probability" (p. 454). The unique characteristics of this "decision-weight function" have been inferred by Tversky and Kahneman from responses by subjects in a large number of settings, and its shape accounts for much of the phenomenon of preference reversal they observed. A number of regularities have been distilled from these studies that Tversky and Kahneman feel may be relied on to govern choice. Several that seem particularly relevant here are: the certainty effect, reference-point adjustment, the endowment effect, and precommitment.

A. Certainty Effect

Laboratory subjects were given the following instructions: "Imagine that you face the following pair of concurrent decisions. First examine both decisions, then indicate the options you prefer."

Decision 1. Choose between:
    A. a sure gain of $240
    B. 25% chance to gain $1,000 and
        75% chance to gain nothing

Decision 2. Choose between:
    C. a sure loss of $750
    D. 75% chance to lose $1,000 and
        25% chance to lose nothing

Although the expected value of choice B in decision 1 exceeds choice A, nearly five times as many subjects chose A as chose B. Similarly, although the expected value of C in decision 2 equals D, nearly seven times as many subjects chose D as chose C. One inference drawn is that people are risk-averse when it comes to gain and risk-seeking in terms of avoiding loss. This result is ascribed to both the S shaped utility curve and the underweighting given in the decision-weighting function to high-probability events. More significantly, it points up the *qualitative* difference between a sure thing and one that is merely highly likely. There is evidently nothing more distressing than to face a certain loss. In the face of such a situation as in decision 2, people overwhelmingly prefer a long shot that might bail them out. It is easy to see how this generalization applies to the specific case of the "trapped administrator" described by Fox and Staw (1979), where additional financial commitments are made to business projects when they fail to live up to expectations. To cut them short would mean taking a sure loss, an outcome not dissimilar to choice C in decision 2. It is equally easy to see the biases that keep banks lending to Mexico despite their default on outstanding loans, or why Penn Square would continue funding the oil industry and Continental Illinois funding Penn Square despite obvious default exposure.

B. Reference-Point Adjustment

Economic analysis treats the outcome of decisions taken under uncertainty as adjustments to the status quo. That is, whatever gains and losses occur in the fortunes of the decision maker affect his wealth as it exists at the moment. There is no memory, no history of past gains and losses. Sunk costs play no role. Tversky and Kahneman (1979, p. 286) characterize this conventional approach in economics as a complete shift of the point of reference. They suggest the following: "Imagine a person who is involved in a business venture has already lost $2,000 and is now facing a choice between a sure gain of $1,000 and an even chance of winning $2,000 or nothing." The question is, will he perceive the outcome of this current opportunity as a chance to erase the lost $2,000 or simply as a choice between a sure $1,000 and a possible $2,000 versus a possible nothing? If he has adjusted his point of reference as conventional marginal analysis says he should, the preference for certainty would lead to the acceptance of the sure $1,000. On the other hand, if his reference point has not shifted and the current choice is considered in the context of the already lost $2,000, he has a chance to eliminate that loss if he accepts the risk. Here the well-documented aversion to certain loss is likely to encourage taking the riskier alternative. It is probable that businessmen using a going-concern concept of a business do not adjust their reference point with the ease suggested by conventional economic theory. This means businesses are likely to undertake riskier options than economic theory suggests they should. Instability encourages further destabilizing activity.

C. Endowment Effect

This is the name given to the often observed fact that people are reluctant to give up anything once they have it. Thaler (1983, p. 64) suggests the following illustration: "Suppose you won a ticket to a sold-out concert that you would love to attend and the ticket is priced at $15. Before the concert you are offered $50 for the ticket. Do you sell? Then, a few weeks later you are offered a chance to buy a ticket to the same concert for $45. Do you buy? Many people say they would not sell for $50 in the first case and would not buy for $45 in the second case. Such responses are logically inconsistent."

A generalization of this is that we often want more when we are selling an item that we have than we would be willing to pay to acquire it in the first place. It is easy to see what violence the endowment effect does to the notion of reserve supply price and the assumption that we have continuous markets where demanders easily become suppliers when the price is right. The endowment effect builds significant rigidities into the market, freezing assets in place when they might be more efficiently allocated elsewhere. On the intrafirm level, it creates a ratchet effect where the overhead of doing business can only move in one direction:

up. There is a built-in asymmetry when organizational change is considered. However reluctant one is to add to overhead, he is that much more reluctant to get rid of it once it is in place. Recession has been observed to be therapeutic for the economy because it forces cost cutting and streamlining by management. Break-even points are lowered by surviving firms and profitability during the next expansion becomes magnified, at least during the early stages. The endowment effect suggests that in the absence of the recession and accompanying financial exigency, none of the described cost cutting readily occurs. Wasteful practices may well accumulate throughout industry, since resources, once in place, are jealously maintained. No wonder profits fluctuate more sharply than gross sales.

D. Precommitment

The likelihood of preference reversal raises the interesting policy question of whether government administrators will execute the policy they plan when a given contingency occurs. If there is a high likelihood that a change in preference will be made as the need for action approaches and that the change will be for the worse, the wisest policy course will be one called rational precommitment. On the fact of it, precommitment seems wholly irrational, because it involves taking away options for action at an early point in time. The classic example dates from Ulysses' encounter with the Sirens, whose song, he knew, would force strong men away from their resolve and onto the rocks. Homer reminds us that Ulysses dealt with the situation by having himself tied to the mast of his ship while it was navigated past the danger point. Doubtless, if he were free, Ulysses would have changed his mind about sailing on and the change would have been for the worse. Hence he eliminated the possibility of one course of action by precommitting himself to another.

Economic policy makers know well the likelihood of preference reversal due to new framing as the time for action comes closer. We have already seen how escalating commitment leads to increased investment in losing causes, and how endowment effects render our resolve to sell an asset difficult to execute. The popular movement to enact a constitutional amendment that would force a balanced budget each year is a form of precommitment that may well bind our choices in the future, because Congress recognizes its inability to curtail spending voluntarily despite its good resolve to do so.

The argument for a constant growth-rate rule instead of discretionary monetary policy also gains credibility because historically, officials were either unwilling or unable to time their policy moves correctly. One interesting attempt at establishing rules for timing policy has been offered by Zarnowitz and Moore (1982). They have developed a system of triggering signals drawn from the rates of change of the leading and coincidental business-cycle indexes. When reached, these signals would automatically trigger appropriate counter-cyclical policies as incipient turning points were indicated. Another indication of the value of pre-commitment is found in a stock-market trading simulation reported by Kwon (1983), where all stocks were sold a fixed number of weeks after the Zarnowitz-Moore signals indicated a trough was approaching and purchases were made a fixed number of weeks after the signals reported an incipient peak. This scheme generated gains in excess of 26 percent annually.[5]

Thaler (1983) discusses the role of precommitment in a variety of policy situations ranging from airline hijacking to tax indexing to personal dieting. Since preference reversal is universal, so is the need to cope with it. We may note that under neoclassical reasoning, not only is precommitment irrational because of its preempting of courses of action, but the need for it also absent, since preference reversal is impossible.

V. COGNITIVE SIMPLIFICATION

In addition to their formulation of prospect theory, Tversky and Kahneman have enriched economics with their analysis of cognitive simplification in decision making. One example of what this entails is found in the economists' stock in trade, modeling. In order to think effectively about complex problems, we have adopted the technique of discarding factors that we acknowledge are present but deem unimportant, and we focus only on a few of the elements present. It is ironic that while engaging in this form of cognitive simplification in dealing with their own problems, most economists implicitly assume corporate decision makers behave otherwise. Even in the face of the most complex internal market and governmental environments, people are presumed by the neoclassical paradigm (and certainly by the new classical economics of the rational-expectation theory) to be complete and perfect information processors. Cognitive simplification means that we decide using "heuristics" and our decisions contain "biases."

We begin our discussion by recognizing that SEU—the decision-making paradigm in mainstream economics—is based on a decision maker accurately appraising the likelihood of an event occurring. In fact, he probably can't. While in most laboratory experiments the probability of an outcome is told to the subject, in real-life decision making there is no experimenter suggesting the probabilities. These must be inferred by the subject from experience. Tversky and Kahneman have demonstrated in their work that, basically, people have little intuitive sense of statistical logic and hence, we may infer, little ability to formulate likelihoods of outcomes. Because of the statistical naïveté found even among sophisticated people, we may infer that business decisions made at or around cyclical turning points are subject to errors in probability perception and, more important, to systematically biased errors.

One of the most frequently described psychological qualities of the cycle is crowd psychology, sometimes giving way to "mania" (see Kindleberger, 1978; McKay, 1914). Over and over we read of contagious animal spirits infusing businessmen with optimism that leads them to estimate future profits generously during boom times and judge them stingily during bad times. Pigou (1927, p. 86) wrote:

> First, among businessmen, even when engaged in different occupations, there often exists a certain measure of psychological interdependence. A change of tone in one part of the business world diffuses itself in quite unreasoning manner, over other and wholly disconnected parts. An expansion of business confidence propagates itself by that sympathetic and epidemic excitement which so largely sways communities of men. There comes into play a quasi-hypnotic system of mutual suggestion:
>
> > One with another, soul with soul
> > They kindle fire from fire.

Pigou goes on to suggest that businessmen's optimism also induces them to extend trade credit in greater measure than their prudence would allow in less ebullient times. This "enormous increase in forward buying against informal promises to pay ... links the fortunes of different businessmen still more closely together. But the forecasts made by businessmen are almost certainly coloured by their present fortune. It follows that interdependence of fortunes carries with it some degree of interdependence of forecasts."

Tversky and Kahneman speak less colorfully of the "representativeness" heuristic. They say "many of the probabilistic questions with which people are concerned belong to one of the following types: What is the probability that event A originates from process B? What is the probability that process B will generate event A?" Rather than apply statistical reasoning to answer this question, most people make a judgement as to whether or not A *resembles* B. A businessman contemplating an investment considers the extent to which similar investments have been successful. During a period of business expansion many similar investments will have already proven to be so. The representativeness heuristic leads to this syllogism: investments we are aware of have been successful; this is an investment; therefore, there is a high probability that it will be successful.

In making this judgment, of course, the businessman will be demonstrating insensitivity to a variety of considerations that are methodo-
logically of importance to statistical reasoning. Tversky and Kahneman
cite among these "prior probability of outcomes." Before jumping to the
conclusion that something belongs to a particular class rather than another, one should analyze the incidence of each class in nature. The
question of how many business investments of the type contemplated
historically have proven successful over the long run should have a
greater influence in determining the likelihood that one's own investment will succeed than the immediate surrounding euphoria of the business expansion. The representativeness heuristic says the likelihood is
that it won't.

People also tend to have an insensitivity to sample size. They treat
information from small samples as being just as representative of populations as that from large samples. For example, a group of subjects
was presented with the following question:

> A certain town is served by two hospitals. In the larger hospital about 45 babies are
> born each day and in the smaller hospital about 15 babies are born each day. As
> you know, about 50 percent of all babies are boys. However, the exact percentage
> varies from day to day. Sometimes it may be higher than 50 percent, sometimes
> lower. For a period of 1 year each hospital recorded the days on which more than
> 60 percent of the babies born were boys. Which hospital do you think recorded
> more such days?

Most subjects judged the probability of obtaining more than 60 percent
boys to be the same in both the small and in the large hospital, "presumably because these events are described by the same statistic and are
therefore equally representative of the general population." Sampling
theory, on the other hand, recognizes that the mean of a small sample
is more likely to depart significantly from the population mean. So too
is the mean performance of a small sample of business investments likely
to differ from the population's performance. In addition to this "law of
small numbers," Tversky and Kahneman note that people are blissfully
unaware of "regression to the mean." Extremely good performances are
not likely to be repeated if they depart from the long-run mean. By not
giving cognizance to the long-run mean, businessmen will behave exactly
as Pigou suggested: they will be overly expansive during good times and
overly conservative during bad.

A second heuristic people employ is "availability," by which they assess
the frequency of a class or the probability of an event by the ease with
which instances of occurrences can be brought to mind. If asked to judge
which is more frequent, suicide or homicide, most people say homicide,

because the newspapers report these more luridly than they do suicides and they are more easily brought to mind. This despite the national statistics that say suicide is the more prevalent, if less publicized, event. Similarly, during a business expansion, there is greater awareness of successful ventures than of failure. At the other end of the cycle, calamitous failures are more likely to be in the papers than new successes; hence the former are available to cognition.

The third major heuristic we want to consider is "anchoring and adjustment." Here it is suggested that once a point of reference is presented, adjustments away from it will be inadequate. In strategic decision making, individuals must often make initial judgements about values of variables critical in particular decisions and revise these judgements as new data come in. Final estimates of values were found to be biased toward the initial values. Individuals involved in the ongoing process of strategy formulation may attend to negative information about the success of present strategy, but they will probably not make full use of it in revising their predictions of company performance. Under the anchoring process, their revisions may be smaller than are justified by the new information (see Schwenk, 1984). It is easy to see how anchoring prevents reversal of a bad decision once one begins with the assumptions that support it. Anchoring narrows the sense of possible outcomes.

One outgrowth of the anchoring process is the bias people have toward overestimating the likelihood of conjunctive events and underestimating disjunctive events. A conjunctive event is one that must be repeated over and over again for an outcome to be successful. One such case would be drawing a red marble seven times in a row from a bag containing 90 percent red marbles. A disjunctive event is one that must be done at least once in many tries, such as drawing a red marble once out of seven tries from a bag containing 90 percent white marbles. When given a choice between these two tasks, a significant majority of subjects preferred to bet on the conjunctive event, whose probability of success is .48, rather than on the disjunctive, which has a .50 probability. The mechanism that appears to be at work here is anchoring, in which the stated probability of the elementary event, 90 percent, is translated onto the set of repetitions. Tversky and Kahneman (1982, p. 15) say, "Since the adjustment from the starting point is typically insufficient, the final estimates remain too close to the probabilities of the elementary events in both cases."

Business management is conjunctive in nature. For a business to succeed a series of ongoing decisions must be made, all of which must be correct and any one of which can produce business failure. The tendency is to overestimate the likelihood of succeeding at such a task. Once again, therefore, psychological biases set the scene for an excessively expansive effort. Businessmen are likely to underestimate the difficulty of repeated and uninterrupted successes in their decision making.

VI. SUMMARY AND CONCLUSION

Writing in 1918, J. M. Clark suggested, "If the economist borrows his conceptions of man from the psychologist, his constructive work may have some chance of remaining purely economic in character. But if he does not, he will not thereby avoid psychology. Rather he will force himself to make his own, and it will be bad psychology."

Behavioral economics recognizes Clark's caveat and attempts to comply with his recommendation for dealing with it. In borrowing three ideas from psychology—cognitive dissonance, prospect theory, and cognitive simplification through heuristics—to gain insight into the dynamics of the business cycle, I have at the same time omitted any number of other borrowings that are possible: learning theory, levels of aspiration, locus of control, and unconscious motivations, to name a few that come to mind. The list of areas that are relatively untapped, and indeed possibly unknown to economists, is both depressingly and excitingly long: depressing because there is so much to be done and exciting because of the possibilities offered.

Some may feel that in this article I have set up a straw man by choosing the rational-expectations explanation of the business cycle as a reference point against which to consider the insights offered by psychology. I don't think so. McCallum (1980, p. 717) writes, "The basic idea of the hypothesis is simply that economic agents behave purposefully in collecting and using information, *just as they do in other activities*, an idea that . . . is hard for an economist to reject without considerable embarrassment" (emphasis added). The trouble is that in collecting and using information in other activities, economic agents fall far short of the neoclassical ideal. Hugh Schwartz (1983) conducted a series of in-depth interviews with business managers in Latin America and the United States. He found errors in their knowledge of technology, prices of raw materials, and prices of equipment. Demand estimates were based on salesmen's judgement rather than on econometrics. The product-mix decision was based on what others did. Estimates of future inflation were based on immediate experiences (anchoring). In brief, firms do what others do. The tendency is to seek redundant information rather than new information that must be integrated. People are more concerned with coherence than objective informativeness, and they seek confirmation of earlier actions rather than opportunities for new initiatives.

Schwartz's findings suggest that perception, judgement, decisions on data and public policy, and internal production decisions are far wide of the mark assumed by economists.

In light of these findings, we can only conclude that McCallum's justification for the rational-expectations paradigm leads away from, rather than toward, neoclassical conclusions. Purposeful information gathering and processing are far from perfect. (See also Morgan's paper in this volume for a discussion of the level of consumer knowledge. It seems that consumers know less of what they are supposed to know than even the businessmen.)

Given the woeful record of the profession in forecasting economic performance, it would appear that mainstream economics itself may suffer from escalating commitment. The worse the results, the more that gets invested in mathematical modeling. The new classical economics is certainly a departure from Keynesian assumptions regarding price adjustments, but it seems like a departure using the return ticket from a round-trip fare. Instead, the repertoire has to be broadened. Back in the days when the *Journal of Political Economy* was publishing simpler fare than it does at present, brain-truster-to-be Rexford Tugwell (1922) wrote, "It is only the study of human nature that can force the great closed door of economic theory. . . . What the behaviorist sees in his laboratory, the economist meets in his fields and the factories and is under obligation to understand." The effort here is to force the door just a bit ajar.

NOTES

1. This classification is drawn from Klein's 1983 article on Mitchell. Klein's complete list includes only two of the names Mitchell listed in his 1913 book as antecedents to his own theories: Beveridge, Spiethoff, Hull, Lescure, Sombart, Carver, Fisher, Johannsen, and England. This underscores the fact that, indeed, the profession has not lacked efforts to explain cyclical phenomena.

2. Mitchell's examination of the facts of business cycles and his lifelong stress on individual behavior certainly place him among the early important figures in behavioral economics. I agree with Klein's contention that the institutionalists deserve recognition as early and resourceful proponents of a behavioral approach.

3. These figures are taken from *Business Conditions Digest* and refer to firms with liabilities in excess of $100,000.

4. This index was developed by Geoffrey Moore at his Center for International Business Cycle Research. Moore has developed a variety of specialized leading indexes that have proven useful in forecasting changes in employment, inflation, foreign trade, individual industry, and regional economic activity.

5. Note that these strategies do not call for the trader to attempt to buy at the bottom in relation to the trough or sell at the top in relation to the peak. Instead they rely on the knowledge that economic events move cyclically. The signal to buy comes automatically

after a lapse of time following a business peak. The signal to sell comes following the previous trough.

REFERENCES

Carswell, J., *The South Sea Bubble*. London: Cresset Press, 1960.

Clark, J. M., "Economics and Modern Psychology," *Journal of Political Economy*, 26 (January 1981), 1–30.

Festinger, Leon, *A Theory of Cognitive Dissonance*. Stanford, CA: Stanford University Press, 1957.

Fox, F. V., and B. M. Staw, "The Trapped Administrator," *Administrative Science Quarterly*, 24 (September 1979), 499–471.

Friedman, M., and L. J. Savage, "The Utility Analysis of Choices Involving Risk," *Journal of Political Economy*, 56 (August 1948), 279–304.

Grether, D. A., and C. R. Plott, "Economic Theory of Choice and the Preference Reversal Phenomenon," *American Economic Review*, 69 (September 1979), 623–638.

Haberler, Gottfried, *Prosperity and Depression*. Cambridge, MA: Harvard University Press, 1958.

Kahneman, D., P. Slovic, and A. Tversky, *Judgement Under Uncertainty: Heuristics and Biases*. Cambridge: Cambridge University Press, 1982.

Kindleberger, C. P., *Manias, Panics, and Crashes*. New York: Basic Books, 1978.

Klein, Philip A., "The Neglected Institutionalism of Wesley Clair Mitchell: The Theoretical Basis for Business Cycle Indicators," *Journal of Economic Issues*, 17 (December 1983), 867–899.

Kwon, O. Y., "Stock Prices, Profits and Interest Rates During Business Cycles." Presented at Atlantic Economic Association, 1983.

Leibenstein, H., "A Branch of Economics is Missing: Micro-Micro Theory," *Journal of Economic Literature*, 17 (June 1979), 477–502.

Lucas, R. E., Jr., "Methods and Problems in Business Cycle Theory," *Journal of Money, Credit and Banking*, 12, Part 2 (November 1980), 696–715.

Lucas, R. E., Jr., "Understanding Business Cycles," in *Studies in Business Cycle Theory*. Cambridge, MA: MIT Press, 1981.

McCallum, B. T., "Rational Expectations and Macroeconomic Stabilization Policy: An Overview," *Journal of Money, Credit and Banking*, 12, Part 2 (November 1980), 716–746.

McKay, C., *Memoirs of Extraordinary Delusions and the Madness of Crowds*. Boston: L. C. Page Co., 1914.

Mitchell, Wesley C., *Business Cycles and Their Causes*. Berkeley: University of California Press, 1941.

Okun, Arthur M., "Rational Expectations with Misperceptions as a Theory of the Business Cycle," *Journal of Money, Credit and Banking*, 12, Part 2 (November 1980), 817–825.

Pigou, A. C., *Industrial Fluctuations*. London: Macmillan, 1927.

Schoemaker, P., "The Expected Utility Model: Its Variance, Purposes, Evidence and Limitations," *Journal of Economic Literature*, 20 (1982), 529–563.

Schwartz, Hugh, "Perception, Judgement and Motivation in Business Firms and Preliminary Hypotheses from In Depth Interviews." Unpublished manuscript, 1983.

Schwenk, C., "Cognitive Simplification Processes in Strategic Decision Making," *Strategic Management Journal*, (1984), 111–128.

Simon, H., *Administrative Behavior*. New York: Macmillan, 1959.

Simon, H., "Rational Decision Making in Organizations," *American Economic Review*, 69 (September 1979), 493–513.

Slovic, P., and S. Lichtenstein, "Preference Reversals: A Broader Perspective," *American Economic Review*, 73 (September 1983), 596–605.

Staw, B. M., "The Escalation of Commitment to a Course of Action," *Academy of Management Review*, 6 (1981), 577–587.

Thaler, R., "Illusions and Mirages in Public Policy," *Public Interest*, 73 (Fall 1983), 60–74.

Tugwell, R. F., "Human Nature in Economic Theory," *Journal of Political Economy*, 30 (May 1922), 330–340.

Tversky, A., and D. Kahneman, "The Framing of Decisions and the Psychology of Choice," *Science*, 211 (January 30, 1981), 453–458.

Tversky, A., and D. Kahneman, "Prospect Theory: An Analysis of Decision Under Risk," *Econometrica*, 47 (March 1979), 263–291.

Wicklund, R., and J. W. Brehm, *Perspectives on Cognitive Dissonance*. Hillsdale, IL: Lawrence Erlbaum Associates, 1976.

Zarnowitz, V., and G. H. Moore, "Sequential Signals of Recession and Recovery," *Journal of Business*, 55 (January 1982), 57–86.

MACROECONOMIC INSIGHTS FROM A BEHAVIORAL PERSPECTIVE

F. Thomas Juster

I. INTRODUCTION

An important set of macroeconomic issues, both scientific and policy oriented, revolved around consumer saving behavior. The literature on this issue goes back a matter of four or five decades and has spawned a number of theories that have had significant impact on professional thinking. These include the original absolute-income theory of Keynes (1936); the sociologically oriented relative-income theory of Duesenberry (1949); the permanent-income theory of Friedman (1957); the life-cycle theory of Ando and Modigliani (1963) and Modigliani and Brumberg (1955); and the recent favorite—the extended life-cycle theory attributable to Feldstein (1974) and Barro (1978). All these theories are based on the standard assumptions of economic theory: that people live in a world characterized by perfect certainty and perfect foresight, or at least in a world where uncertainty can be treated as a distribution of expectations with an expected value that dominates decisions[1] and where expectations are unbiased; that there are long-term income, consumption, labor-supply, and bequest plans; that changes in family circumstances and in the general economy are foreseen and embedded in the plans; and that all consumers are busily making small adjustments in their consumption and saving behavior as new information emerges and different circumstances occur over their lifetimes.[2] Conventional theory,

51

despite its occasional references to forward-looking phenomena, has a
static flavor—it assumes fixed expectations and goals and does not provide for much in the way of learning, adaptation, or other dynamic processes. To many economists, certainly including this writer, models of this
sort are not very plausible representations of how people actually make
consumption and saving decisions, given the uncertainties and vicissi-
tudes of the real world.

Theories of this sort, and theories generally, have a powerful influence
on policy. For example, the strong professional consensus in favor of
the life-cycle view of saving behavior is the basis for much of the debate
about the implications of an aging population structure on aggregate
saving and underpins much of the discussion about whether the rate of
capital formation can be significantly increased in the future (Leiberman
and Wachtel, 1980; Wachtel, 1980). The general life-cycle idea certainly
sounds plausible: younger people tend to save little or dissave because
they are in the process of acquiring durable goods and are thus expanding debt of one kind or another; older people are using up the
assets they have accumulated during their working lifetime and are thus
either saving little or dissaving; and middle-aged people whose children
have grown and whose durable good stocks are adequate for their needs
are relieved from expenditure pressures, are looking toward retirement,
and are saving at relatively high rates. As a rational way of acting in a
perfectly certain world, that picture seems believable. But does it accord
with the way that people actually behave? Or do preferences for managing one's own assets rather than acquiring a riskless annuity, or concern about the uncertainties associated with aging (health, spouse's
health, date of death), or the habits generated by a lifetime of spending
less than income and thus adding to capital, or the need for safeguarding
one's financial situation against unspecified bad luck, and the like, result
in a pattern of saving behavior for most households that is inconsistent
with the life-cycle model?

Most of the evidence used to test saving theory is based on time-series
analyses of aggregate data. The analysis in this paper will also be based
on the same kind of data. At the same time, I should note a disclaimer:
for a variety of well-known technical reasons having to do with the
smoothness of time series and the collinearity problems involved in trying
to sort out the net effects of what are really a large number of averages,
all attempts to estimate saving functions from time-series data are unstable and, in my judgment, fundamentally unpersuasive. That applies
to my own analyses as well as to those of others. In principle, one would
like to find evidence, at the level of individual behavior, that has much
better prospects of either confirming or disconfirming theory. The problem is that good data on individual saving behavior are extremely hard

to come by, and all such data available for the United States are subject to potentially serious biases arising out of very substantial measurement errors. There is not much that can be done about that except to design better measurements that have some prospect of identifying regularities and are not totally swamped by measurement error problems.

II. PLAN OF THE PAPER

The first part of this paper takes a look at the relevant aggregate time-series data on personal saving, using data both from the Flow of Funds (FOF) system and from the National Income and Product Accounts (NIPA). The definitions of financial flow variables used throughout the paper are summarized in Table 1. The next part of the paper examines a variety of consumer survey data that bear on some of the behavioral forces that seem to have been at work during the last several decades and attempts to interpret observed movements in light of these behav-

Table 1. Definitions of Financial Flow Variables
(All Ratios to Disposable Personal Income)

SNIA	Saving as defined in the U.S. National Income and Product Accounts (NIPA)
SFOF	Saving as defined by Flow of Funds (FOF) measurements, but using NIPA concepts (excludes increases in public pension reserves, net investment in consumer durables, and a few minor items)
NAFA	Net acquisition of financial assets from FOF data, less increases in public pension reserves
NAFA*	NAFA plus statistical discrepancy between FOF and NIPA
NIL	Net increase in liabilities from FOF data
NIL*	NIL plus statistical discrepancy between FOF and NIPA
NFI (net financial investment)	NAFA − NIL
NFI*	NAFA − NIL + statistical discrepancy
SCON	Net increase in private pension reserves plus net increase in life insurance reserves
SCON*	SCON plus net increase in public persion-fund reserves
VFI* (variable financial investments)	NAFA* − NIL − SCON
NTI	Net investment in tangible assets (except consumer durables) from FOF data
NTI*	NTI plus net investment in consumer durables

ioral phenomena. The last part of the paper contains some tentative conclusions, as well as some recommendations for policies that might be expected to have some influence on saving behavior, given what we know about actual behavior and behavioral perspectives.

III. AGGREGATE SAVING DATA

There are two basic sources of personal saving data in the United States. One is derived from the NIPA, in which saving is defined as the difference between disposable personal income and consumer outlays. Outlays, in turn, include consumer expenditures that are part of final product and other payments (largely interest) that are not counted as part of final product but are a use of disposable income. The important points are that saving is a residual, that the income and outlay numbers are both very large compared with the residual, and that relatively small errors in either the income or the outlay data will result in relatively large errors in the data on saving.

A second source of data, less widely used by economists, seems to me substantially more valuable in that they enable us to decompose saving into components that have more behavioral relevance than does the total. The FOF data are derived, as the name implies, from data supplied by financial institutions. In these data, saving is defined as the difference between net acquisitions of financial assets (additions to checking and savings accounts, net purchases of common stock and bonds, additions to money-market funds, etc.), and net increases in liabilities (increases in consumer installment debt, mortgage debt, debt on securities, etc.), along with net investment in tangible capital in the household sector (housing and durables) and in the nonprofit sector of the economy.

Before looking at the relevant components of saving, it is well to note a couple of important differences both on the conceptual and on the measurement side. There are two major conceptual differences between saving as defined in the FOF system and in the NIPA: the FOF system treats increases in the reserves of government pension funds (federal, state, and local) as additions to assets and thus as flows of saving, paralleling the treatment of additions to private pension-fund reserves. The NIPA, in contrast, counts increases in private pension reserves as saving, but for obscure historical reasons does not count increases in public pension reserves as either income or saving. Second, the FOF system treats net increases in the stock of consumer durable goods (expenditures less capital consumption allowances) as a form of saving, while the NIPA does not. There are other small conceptual differences between the two, but public pension reserves and net investment in consumer durables are the two major ones.

On the measurement side, the saving numbers are derived in totally different ways, as already noted, although both are estimated as residuals: NIPA calculates saving as the difference between income and outlay, while the FOF system calculates household savings as total financial flows minus estimates for other sectors—noncorporate business, financial institutions, and the like. Thus all the measurement errors in FOF data dealing with sectors other than the household sector will show up as errors (with opposite sign) in the household sector accounts.

The FOF system calculates a statistical discrepancy, which is simply the difference between conceptually comparable measurements of saving based on NIPA and FOF. That discrepancy is sometimes extremely large—in a couple of quarters during the early 1980s, for example, the discrepancy was just about as large as the total NIPA saving. Typically, the discrepancy has a negative sign, in that FOF data estimate household saving to be larger than does the NIPA.

Time series of the two estimates of personal saving, adjusted to be conceptually comparable, are shown in Figure 1. SNIA/Y is NIPA saving divided by disposable personal income, while SFOF/Y is FOF measurement (of the NIPA saving concept), also divided by disposable personal income. As indicated above, FOF savings are typically larger than NIPA savings, and the difference became extremely large in 1982 and the first few quarters of 1983. By the fourth quarter of 1983, the discrepancy had just about disappeared. But the implied pattern of saving behavior over the last decade and a half is very different if one regards NIPA data as reliable than if one judges FOF data to represent a closer approximation to the truth.[3]

Before returning to aggregate saving, we can take advantage of the decomposition of saving figures available from FOF data to examine the question of behaviorally relevant saving components as well as the question of measurement error as it relates to the statistical discrepancy. Let me first turn to the latter.

One way to resolve the measurement-error issue is to ask whether the FOF component series, adjusted by the statistical discrepancy between FOF and NIPA, appear to be behaviorally more plausible than the original FOF series. If it turns out that the adjusted FOF series looked like a better representation of behavior, it could be inferred that the measurement error is likely to be lodged in that FOF comonent. But if the reverse were true, the inference is that the measurement error must be in other components of the FOF series or in the NIPA data. If none of the FOF series looks more plausible behaviorally when adjusted by the

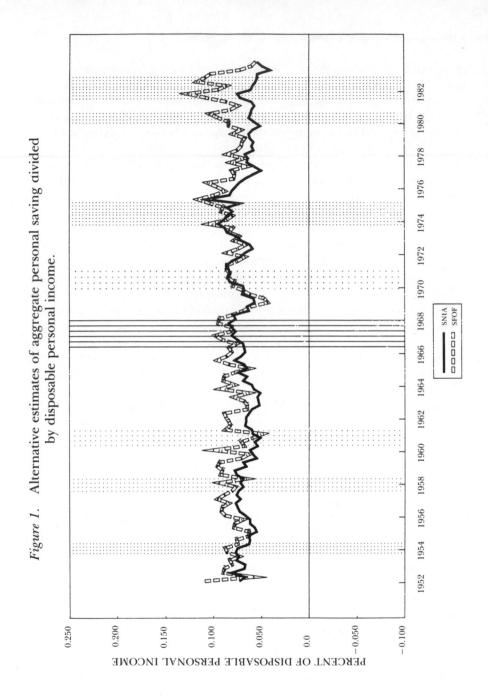

Figure 1. Alternative estimates of aggregate personal saving divided by disposable personal income.

56

discrepancy, the inference is that the measurement error is likely to be lodged in the NIPA series.

Figures 2 and 3 examine this issue for the two principal components of the FOF saving data. Figure 2 contains estimates of the net acquisition of financial asset component of FOF data, both in its original form (NAFA) and with the statistical discrepancy added (NAFA*), while Figure 3 contains similar data for the FOF net increase in liabilities (NIL) series. For the data in these charts, we have adopted the NIPA concept of saving and have therefore excluded increases in government pension-fund reserves as part of the NAFA series.

The data portrayed in Figures 2 and 3 lead to a relatively straight-forward conclusion. In Figure 2, the net increase in the asset series in its original form appears to be a much less plausible picture of consumer responses to various economic circumstances than the same series adjusted for the statistical discrepancy. It is not only that the series is a good bit smoother with the discrepancy added, but it seems to have a more plausible cyclical pattern as well as representing a better-defined response to known external circumstances. Modeling both series with a fairly simple equation designed to explain consumer asset acquisition yields the conclusion that the series in its original form has substantially more unexplained variation than does that series adjusted by the discrepancy. For example, a model in which the net acquisition of financial assets responds to the detrended index of leading indicators, net investment in consumer tangible assets, rate of change in real income, and rate of change in price generates an adjusted R^2 of 0.67 and a residual error of 0.0144; the same model, using the NAFA series adjusted for the statistical discrepancy, yields an equation with an $\overline{R}^2$ of 0.80 and a standard error of 0.0100—40 percent *lower*.

In contrast, using the same adjustments for the net increase in liability series produces exactly the opposite conclusion. Here, modeling liabilities by the same set of explanatory variables generates an adjusted R^2 of 0.69 and a standard error of 0.0124. But modeling the liabilities series adjusted by the discrepancy produces an explained variance of 0.64 and a standard error of 0.0158—almost 30 percent *higher*. Without worrying about the correlations or standard errors associated with the simple models used for this test, it is clear even to the naked eye that the asset acquisition series seems very erratic in its original form and substantially less so when adjusted by the discrepancy. Again, in contrast, the liability series seems quite erratic when adjusted for the discrepancy and substantially less erratic in its original form. The same analysis applied to the net tangible investment series in the FOF data yields results similar to those shown by the analysis of liabilities.

These simple empirical tests are buttressed by some a priori consid-

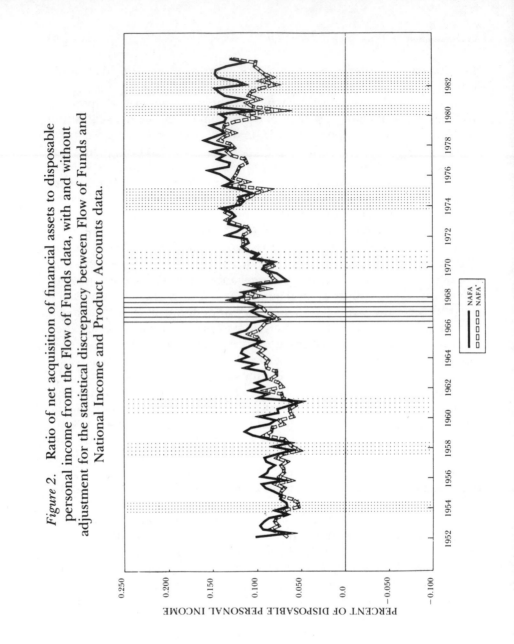

Figure 2. Ratio of net acquisition of financial assets to disposable personal income from the Flow of Funds data, with and without adjustment for the statistical discrepancy between Flow of Funds and National Income and Product Accounts data.

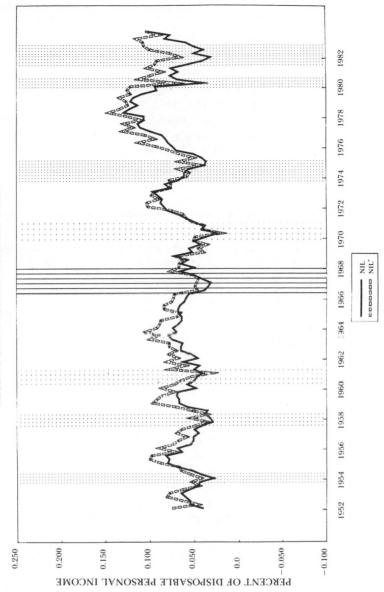

Figure 3. Ratio of net increase in liabilities to disposable personal income from the Flow of Funds data, with and without adjustment for the statistical discrepancy between Flow of Funds and National Income and Product Accounts data.

erations. We know that the liabilities data in the FOF series come from sources that provide relatively reliable data, and we also know that the distinction between various liability series that relate to consumer behavior and those that relate to business or financial institutions' behavior are relatively well defined. Put most simply, changes in consumer installment credit and in housing mortgage debt are dominantly associated with consumer decisions relating to the acquisition of tangible assets. But the same is not true for the acquisition of financial assets. Here, holdings of checking and savings accounts, various kinds of bonds, and so on are common in both the household and the business sectors, as well as in the foreign sector, and the estimated share of these asset increases that go to households can be badly estimated if the shares of other sectors are badly estimated. Thus it would not be surprising if most of the errors in the FOF data on household-sector saving were associated with the behavior of financial-asset holdings rather than with the behavior of liabilities, and the discrepancy analysis suggests that this is indeed so.

Although the evidence suggests that measurement errors are much more likely to be associated with the NAFA series than with the NIL series, that conclusion does not really tell us whether the full amount of the statistical discrepancy is properly associated with errors in the NAFA series. The data in Figure 2 make that assumption, and the resulting NAFA series looks plausible. But the series would also look plausible if much but not all of the statistical discrepancy were assumed to be associated with the NAFA estimate. There is no clear-cut way to resolve that issue. For purposes of this paper I will assume that the original NAFA series as estimated from FOF data is in error by the full amount of the statistical discrepancy between FOF and NIPA data, hence that the NIPA are the appropriate measures of total personal savings.

While previous analysis suggests that the NIPA estimate of personal saving is more likely to be valid than the FOF estimate, the FOF data have the great advantage of permitting us to identify the principal components of saving, shown in Figures 4 and 5. Figure 4 divides saving into net increases in financial assets adjusted by the statistical discrepancy (NAFA*), NIL, and net tangible investment (NTI).[4] Figure 5 combines the two financial series into a single net financial investment (NFI*) series (again, adjusted by the statistical discrepancy) and plots those data along with the NTI series.

A number of conclusions emerge from observing the data in Figures 4 and 5. First, the dominant source of cyclical movement in the behavior of personal saving is associated with changes in liabilities: as might be expected, these changes are closely associated with changes over time in investment in tangible assets—the NTI series. While changes in financial-

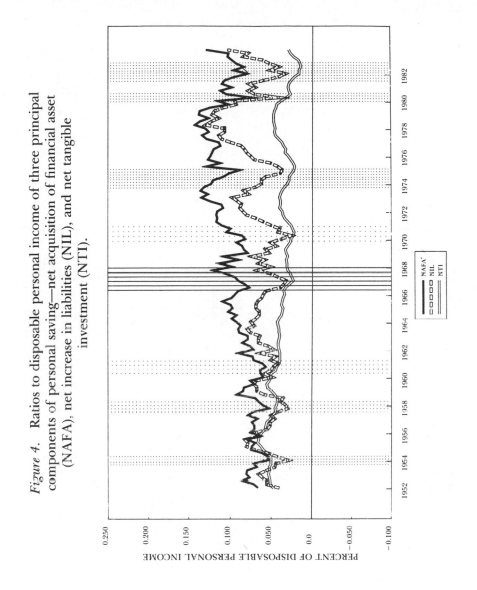

Figure 4. Ratios to disposable personal income of three principal components of personal saving—net acquisition of financial asset (NAFA), net increase in liabilities (NIL), and net tangible investment (NTI).

61

Figure 5. Ratios to disposable personal income of net financial investment (NFI) and net tangible asset investment (NTI).

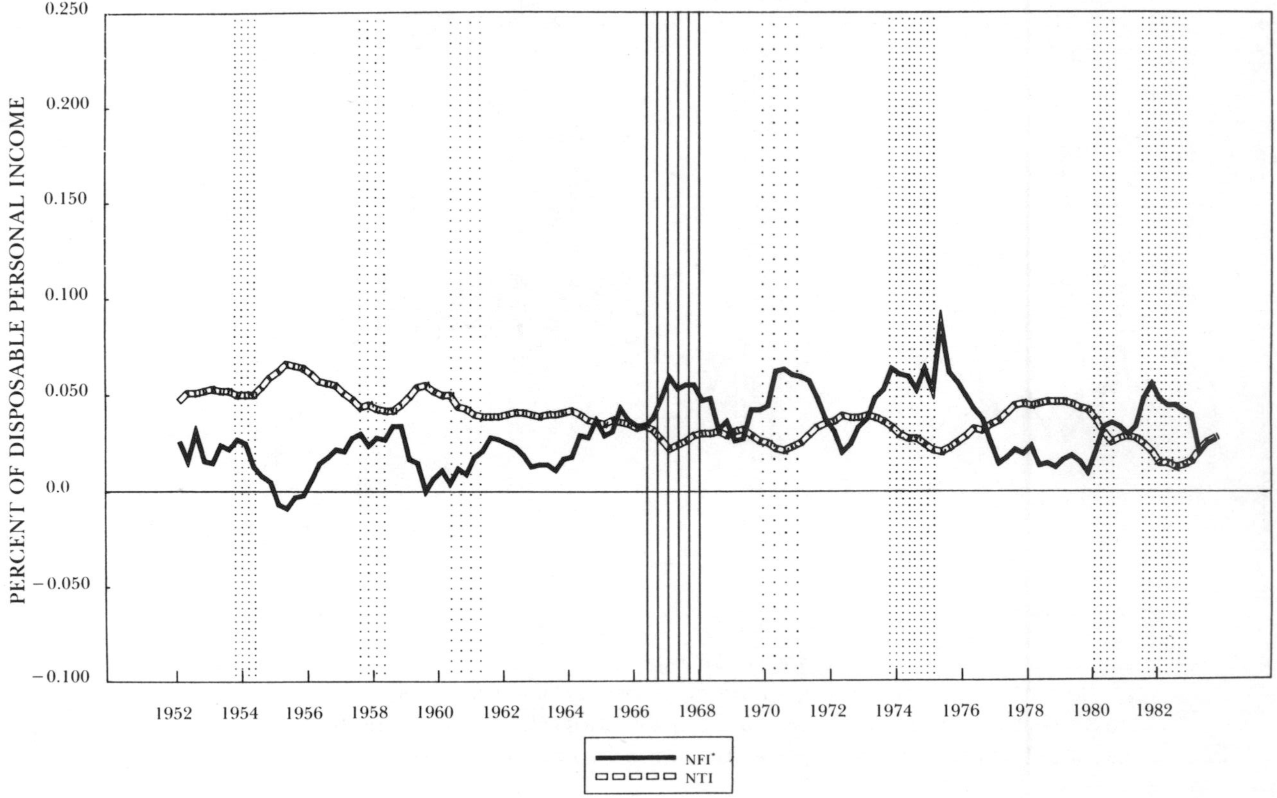

62

asset acquisitions also have some cyclical association with changes in tangible-asset holdings—the relationship is inverse rather than direct as with changes in liabilities—the association appears to be substantially weaker. Second, there seems to have been a distinct secular trend throughout the post-World War II period in the two principal components of saving (Figure 5). Net financial investments have a distinctly positive time trend over this period, while NTI has a distinctly negative trend; both trends are statistically significant. The cyclical movement in these two major components are negatively correlated: the changes in NFI are dominated by the (negative) changes in financial investment resulting from changes in liabilities, and these vary inversely with changes in tangible-asset holdings.

As shown earlier in Figure 1, there is little evidence of any overall trend during the entire post-World War II period in the aggregate ratio of total personal saving to disposable personal income: what little trend appears in the data is slightly negative and is not significant.[5] (In contrast, the time trend in the FOF data is slightly positive but also nonsignificant.) And if the same series could be extended backward into the nineteenth century, the evidence from the careful studies of Goldsmith (1955) and Kuznets (1961) is that the same general pattern (no long-term trend) in the ratio of saving to income would be observed.

We turn next to an examination of the contractual components in the personal-saving rate. In the FOF data, contractual savings can be represented by the sum of two components: changes in life-insurance reserves, and changes in reserves of pension funds. In the NIPA concept, as noted earlier, changes in contractual saving exclude changes in the reserves of public pension funds but include changes in the reserves of private pension funds. The two contractual savings-to-income ratios are shown in Figure 6. The more narrow definition associated with the NIPA definition of saving has a slight (significant) upward trend during the post-World War II period, while the broader definition, which includes saving in the form of public pension funds, has a larger (also significant) upward trend that appears to accelerate during the latter part of the period.

It is hard to see the justification for the treatment of pension funds in the NIPA data. There is virtually no difference in the behavioral content of changes in either public or private pension-fund reserves: in neither case do households have any direct ability to control such reserves; in neither case are all of the reserves fully vested or fully guaranteed; and there appears to be no systematic difference in the degree to which either public or private pension funds underaccrue the reserves needed to discharge future liabilities. The distinction between the two drawn in the NIPA data was apparently the result of a reluctance to

Figure 6. Alternative estimates of the ratio of contractual saving to disposable personal income.

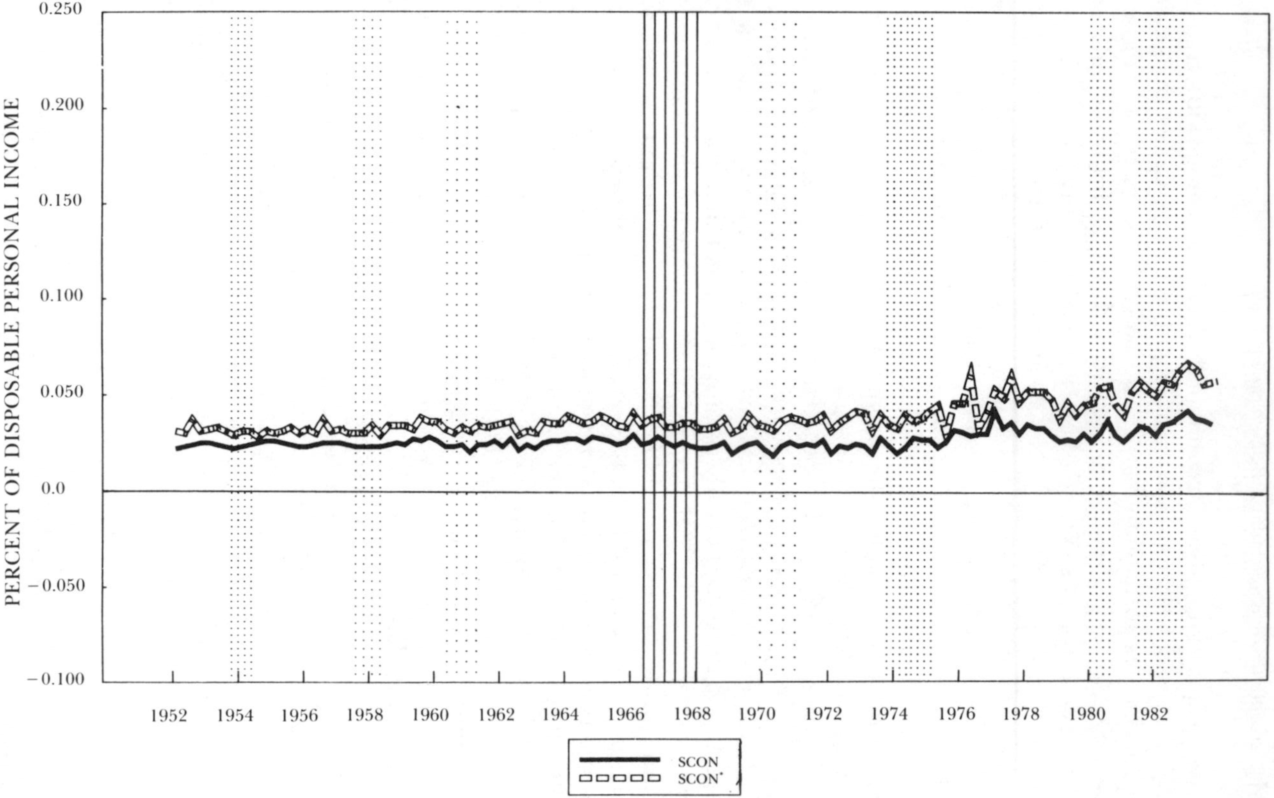

include public pension funds in saving because of the way in which social security payments are treated in the accounts. These are handled as straight tax and transfer transactions, as seems appropriate given the way in which the system developed. But pension funds available to both federal and state and local government employees should not really be treated in the same way, and there seems little justification for the differing NIPA treatment of public and private pension funds. Thus the FOF definitions seem more appropriate for behavioral analysis.

Figure 7 divides the NFI component of personal saving into its two major parts—contractual financial saving and the rest (variable financial saving). Net tangible asset investments are also shown in Figure 7. What we observe is hardly surprising: most of NFI takes the form of contractual saving, and virtually all net saving takes the form of either contractual financial saving or net increases in tangible-asset holdings: variable financial-asset saving has a strong cyclical component, is dominantly influenced by the behavior of changes in liabilities, and has a cumulative net negative change over the entire post-World War II period.

It is useful to note that the data in Figure 7 do not quite reflect the difference between contractual saving and discretionary saving, since the liability series embedded in the variable financial investment series is in turn the sum of two components, one of which is partly contractual and the other, discretionary. The contractual component consists of debt repayments resulting from prior decisions to acquire tangible assets like houses and cars, while the variable component consists of decisions to acquire new debt, usually simultaneously with acquisition of a tangible asset. Thus the net increase in liability series really has a contractual component and a discretionary component, and the data that we have been using shows the net influence of the two combined. If we had broken out contractual changes in liabilities from total change in liabilities, the contractual component would show large positive saving (debt repayment), while the discretionary part would show even larger negative saving (new debt acquisition).

The final adjustment to the data on personal saving that seems warranted on behavioral grounds involves the treatment of consumer durables. In the NIPA saving data, acquisition of consumer durables is treated as consumer spending rather than as investment, although the liabilities incurred to acquire such products are included (negatively) in personal saving. It has long been noted that there is little warrant for a difference in the treatment of owner-occupied housing from that of cars and other long-lived consumer assets, and that treating such assets as investment and saving provides a better picture of how consumers actually make decisions about the future (Ruggles and Ruggles, 1970;

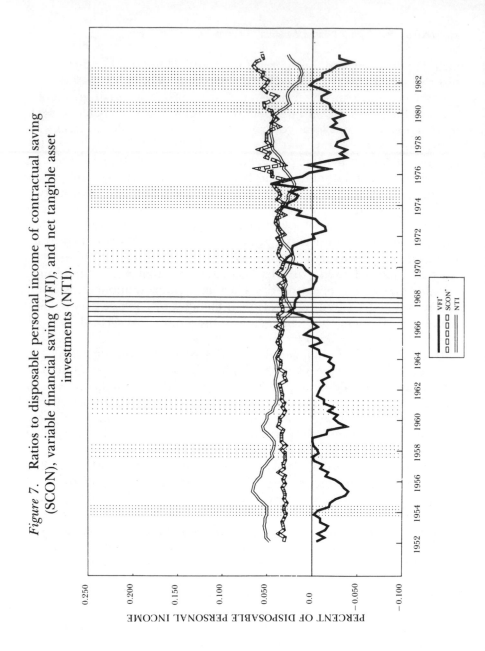

Figure 7. Ratios to disposable personal income of contractual saving (SCON), variable financial saving (VFI), and net tangible asset investments (NTI).

66

Juster, 1966; Kendrick, 1976). Thus Figure 8 portrays two versions of NTI investment: one is the conventional measure embedded in the NIPA saving data, while the other adds net investments in consumer durables to the housing and nonprofit investment included in the NIPA data. The resulting series shows a bit more variability in cyclical movement and about the same (negative) time trend.

Finally, Figure 9 shows the major components of my preferred definition of personal saving; Table 1 summarizes the definitions used throughout. Figure 9 displays variable financial investments, contractual financial investments, and net tangible asset investments. The first variable combines increases in financial assets exclusive of contractual saving with net increases in liabilities and adjusts for the statistical discrepancy; the second includes changes in contractual saving reflected by growth in life insurance reserves and in both public and private pension-fund systems; and the third includes net investments in housing, consumer durables, and nonprofit organizations. These data are only slightly different from those portrayed in Figure 7; the only difference is the addition of net investments in consumer durables in Figure 9. Contractual financial savings show a slight upward trend, net tangible asset investments show a slight downward trend, and variable financial investments show very substantial cyclical variability but no particular trend over the entire period. To me, these seem to be the set of data relating to personal saving behavior that must be explained.[6]

IV. BEHAVIORAL RELATIONSHIPS

For the study of behavioral relationships, we will concentrate largely on the decades of the 1970s and 1980s. We start with an examination of the variable components of saving, reflected by net investments in tangible assets and the variable component of consumer financial investment—the latter dominated by the liabilities series. Figure 10 shows the data.

The close correspondence between the two series is evident: cyclical movements in variable financial investment (VFI) are almost the mirror image of cyclical movements in net acquisitions of tangible assets, due, of course, to the close association between changes in tangible asset acquisitions and the changes in liabilities ordinarily associated with such acquisitions. However, some of the broader movements in the two series, especially during the 1970s, warrant closer examination. In particular, it is interesting to look at the influence of inflation rates on both financial and tangible asset investments.

The 1970s can be described as a decade when NFIs by households

Figure 8. Ratios to disposable personal income of alternative measures of net tangible asset investments (NTIs) by households.

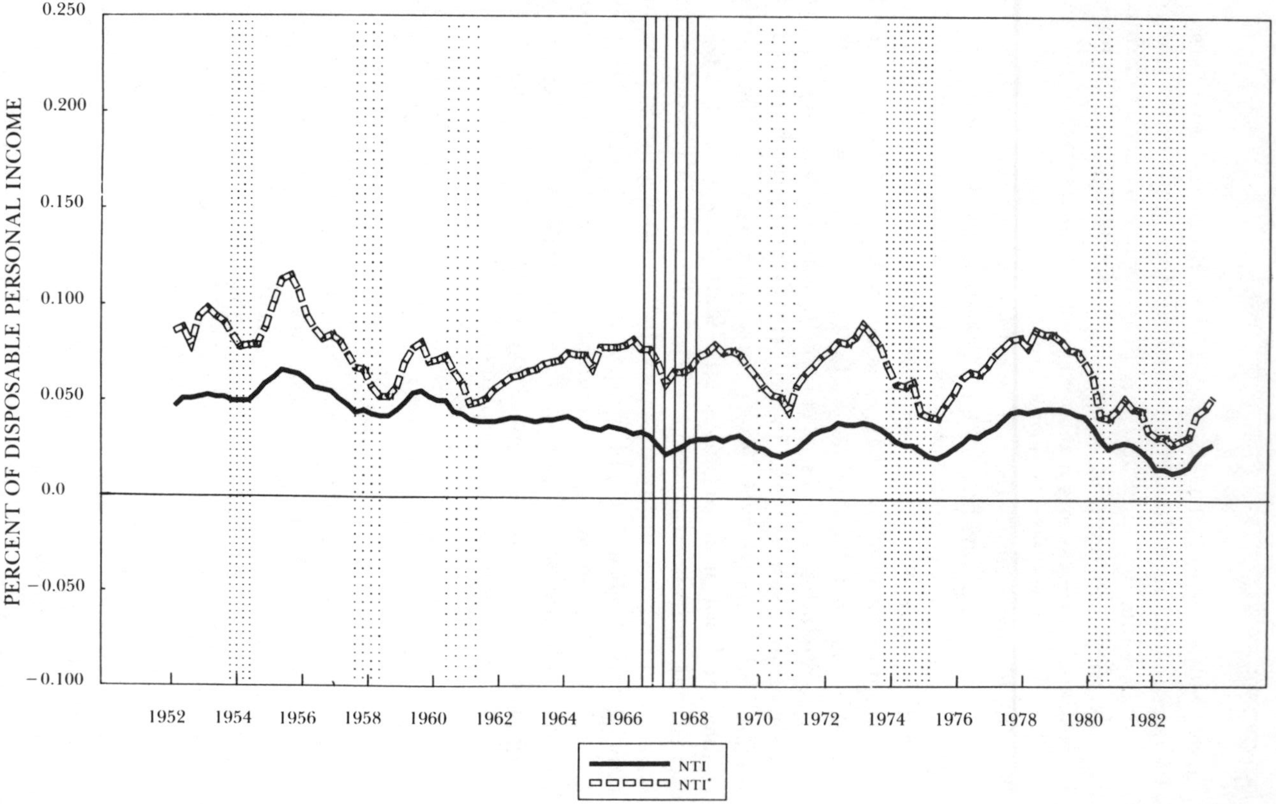

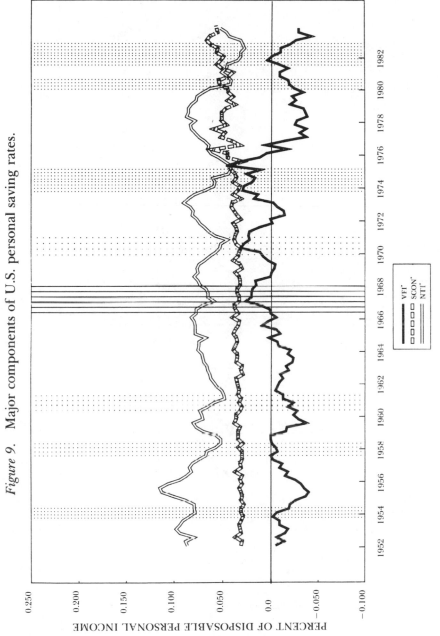

Figure 9. Major components of U.S. personal saving rates.

PERCENT OF DISPOSABLE PERSONAL INCOME

69

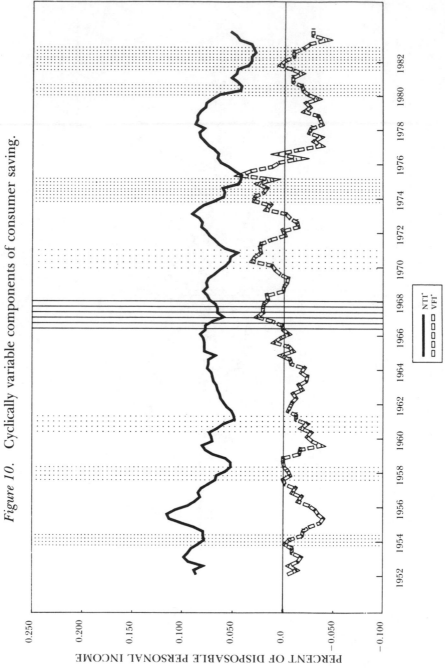

Figure 10. Cyclically variable components of consumer saving.

70

were well above average during the first half of the decade and somewhat below average during the second half. A simple association between NFIs and either actual or expected inflation rates clearly cannot explain the facts: inflation rates were relatively stable during the 1950s and most of the 1960s, accelerated substantially during the late 1960s and during the early and middle 1970s, and reached double-digit levels for the first time in many decades during 1974 and again in the late 1970s; VFIs were generally negative during the 1950s and most of the 1960s, generally positive during the late 1960s and early or middle 1970s, and negative in the late 1970s.

A significant element in the explanation of the high financial asset net acquisition rate in the early part of the 1970s and the lower rate in the latter part seems to be the way in which consumers reacted to inflation. In the early part of the 1970s, as well as in the late 1960s, consumers seemed to react to the prospects of inflation by retrenching on spending and adding to their savings (Juster and Taylor, 1975; Juster and Wachtel, 1972). High inflation rates induce uncertainty about future real income prospects, and consumers reacted to that uncertainty by retrenchment. There were a few key markets—cars and houses—where inflation prospects occasionally appeared to have the opposite effect—acceleration of purchases rather than entrenchment—but the dominant influence appears to have been the uncertainty created by the inflation.

In sharp contrast, during the latter part of the 1970s, when inflation began to accelerate again after cooling off in the aftermath of the 1974–1975 recession, the dominant reaction of consumers appeared to be speculative buying fueled by the anticipation of future price increases. That reaction was pervasive across all consumer markets—cars, houses, durable goods, and so on.

The proposition that the reaction of U.S. consumers to inflation has changed markedly from the early and middle 1970s to the late 1970s is examined in Table 2 and Figure 11. Table 2 shows the results of an attempt to discover whether the behaviorally plausible reaction of consumers to high inflation rates—retrenchment due to uncertainty—could be found in behavioral responses from a cross-section of consumers. We designed a survey question that asked consumers directly about two possible reactions to inflation—buy in advance before prices go up, and retrench on spending in order to conserve resources. When the question was first asked in the mid–1970s, the results were strongly consistent with the proposition that retrenchment on spending was the dominant consumer reaction: by margins of five or six to one, consumers reported that their reaction to inflation was to retrench on spending rather than to buy in advance.

But toward the latter part of the 1970s the movement of these data

Table 2. Survey Responses: Reactions To Inflation[a]

| Yr:Qtr | Buy Before Prices Go Up | | Both Reactions | Try to Cut Down Spending | | No Indication of Either[d] | Don't Know, Not Ascertained |
	All	Qualified[b]		All	Qualified[c]		
1975:2	8%	2	3%	56%	5%	28%	5%
1975:3	9	2	5	66	5	16	4
1976:3	11	4	6	43	2	37	3
1977:2	10	1	5	49	1	33	3
1977:3	9	2	4	47	2	36	4
1977:4	11	1	5	51	1	30	3
1978:1	9	2	7	46	2	35	3
1979:1	12	4	7	39	3	40	2

Notes:

[a]The question posed to respondents during 1975 was: "When prices go up, some people react by figuring that they should buy things they need before prices go up further, while others react by trying to cut down their spending because they are worried about making ends meet. How is it with you?" After 1975, the phrase "react by figuring they should" was omitted.

[b]Typical responses were that buying before prices go up was the desired behavior, but respondents felt that money was short, or they wanted to save.

[c]Typical responses were that saving was the desired behavior, but respondents found that inflation made it hard to save, or they had to spend regardless of prices.

[d]No choice detected, or neither response important.

Source: *Surveys of Consumer Attitudes*, Survey Research Center, The University of Michigan.

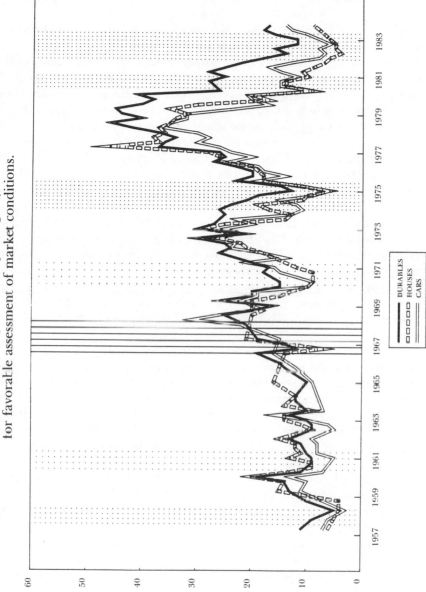

Figure 11. Percent of survey respondents reporting buy-in-advance rationale tor favorable assessment of market conditions.

73

shows an interesting pattern—one that is consistent with a shift from spending retrenchment to buy in advance. The data do not show that buy-in-advance reactions become stronger than uncertainty and caution reactions, but they do show an appreciable shrinking of the margin by which uncertainty responses exceed buy-in-advance responses. In short, the late 1970s has many more buy-in-advance responses than was true of the middle 1970s, and many fewer uncertainty responses.

The same pattern is shown by Figure 11, which contains a somewhat different measure of the strength of buy-in-advance reactions. The data represent the time-series patterns of joint responses to two survey questions for three products—cars, houses, and durable goods. Figure 11 plots the proportion of households that report *both* that this is a good time to buy (houses, cars, durables) *and* that the reason is that prices are expected to be higher in the future. That is, it is the proportion of consumers who report that this is a good time to buy houses, cars, and durables because prices for these products are rising. The data show a very sharp increase in buy-in-advance psychology in the late 1970s, consistent with the time-series evidence as well as the declining margin of uncertainty over buy-in-advance responses obtained from the cross-section data.

The reader may ask whether the cross-section data in Table 2 are consistent with the hypothesis that buy-in-advance responses dominated uncertainty reactions in the late 1970s, since the table shows that uncertainty responses continued to be more frequent. The answer is that buy-in-advance responses may well have been dominant despite the fact that uncertainty responses appear to be more numerous: all survey questions contain perceptual biases—there may be socially acceptable responses that tend to show up in particular response categories. All one can really tell from survey responses is the change over time in the relative importance of different responses, and the data clearly show that buy-in-advance responses grew in strength substantially during the latter part of the 1970s. Figure 11 tells the same story.

One way to characterize the 1970s from the perspective of consumer reactions to inflation is that the double-digit inflation of the early part of the decade gave rise to what has been the traditional reaction of U.S. consumers to inflation—retrenchment on spending and an attempt to build reserves as a contingency against uncertainty.[7] But consumers appear to have learned that inflation rates did not result in as much damage to their real-income position as they had feared; they also learned to take advantage of the prospect of rising prices by accelerating purchases. Once that lesson has been learned, it seems unlikely to be unlearned: the typical reaction of consumers to inflation in the 1980s is more likely to be speculative buying than retrenchment due to uncertainty.

A second interesting feature of the post-World War II saving data relates to the trend of contractual savings. As shown in Figure 6, the preferred definition of contractual saving shows a slight upward tilt in the ratio of contractual saving to income during the 1970s and the early 1980s. These data presumably correspond to the growing incidence of pension plans in both the public and the private sectors, reflecting both more generous pension arrangements as well as the spread of employment situations with associated pension arrangements. There seems to be little evidence in the data (see Figure 9, e.g.) that this rising trend in contractual savings had a negative affect on the trend of noncontractual savings. The latter have often been negative, are dominantly influenced by changes in liabilities, and seemed to be no more negative in the latter part of the period than they were during the 1950s or 1960s.

These data seem to me to call into question the conclusions reached by recent analyses of the trade-offs among various forms of saving, especially between private saving and saving in the form of social security entitlements (Munnell, 1974; Feldstein, 1974; Leimar and Lesnoy, 1980). If there were trade-offs between larger flows of future social security benefits that take the form of higher values of something called "social security wealth," then private contractual savings should have shown a tendency to decline over the post-World War II period. During this entire postwar period, social security wealth has risen appreciably. If that development made consumers less willing to save in other forms, we should have expected to see some weakening of the flow of contractual saving outside of the social security system. But the data show no evidence of this effect; in fact, they show, if anything, exactly the reverse—a tendency for contractual financial saving to rise, relative to income, over the postwar period.

How might one explain the tendency for private contractual saving to grow in the face of enhanced social security benefit flows and thus intangible assets in the form of "social security wealth?" Possible answers to that question were advanced a good many years ago by George Katona (1965) and Philip Cagan (1965). Katona hypothesized that psychological theory related to goal attainment would have predicted a positive influence of larger social security wealth on other forms of saving. Simply put, if a goal is perceived to be totally unreachable, there is little incentive on the part of people to take actions designed to reach it. But once people perceive that a goal is within reach, more intensive, rather than less intensive, efforts to reach it are the appropriate response. In the case of provision for retirement, it would thus be argued that prior to the establishment of the social security system an attempt to provide an adequate income during retirement years would have been regarded by most members of the population as unattainable. But establishment of the social security system made the goal reachable, and thus efforts to realize a satisfactory living standard during retirement have resulted in a rise in other forms of saving, rather than a decline. Cagan argued that the initiation of private pension plans resulted in a recognition effect (greater awareness of retirement needs), with the result that saving non-pension forms increased rather than decreased. Both are striking illustrations of the different conclusions reached by economists working within a fixed goal—constrained optimization framework—and others working within a learning/adaptation framework.[8]

It is worth noting that neither the goal-attainment nor the recognition-effect interpretation of the past precludes the possibility that a more conventional trade-off interpretation may be operative in the future. Suppose it were true, for example, that current levels of prospective social security benefits in conjunction with current levels of private provisions for retirement added up to a retirement income widely judged as satisfactory. It would then be true that any future expansion of the social security benefit structure might well result in reduced incentives to accumulate assets in the form of private pension reserves, since the incentives associated with scrambling to reach a goal judged to be attainable would be less important once it is widely believed that the goal had been reached.

Of course, other types of learning theory argue against that conclusion: there is no reason to believe that goals of any sort, including retirement goals, are fixed and immutable over time and are unresponsive to current living standards. The dynamics of rising real incomes might well generate continued strong incentives to accumulate in the private pension systems even if it were the case that social security pension benefits also tended to expand. The principal point is that, while one might see as a behaviorally satisfactory explanation the past tendency of private pensions to increase during a period when social security benefits were rising, that model does not necessarily require that the future be like the past. It depends on how aspirations change with outcomes, and on the relative importance of retirement goals versus other types of goals.

The final behavioral issue that can be examined with the data on post-World War II saving relates to another issue that has been widely discussed during recent years in the conventional economic literature—the influence of tax and budget policy on private saving and, in particular, the influence of rates of return on saving.[9] The data discussed above provide us with some insight into this issue.

One important characteristic of consumer response to interest rates can be inferred from the data in Figure 9, where the contractual and noncontractual components of private saving are displayed, and by Figure 4, where the financial component of consumer saving is divided between financial asset changes and liability changes.

The financial-asset change data contain an interesting implicit story about the interest-rate response of consumer saving. Between about 1977 and 1981, consumer saving in the form of financial investments showed a general tendency to increase slightly: this phenomenon was the result of two quite strong offsetting movements—a substantial *decline* in financial-asset acquisitions relative to income and an even more substantial *decline* in the ratio of increases in consumer liabilities to income. During the same period, the nominal yield on corporate securities went from about 8 percent to roughly 16 percent, while the yield on treasury bills went from about 5 percent to about 15 percent. And the holdings of consumers in money-market funds rose from approximately zero to roughly $200 billion.

While the 1977–1981 period can generally be characterized as one in which nominal interest rates rose rapidly and real interest rates rose somewhat, from the point of view of consumers it is best characterized as a period when the nominal cost of liabilities rose rapidly, with real costs perhaps rising somewhat, while at the same time both nominal and real rates of return on fixed-price assets were rising rapidly and virtually in tandem. That is, although much of the rise in borrowing cost can be represented as a rise in nominal rather than real costs, that was not true (for most of the population) with regard to the return on financial assets—such returns rose rapidly for most consumers in both nominal and real terms.

The reason that the rate of return on saving in the form of fixed-price assets rose substantially in real terms during this period was the initiation of a new market instrument—the money-market fund. Prior to the existence of such funds, consumers who wished to obtain market rates of return on assets had to be sufficiently wealthy to be able to afford assets denominated in relatively large units. Most consumers were thus precluded from obtaining market rates of return on assets and were forced to settle for the conventional rate of return on savings accounts. But money-market funds changed that situation entirely, and after 1977 many more consumers had access to market rates of return than had been the case previously. The effect, over a three- or four-year period, was a virtual tripling of the real rate of return to many consumers in the U.S. economy, since the rapid rise in market rates on money-market funds translated into a one-for-one increase in real rates of return.

If one looks at the data to determine what effect this enormous increase in real rates of return had on consumer saving in the form of financial assets, the answer appears to be: almost none. There was, of course, an explosion of holding of money-market funds, but there was an almost equally large reduction in holdings of other asset forms with lower yields. The fact that saving rates rose somewhat over the period is apparently due, either largely or entirely, to the sharp decline in the rate at which consumers increased liabilities.

More generally, the picture projected by the post-World War II data on changes in consumer holdings of assets and in liabilities is that most of the movement in net financial investments is associated with a change in liabilities. There is abundant evidence that consumer indebtedness is strongly influenced by changes in income, the cyclical phase of the economy, and borrowing costs. Thus interest rates do have an impact on consumer saving, but it appears that the primary channel is via its impact on the liability side of consumer balance sheets. There is virtually no evidence that changes in rates of return on assets have a significant influence on the asset side of consumer balance sheets, although differences in rates of return among types of assets will have dramatic effects on the composition of consumer portfolios.

V. CONCLUSIONS

What can we learn from this brief overview of the characteristics of consumer saving behavior in the United States? For one, we can find evidence that the behavioral responses of consumers to the same external stimuli are quite likely to change over time with experience. The evidence here consists of the behavioral responses of consumers to inflation, which appeared to have been quite different during the earlier episodes of escalating inflation rates (during the late 1960s and the early and middle 1970s) than was the case during the most recent and most sustained experience with rising inflation rates. Second, there is some reason to be skeptical about an analysis of secular trends in saving behavior that relies heavily on the presumption that consumers retain an unchanged set of savings objectives such that an increased likelihood of attaining the objective by one means lowers incentive to move toward the same objective by other means. Not only is the evidence (inconclusive, to be sure) on the long-term stability of the saving/income ratio inconsistent with the behavior implied by constrained optimization models, but the component of saving that ought to be most closely related to public provisions for retirement security (private contractual saving) goes in the wrong direction over the post-World War II period.

Finally, the data suggest that the response of consumers to rate-of-return factors is much stronger on the liabilities side of consumer balance sheets than on the asset side: there is little evidence to suggest that consumer asset acquisition is significantly impacted by changes in rates of return. If so, policies designed to increase the flow of personal saving would seem to have better prospects of success if they operated on the liabilities side rather than on the asset side. In the very long term, the evidence implies that no set of public policies is likely to have much effect on aggregate personal saving. But in the short-to-intermediate term, the sensitivity of the liabilities side of consumer balance sheets suggests that policies designed to change the cost of borrowing, or the terms on which borrowing is permitted, are much more likely to impact consumer saving than policies designed to modify the return on assets.

ACKNOWLEDGMENTS

Prepared for presentation at the First Annual Conference on Behavioral Economics. The conference was held at Princeton on May 22 and 23, 1984, supported by a grant from the Sloan Foundation and sponsored by: Department of Economics, Rutgers, The State University of New Jersey; Woodrow Wilson School, Princeton University; and Society for Advancement of Behavioral Economics.

This paper grows out of work supported by the National Science Foundation (Grant SOC 74–22104).

NOTES

1. An early and vigorous treatment of the importance of worrying about dispersion can be found in Hart (1940). More recent work on consumer saving behavior (Juster and Taylor, 1975) has a similar flavor.

2. For a thorough review of the literature on saving behavior up through the late 1960s, see Mayer (1972).

3. It should be kept in mind that there is no basic statistical disagreement about the trend of movement over time in *total* national saving. The difference in FOF and NIPA estimates for the household sector largely represents offsetting differences in estimates of sectoral (household, business, foreign) contributions to a national saving estimate that must be related to an accurately measured estimate of total national investment. But the FOF versus NIPA issue is important for resolution of the behavior of personal saving.

4. In the FOF data, two components that are not really part of the household sector are incorporated into the estimates of household saving. One is the NFI for the noncorporate sector, which is part of the change in financial assets assigned to the household sector, and the other is the net investment in nonprofit institutions, which is part of the NTI series.

5. Benchmark revisions of the NIPA data appear periodically and have usually raised the level of saving during the last few years prior to the revision date. Thus the negative trend is likely to be overstated.

6. There are other elements that should be considered as part of any full story about

personal saving behavior but that are not treated here—for example, saving in the form of human capital accumulation, research and development expenditures, and so on.

7.   That reaction can be observed as far back as the early 1950s, during the high inflation-rate period associated with the Korean War.

8.   There is a very illuminating paragraph in Feldstein's (1974) original article dealing with this issue, in which he notes the goal-attainment argument but essentially says that since the argument amounts to allowing for changing tastes, it is outside the framework of the theory. Is the endogenizing of tastes, which is what both the goal-attainment theory and the recognition effect amount to, outside the purview of economic theory or uninteresting?

9.   The literature is discussed in a recent working paper by Kotlikoff ("Taxation and Saving—A Neoclassical Perspective," Lawrence J. Kotlikoff, Working Paper No. 1302, NBER).

REFERENCES

Ando, Albert, and Franco Modigliani, "The 'Life-Cycle' Hypothesis of Saving," *American Economic Review*, 53 (March 1963), 55–84.

Barro, Robert J., *The Impact of Social Security on Private Saving*. Washington, D.C.: American Enterprise Institute for Public Policy Research, 1978.

Cagan, Philip, "The Effects of Pension Plans on Aggregate Saving: Evidence from a Sample Survey." Occasional Paper No. 95, National Bureau of Economic Research, 1965.

Duesenberry, James, *Income, Saving and the Theory of Consumer Behavior*. Cambridge, MA: Harvard University Press, 1949.

Feldstein, Martin, "Social Security, Induced Retirement and Aggregate Capital Accumulation," *Journal of Political Economy*, 82 (September–October 1974), 905–926.

Friedman, Milton, *A Theory of the Consumption Function*. Princeton, NJ: Princeton University Press for the National Bureau of Economic Research, 1957.

Goldsmith, Raymond W., *A Study of Saving in the United States*. Princeton, NJ: Princeton University Press for the National Bureau of Economic Research, 1955.

Hart, Albert G., "Anticipations, Uncertainty and Dynamic Planning," in *Studies in Business Administration*, Vol. II, no. 1. Chicago: University of Chicago Press, 1940.

Juster, F. Thomas, "Current and Prospective Financial Status of the Elderly Population," in P. Cagan, ed., *Saving for Retirement*. Report on a Miniconference on Saving held for the White House Conference on Aging, 1981.

Juster, F. Thomas, *Household Capital Formation and Financing, 1897–1962*. New York: Columbia University Press for the National Bureau of Economic Research, 1966.

Juster, F. Thomas, and Lester D. Taylor, "Towards a Theory of Saving Behavior," *American Economic Review*, 65 (May 1975), 203–209.

Juster, F. Thomas, and Paul Wachtel, "Inflation and the Consumer," *Brookings Papers on Economic Activity*, (1972), 1, 71–114.

Katona, George, *Private Pensions and Individual Saving*. Ann Arbor, MI: The University of Michigan, Survey Research Center (Monograph No. 40), 1965.

Kendrick, John, *The Formation and Stocks of Total Capital*. New York: Columbia University Press for the National Bureau of Economic Research, 1976.

Keynes, John Maynard, *The General Theory of Employment, Interest and Money*. New York: Harcourt, Brace & Co., 1936.

Kuznets, Simon, *Capital in the American Economy*. Princeton, NJ: Princeton University Press for the National Bureau of Economic Research, 1961.

Leiberman, Charles, and Paul Wachtel, "Age Structure and Personal Saving Behavior," in G. von Furstenberg, ed., *Social Security versus Private Saving*. Cambridge, MA: Ballinger, 1980, chapter 9.

Leimer, Dean R., and Selig D. Lesnoy, "Social Security and Private Saving: A Reexamination of the Time Series Evidence Using Alternative Social Security Wealth Variables." Working Paper No. 19, Social Security Administration, Office of Research and Statistics, November, 1980.

Mayer, Thomas, *Permanent Income, Wealth, and Consumption*. Berkeley, CA: University of California Press, 1972.

Modigliani, Franco, and Richard Brumberg, "Utility Analysis and the Consumption Function: An Interpretation of Cross-Section Data," in K. Kurihara, ed., *Post-Keynesian Economics*, London: George Allen and Unwin, 1955.

Munnell, Alicia H., *The Effects of Social Security on Personal Saving in the U.S.* Cambridge, MA: Ballinger, 1974.

Ruggles, Nancy, and Richard Ruggles, *The Design of Economic Accounts*. New York: Columbia University Press for the National Bureau of Economic Research, 1970.

Wachtel, Paul, *Household Saving and Demographic Change, 1950–2050.* New York: New York University Graduate School of Business Administration, October 1980.

PART II

ECONOMIC POLICY

INTRODUCTION TO PART II:
ECONOMIC POLICY

Doing economics without prescribing policy is similar to practicing psychiatry but refusing to buy a sofa. The temptation to recommend "corrective" measures, usually in the form of government intervention, is too strong for mortals to resist. The result when the advice is heeded is frequently wasteful and sometimes disastrous. The problem is that *effective* policy is impossible without an understanding of the behavioral variables involved in the implementation of intervention. That does not imply that there are no theoretical difficulties underlying the failure, as any economist of the *other* "camp" will quickly point out. The point is that, regardless of the stand one takes in relation to public policy aimed at correcting the real or imagined "market failures," it is imperative, to use Howard Kunreuther's words (from his paper, which follows), that we understand the importance of "descriptive analysis as a prelude to prescriptive recommendations." The three papers in this part address, to a lesser or greater degree, this aspect of "behavioral public policy."

Howard Kunreuther's paper, which opens this part, is based largely on the work of the Wharton group, which he heads. The group has recently found an institutional base in the new Risk and Decision Processes Center at The Wharton School. After reading Kunreuther's paper it becomes clear why the center is playing such a pivotal role in the development of behavioral economics and why it can be expected to continue to do so in the future.

Alan Lewis's paper is about the field its author founded—fiscal psychology. The essence of the message of the paper is captured in the following words from its section IV: "A behavioral approach does not take issue with the notion that [tax] evasion is a function of opportunity, probability of detection, and the size of the fine; instead it stresses the way these factors are mediated through attitudes and perceptions." The difference between Gary Becker's approach to behavior and Alan Lewis's view is the difference between the elegant predictions of a stylized model employing theoretical parameters and the much more restricted predictions of a dynamic model employing subjective (i.e., real) factors.

Richard Coughlin's paper attempts to reconcile the apparent contradiction of unfaltering public support for the current system of social security and the neoclassical assumption of rationality. Despite important criticism of its goals, methods, and value, social security enjoys widespread public support, as revealed by various surveys. To explain the paradox, Coughlin proposes a modification of the rational-choice model to include some psychological and sociological insights about the extended self and the attitude of the individual as part of the sociopolitical climate of the time.

The last paper, by McGonagle, is based on the author's firsthand experience in the insurance industry. The paper suggests that the Heisenberg principle (one cannot observe a phenomenon without changing it) has an application in economic regulation. The phenomena reported in the paper raise some interesting questions. Why do insurance executives want to disguise their weak condition from the regulator even though in doing so they may kill their respective firms? This is analogous to lying to your doctor about your symptoms when you are taking a physical. Furthermore, what changes can be made in the regulatory process that will give the company a behavioral incentive to want to cooperate with the regulator? All these are issues related to the basic question of how to make a policy effective. The answers will not be found unless economists delve into behavioral considerations.

BEHAVIORAL INSIGHTS FOR PUBLIC POLICY:

EX ANTE/EX POST CONSIDERATIONS

Howard Kunreuther

I. INTRODUCTION

An important theme in Behavioral Economics is the appropriate role of the market system in dealing with problems of uncertainty. Economists traditionally use market systems as a benchmark to evaluate other policy options that are used in the real world. Although a price system may be highly appropriate for private-market transactions such as buying and selling consumer goods, it is less appropriate for coping with problems that have a societal impact (Stokey and Zeckhauser, 1978). There are two elements that are of particular concern here:

1. *Uncertainty with respect to different outcomes.* Many problems involve elements of risk to different interested parties. For example, an individual living in a floodplain or near a new technological facility faces a risk of a potential disaster. Passengers or drivers of automobiles face the chance of a car accident. Frequently these risks are not well specified or understood by the relevant interested parties. This misinformation or misperception can lead to problems in market failure (see Akerlof, 1970; Arrow, 1982).
2. *The public good or public bad nature of certain problems.* Each taxpayer may subsidize potential victims for the costs associated with disasters.

For example, those suffering losses from natural disasters may receive liberal relief from the federal government in the form of grants and low-interest loans. Those injured in automobile accidents may receive subsidized health care. To the extent that these *ex post* payments discourage *ex ante* protective action, there is a type of market failure. Another type of public goods problem relates to the siting of technological facilities that promise to yield benefits to many but imposes costs on a (relatively) few individuals. Without some compensation mechanism for sharing potential gains between winners and losers, these projects may never receive final approval.

This paper examines a class of problems that involve risk and uncertainty or have the character of a public good/bad. Particular attention will be given to problems where there is a low probability of a negative outcome to the individual and/or society. There will normally be an opportunity for taking action in anticipation of the negative event (i.e., *ex ante* policies) as well as after the event occurs (*ex post* policies). Our primary focus will be on how the decision processes of individuals impact on the design of alternative *ex ante* and *ex post* programs. The paper also raises a set of questions about the types of alternative social institutions that may emerge when the market fails to allocate resources efficiently.

To motivate the analysis of market and nonmarket mechanisms, consider the following areas of current interest:

- *Automobile safety*: What are the appropriate roles of market mechanisms and regulations with respect to reducing injuries and fatalities on the road? Specifically, should there be formal requirements that some type of passive restraint (e.g., automatic seat belts, air bags) be installed in all new cars, or can market mechanisms achieve desirable outcomes? This issue currently faces the National Highway Traffic Safety Administration in the U.S. Department of Transportation.
- *Natural disasters*: What role should the federal government play with respect to providing relief for natural-hazard victims? Specifically, what role should insurance play in relation to disaster relief in coping with these problems?
- *Hazardous-waste siting*: What is the appropriate role of government at the state and federal levels with respect to the siting of hazardous-waste facilities? Specifically, can one develop meaningful marketlike mechanisms such as compensation for helping to successfully negotiate a feasible site?
- *Nuclear power plants*: What role should the government play with respect to facilitating the development of nuclear power as a source

of energy? Specifically, should the current federally subsidized insurance program (i.e., the Price-Anderson Act) be renewed in its present form?

The next section develops a conceptual framework for understanding the interaction among consumers, firms, and government agencies facing these problems. A simple model will be developed that addresses the relationship between *ex ante* actions and *ex post* behavior. We have focused on this aspect of the problem because it raises a set of questions regarding the decision processes of the interested parties and the role of misinformation and asymmetric information in their final choices. Section III introduces a set of strategies linking *ex ante* and *ex post* behavior. These strategies range from market-like mechanisms such as information provision and compensation to more centralized problems such as formal regulations. The concluding section summarizes the implications of the analysis for future research. Throughout the paper the above four problems will be used to illustrate the importance of incorporating descriptive analysis in the development of strategies.

II. A WELFARE-MAXIMIZING FRAMEWORK

A. Basic Assumptions

The class of problems outlined above involves the possible occurrence of an event that will produce adverse effects to a given class of individuals. To simplify the analysis, the world is divided into two groups with respective populations N_i ($i = 1, 2$):

Potential victims (N_1): Those who face a given event that occurs with known probability (Φ) and creates a potential loss (L). If there is an opportunity for an individual to reduce the impact of the loss to him or her through some type of protection, we assign two potential outcomes—L_y (if protection is adopted) and L_n (if protection is not adopted), where $L_n > L_y$.

Other individuals (N_2): Those who do not face the threat of a loss but may subsidize the potential victims *ex ante* and/or assist in *ex post* payments following the occurrence of a loss. *Ex ante* payments can take the form of lump-sum transfers such as compensation for individuals living near a hazardous technological facility or subsidizing protective activities like air-bag installations or flood insurance. Examples of *ex post* payments are subsidized disaster relief or health care.

If protective activities are available, they are provided by suppliers in the form of a physical product such as a safety device or as a contingent claim such as an insurance policy. The type of protection will vary depending on the nature of the problem. Here we will assume that only one option is available at a cost of C dollars. Thus automobile companies supply only one type of air bag, and insurance companies offer one type of policy with a given stated loss.

The *ex ante* and *ex post* payments will be a function of the costs of protection and the magnitude of the loss inflicted on the victim. More specifically, let:

$S_{A1}(C)$ = *ex ante* subsidy to each potential victim in group 1 as a function of the cost of protection (C)

S_{A2} = *ex ante* subsidy provided by each individual in group 2

$S_{P1}(L_i)$ = *ex post* subsidy to each victim in group 1 as a function of the loss L_i i = y, n

S_{P2} = *ex post* subsidy provided by each individual in group 2.

Naturally, as the number of potential victims increases relative to the rest of the population there will be an increasing burden placed on the general taxpayer if disaster-related activities are subsidized.

The problem confronting the policymaker is to select a strategy that reflects the values of society. There are obviously a number of problems in choosing among alternative strategies. First, some measure(s) of welfare must be agreed on to help rank alternative policies. Second, since such welfare measures may be expected to depend on the actual behavior of consumers and firms, one must also understand what each actor's behavioral response will be to alternative free-market and governmental policies. These problems of representation of welfare and of predicting behavioral adjustment are central to public-policy analysis. At the outset, it is instructive to sketch the traditional framework for dealing with these issues.

In the traditional approach of neoclassical economics, individuals are assumed to be rational. This means that each individual or firm acts as if it were maximizing utility. In the above formulation all potential victims are assumed to be identical with respect to utility function U and initial wealth W_1; the other individuals are also identical and have a utility function V and initial wealth W_2. One of the controversial issues in welfare economics is what weight should be given to different segments of society. In this simplified example, suppose that the policymaker arbitrarily determines that potential victims are given a weight so that other individuals are assigned a weight $1 - \Psi$.[1]

The adjustment process is typically characterized by assuming that potential victims behave as if they were maximizing their expected perceived welfare, taking everyone else's behavior as fixed. The basic data required for the traditional descriptive analysis are the perceptions and associated utility functions of each party. Traditional welfare theory also assumes that each economic agent involved is the best judge of his or her own utility. There are, of course, many problems in choosing a welfare function, and these issues have been the subject of considerable debate in the economics literature. There seems to be general agreement in the literature on one important point, however: the utilities in the welfare function are evaluated under the assumption that individuals and firms are well-informed and rational.

A number of alternative programs can be formulated in the context of the simplified world constructed above. We will develop several of them in the following subsections.

B. Programs for Adopting Protective Activities

In order to determine whether market-based systems are likely to achieve a desired effect, it is necessary for individuals to have a choice between adopting or not adopting a protective activity. Suppose potential victims purchased *ex ante* protection and other individuals subsidized a certain proportion of its costs and a certain proportion of *ex post* losses. If potential victims voluntarily protected themselves under such policies (program I), the resulting societal welfare (F_I) is given by:

$$F_I = \psi[\Phi \, U(W_1 - C - L_y + S_{A1}(C) + S_{P1}(L_y)]$$
$$+ (1 - \Phi)U(W_1 - C + S_{A1}(C))] + (1 - \psi)[\Phi \, V(W_2 - S_{A2}(C) \quad (1)$$
$$- S_{P2}(L_y)] + (1 - \Phi) \, V(W_2 - S_{A2}(C)]$$

On the other hand, potential victims may decide not to purchase the product voluntarily, so that potential losses increase to L_n, but the cost of protection (C) is avoided. An analysis of the welfare effects of such an action, which is equivalent to the situation where no protection is available (program II), yields:

$$F_{II} = \psi[\Phi \, U[(W_1 - L_n + S_{P1}(L_n)] + (1 - \Phi) \, U(W_1)$$
$$+ (1 - \psi) \, [\Phi \, V[(W_2 - S_{P2}(L_n)] + (1 - \Phi) \, V(W_2)] \quad (2)$$

The programs presented above characterize both the auto-safety problem as well as the natural-disaster insurance question. In the case of automobile safety, the difference between L_n and L_y represents the reduction in the severity of injuries from a particular type of accident from the use of an air bag or passive restraint. In the case of natural disasters, the actual loss is L_n and the purchase of I dollars of insurance is equivalent to reducing the loss to $L_y = L_n - I$. The relative performance of programs I and II for these two problems depends on how individuals perceive risk, their decision processes, and how society views its obligation to protect individuals from misfortune through *ex ante* and/or *post ante* payments. Let ϕ represent the perception of the probability of an accident and ℓ_y and ℓ_n the respective perceived losses when protection is adopted or not adopted. If $\phi < \Phi$ and $\ell_y - \ell_n < L_y - L_n$, then the value of protection is considered by individuals to be less than if they had "objective" data.

High *ex ante* subsidies (S_{A1}) should encourage adoption of protection, while large *ex post* subsidies (S_{P1}) should discourage voluntary purchase. here again, actual behavior depends on the knowledge of these payments by potential victims and how it is incorporated into their decision processes. Suppose individuals utilize threshold models of choice by not worrying about events which they perceive to have a probability of occurrence below some prespecified value of ϕ.* The magnitudes of S_{A1} and S_{P1} will then be irrelevant to the choice process if $\phi < \phi^*$.

As an alternative to a voluntary program, the government might require individuals to purchase the protective activity. Air bags would be installed in all new cars, flood insurance would be required for all homes in the flood plain. If no *ex ante* subsidies are provided under such a program but *ex post* subsidies remained the same as before, the welfare impact of this regulatory scheme is given by:

$$F_{III} = \psi \left[\phi \ U[W_1 - C - L_y + S_{P1}(L_y) + (1-\phi) \ U(W_1 - C)] \right. \\ \left. + (1-\psi) \left[\phi \ V(W_2 - S_{P2}(L_y)) + (1-\phi) \ V(W_2) \right] \right. \tag{3}$$

Under this type of program, potential victims will feel worse off than if they had the choice of voluntarily adopting protection with an *ex ante* subsidy. Their actual expected welfare, however, may be improved if they decide not to protect themselves voluntarily because of their misperceptions of the risk (i.e., their underestimation of Φ and/or $L_n - L_y$) or the use of heuristics such as threshold models of choice. A comparison of the above programs is an important step in evaluating the desirability of regulations with respect to safety measures such as air bags. One must understand how individuals determine whether to purchase these products, what type of information they collect, and how they incorporate the data into their choice models.

Recent work in behavioral decision theory by psychologists and economists suggest that individuals possess considerable misinformation on risks (see Fischhoff et al., 1982) and that people do not behave as if they have maximized their expected utility (Kahneman and Tversky, 1979; Schoemaker, 1982). Furthermore, there is a growing body of evidence that suggests that the context in which information is framed will influence preferences (Hershey, Kunreuther, and Schoemaker, 1982) and choices (Tversky and Kahneman, 1981). One of the reasons for this behavior is that individuals may undertake a form of mental accounting in which the same data are perceived differently as a function of how they are presented (Thaler 1980, 1983). These behavioral findings suggest that when evaluating the welfare impacts of alternative programs, it is important to recognize that individuals may not maximize their expected utility. We will return to this general point in section III.

C. Compensation Programs for Siting Hazardous Facilities[2]

In the case of locating potentially hazardous facilities it is extremely difficult to reach acceptable solutions, for both normative and strategic reasons. From a normative perspective, conflict and disagreement stem from the fact that society lacks unanimity regarding some fundamental ethical issues raised by these siting problems. These issues include:

- What is a "fair" distribution of risks, benefits, and costs over time, space, and income classes?
- Who is responsible for the creation of safe production facilities?

According to O'Hare (1977), the strategic reason for resistance to facility siting is the condition of "public impotence." Society is unable to prevent a minority coalition of narrow (though legitimate) opponents from delaying or blocking the siting of otherwise socially worthwhile technological projects. In other words, society (the government) is currently unable to strike an acceptable balance among the democratic notions of protecting and giving expression to individual rights, protecting the rights of vocal interest groups, and rule by majority. The problems of resolving conflicts often revolve around the risks to human health, safety, and environment. Recent empirical research by Edwards and von Winderfeldt (1983) has shown that public movements can lead to disruption, halting, or abandonment of new technologies. Thus there is an urgent need to design appropriate public decision-making processes for reducing the conflict surrounding the siting of hazardous facilities.

As an example, consider the decision concerning where to locate a hazardous-waste disposal facility (HWDF). Figure 1 depicts the institutional arrangements for negotiating an acceptable agreement. There are three key stakeholders in the process: a set of eligible communities, the developer, and governmental agencies. The linkage among these three

Figure 1. Institutional arrangements for the siting process.

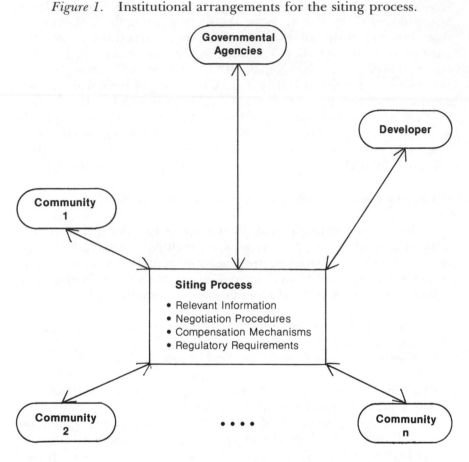

parties is determined by the siting process, which consists of the following features: (1) the *relevant information* upon which communities base their actions, as well as other data used in the siting process; (2) the *negotiation procedures* for siting the facility; (3) the *compensation mechanisms* for providing benefits to the selected community; (4) the *regulatory requirements* that will insure that health and safety standards are obeyed.

Figure 1 suggests two broad problems that should be studied:

- *Problem 1: The intercommunity process.* Given that a number of communities are possible HWDF sites, what impact will different information bases, procedures, and compensation mechanisms have on the siting process?
- *Problem 2: The intracommunity process.* How does a given community

determine under what circumstances it would be willing to have an HWDF site located within its boundaries?

The focus in this paper will be on problem 1. Using the notation for the welfare-maximizing model structured above, N_1 represents the set of identical individuals in a community that is being considered as a potential site while N_2 represents all the other individuals in communities that benefit from the site. One way of facilitating the siting process is to have the other communities provide *ex ante* compensation to the N_1 residents (S_{A1}) so that the latter are willing to accept the additional risk of a loss of L dollars from a potential accident. In addition, certain *ex post* compensation arrangements can be specified with respect to reimbursement in the case of a loss (S_{P1}).

Ex ante compensation can take the form of monetary payments such as tax rebates, or it can be in terms of in-kind services such as a new hospital that increases the utility of each of the community residents. *Ex post* compensation can also take similar forms—either monetary payments to individuals or special services to the community for improving the quality of life. Examples of these types of compensation are discussed in Kunreuther, Linnerooth et al. (1983).

To simplify the model formulation, assume that the question of designing a sufficiently safe facility has been dealt with as a separate problem, so that the only open issue is to determine whether there is a feasible compensation package that can be designed between the community in which the site is to be located and other individuals. Using the same notation as before, a given set of *ex ante* and *ex post* subsidies to potential victims yields the following societal welfare incorporated into program III. If individuals have perceived probability of an accident ϕ:

$$F_{IV} = \psi \left[\phi \ U(W_1 - L + S_{A1} + S_{P1}(L)) + (1 - \phi)U(W_1 + S_{A1}) \right]$$
$$+ (1 - \psi) \left[\phi \ V(W_2 - S_{A2} - S_{P2}(L)) + (1 - \phi) \ V(W_2 - S_{A2}) \right] \quad (4)$$

The importance of understanding the decision process if individuals who are involved in the siting process cannot be overemphasized. There is considerable theoretical work in the collective-choice literature that stresses the importance of *ex ante* compensation as a way of allocating a public good or bad (see Groves, 1979). The essential idea can be explained as follows: A central agency (e.g., a state siting authority) has the task of choosing among several alternatives (e.g., several HWDF sites). To do so, the agency collects information on available alternatives and on the preferences of its constituency. After collecting the necessary information (e.g., the minimum compensation each community would require to have an HWDF sited within its boundaries), the central agency chooses one of the alternatives by some prespecified formula (e.g., site the HWDF in the community with the lowest required compensation). The central agency would then finance the chosen alternative by some taxation formula.

An important issue raised by the above discussion is whether individuals or communities will misrepresent their preferences (e.g., by overstating the minimum compensation they would require for accepting an HWDF). Such misrepresentation may make it appear that no alternative to the status quo is desirable when this in fact is not the case. Recent research (see Green and Laffont, 1979 for a survey) has dealt with this issue. For certain types of problems, taxes and subsidies (coupled with compensation) can avoid misrepresentation and lead to efficient and equitable choice. The relative success of these demand-revealing procedures depends on the way potential victims and other individuals perceive the risks of the facility, their behavioral decision rules, and the degree of common knowledge regarding the "willingness-to-pay" and "willingness-to-accept" functions of the relevant stakeholders.

For example, suppose there are m potential sites for a hazardous facility. What does each community know about the minimum *ex ante* compensation amount they would require to have the plant in their backyard and the maximum they would be willing to pay for it to be located elsewhere? Several questions regarding existing procedures should be examined:

- What information and rationality assumptions do these theories make? Are they credible when applied to the hazardous-waste siting problem?
- Do these procedures motivate participants to misrepresent privately held information?
- What are the efficiency and equity properties of these procedures?

A related set of questions applies to the problems associated with location of nuclear power plants, except that the principal issues relate to the magnitude of *ex post* compensation to victims of an accident. The Price-Anderson Act of 1975 established a complex program of private financial protection through a nuclear liability insurance pool and government guarantees covering total claims up to a maximum of $560 million in the event of a nuclear accident. This limitation is of some importance, since virtually all property-liability insurance policies issued in the United States exclude nuclear damage. Residents who have suffered property damage from radiation or contamination from a nuclear facility currently collect under their own personal-line policy.

Suppose potential victims of a nuclear power plant accident perceive that they will be only partially covered for losses and/or that the designers of a nuclear facility do not have sufficient concern about plant safety because of the limited-liability features of the Price Anderson Act. Then these individuals may be opposed to the construction of new facilities or the operation of existing ones near their community. At the other extreme, if victims are fully compensated for losses so that $S_{P1} = L$, then the other individuals (e.g., the stockholders of the utility company) may express a reluctance to build a new facility or operate existing ones. Hence the question of whether the upper liability limits associated with the Price-Anderson Act should be increased depends on the ways different stakeholders perceive the financial risks to them of a severe accident.

III. *EX ANTE/EX POST* STRATEGIES

The above framework with a set of alternative programs suggests a number of different approaches for coping with low-probability-event problems that have a potential societal impact. They range from marketlike mechanisms such as providing better information to the use of strict requirements such as installing air bags in all new automobiles or legislating the design and location of a hazardous-waste facility. In evaluating these different approaches it is important to understand the perceived and actual relationship between *ex ante* actions and *ex post* behavior.

In what ways are *ex ante* decisions by individuals influenced by their expectations about the level of *ex post* subsidies? Are *ex ante* decisions by the public sector regarding intended aid to victims likely to be modified after the catastrophe occurs? In other words, will the best intentions go by the board after the actual impacts of a disaster are examined from the vantage point of the different stakeholders?

By formulating alternative testable hypotheses regarding the behavior of the private and public sectors, we may be able to develop more meaningful strategies for improving social welfare. Specific hypotheses regarding *ex ante/ex post* relationships are illustrated in the context of natural-hazards policy in the United States. A key question that motivated a large-scale field study and controlled laboratory experiments on disaster-insurance purchase decision was why individuals had not voluntarily purchased coverage against low-probability – high-consequence events (Kunreuther et al., 1978; Slovic et al., 1977). In the case of flood insurance this behavior was particularly surprising, since coverage was highly subsidized by the federal government. At least two alternative hypotheses could account for this behavior:

HYPOTHESIS 1. *Individuals did not insure because they expected liberal disaster relief from the federal government should they suffer damage.*

HYPOTHESIS 2. *Individuals did not insure because they misperceived the relevant parameters associated with insurance purchase and/or they used a decision process that differed from expected utility maximization.*

Evidence from the survey data support Hypothesis 2. Of particular interest is the lack of anticipation by uninsured homeowners of receiving relief from the government should they suffer property damage. During the predisaster period, most individuals do not even consider where they will obtain aid should they suffer losses. On the other hand, Congress feels itself under great pressure to provide liberal relief should a large number of victims be uninsured. This example illustrates the importance of understanding the decision process of individuals and government before and after a disaster when designing welfare-improving strategies. Let us *now* consider a set of possible approaches for linking descriptive and prescriptive analyses.

A. Providing Better Information

There are considerable laboratory and field data suggesting that individuals have limited knowledge of the risk associated with low-probability events. For example, individuals may misestimate the chances of certain events occurring because of their limited experience as well as the difficulties of obtaining these data even if they are available. In certain cases, individuals' perception of the probability of an event (ϕ) is less than the actual probability (Φ), so that even if they maximized expected utility their behavior might differ from the intention of a particular program. Similarly, their perception of the loss (ℓ) may differ from actual losses (L). For example, a study by Svenson (1981) revealed that 80 percent of all drivers believed they were better than the average driver. If they translated this attitude toward their ability into a $\phi < \Phi$, this would discourage their demand for air bags in cars.

Similarly, many individuals in flood- and earthquake-prone areas feel they are on more solid ground then they actually are. Insurance may be less attractive to these individuals than it would be if they had correct perceptions of the probabilities. This type of behavior can be understood in terms of cognitive dissonance (Festinger, 1957; Aronson, 1979). People prefer not to acknowledge potential dangers they cannot avoid, and hence they underestimate the chances of events occurring (Akerlof and Dickens, 1982).

For other events such as accidents connected with technological facilities, individuals tend to consider such plants too dangerous for their own backyard. Among the factors that trigger this attitude may be a tendency to focus on potential losses rather than on the probability of an accident and/or failure to see any benefits that would be provided by the technological facility. Because statistical data to determine the risks associated with these accidents are limited, there are substantial differences between the experts in their estimate of ℓ and L. For example, there were large discrepancies among the experts concerning the probability and magnitude of losses from a liquified natural gas explosion. Hence communities that were opposed to potentially hazardous facilities in their backyard could defend their preferences by using data from an expert who estimated the risk to be relatively high (Kunreuther et al., 1983).

These data taken alone suggest that information presented in a more meaningful form may alleviate some of the problems associated with individuals' lack of interest in protection and the negative reaction of communities toward locating technological facilities in their backyard. Slovic, Fischhoff, and Lichtenstein (1978) hypothesized that individuals may not use seat belts because they perceive the probability that an average trip will end in a fatality as so small (according to the statistical data, .0000025) that it is not worth worrying about. By demonstrating to them that this low probability compounds to a lifetime probability of .01, people may view the use of seat belts more favorably.

With respect to technological facilities, there is a need to develop rules of evidence that provide a clearer picture concerning what we know and do not know about the risk of specific accidents. For relatively new technologies it may be important to indicate what low-probability accidents fall into the class of what Weinberg (1972) calls transcientific events. This implies that there is no practical basis for estimating the statistical chances and consequences of the occurrence of certain types of accidents although, epistemologically speaking, they are questions of fact. Under these circumstances it is difficult to evaluate the welfare implications of alternative programs using the probabilistic model described in section II. Decisions may then have to be made by assuming that the value of ϕ is below some prespecified level rather than assigning it a specific value.

The importance of past experience as a variable in the adoption of protective activities, coupled with the availability bias (see Kahneman, Slovic, and Tversky, 1982), suggests that one way to increase concern about a hazard is to use vivid films or visual displays. Evidence regarding the extent to which media publicity has generated interest in protection is not very reassuring, however. Films on the dangers associated with not wearing seat belts or the nature of the flood hazard and ways to protect oneself have had limited impact on protection. A much more effective source appears to be learning from friends and neighbors (Kunreuther, Sanderson, and Vetschera, 1983).

In summary, we need to understand whether presenting information on probabilities and losses will produce changes in the decision processes of individuals and communities. These strategies are costly and in this sense represent an *ex ante* subsidy from other individuals to potential victims. Potential benefits from this strategy may be significant enough to justify its use. The empirical evidence on the efficiency of different approaches is not yet in. Currently there is considerable interest in trying to promote adoption of protective activities through information campaigns, as evidenced by recent attempts to induce seat-belt usage through media messages.

B. Incentive Systems

The welfare models developed in section II imply that specific monetary incentives such as *ex ante* subsidies may induce individuals to protect themselves against negative events. Similarly, *ex ante* compensation may convince a community to accept the siting of a hazardous-waste facility or nuclear power plant within its borders. There is limited empirical evidence as to whether offering the same monetary incentives in different forms will influence final choices. Experimental results of the framing and context effects discussed above suggests that this may make a difference in final choices. Consider the problem of convincing a consumer to purchase a car with an air bag. Suppose the automobile insurance with and without air-bag protection is P_y and P_n respectively. If the insurance required on all cars is such that loss is fully covered, the perceived utility to each potential victim would be:

$$\phi \, U(W_1 - P_y - C) + (1 - \phi) \, U(W_1 - P_y) \qquad \text{(Buy Air Bag)}$$
$$\phi \, U(W_1 - P_n) + (1 - \phi) \, U(W_1 - P_n) \qquad \text{(Don't Buy Air Bag)} \tag{5}$$

By framing the problem in terms of insurance costs rather than potential losses, the *ex post* consequences are translated into *ex ante* payments. If $P_y + C < P_n$, individuals should automatically see the advantage of air bags as long as the car-purchase decision is explicitly coupled with insurance. If the two transactions are kept separate, this benefit/cost comparison may never be made.

Standard welfare analysis normally considers utility in terms of a single attribute—wealth. Bell (1982, 1983) and Loombs and Sugden (1982) suggest that other attributes such as regret may play an important role in individual choices under uncertainty. Protective activities such as safety devices and insurance are particularly open to regret, since the product has no tangible return on its own. Only if a particular state of nature occurs does the individual receive a return. Otherwise, the person may regret investing funds in this activity. The Toro Corporation recognized the potential for regret and markets their snowblowers under a S'N$_o$ Risk Program. For example, if you buy their machine and the annual snowfall for your area is less than 20 percent of the average (based on statistical records) you will receive a full refund for the snowblower and can keep the machine. Refunds on insurance policies against which there are no claims during a year or over a period or years may be viewed more favorably by individuals than rate reductions in future years (i.e., experience rating) for similar reasons related to regret. Specific hypotheses need to be developed to predict the relative outcomes of different incentive schemes if regret is an important variable.

The potential for regret also suggests that there is a close connection established in a person's mind between *ex ante* behavior and *ex post* consequences. If individuals read that they would receive limited *ex post* subsidies (S$_{P1}$) after a disaster and believe this information, they may take more *ex ante* precaution. Given political pressures for *ex post* subsidies to victims, it may be difficult to make a convincing case for such a program.

A more politically palatable step is for government agencies to link subsidized relief with *ex ante* protection. A step in this direction was taken by the Federal Energy Management Agency, which required all flood victims obtaining a low-interest loan from the Small Business Administration to purchase flood insurance on their property. General Motors has recently taken a step to encourage seat-belt usage by offering to pay $10,000 to the estate of anyone who suffers fatal injuries while wearing a seat belt in a new GM car. The intention of the GM program is to link *ex-ante* protection with ex-post returns should the safety device fail, a technique similar to one utilized by Toro. Whether consumers will make the desired connection remains to be seen.

C. Ex Ante Compensation[3]

Turning to the siting of hazardous facilities, the development of appropriate *ex ante* compensation systems depends on both equity and efficiency considerations. *Efficiency* refers to the optimal allocation of resources associated with locating the facility in one of the potential sites. If the cost associated with the construction of the facility and its use (e.g., disposal of waste by different industries) is identical in each of the eligible sites, then the efficient solution is to locate the project in the community that requires the smallest compensation payment.

The *equity* criterion, however, is concerned with the impact of the siting decision on the distribution of resources among eligible communities, the developer, and the government. The specific concern is about how the total "pie" is shared between winners and losers. Questions are also raised as to whether it is fair to site a facility in the poorer community, which may require less money to find it acceptable.

The trade-offs between equity and efficiency depends on the type of procedures that will be used first to reveal community preferences and then to allocate resources among potential victims and other individuals. The following selected procedures for negotiating siting agreements can be considered from a theoretical and experimental viewpoint.

Procedure 1: Random Lottery. If a state is forced to accept a site somewhere within its boundaries and all the local communities feel it should "not be in their backyard," then a random draw from among the sites the state government has designated as acceptable locations may be deemed appropriate. The "unlucky" community in which the facility is located receives a designated compensation sum.

Procedure 2: Two-Stage Lottery. This procedure resembles procedure 1, with the following major difference: each community specifies an amount of compensation it would have to receive in exchange for having the facility located within it, if it were chosen. Suppose a community specified that compensation in the amount of S dollars would make it indifferent to having the site in its own backyard or elsewhere. If it is chosen, it will receive S dollars. However, communities not selected are allowed to resubmit their bids. A second lottery is then held among those communities whose bids are less than S. The community chosen by lottery at any stage in this process cannot change its bid. We hypothesize that communities participating in this would have an incentive to reveal their true indifference levels of compensation.

Procedure 3: Arbitration Procedure. Each community specifies to an arbitrator the amount of compensation it would require to have a site located within its boundaries. Alternatively, this figure can be viewed as the amount of money each community would be willing to pay to have the site located somewhere else. Under these arrangements, the probability of a particular community being chosen as the site will be reduced as the amount the community bids, relative to others, is increased. The community chosen as the site will receive the amount of money it requires, with such funds obtained either through general tax revenues or (by a formula) from those communities not selected for siting.

Procedure 4: Iterative Procedure. Each community makes an initial bid that reflects its indifference toward having the facility located in its backyard or having to pay this same amount to have it located elsewhere. The community has an opportunity to change its bid on the next iteration. The process stops when each community maintains the same bid on any two successive rounds. The site goes to the lowest bidder as long as the total sum the other communities are willing to pay exceeds that amount.

Procedure 5: Dutch Auction. In this procedure, each community indicates the minimum amount it would be willing to accept as compensation for allowing a facility to be sited within its boundaries. It then receives the second lowest bid as its compensation. The state government would pay the compensation through tax revenues.

Procedure 6: Buyer–Seller Negotiation. In this procedure, the developer and the community negotiate a mutually acceptable deal for locating the facility within the community's boundaries. The Massachusetts Siting Act is designed in this spirit, with the additional proviso that if a community and developer are unwilling to initiate the process, binding arbitration may be invoked to reach an agreement. Hence both parties have the incentive to try and work out a mutually acceptable agreement.

D. Criteria for Judging Alternatives

The performance of these procedures can be analyzed using the following criteria:

- *Information processing costs*: How difficult is it for different interested parties (communities, developer, arbitrator, state) to process information for a given procedure?
- *Efficiency*: How close does the proposed solution come to making everyone in the state better off without making anyone worse off (Pareto optimality)?
- *Equity*: What impact does the proposed solution have on the distribution of resources among different communities? The Ψ weighting function in the welfare model of section II reflects this consideration.
- *Time to solution*: How long is it likely to take to reach a solution for a given procedure? When will negotiation fail so that the undesirable status quo is maintained?
- *Degree of misrepresentation of preference*: How likely is it that a given procedure will lead communities and developers to represent their preferences truthfully through stated compensation levels?

As part of an *ex ante* compensation program, it may be important to provide a set of incentives that reassure individuals that the new facility will remain acceptably safe. Well-specified liability arrangements indicating how much *ex post* compensation will be paid to victims of a given accident may help in this regard. In addition, residents will want to know that the facility is regularly inspected and that it will be repaired or temporarily shut down if the risk of an accident is above a given level. This concern that the community have an active role in the siting process suggests that one must couple decision processes with outcomes in evaluating alternative proposals.

E. Regulations and Requirements

The use of specific requirements as a way of improving welfare must be evaluated in relation to the other mechanisms proposed above. In particular, it is important to understand how well consumers process information and the type of data utilized in order to determine whether certain regulations improve welfare. Colantoni, Davis, and Swaminuthan (1976) make this point when evaluating policies that impose certain standards (e.g., auto safety features) rather than provide consumers with better information.

Consider the problem of evaluating whether a passive-restraint feature such as the air bag should be required as standard equipment for all new automobiles. Kleindorfer and Kunreuther (1981) have analyzed the welfare implications of this proposal in relation to optional installation of this safety feature under different informational assumptions. They show that the citizenry might be willing to accept mandatory air bags if it knew and believed the actual figures, but it might be opposed to such action if consumers underestimated the probability of an accident. Colantoni, Davis, and Swaminuthan (1976) also point out that any type of regulation may harm a group of consumers who are already taking protective action on their own. For example, those who currently wear seat belts may be unduly penalized for having to purchase a car with an air bag. This welfare loss must be compared with a policy of optional standards, whereby many drivers do not avail themselves of protection because they underestimate the risk.

The issue of the political feasibility of mandatory requirements has also been analyzed by Pauly, Kunreuther, and Vaupel (1984). Politicians may not support regulations even if these regulations yield potential net benefits to society, because the achievement of the politicians' goals (which includes staying in office) depends on pleasing the same consumers whose misperceptions are the source of the problem. Consequently, compelling the voters to do things they believe are not in their interest is unlikely to enlist their political support. For this reason politicians may do nothing with respect to regulations and instead may favor methods such as *ex post* compensation to disaster victims.

This negative attitude by politicians toward regulations may also explain the reluctance of state and federal agencies to regulate a solution to the hazardous-waste facility problem. Rather than forcing a particular community to "accept" a waste treatment plant in its backyard, they prefer efforts to reach settlements through some type of buyer-seller negotiation (see O'Hare, Bacow, and Sanderson, 1983; Raiffa, 1982). The areas in which regulation is most likely to be supported are those concerning the safety of public goods such as a nuclear power plant, where citizens feel that they have limited understanding of the technical issues and that under traditional market mechanisms, including liability, there may not be an incentive for developers to make the facility safe enough. Similar arguments could be used for legislation on consumer product safety such as drug regulation, although the potential benefits of such legislation to consumers has been questioned (Peltzman, 1973).

IV. CONCLUSIONS AND SUGGESTIONS FOR FUTURE RESEARCH

The principal theme of this paper is the importance of understanding descriptive analysis as a prelude to prescriptive recommendations. At the descriptive level there is a need to understand the decision process of the relevant stakeholders with respect to problems involving protection against potential disasters that affect individuals and communities. What type of information is collected on risk and how are these data utilized in making choices?

The evidence from field studies and laboratory experiments suggests that individuals exhibit systematic biases and heuristics with respect to probabilistic information and that problem context and framing of outcomes influence choices. We have limited knowledge, however, about whether these factors are important in a market setting. One of the next steps is to collect empirical data from the field as well as to conduct market-based experiments to gain a better understanding of the decision processes associated with problems such as those described in section I. These efforts must be guided by theoretical work in economics and behavioral-decision theory that will yield a set of testable hypotheses. Several directions are being taken in this spirit as part of the work at the new Risk and Decision Processes Center at The Wharton School: these are discussed below.

Building on the pioneering work in experimental economics by Charles Plott, Vernon Smith, and their colleagues (see Smith, 1982), there is an opportunity to study the effect of individual biases and heuristics on the performance of markets. Some recent studies on misinformation and information asymmetry have been undertaken in this spirit on information aggregation (Plott and Sunder, 1982), warranties and consumer search (Palfrey and Romer, 1984), and information asymmetry (Miller and Plott, 1982; Lynch, Plott, and Porter, 1983). Experiments in insurance and asset trading are now being undertaken at The Wharton School to determine the impact on market performance of individual behavior under different informational conditions. For example, what effect does providing ambiguous information on the probability of certain outcomes to buyer and/or sellers in the spirit of Ellsberg (1961) and Einhorn and Hogarth (1983) have on the equilibrium market price and the level of trading? The design of these experiments and a set of testable hypotheses are discussed by Camerer and Kunreuther (1984).

A second area of emphasis is the gathering of empirical data on the performance of different policy tools in real-world markets. For example, with respect to consumer goods, Russel and Thaler (1985) show how information-processing limitations may prevent profitable arbitrage of prices in a market setting. Individual processing limitations with respect to adoption of protective activities may also lead to market failure. Can specific information campaigns significantly improve the situation? The results of previous efforts to promote disaster insurance and auto safety have not been very encouraging in this regard. There is a need to study alternative strategies that are designed to deal with features such as potential regret and cognitive dissonance. For example. how well will the new GM campaign, which links life insurance with use of seat belts, fare?

Another area is the need to integrate field experience with experimental markets in the area of public-good problems. The important work by Ferejohn, Forsythe, and Noll (1979) on allocating programs to public television stations suggests that collective-choice procedures can be studied in both settings. With respect to hazardous-waste siting, there is currently a project at the University of Pennsylvania designed to link field experience with prototype laboratory experiments on the role of compensation in siting hazardous-waste facilities (Kunreuther and Kleindorfer, 1985).

Finally, we should attempt to gain a better understanding of the institutional realities associated with alternative strategies for dealing with problems in which there are potential conflicts between relevant stakeholders. The work of Williamson (1975) with respect to information asymmetries and transaction costs between stakeholders may be a useful way of structuring the problem. The multidisciplinary project conducted at the International Institute of Applied Systems Analysis on siting LNG facilities (Kunreuther, et al., 1983) may also provide insights into the conflicts between stakeholders with different agendas and information bases. Current questions facing Congress about what form the renewal of the Price-Anderson Act should take with respect to potential liability arrangements for nuclear power plants could be studied in this context.

The emerging field of behavioral economics offers an opportunity to pursue the above research in a systematic manner. The four examples that motivated this paper are illustrative of the type of problems that require an understanding of individual behavior and decision processes as inputs to prescriptive analysis. The design of policies for dealing with *ex ante* and *ex post* choices may produce fruitful linkages between theory and practice in the public policy arena.

ACKNOWLEDGMENT

The ideas in this paper were stimulated by informal discussions with participants in the decisions-processes lunch at The Wharton School. These individuals include Jon Baron, Colin Camerer, Joshua Eliashberg, Jack Hershey, Paul Kleindorfer, and James Laing. Support from NSF Grant SES–8312123 is gratefully acknowledged.

NOTES

1. If each person is given equal weight, then $\Psi = W_1/(W_1 + W_2)$ and $(1 - \Psi) = W_2/(W_1 + W_2)$

2. The material in this section draws heavily on the work of Kunreuther and Kleindorfer (1983).

3. The material in this subsection draws heavily on Kunreuther and Kleindorfer (1983).

REFERENCES

Akerlof, G., "The Market for 'Lemons': Quality Uncertainty and the Market Mechanisms," *Quarterly Journal of Economics*, 84 (1970), 488–500.

Akerlof, G., and W. T. Dickens, "The Economic Consequences of Cognitive Dissonance," *American Economic Review*, 72, no. 3 (1982), 307–319.

Aronson, E., *The Social Animal*, 3rd ed. San Francisco: W. H. Freeman, 1979.

Arrow, K., "Risk Perception in Psychology and Economics," *Economic Inquiry*, 20, no. 1 (1982), 1–9.

Bell, D. E., "Regret in Decision-Making under Uncertainty," *Operations Research*, 30, no. 5 (1982), 961–981.

Bell, D. E., "Risk Premiums for Decision Regret," *Management Science*, 29, no. 10 (1983), 1156–1166.

Camerer, C., and H. Kunreuther, "Linking Individuals and Markets Through Behavioral Decision Theory: An Experimental Approach." Decision Sciences Dept. Working Paper No. 84–05–03, The Wharton School, University of Pennsylvania, 1984.

Colantoni, D., O. Davis, and M. Swaminuthan, "Imperfect Consumers and Welfare Comparisons of Policies Concerning Information and Regulation," *Bell Journal of Economics*, 2 (1976), 602–615.

Edwards, W., and D. von Winterfeldt, "Public Disputes about Risky Technologies: Stakeholders and Arenas." Mimeo, 1983.

Einhorn, H. J., and R. M. Hogarth, "Ambiguity and Uncertainty in Probabilistic Inference." Working Paper, University of Chicago, 1983.

Ellsberg, D., "Risk, Ambiguity, and the Savage Axioms," *Quarterly Journal of Economics*, 75 (1961), 643–669.

Ferejohn, J., J. Forsythe, and R. Noll, "An Experimental Analysis of Decision Making Procedures for Discrete Public Goods," in V. Smith, ed., *Research in Experimental Economics*, Vol. 1. Greenwich, CT: JAI Press, 1979, pp. 1–58.

Festinger, L. A., *A Theory of Cognitive Dissonance*. Stanford: Stanford University Press, 1957.

Fischhoff, B., S. Lichtenstein, P. Slovic, R. Keeney, and S. Derby, *Approaches to Acceptable Risk: A Critical Guide*. Cambridge: Cambridge University Press, 1982.

Green, J., and J. J. Laffont, "Incentives in Public Decision Making," in *Studies in Public Economics*, Vol. 1. Amsterdam: North-Holland, 1979.

Groves, T., "Efficient Collective Choice with Compensation," *Review of Economic Studies*, 46 (1979), 227–241.

Hershey, J., H. Kunreuther, and P. Schoemaker, "Sources of Biases in Assessment Procedures for Utility Functions," *Management Science* 28 (1982), 936–954.

Kahneman, D., P. Slovic, and A. Tversky. *Decision Making under Uncertainty: Heuristics and Biases*. Cambridge: Cambridge University Press, 1982.

Kahneman, D., and A. Tversky, "Prospect Theory: An Analysis of Decision Under Risk," *Econometrica*, 47, no. 2 (1979), 263–291.

Kleindorfer, P., and H. Kunreuther, "Descriptive and Prescriptive Aspects of Health and Safety Regulation," in A. Ferguson and R. Leveen, eds., *The Benefits of Health and Safety Regulations*. Cambridge, MA: Ballinger, 1981.

Kunreuther, H., R. Ginsberg, L. Miller, et al., *Disaster Insurance Protection: Public Policy Lessons*. New York: Wiley, 1978.

Kunreuther, H., and P. Kleindorfer, "A Sealed Bid Auction Mechanism for Siting Noxious Facilities," *American Economic Review Papers and Proceedings* (May 1986).

Kunreuther, H., J. Linnerooth, et al., *Risk Analysis and Decision Processes: The Siting of LEG Facilities in Four Countries*. New York: Springer-Verlag, 1983.

Kunreuther, H., W. Sanderson, and R. Vetschera, "A Behavioral Model of the Adoption of Protective Activities." *Journal of Economic Behavior and Organization* 6 (1985), 1–15.

Loombs, G., and R. Sugden, "Regret Theory: An Alternative Approach to Rational Choice under Uncertainty," *Economic Journal*, 92, 805–824.

Lynch, M., R. Miller, C. Plott, and R. Porter, "Product Quality, Informational Efficiency and Regulations in Experimental Markets." Working Paper No. 39/83, Boston University, School of Management, December, 1983.

Miller, R., and C. Plott, "Product Quality Signaling in Experimental Markets." Working Paper No. 447, California Institute of Technical Social Science, 1982.

O'Hare, M., "Not on My Block You Don't: Facility Siting and the Strategic Importance of Compensation," *Public Policy*, 25 (1977), 409–458.

O'Hare, M., L. Bacow, and D. Sanderson, *Facility Siting and Public Opposition*. New York: Van Nostrand-Reinhold, 1983.

Palfrey, R. T., and T. Romer, "An Experimental Study of Warranty Coverage and Dispute Resolution in Competitive Markets." Working Paper No. 34–83–84, Carnegie-Mellon University, 1984.

Pauly, M., H. Kunreuther, and J. Vaupel, "Public Protection Against Misperceived Risks: Insights from Positive Political Economy." *Public Choice* 43 (1984), 45–64.

Peltzman, S., "An Evaluation of Consumer Protection Legislation: The 1962 Drug Amendments," *Journal of Political Economy*, 81 (1973) 1049–1091.

Plott, C. R., and S. Sunder, "Efficiency of Experimental Security Markets with Insider Information: An Application of Rational Expectations Models," *Journal of Political Economy*, 90 (August 1982), 663–698.

Raiffa, H., *The Art and Science of Negotiation*. Cambridge, MA: The Belknap Press, 1982.

Russell, T., and R. Thaler, "The Relevance of Quasi Rationality in Competitive Markets."

Shoemaker, P. J. H., "The Expected Utility Model: Its Variants, Purposes, Evidence, and Limitations," *Journal of Economic Literature*, 20 (1982), 529–563.

Slovic, P., B. Fischhoff, and S. Lichtenstein, "Accident Probabilities and Seat Belt Usage: A Psychological Perspective," *Accident Analysis and Prevention*, 10 (1978), 281–285.

Slovic, P., B. Fischhoff, S. Lichtenstein, B. Corrigan, and B. Combs, "Preference for Insuring Against Probable Small Loss: Implications for the Theory and Practice of Insurance," *Journal of Risk and Insurance*, 44 (1977), 237–258.

Smith, V., "Microeconomic Systems as an Experimental Science," *American Economic Review*, 72 (1982), 923–955.

Stokey, R., and R. Zeckhauser, *A Primer for Policy Analysis*. New York: W. W. Norton & Company, 1978.

Svenson, O., "Are We All Less Risky and More Skillful than Our Fellow Drivers Are?" *Acta Psychologica*, 47 (1981), 143–148.

Thaler, R., "Toward A Positive Theory of Consumer Choice," *Journal of Economic Behavior and Organization*, 1, no. 1 (1980), 39–60.

Thaler, R., "Using Mental Accounting in a Theory of Consumer Behavior." Working Paper, Cornell University, 1983.

Tversky, A., and D. Kahneman, "The Framing of Decisions and the Psychology of Choice," *Science*, 211 (1981), 354–458.

Weinberg, A., "Science and Trans-Science," *Minerva*, 10 (1972), 209–222.

Williamson, O. E., *Markets and Hierarchies*. New York: The Free Press, 1975.

FISCAL POLICY:

THE IMPORTANCE OF PERCEPTIONS
AND ATTITUDES

Alan Lewis

I. INTRODUCTION

Governments have a major influence on the economy of nations through their budgeting of taxation and public expenditure, the central concern of fiscal policy. The level of taxation and the relative size of the public sector are determined by many factors, not least among them being the economic theories favored by policy makers. For Keynesians, consumer and other elements of aggregate demand can be increased through budget deficits, whereby public expenditure exceeds revenue. Similarly, where demand is excessively high, it can be reduced by a budget surplus. The Keynesian approach has come under sharp criticism from monetarists in the past fifteen to twenty years in both the United States and the United Kingdom. The relative growth of the public sector's contribution to the gross national product (GNP) has caused considerable alarm among monetarists; as they see it, this growth adds to inefficiency in the economy and the crowding out of the private sector (Cook and Jackson, 1979).

Fiscal policy is not determined solely by the ascendence of particular economic theories; it also depends on political expediency. In a democracy, governments must pay close attention to public opinion, especially as an election approaches (Tufte, 1978). Enthusiasm for cuts in public expenditure on the part of policy makers may be tempered if there is little support for such cuts among the electorate. Indeed, one of the most popular explanations for the growth of the public sector relies on the so-called fiscal illusion to which the general public is supposedly susceptible. To summarize, demand for public expenditure may be buoyant because people underestimate the true "tax-price" of these benefits (Puviani, 1903). As this example—and others concerning tax incentives and tax evasion—show, justifications for fiscal policies and their success or failure, when implemented, are often based on the hypothesized preferences and beliefs of voters and taxpayers; yet rarely are those preferences and attitudes investigated directly. As a partial remedy for this imbalance, the present paper concentrates on a critical review of the social survey literature concerning peoples' tax attitudes, tax perceptions, and preferences for public expenditure.

II. PERCEPTIONS OF TAXATION AND PUBLIC EXPENDITURE

Which are the most "visible" taxes? A poll conducted by Marplan Ltd., using a quota sample of 900 respondents in the United Kingdom, asked people where they thought the government gets the money to pay for services. In free responses, over 93 percent of the sample mentioned income taxation and 56 percent, taxes on goods; over 30 percent separately named taxes on vehicles, tobacco, petrol, and alcohol (Cullis and Lewis, 1985). It should be mentioned that this question followed one about preferences for public expenditure, so the "fiscal connection" between taxes and benefits was already in peoples' minds—the answers may well have been more bizarre if the ordering of questions was different. Nonetheless, the high visibility of income taxation is abundantly clear although the actual revenue collected through income tax in the United Kingdom is approximately 34 percent; value-added tax (VAT) and other indirect taxes, 41 percent, insurance contributions, 16 percent, and rates (local property taxes), 9 percent.

In a comparable study, Beedle and Taylor-Gooby (1983) reported on the tax perceptions of 240 respondents from Kent, the United Kingdom. People were shown a card that listed five ways of financing services and were asked which way "most money is raised at present." Although, unlike those participating in the Marplan poll, respondents were not allowed a free response, the results were consistent: 75 percent mentioned income tax; 9 percent, VAT; 9 percent, national insurance; 6 percent, rates; each person being allowed one choice only.

The modern empirical evidence suggests that people may underestimate their total tax burdens, as they are comparatively unaware of the incidence of indirect taxes. And although income tax is highly visible, this does not mean that people have a realistic idea of how much income tax they actually pay. In a survey of 200 voters in the city of Bath, United Kingdom, Lewis (1978) asked respondents how much they would lose in income tax if they earned an extra pound sterling (i.e., an estimate of the marginal rate of taxation). The results showed consistent under-estimation of the marginal rates of income taxation.

Empirical results dealing with the visibility of various taxes are not only informative when the demand for public expenditure is considered but also with respect to the effects of taxation on the supply of labor. Theoretically, taxation may act either as a disincentive for hours worked and work effort generally or as an incentive (Brown, 1981). However, recent monetarist policy makers have virtually taken it for granted that high income-tax rates are a disincentive and a reduction in such rates would release, in particular, risk-taking businessmen and entrepreneurs to expand, thus providing more jobs and contributing to economic growth. However, when people are actually asked, the majority of respondents from studies conducted both in the United States and the United Kingdom report that taxation has no effect on their work effort (in the United States: Barlow, Brazer, and Morgan, 1966; Sanders, 1951; and Holland, 1969; in the United Kingdom; Break, 1957; Fields and Stanbury, 1970). The disincentive effect of taxation is a simple expla-nation that may be considered appropriate in the interpretation of an-other's behavior but rarely of one's own (cf attribution theory, Kelley and Michela, 1980). The Royal Commission on the Taxation of Profits and Income (1954) reported that three quarters of respondents thought income tax was a deterrent to work effort; yet, as has been found in the other research reviewed, less than 30 percent of people claimed that tax had any effect on their own behavior.

Perceptual data concerning government spending provides informa-tion about the comparative visibility of public expenditure. In a national quota sample in the United Kingdom, a Marplan poll question enquired: "All governments spend money on a variety of different things. What are the main things governments spend money on?" Fifty-three percent of the respondents mentioned defense and the armed forces; this was the most frequently cited expenditure. It was closely followed by hos-pitals and the health service (51 percent) and schools and education (44 percent). Far fewer people mentioned social security (26 percent), roads (21 percent), unemployment benefits (19 percent), and the nationalized industries (19 percent) (Jones and Cullis, 1984). While the results show that most people can bring several forms of government spending to mind, the case for high visibility of public expenditure should not be overstated—Auld (1978) found that only about 20 percent of 1,294 individuals in Ontario had even a general awareness of the actual size of the provincial budget and the shares allocated to social welfare, health, and other items.

III. PUBLIC EXPENDITURE PREFERENCES AND TAX ATTITUDES

Both fiscal referenda and social survey results have shown some consistency in both the United States and the United Kingdom: people generally show a dissatisfaction with the level of taxes, yet indicate widespread support for favored expenditures on health, education, and provisions for the elderly (Coughlin, 1980; Lewis, 1982). As Beedle and Taylor-Gooby (1983) have reported, the general public shows an ambivalence toward the public sector and the welfare state: on the one hand people are loathe to see a general increase in the size of the public sector, yet on the other they are greatly concerned about cuts in public expenditure when specific provisions are put to them. This ambivalence has also been portrayed in referenda results in the United States. The now-famous Jarvis-Gann Amendment, Proposition 13 in California, showed over a two-to-one majority in favor of cutting property taxes; but this may have been a special case (Levy, 1979). Subsequent referenda results have revealed a dampening of "fiscal conservatism" where voters may have become more cognizant of the fiscal connection between desirable tax cuts and their possible undesirable consequences in terms of reduced social benefits.

At first sight, attitudes toward taxation are less ambivalent. As Keene (1983) has pointed out, nearly every survey of its kind conducted in the United States since World War II has recorded a majority view that taxes are too high. This indicates support, albeit lukewarm, for progressive income taxation in both the United States and the United Kingdom (Keene, 1983; Lewis, 1978; Beedle and Taylor-Gooby, 1983). It is also revealing to examine what has been described as the "tax mentality" of individuals, by which is meant people's perceptions of the purposes of taxation, its fairness, and their willingness to comply with the tax system or their propensity to illegally evade paying taxes (Schmölders, 1970).

It has been argued that people are becoming more aware of the "fiscal connection," partly because of fiscal referenda, partly because of political pressure to reduce the size of the public sector, and partly because of increased media coverage of public-expenditure issues. Nevertheless, the wording of questions in social surveys can have an important influence on the results recorded, depending on whether or not the fiscal connection is made explicit. A simple question concerning attitudes toward taxation invariably produces an antipathetic response, antipathy that can be reduced when the benefits of public expenditure are mentioned. Conversely, attitudes toward expenditures on education and health are generally favored, and while a majority frequently favor keeping spending at present levels, of the remainder more favor increased, rather than decreased, spending (Coughlin, 1980; Lewis and Jackson, 1985; Edgell and Duke, 1982). The enthusiasm for increased spending can be readily dampened by mention of the "tax price" in the social survey question posed (Lewis, 1982; Mueller, 1963; Seldon, 1980).

While it is likely that a sizable minority will mention provisions for public expenditure as one of the purposes of taxation, only a small number are likely to mention its use in the redistribution of wealth, and still fewer will cite the use of fiscal policy in the demand management of the economy. This lack of fiscal consciousness has important implications for both people's perceptions of the fairness of the tax system and their willingness to comply with it generally. Tax evasion appears to be a growing problem both in North America and Europe; the loss of revenue may even be as high as 10 percent of the GNP (*Newsweek*, 1983), although the extent of tax evasion is extraordinarily difficult to assess (O'Higgins, 1981). In an imaginative survey, using "locked box" and "randomized response" techniques the Internal Revenue Service (IRS) commissioned research to assess the degree of underreporting of income and other forms of evasion among a sample of 4,888 Americans (Aitken and Bonneville, 1980). The results revealed that 13 percent said they sometimes underreported income on their tax returns, 4 percent said they listed more tax deductions than they were entitled to, and 3 percent made illegal claims for dependents. The results closely resemble those reported by Mason and Calvin (1978) of a study of 800 Oregon adults, in which 14 percent admitted underreporting of income and 5 percent, overstatement of deductions. Another common form of tax evasion, and one in which people feel confident about underreporting income, is through "cash-in-hand" transfers, so difficult to trace by the tax authorities. In a study of 426 Swedish male taxpayers, fully 42 percent of the sample admitted paying "black money" to traders that they suspected went untaxed (Warneryd and Walerud, 1982). Public attitudes differ toward the evasion of small as opposed to large amounts (Aitken and Bonneville, 1980; Vogel, 1974; Lewis, 1979). Evasion of paying large amounts is considered to be ethically wrong and a serious offense warranting heavy fines and even imprisonment. Aitken and Bonneville (1980) found that 58 percent of their respondents considered evasion of $500 a very serious offense. In comparison, evasion of paying small amounts is still considered wrong by the majority but only about as serious as stealing a bicycle (Song and Yarbrough, 1978) and less serious than pilfering at work, not repaying a friend, or fiddling with social security and welfare payments (Keenan and Dean, 1980). In their Scottish study, Keenan and Dean found that a sizable minority of taxpayers felt tax evasion was justified because there was a certain inequity in the ways different people were treated by the tax authorities. In the United States, Aitken and Bonneville found 42 percent of respondents believed that high-income earners receive more lenient treatment from tax-enforcement agencies and, because people with lower incomes generally receive most of their income in salaries and wages taxed at source, tax evasion is the poor man's tax avoidance.

IV.   FISCAL-POLICY IMPLICATIONS AND FUTURE RESEARCH

A. Macroeconomics and Attitudes

The macroeconomics of fiscal policy by necessity is painted with a broad brush; however, the distinction between macroeconomics and behavioral microeconomics can be a blurred one. The traditional axiomatic approach to the interpretation of choice and economic behavior could be made more realistic by recourse to perceptual and attitude data. The success or failure of fiscal policies can depend on many factors, but a neglected one relates to people's perceptions of fiscal changes and the effects people believe such changes are likely to have on their behavior. Such studies need not be entirely microeconomically based, and a lead may come from Katona's work on "consumer sentiment" (Katona, 1980). For Katona, people's economic expectations are not necessarily what one would expect them to be based on rationality theory; consequently, there is no substitute for direct examination of consumer sentiment—consumers' expectations and their economic optimism and pessimism. The consumer-sentiment measure consists of five interview questions: (1) whether respondents feel financially better or worse off than a year ago; (2) whether they think they will be financially better off in a year from now; (3) whether it is a good time for buying things; (4) whether the next twelve months and (5) the next five years will be better or worse for the economy as a whole. The index has proved a success in short-term forecasts of consumer demand. For the years 1952 to 1962, Katona (1967) was able to record some impressive results from regression studies of time-series data. The index, combined with income level, explained 91 percent of the variance in consumer expenditure on durables. The success of this measure points to the development of an "index of labor sentiment," which could be of considerable help in understanding trends in labor supply. People's willingness or otherwise to work longer hours and increase productivity, and their optimism and pessimism about the future, could be linked and compared with fiscal changes. In the long term, this kind of analysis might lead to the development of a "behavioral" fiscal theory that could improve predictions and fiscal management.

B. Attitudes and Tax Evasion

An emphasis on the variables intervening between economic antecedents and economic consequences is also of direct relevance when considering tax-evasion behavior. In a recent report by the American Bar Association on tax compliance, three main themes were identified (Katz, 1983). The first theme concerned the need for research into the causes of noncompliance; the second, an analysis of the success or failure of differing tax-enforcement procedures; and the third, an examination of taxpayers' attitudes and how they might be changed. These themes go somewhat further than the common economic approach, which concentrates on utility maximization under uncertainty (Allingham and Sandmo, 1972). A behavioral approach does not take issue with the notion that evasion is a function of opportunity, probability of detection, and size of the fine; instead, it stresses the way these factors are mediated through attitudes and perceptions. Models that stress these mediating factors have been proposed by Strumpel (1969), Lewis (1982), Groenland and van Veldhoven (1983), and Warneryd and Walerud (1982). Recent research has underlined the importance of concentrating on attitudes toward tax evasion specifically rather than on tax attitudes generally. Ajzen and Fishbein (1980) have developed a restricted measure of attitudes designed to improve predictability between attitudes and behavior. An adaption of Ajzen and Fishbein's model for tax evasion is represented in Figure 1 (Lewis, 1982, p. 172). In this case, demographic variables and attitudes toward fiscal authorities are treated as external variables. Specific attitudes toward tax evasion, behavioral intentions, subjective norms, and the relative importance given to attitudinal and normative components are the mainstays of the approach. The adaptation of Ajzen and Fishbein's model for the case of tax evasion gains support from the work of Warneryd and Walerud (1982) and Vogel (1974). Warneryd and Walerud found that their general measure of tax attitude was not as good a predictor of admitted tax-evasion behavior as was a more specific measure of attitudes toward tax evasion. Both Vogel and Warneryd and Walerud have underlined the importance of perceived opportunities (included in Ajzen and Fishbein's notion of out-

Figure 1.   Model for the case of tax evasion. (Reproduced from
Lewis, 1982, p. 172; and adapted from Ajzen and Fishbein, 1980).

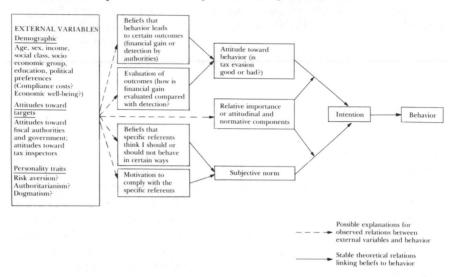

come evaluation) and normative influence ("subjective norms" as defined
by Ajzen and Fishbein). Tax evaders think, probably rightly, their
chances of being caught are less than those of other people and are more
likely to have friends and acquaintances who are tax evaders themselves.

Experimental simulation studies have also been undertaken that are
more closely allied to economic theory in that they concentrate on tax
rates, probability of detection, and size of fines and that these factors
are made "objective" by informing the subjects of the "facts" before the
simulation begins (cf Friedland, Maital, and Rutenburg, 1978; Spicer
and Becker, 1980; Friedland, 1982).

Future studies need to be more realistic. To quote Katz (1983):

> Theoretical models, surveys and taxpayers' attitudes, game simulation studies, and
> a few empirical studies of tax compliance behaviour illustrate the difficulties of
> drawing conclusions. The theoretical and empirical bases for sound contribution
> from the social sciences is inadequate. While policy issues involving such matters as
> privacy may be better left to policy makers than to social scientists, the contribution
> which social scientists can make is to design real world experiments to test theories
> for improving tax administration (p. 3).

Model building in this area is in its early stages. Models in the future
should include attitudinal and perceptual components, but these must
place greater stress on objective and cultural factors and the link between
mediating factors and behavioral constraints.

C. Better Communications

The quality of the communication between government departments and citizens has an important influence on the relationship between voters and the state. The direct experience of claimants of social security and unemployment benefits and communication between taxpayers and tax-administration agencies influence attitudes toward the public sector and spread waves far beyond those caused by a single stone cast into an individual pool: they help develop a shared fiscal subculture. This has been recognized by the IRS in the United States, the Inland Revenue and Department of Health and Social Security in Britain, and elsewhere in Europe (Delormé, 1980). Generally, a higher proportion of professional, well-educated people contact the official sources for information; people who know least about taxes tend to have less positive feelings toward tax-administration agencies and are more likely to contact "unofficial" sources of information (i.e., friends, newspapers, and advice bureaus) (Allison, James, and Lewis, 1986).

There has been a prolific growth of academic literature concerned with document and form design (Felker, Pickering, Charrow, Holland & Redish, 1981; Allison, James, and Lewis, 1986). Special leaflet- and form-design units have been inaugurated within the IRS in the United States and the Inland Revenue and DHSS in the United Kingdom, as well as in Sweden. Aitken and Bonneville (1980) have shown that the most frequent reason for not completing a tax return is that the forms are considered too complicated.

The advantages of improved communication are manifold: not only do they improve the impression of the general public toward the public sector, enhance tax compliance, and reduce personal-compliance costs; simplified forms of communication reduce administrative costs as well.

D. Public Opinion and Public Choice

Fiscal policies are influenced by the fiscal preferences of the general public. It is not appropriate in the present context to debate the influence these preferences *should* have on the size of the public sector and its administration, but the implications of survey research, should they be adopted, are clear. First of all, if revenue must be increased, the increase will be less "visible" if it is added to "indirect taxes." The economic consequences of such a move may be inequitable and its influence inflationary, but in the short term people would notice this kind of tax increase the least. "Informed" fiscal choices would become more prevalent through fiscal education, by which the connection between taxation and public expenditure was made explicit. The participative role of fiscal referenda enhances this consciousness but on occasion can be disruptive to harmonious and consistent fiscal policy making. Fiscal preferences cannot adequately be predicted from rationality and self-interest assumptions (Lewis, 1982; Cullis and Lewis, 1985; Hochman and Rodgers, 1974). People have preferences that can be predicted not only from their self-interest, narrowly or broadly defined, but from changes in the political climate. Comparatively wealthy individuals who are fiscally informed make choices that may not directly be in their self-interest. Furthermore, ideological differences have the greatest effects of all, and these cannot be simply reduced to income and social-class differences. A public sector under threat breeds, if anything, more converts than critics. This said, social survey evidence can be misleading, as choices made on the street corner are greatly affected by the form of the question posed.

V. CONCLUSIONS

Recommendations for future research have been proposed. These include the employment of attitudinal components in macroeconomic analyses of fiscal policy; attitudes toward tax authorities and legislation with regard to curbing tax evasion; an improvement in communication between citizens and government departments; and an increased appreciation of the influence of public opinion and public preferences on fiscal policy making. The relevance of attitude data, also a central theme of the present paper, should not be overemphasized. There are many factors involved in fiscal policy making; stress is placed on opinion data because of the frequency with which such data have been ignored in previous studies. Future attitudinal research should be less "atomistic." Public opinion, or the "general will," is not a simple function of the aggregation of individual preferences derived from social survey data. Preferences so expressed are themselves a function of economic and fiscal policy. To an extent, the influence of "opinion leaders" creates what is to be learned. For example, a "monetarist" economy in ascendence can create a monetarist consciousness among the general public. If nothing else, the truth or falsity of the above statement requires empirical verification, given its influence on the economy. Furthermore, public opinion is dependent on many influences besides those of fiscal policy makers, such as trade-union leaders, politicians, and media representatives. The views expressed by these influential groups also merit future research attention.

REFERENCES

Aitken, S., and L. Bonneville, *A General Taxpayer Opinion Survey*. Washington, D.C.: CSR Inc., 1980.

Ajzen, I., and M. Fishbein, *Understanding Attitudes and Predicting Social Behavior*. Englewood Cliffs, NJ: Prentice-Hall, 1980.

Allingham, M., and A. Sandmo, "Income Tax Evasion: A Theoretical Analysis," *Journal of Public Economics*, 34, no. 1 (1972), 323–338.

Allison, F., S. James, and A. Lewis, *Communicating with Bureaucracy: The Case of Taxpayers and the Inland Revenue*, Mimeo. University of Bath, 1986.

Auld, D., "Public Awareness and Preferences in Ontario." Discussion paper, Department of Economics, University of Guelph, Ontario, 1978.

Barlow, R., H. Brazer, and J. Morgan, *Economic Behavior of the Affluent*. Washington, D.C.: Brookings Institution, 1966.

Beedle, P., and P. Taylor-Gooby, "Ambivalence and Altruism: Public Opinion About Taxation and Welfare," *Policy and Politics*, 11, no. 1 (1983), 15–39.

Break, G., "Income Taxes and Incentives to Work: An Empirical Study," *American Economic Review*, 45, no. 5 (1957), 529–549.

Brown, C., *Taxation and the Incentive to Work*. Oxford: Oxford University Press, 1981.

Cook, S., and P. Jackson, eds., *Current Issues in Fiscal Policy*. Oxford: Martin Robertson, 1979.

Coughlin, R., *Ideology, Public Opinion and Welfare Policy*. Berkeley, CA: Institute of International Studies, University of California, 1980.

Cullis, J., and A. Lewis, "Some Evidence on Tax Knowledge and Preferences," *Journal of Economic Psychology*, 6 (1985), 271–287.

Delormé, G., "General Report of the XXXIV Congrès International de Droit Financier et Fiscal 1980," *Cahiers de Droit Fiscal International*, LXVa (1980), 43–67.

Edgell, S., and V. Duke, "Reactions to the Public Expenditure Cuts: Occupational Class and Party Realignment," *Sociology*, 16, no. 3 (1982), 431–439.

Felker, P., F. Pickering, V. Charrow, C. Holland, and J. Redish, *Guidelines for Document Designers*. Washington, D.C.: American Institute for Research, 1981.

Fields, D., and W. Stanbury, "Incentives, Disincentives and Income Tax: Further Empirical Evidence," *Public Finance*, 25, no. 3 (1970), 381–415.

Friedland, N., "A Note on Tax Evasion as a Function of the Quality of Information about the Magnitude and Credibility of Threatened Fines," *Journal of Applied Social Psychology*, 12, no. 1 (1982), 54–59.

Friedland, N., S. Maital, and A. Rutenberg, "A Simulation Study of Income Tax Evasion," *Journal of Public Economics*, 10 (1978), 107–116.

Groenland, A., and G. van Veldhoven, "Tax Evasion Behavior: A Psychological Framework," *Journal of Economic Psychology*, 3, no. 2 (1983), 129–144.

Hochman, H., and R. Rodgers, "The Simple Politics of Redistribution." Working Paper No. 9, University of California Graduate School of Public Policy, 1974.

Holland, D., "The Effects of taxation on Effort: Some Results for Business Executives," in National Tax Association, *Proceedings of the Sixty-Second Annual Conference*, September 1969.

Jones, P., and J. Cullis, "Fiscal Preferences: Some Theory for Some Evidence and Some Evidence for Some Theory," Mimeo. University of Bath, 1984.

Katona, G., "Anticipations Statistics and Consumer Behavior," *American Statistician*, 21 (1967), 12–13.

Katona, G., *Essays on Behavioral Economics*. Ann Arbor, MI: Institute for Social Research, 1980.

Katz, M., "Main Themes of the Conference," in P. Sawicki, ed., *Income Tax Compliance*. Reston, VA: American Bar Association, 1983.

Keenan, A., and P. Dean, "Moral Evaluations of Tax Evasion," *Social Policy and Administration*, 14, no. 3 (1980), 209–220.

Keene, K., "What Do We Know about the Public's Attitudes to Progressivity," *National Tax Journal*, (September 1983), 371–376.

Kelley, H., and J. Michela, "Attribution Theory and Research," *Annual Review of Psychology*, 31 (1980), 457–561.

Levy, F., "On Understanding Proposition 13," *Public Interest*, 56 (1979), 66–89.

Lewis, A., "Perceptions of Tax Rates," *British Tax Review*, 6 (1978), 338–366.

Lewis, A., "An Empirical Assessment of Tax Mentality," *Public Finance*, 2 (1979), 345–357.

Lewis, A., *The Psychology of Taxation*. Oxford: Martin Robertson, 1982; New York: St. Martin's Press, 1982.

Lewis, A., and D. Jackson, "Voting Preferences and Attitudes to Public Expenditure", *Political Studies*, XXXIII (1985), 466–475.

Mason, R., and L. Calvin, "A Study of Admitted Income Tax Evasion," *Law and Society Review*, 13, (1978), 73–89.

Mueller, E., "Public Attitudes Towards Fiscal Programs," *Quarterly Journal of Economics*, 77, no. 2 (1963), 210–235.

Newsweek, "Europe's 'Black Economy,' "*Newsweek*, (July 25, 1983), 12.

O'Higgins, M., "Aggregate Measures of Tax Evasion: An Assessment," *British Tax Review*, 5 (1981), 286–302.

O'Higgins, M., "Tax Evasion and the Self-Employed: An Examination of the Evidence," *British Tax Review*, 6 (1981), 367–378.

Puviani, A., *Teoria Della Illusione Finanziana*. Milan: Remo Sandron, 1903.

Royal Commission on the Taxation of Profits and Income, "PAYE and Incentives," Cmnd. 9105, Appendix 1. London: Her Majesty's Stationery Office, 1954.

Sanders, T., "Effects of Taxation on Executives," Harvard University Graduate School of Business Administration, 1951.

Schmölders, F., "Survey Research in Public Finance: A Behavioral Approach to Fiscal Policy," *Public Finance*, 25, no. 2 (1970), 300–306.

Seldon, A., "Price-less Opinion Research," *British Public Opinion*, 1, no. 2 (1980), 8.

Song, Y. D., and T. Yarbrough, "Tax Ethics and Taxpayers' Attitudes," *Public Administration Review*, (September/October 1978), 442–452.

Spicer, M., and L. Becker, "Fiscal Inequality and Tax Evasion: An Experimental Approach," *National Tax Journal*, 33, no. 3 (1980), 171–175.

Strumpel, B., "The Contribution of Survey Research to Public Finance," in A. Peacock, ed., *Quantitative Methods in Public Finance*. New York: Praeger, 1969.

Tufte, E., *Political Control of the Economy*. Princeton, NJ: Princeton University Press, 1978.

Vogel, J., "Taxation and Public Opinion in Sweden: An Interpretation of Recent Survey Data," *National Tax Journal*, 28, no. 4 (1974), 499–513.

Warneryd, K., and B. Walerud, "Taxes and Economic Behaviour: Some Interview Data on Tax Evasion in Sweden," *Journal of Economic Psychology*, 2, no. 3 (1982), 187–211.

THE UNCERTAINTY PRINCIPLE AND REGULATION

John J. McGonagle, Jr.

Slip sliding away, slip sliding away. The nearer your destination the more you slip slide away.

—Paul Simon

I. INTRODUCTION

In physics, there is a principle known as the Heisenberg principle of uncertainty/indetermination. Stated one way, it holds that two characteristics of an item cannot be measured at the same time, for to measure one, you cannot measure the other (Wolf, 1981). As Heisenberg himself (1974, pp. 19–20) put it in his work on physics and its relationship to other disciplines, "We know from the uncertainty relations that to determine a position requires an intervention of ever-increasing sharpness, the more accurately it is to be carried out. An infinitely sharp determination of position would actually presuppose an infinitely large intervention, and so cannot be realized at all."

The same principle, under other names, has been found to apply in other fields such as psychoanalysis (Freud, 1963, pp. 135–136), environmental studies, and management efficiency studies. In those disciplines, it is more commonly designated as the concept of the nonneutral observer, whereby the experimenter's choice of the design of the experiment determines which one of the mutually exclusive aspects of the same phenomenon will manifest itself. "Heisenberg's uncertainty principle demonstrates that we cannot observe a phenomenon without changing it" (Zukav, 1979, p. 308). This means that during the observation of an environment, such as economic performance, to establish a baseline against which to measure future changes, the known presence of the observer actually changes the environment so that we cannot know the actual untouched state of the environment—the state it would have shown with the attempt to measure it absent.

II.   CURRENT ECONOMIC THEORY

These faces of the Heisenberg uncertainty principle have a particular application in the economics of regulation.[1] They mean that the common requirement that information be filed with an agency produces a by-product. Not only is the requirement a way for regulators to supervise the industries they regulate, but in fact it also has a direct impact on the businesses' operations being reported on.

In general, economic, governmental, legal, and political analyses of regulation (Kahn, 1970, 1971; Phillips, 1978; Stigler, 1971; Posner, 1974; U.S. Department of Commerce, 1978; Smead, 1969; Morgan, 1976; Steiner, 1982; U.S. Government Accounting Office, 1981; National Association of Insurance Commissioners, 1974; Maskaw, 1979; Frohnmayer, 1981) have not identified this second aspect of disclosure. Instead they cite two purposes of information collection and production by the regulated company: providing the regulator with information to permit it to make decisions about the industry or company being regulated and providing consumers with additional information they would not otherwise receive to permit better decision making. For example, law professor Peter Schuck (1979) has commented:

> One of the principal justifications for regulation is the market failure that results from inadequate consumer information. Yet regulation does not obviate the need for such information; it simply shifts the locus of that need from the consumer to the regulator, while vastly increasing the quantity, quality, and types of information needed (p. 714).

In 1978, the U.S. Senate Committee on Governmental Affairs commissioned inquiries into the current effectiveness of federal regulation. In describing the current alternatives available, the committee staff compared performance standards and information disclosure:

> Still another alternative to the standard-setting approach is the increased use of information regulation. For example, rather than banning outright a product which does not meet a particular standard, it may make sense to allow distribution of the product provided that it is accompanied by information disclosing the hazards or problems associated with its use. This approach is now taken with numerous products, notably cigarettes, thereby allowing consumers who are willing to take certain risks the opportunity to purchase the product.... Information thus has some of the automatic quality of incentives; in other words, it can naturally prompt a certain response. However, like incentives, the existence of a potentially severe risk or irreversible consequences suggests that information without something more is inadequate. Also, if the recipient of the information is different than the ultimate users of a product, information regulation alone may not be enough. Under these circumstances, information might be properly supplemented with vigorously enforced standards and suitably designed incentives (pp. xxi–xxii).

This classic attitude toward the relationship between information and regulation reflects Charles L. Schultze's 1976 Godkin lectures (Schultze, 1977, pp. 36–40).

In fact, even in the 1980 National Bureau of Standards study on securities regulation and the venture capital markets, there is no recognition of the regulatory role that mere reporting can have. That study considered several questions dealing with the impact of the Securities and Exchange Commission's disclosure rules on capital markets, but never asked whether the act of requiring disclosure resulted in changes in the behavior of those companies that would have to make the disclosures (Barth, Cordes, and Tassey, 1980, pp. 22–23, 34–35).

However, there is some evidence that economists and regulators are beginning to recognize that there is a special relationship between mere reporting and regulation, but that recognition is not emerging in any formal manner. For example, former President Carter created the United States Regulatory Council. In 1980, the council reported that the Environmental Protection Agency was using labeling as an information strategy to protect the public health by informing workers of the risks posed by different chemicals. As an aside, the council also noted that the labeling requirement "may also act as an incentive for manufacturers to develop safer products" (U.S. Regulatory Council, 1980, p. 13). In addition, in a comprehensive review of the economics of advertising, a former senior official of the Federal Trade Commission implied that the federal government's rules requiring reporting of nicotine and tar content of cigarettes to the federal government and requiring disclosure of these results to consumers may have influenced the development and marketing of low tar and nicotine cigarettes (Pitofsky, 1978, pp. 27, 38].

III.   CASE STUDY—INSURANCE

Today, state insurance commissioners use a set of operating ratios to determine whether or not to examine particular insurance companies. These ratios are applied to the financial data of the insurers displayed in their annual financial statements filed with the state insurance departments. The actual ratios to be applied are known to the insurers, as are the standards used by the insurance departments in analyzing the results. This means that the insurers can determine how they will look to the insurance departments before the latter have had the chance to apply and analyze the ratios. One result is that insurers sometimes make economically unsound decisions, and may even be compelled to take improper actions (i.e., they may violate other aspects of the state insurance law) to avoid triggering the application of the ratios.

A.   Insurance Department Oversight

In 1982, the governor of New York State received a report from the (state) Executive Advisory Commission on Insurance Regulatory Reform on regulatory reform in the insurance industry (New York, 1982). The importance of such a report cannot be overestimated, since New York has always been a landmark state in effective insurance supervision and regulation.

In that report, the commission summarized the current state of financial regulation and supervision in New York State. It noted that the first stage in the state insurance department supervision of the financial condition of insurance companies is the "desk audit." In a desk audit the department reviews in detail the annual statements filed by all companies, as well as the quarterly statements required to be filed by most companies. During this review, the insurance department applies its early-warning system, which is somewhat similar to that of the National Association of Insurance Commissioners (NAIC) Insurance Regulatory Information System (IRIS).

In New York State's system (as well as in the NAIC IRIS), a series of financial ratios is computed. Ratios for a particular company falling outside specified ranges, while not necessarily demonstrating that a problem exists, indicate areas for further review by experienced financial examiners. If a problem exists, it could lead to discussions between insurance department personnel and the management of the insurance company, a special field examination, or continuing "priority review."

Summarizing its analysis of the financial supervision system, the commission concluded:

The time now spent by the Department in lengthy examination of companies that are clearly sound should be redeployed in more intensive examinations of companies showing evidence of hazardous condition. A related issue is the method of assessing the cost of examination. New York (like most states) now assesses that cost against the company being examined. *Companies in hazardous condition may be least able to afford the intensive examinations they require* (pp. 73–74, emphasis added).

B. The Insurance Early Warning System

In the early 1970s, the National Association of Insurance Commissioners, the umbrella organization representing all state insurance departments, developed what is known as the Early Warning System, or the Insurance Regulatory Information System (or IRIS) (U.S. Congress, 1977, p. 156). That system is intended to assist the various state insurance departments in identifying insurance companies (primarily those dealing with property and liability insurance) requiring "particularly close surveillance" (NAIC, 1973). In the language of insurance regulation, the term *close surveillance* means that the insurance company to which it is applied is believed to be close to insolvency. If the company is insolvent or may soon become insolvent, the insurance commissioner is permitted to move in and take control of the company.

For the insurer, having the insurance commissioner take control of the company can have several consequences. First, the entire company may be put under the control of a receiver and its current management removed by the insurance department. Second, the insurance department may determine that the financial condition of the insurance company is so weakened that it should be dissolved. Third, even if the insurance commissioner does not elect one of these options, the mere fact that the company is under the control of the state may put the company out of business: old customers may take their business elsewhere; potential customers may not want to buy from a company "in trouble"; insurance agents will steer clients elsewhere, fearing they may not collect their commissions from a company in trouble; and other insurance companies might not reinsure the risks of the company under supervision, cutting off its ability to spread its risks around (NAIC, 1986; McGonagle, 1983).

The Early Warning System, as first designed, was intended to assist insurance department personnel in quickly identifying companies in need of this close surveillance. While the creators of the system disavowed any intention to have the system replace in-depth financial analyses or on-site examination, in fact it has done so (U.S. Government Accounting Office, 1979, Chaps. 3–4), because the insurance departments are reluctant to undertake in-depth analyses or on-site examinations. Departments avoid in-depth analyses because of personnel and budget limitations (*NBC Reports*, 1982; Anonymous, 1974), and they avoid on-site examinations for the additional reason that the direct costs of these examinations are almost always shifted to the insurer being examined, a situation that can make a solvent insurer insolvent (New York, 1982, p. 74).

Essentially, the Early Warning System consists of an analysis of financial ratios designed to compare the performance of insurers, based on the data presented in their annual reports, with that of companies which became "problem" companies during the time the ratios were established (NAIC, 1973, p. 2). When created, the ratios were tested against the current experience. The system's advocates suggested that if a company failed four of the eleven ratios, it be classed as a "priority" company—that is, one whose financial situation should be more closely examined (NAIC, p. 2). In reviewing the percentage of insurance companies that became insolvent in the five years prior to the initiation of the system, the NAIC found that 96 percent of them would have been given priority classification 1 year prior to insolvency using the four of eleven standards; 82 percent, three years prior to insolvency; and 82 percent, five years prior to insolvency.

Just two years after the system was in place, in 1974, the NAIC engaged in fine-tuning it (NAIC, 1973, pp. 67–74). The reason was the perception that the system was not working as effectively as had been predicted in targeting problem companies. The Early Warning System was revised and continued in use. However, even after the revision, all insurance companies continued to be aware of the ratios used by the NAIC, the ranges of acceptable performance, and the number and types of tests that had to be passed each year. In fact, the manual summarizing the system has two objectives: to help state insurance departments understand and fully utilize IRIS, and to help participating insurance companies understand IRIS so that each will be able to verify its own ratios and data. To help achieve the latter goal, each insurer receives a copy of its own test results *before* the state insurance departments do (NAIC, 1983a, p. 1; 1983b, p. 1).

Use of the NAIC IRIS increased rapidly after 1974, and by 1979 about half the states were using the NAIC system (U.S. Government Accounting Office, 1979, pp. 37–38). A report commissioned by the American Insurance Association to review the performance of IRIS over that period proposed some changes be made. It found that the system had correctly identified only 52 percent of insolvent insurance companies in year 3 (that is, three years prior to legal action being taken against the company because of its insolvency) (American Insurance Association, 1978, p. 4). The system identified only 82 percent of the insolvent insurance companies in year 5 (that is, one year prior to legal action being taken against the insurer). Curiously, the changes proposed at that time would have raised the accuracy to 68 percent in the third year and 94 percent in the fifth year (American Insurance Association, 1978, p.4). This is very close to the original level of accuracy predicted for the system—that is, 96 percent one year prior to insolvency and 82 percent three years prior to insolvency (NAIC, 1973, p. 3)—and may well be indirect evidence that the insurers rapidly adapted their behavior to the test being applied. Discussing the efficacy of the IRIS system at the same time, the Illinois Insurance Department compared its effectiveness with that of a modified version the department used (the Illinois System) and that proposed by the American Insurance Association. The Illinois Insurance Department concluded that the two systems then in operation, IRIS and that of its own state, tended to identify the same insurance companies. The American Insurance Association's proposed system, not in use anywhere, was described as the system that "potentially performs best in capturing insolvents" (Illinois, 1979, p. 11).

The NAIC has now openly acknowledged the continuing need to modify the ratios it uses. "Through the years, the effectiveness of the ratios has been improved. Studies have shown that IRIS had been reasonably effective in identifying troubled companies. However, economic conditions are not so static, so research continues. The components of each ratio are reviewed annually and revised whenever revision is necessary" (NAIC, 1983a, pp. 1–2; 1983b, pp. 1–2). Reading the history of the need for constant changes in the ratios being applied, we must conclude that they have not consistently lived up to their intended purposes and in fact have not even met the degrees of accuracy they had been expected to meet.[2]

There are two reasons for this. First, the insurers covered by the system are permitted to see the results of the tests as calculated by the NAIC prior to their being received by the state insurance departments and to amend their annual statements, and thus alter the results of the tests, *before* the results are available to the states. Second, the insurers can compute their own ratios before they even complete their annual report by using the NAIC materials, which also specify the acceptable ranges for changes in the ratios (NAIC, 1983a, 1983b).

Personal observation confirms that insurers review the ratios their annual reports to insurance departments can be expected to produce. Since the annual statement on which these ratios are based is as of December 31 of each year, companies that are in danger of exceeding too many ratios, and thus becoming targets of increased insurance department interest, have the ability to make operational changes that can improve their posture. These changes, made to avoid automatic insurance department review, are not necessarily in the best financial or economic interests of the insurer.

For example, a life insurer may find, in previewing its potential results prior to the end of the year, that its operations violate four tests, a result that generally triggers examination by the insurance departments. If one of the tests violated is ratio 7, the insurer may be able to take "corrective" action. Ratio 7 measures the ratio of investments in affiliates to capital and surplus. An "unusual value" is one over 100 percent (NAIC, 1983b, pp. 18, 26). If needed, an insurer can reduce this value by selling bonds of its affiliates prior to December 31. However, since these bonds may not be registered, that sale may be at a severe discount. The result is that the insurer takes a loss to avoid an examination. Taking the case even a step further, if the insurer wishes, it can buy back the bonds on January 2 and thus keep its position in the affiliate unchanged (except for the costs and taxes associated with "parking" the securities, which may be substantial).[3]

The existence of the test and the reports to be made by the insurer both force an insurer to review and limit the overall investment in its affiliates without any insurance department action. Thus the mere existence of the test has a regulatory impact in and of itself. On the other hand, since the test is known in advance, and is a static measurement, an insurer in difficulty, knowing what its own ratios will be, can modify many of them by transactions near the end of the year (in some cases, they may be violations of the insurance laws) and effectively conceal its poor financial situation (Illinois Insurance Guaranty Fund, 1979, p. 4).

IV. CONCLUSION

One conclusion must be that the insurers, except those in the very last stages of a losing struggle against insolvency, study the ratios being applied by state insurance departments and adapt their behavior to them, at least as far as they can. As the Illinois Insurance Department (1979) casually observed, "The most important testing consideration may center on a ratio that is not within the immediate and direct control of the [insurance] company management" (p. 7). This adaptation may conceal a great percentage of the problems that may eventually lead to insolvencies. However, one question that must also be asked is whether the actions taken by insurers to conceal their problems from the IRIS merely delayed the inevitable, accelerated the insolvency, or was corrective behavior of a kind that might also prevent those same problems.

NOTES

1. On the limits of modern economics and the need for behavioral inputs, see Thurow (1983, pp. 87, 115, 163, 209, 211, and 219) and Scitovsky (1976).

2. For additional criticism of the use of hard-and-fast ratios, see Hammond (1978).

3. For examples of insurance companies concealing problems from state insurance departments prior to the widespread use of the IRIS, see U.S. Congress (1977, pp. 31–33, 506–508).

REFERENCES

American Insurance Association, "Property/Liability Early Warning System Proposal," Prepared by Aetna Life & Casualty, July 1978.

Anonymous, "Regulation of the Financial Condition of Insurance Companies," *Best's Review, Property-Liability Edition*, (October 1974).

Barth, James R., Joseph J. Cordes, and Gregory Tassey, "Evaluating the Impact of Securities Regulation on Venture Capital Markets." Monograph 166, National Bureau of Standards, U.S. Department of Commerce, June 1980.

Freud, Sigmund, *Three Case Histories*. New York: Collier Books, 1963.

Frohnmayer, David B., "Regulatory Reform: A Slogan in Search of Substance," *American Bar Association Journal*, 66 (1981).

Hammond, J.D., Arnold F. Shapiro, and N. Shilling, "The Regulation of Insurer Solidity through Capital and Surplus Requirements." Summary Report, NSF Grant APR75–16550, April 1978.

Heisenberg, Werner, *Across the Frontiers*. New York: Harper & Row, 1974.

Illinois Insurance Guaranty Fund, Illinois Department of Insurance, "Property and Liability Solidity Testing Programs: An Analysis," 1979.

Kahn, Alfred E., *The Economics of Regulation*, Ann Arbor: Books Demand, 2 vols. 1970, 1971.

Maskaw, Jerry L., "Regulation, Logic, and Ideology," *Regulation* (November/December 1979).

McGonagle, John J., Jr., "Loud and Clear: Whistle Blowers and State Regulated Businesses—The Case of Insurance." Unpublished manuscript, 1983.

Morgan, Thomas D., *Economic Regulation of Business*, St. Paul: West, 1976.

National Association of Insurance Commissioners (NAIC), *Using the Early Warning System*, 1973. Reprinted in *Federal Insurance Act*, Hearings on S.1710 before the U.S. Senate Commission on Banking, Housing, and Urban Affairs, 95th Congress, 1st Session on S.1710, September 12–14, 1977.

NAIC, Staff of the Central Office, *Monitoring Competition: A Means of Regulating the Property and Liability Insurance Business*, 2 vols., May 1974.

NAIC, "Using The NAIC Insurance Regulatory Information System—Property and Liability Edition—1982," 1983a.

NAIC, "Using The NAIC Insurance Regulatory Information System—Life and Health and Fraternal Edition—1982," 1983b.

NAIC, "Insurers Supervision, Rehabilitation, And Liquidation Model Act," *II Official NAIC Model Laws, Regulations and Guidelines* 555–33–35, 1986.

"NBC Reports: Protection For Sale—The Insurance Industry," April 17, 1982 (Transcript).

[New York] Executive Advisory Commission On Insurance Regulatory Reform, *Report* (May 6, 1982).

Phillips, Almarin, "Regulation and Its Alternatives," in Donald P. Jacobs, ed., *Regulating Business: The Search for an Optimum.* Washington, DC: ICS Press, 1978.

Pitofsky, Robert, "Advertising Regulation And The Consumer Movement," in David G. Tuereck, ed., *Issues in Advertising—The Economics of Persuasion.* Washington, DC: American Enterprise Institute, 1978.

Posner, Richard A., "Theories of Economic Regulation," *Bell Journal of Economics* (Autumn 1974).

Schuck, Peter H., "Regulation: Asking The Right Questions," *National Journal,* (April 28, 1979), 714.

Schultze, C.L., *The Public Use of Private Interest.* Washington, DC: Brookings Institution, 1977.

Scitovsky, Tibor, *The Joyless Economy.* New York: Oxford University Press, 1976.

Smead, Elmer E., *Governmental Promotion and Regulation of Business.* New York: Appleton-Century-Crafts, 1969.

Steiner, Peter O., "The Legalization of American Society: Economic Regulation," *Law Quadrangle Notes* (Winter 1982).

Stigler, George J., "The Theory of Economic Regulation," *Bell Journal of Economics* (Spring 1971).

Thurow, Lester C., *Dangerous Currents.* New York: Random House, 1983.

U.S. Congress, Senate Committee on Banking, Housing, and Urban Affairs, "Federal Insurance Act, Hearings on S. 1710," 95th Congress, 2nd Session, September 12–14, 1977.

U.S. Congress, Senate Committee on Governmental Affairs, "Study On Federal Regulation," Vol. VI, 95th Congress, 2nd Session, December 1978.

U.S. Department of Commerce, *Regulatory Reform Seminar—Proceedings and Background Papers* (October 17, 1978).

U.S. Government Accounting Office, "Issues and Needed Improvements in State Regulation of the Insurance Business," PAD–79–72, October 9, 1979.

U.S. Government Accounting Office, "An Economic Overview of Bank Solvency Regulation," PAD–81–25, February 13, 1981.

U.S. Regulatory Council, *Regulating with Common Sense: A Progress Report on Innovative Regulatory Techniques* (October 1980).

Wolf, Fred Alan, *Taking the Quantum Leap.* New York: McGraw–Hill, 1981.

Zukav, Gary, *The Dancing Wu Li Masters.* New York: Wm. Morrow & Co., 1979.

UNDERSTANDING (AND MISUNDERSTANDING) SOCIAL SECURITY:

BEHAVIORAL INSIGHTS INTO PUBLIC POLICY

Richard M. Coughlin

I. INTRODUCTION

At no time since its inception has the U.S. social security system been the subject of close scrutiny and sharp disagreement more than in recent years.[1] Resurgent interest in social security coincided with, and probably resulted from, revelations in the mid–1970s about an impending crisis in the system's financing.[2] As the debate developed, several facts became clear. The first was that in every respect—social, political, and economic—social security is a program of immense national importance. In its 50 years of operation, social security has grown dramatically in size and scope. What started out in 1935 as a program designed to provide modest retirement benefits to workers in private industry subsequently evolved into a system of extensive coverage and high costs. Among all federal expenditures, social security now ranks second only to the entire defense budget: in 1983, spending for Old Age, Survivors, and Disability Insurance (OASDI) amounted to $166.8 billion, with another $39.3 billion spent for Medicare (U.S. Department of Health and Human Services, 1983). Second, it became apparent to all observers that social security had expanded in ways that stretched existing financing mechanisms to the breaking point and necessitated major reforms in the program's benefit structure, method of financing, or both. Third, increased attention to social security's financial predicament revealed widespread confusion among the public about the system's current status and future prospects. Extensive media coverage of the "social security crisis" brought many issues to public attention for the first time, raising the question of whether more information about the program would serve to strengthen or weaken its traditional base of support. A fourth and concomitant outcome of the renewed debate was the discovery of how little consensus exists among economists and other policy experts on how to go about reforming social security, even in the face of widespread agreement over the proximate causes of the system's financial problems.

This paper examines the development of social security in the United States with the intent of clarifying the origins and implications of the controversies that have enveloped the program in recent years. The discussion will focus on social security topics identified by economists as crucial to understanding the system. We shall first look at how economists, acting either as program advocates or critics, have argued the case for or against social security on theoretical grounds as well as on the basis of research into the system's effects. Second, the discussion will explore the underlying assumptions about economic rationality and individual behavior that have guided economic studies of the social security system's development, present circumstances, and future prospects.

II. PURPOSES OF SOCIAL SECURITY

The purpose of social security is ostensibly to provide income security for retired workers. Functional simplicity, however, has never characterized the social security system, and there continues to be widespread disagreement over what the program's purposes are and what they should be. In part this disagreement is a result of elements peculiar to the current program. At times social security has been portrayed as analogous to a private insurance scheme with narrowly circumscribed goals of replacing part of earnings lost through retirement. At the same time, social security's scope of coverage and level of benefits have expanded far beyond this limited goal. Insofar as purposes are concerned, social security has evoked so much controversy because it contains so many complicated and contradictory features and because it presents so many different faces to expert and layman observers alike (see Derthick, 1979a). It has served—if the debate can withstand one more analogy—as a kind of Rorschach ink blot into which observers can readily project a multitude of preconceptions and ideological values, and the closer its details are scrutinized the more the broad outlines of the image seem to dissolve into a blur.

A. Historical Roots

Controversy over social security's identity and purposes dates back to
the 1930s and the victorious effort by members of the Committee on
Economic Security (CES) and, later, the Social Security Board to impose
a particular model of old-age insurance (OAI) on the new federal program. Although now widely regarded as the centerpiece of liberal social
legislation, the approach settled upon by the CES and later enacted into
law as Titles II and VIII of the Social Security Act of 1935 reflected a
"conservative" strain of social insurance. In planning social security, the
CES drew heavily on the work of institutional economist John Commons
and reform leader John Andrews, who a few years earlier had laid the
foundation of 1920s social insurance legislation in Wisconsin. The Wisconsin model of social insurance emphasized principles of risk selection
(i.e., limitation of coverage to the risk of loss of earned income because
of retirement), the linking of coverage to prior employment, financing
by payroll taxes falling on both the employee and the employer, and a
structure of wage-related benefits (Lubove, 1968; Cates, 1983). The conservatism of this model was to be found in its contrast to the more liberal
philosophy of social insurance expounded by Abraham Epstein and Isaac
Rubinow, as well as in contrast to radical schemes for income redistribution that sprang up in the 1930s in the form of the Townsend Plan
and Huey Long's Share Our Wealth.

But political judgments are all relative, and measured solely against
existing income-support provisions for the aged—which prior to 1935
were restricted to coverage under state public assistance programs—the
federal social security program represented a move toward greater governmental intervention in the social and economic life of the nation that
was anything but conservative. Subsequently, a long series of legislative
actions wrought important changes in the structure of the OAI program,
broadening its coverage, liberalizing benefits, and further contributing
to the ambiguity surrounding its purposes.

B. The Insurance Analogy

One important element of the early debate over social security concerned the development of the insurance analogy. The original architects
of social security rationalized their actions as much or more in terms of
political expediency than economic principles. Much of their efforts went
toward selling the idea of a federally sponsored program to the Congress
and the electorate. The original social security legislation contained no
reference to insurance principles of any kind, because it was feared that
such terminology might lead to the program being declared unconsti-

tutional. Immediately following the favorable 1937 decision by the U.S. Supreme Court, however, the program began to be infused with a terminology reminiscent of private insurance. Government pamphlets, other official documents, and pronouncements by social security administrators started to refer to payroll taxes as "contributions." Each participating worker received an identification number to record earnings in covered employment, giving the impression that social security numbers were tied to individual retirement accounts. Moreover, the establishment of the Old Age Reserve Account, later joined by trust funds for disability insurance and Medicare, into which contributions were paid further reinforced the perception that social security was like a fully funded private insurance scheme. And perhaps most important of all, proponents of social security offered the repeated and insistent reminder to the public that only those workers who had paid into the system would be entitled to receive benefits later on.

Ironically, the private insurance analogy came into widespread use just as major reforms were occurring that would push the program ever farther away from narrow insurance principles. In the original legislation the relationship between taxes paid and benefits received under the OAI program was at least roughly similar to private annuity insurance, favoring the preservation of *individual equity* over welfare objectives in the system. For example, only one beneficiary, the retired worker, was to be eligible for benefits, which ranged from $10 to a maximum of only $85 per month (Weaver, 1982). Benefit tables further reflected the equity principle of equal benefits for equal contributions irrespective of individual need or family circumstance. Coverage under OAI was limited, moreover, to only about 60 percent of the labor force.

But even at the beginning, misleading terminology and crude similarity could not conceal the elements of OAI that diverged sharply from private insurance. From the start, benefits were progressively weighted in favor of workers with a history of low earnings; although the absolute level of benefits increased at higher earnings levels, the ratio of benefits to covered earnings decreased. Furthermore, the entire benefit structure was artificially elevated to provide higher benefits to the first retirement cohort, resulting in an even greater disjunction between taxes paid in and benefits received than would have been produced by the progressive benefit structure alone. Together these elements constitute what has come to be known as the *social adequacy* component of social security.

In subsequent years, two opposing forces further altered the balance between individual equity and social adequacy in social security. On the one hand, amendments to the Social Security Act beginning in 1939 and in years following served to weaken the relationship between taxes paid to social security and benefits received by altering the way in which the earnings base was calculated, by inclusion of survivors and dependents in the program, by the introduction of disability and Medicare coverage and, most of all, by periodic upward adjustments in benefit levels at a rate exceeding increases in the payroll tax. Considered in isolation, these actions served to augment the transfer (or "welfare") component of social security. On the other hand, as the system matured and each new cohort of retiring workers paid taxes over a longer period of time than the cohort before it, the tendency was toward a steady reduction of the relative size of the welfare component. Evidence suggests that the net trend was toward an overall reduction in the welfare component of social security from almost 98 percent of average benefits in 1940 to about 70 percent in 1970 (Parsons and Munro, 1977). However, these data do not take into account the very large benefit increases that were enacted during the 1970s, nor do they reflect large discrepancies of the equity/adequacy balance within retirement cohorts resulting from the progressive benefit formula, the impact of survivors' and dependents' benefits, variations in the timing of retirement, or differences in longevity—all of which further distort the simple equity principle implied by the insurance analogy.

In sum, the enduring presence of a large social adequacy component in social security has rendered the analogy to private insurance untenable. Today its usefulness as a defense of social security is dubious. If all that can be said about social security is that it is like a private annuity, it is hard to see any valid reason for providing benefits higher than those justified by actual individual contributions. Moreover, adhering strictly to the private insurance analogy, one might just as well argue that individuals should be free to choose how to allocate their own resources, including foregoing current individual consumption in order to save for retirement—or not, as they desire (see, e.g., Friedman, 1962). Pursuing this logic, conservative and libertarian critics of social security have seized on the insurance analogy as an inviting point of attack on the system as a whole. They correctly point out that social security is not voluntary, that it imposes substantial tax burdens on current workers to pay benefits to those currently retired, and that future benefits are not guaranteed on the basis of individual contributions but by the willingness of future working generations to bear the tax burden to support future retirees. In the view of these critics, comparing social security to private insurance is little more than "fraud" (Shore, 1975; see Friedman, 1977).

C. *Rationales for Social Insurance*

While few, if any, contemporary proponents of social security have attempted to defend the system on the basis of the private insurance analogy, the notion that social security provides essential risk protection *qua* social insurance is far from dead. The focus of debate over the justification for social security has shifted from the discredited private insurance analogy to the examination of more valid social insurance rationales, the most important of which are reviewed below.

Individual Myopia. In the absence of a mandatory savings system, there is the danger that individuals will fail to insure adequately for retirement (Manser, 1981; Pechman, Aaron, and Taussig, 1968). This argument can take several forms. One explanation attributes savings failure to *individual myopia*, involving the tendency of individuals to underestimate their retirement savings needs (Schulz, 1980). A slight variant of this explanation identifies individual irresponsibility or simple bad judgment as the cause of insufficient savings (Diamond, 1977; Viscusi and Zeckhauser, 1977; Stein, 1980; cf. Feldstein, 1977). Still another version of this explanation elaborates the concept of myopia to include the role of uncertainty in individual decision making (Diamond, 1977; Viscusi and Zeckhauser, 1977). Schulz (1980, p. 74), for example, enumerates the following conditions that interfere with the individual's ability to make adequate plans for retirement:

1. He doesn't know with certainty when he will die.
2. He doesn't know exactly what his future income flow will be.
3. He doesn't know what his basic retirement needs will be or what lifestyle he will ultimately prefer for that period.
4. He doesn't know when he will retire.
5. He cannot easily predict the future rate of inflation.
6. He cannot easily predict the rate of economic growth.

It follows that to compensate for uncertainties and to ensure that individuals will be protected from destitution in old age, paternalistic strategies are justified to enforce savings via social insurance or some functionally similar strategy.

Opposing this rationale are arguments questioning both the prevalence of individual savings myopia and the presumed obligation of society to protect those who fail to protect themselves. Browning (1973) notes the lack of good information on the extent to which people would fail to accumulate sufficient savings in the absence of paternalistic government policies; if the actual number were small—on the order of a few percent—the myopia rationale would, in his words, "hardly be considered convincing" (p. 236).[3] Friedman (1962) challenges not only the need for policies to enforce savings but also the morality of governmental paternalism. Consider the following excerpt from *Capitalism and Freedom*:

Those of us who believe in freedom must believe also in the freedom of individuals to make their own mistakes. If a man knowingly prefers to live for today, to use his resources for current enjoyment, deliberately choosing a penurious old age, by what right do we prevent him from doing so? We may argue with him, seek to persuade him that he is wrong, but are we entitled to use coercion to prevent him from doing what he chooses? Is there not always the possibility that he is right and that we are wrong? Humility is the distinguishing virtue of the believer in freedom, arrogance of the paternalist (p. 188).

Market Failure. Government intervention may also be justified on grounds of market failure. Social security, of course, came into being during the Great Depression largely as a result of a prolonged and disastrous failure in the private market. Although the dire conditions that marked that era are gone, there is evidence that the private market still does not provide adequate protection against the loss of income in old age. Diamond (1977) offers several examples of market failure in the area of retirement income security: first, investment opportunities to provide a reasonably safe real return on investment may not exist, and even if they do individual investors may not have sufficient assets or knowledge to take advantage of them; second, there may be an absence of investment opportunities in annuities indexed to changes in the level of prices; and third, it may not be possible for the individual to insure against the risks associated with the length of working life, such as ill health, declining energy, and obsolescent skills.

Feldstein (1977) and Rosen (1977) also cite examples of market failure as a rationale for social security, identifying the "adverse selection" problem as a limiting factor in the ability of private insurance to offer adequate coverage to high-risk individuals who need protection the most.

Schulz (1980) points to the poor performance record of pension plans in private industry, which historically have offered uncertain and inadequate retirement protection to workers and which still cover less than half of all workers. Based on analysis of a recent Social Security Administration Retirement History Survey, Thompson (1978) underscores this point, reporting that 28 percent of men and fully 45 percent of women covered by private pension plans never received any benefits from the plans after retirement.[4]

The idea that adequate retirement security cannot be insured through private market mechanisms has not gone entirely unchallenged. A number of proposals have been put forward by libertarians and fiscal conservatives to reform social security by replacing most or all of its coverage with market-based alternatives. A notable example is Buchanan (1968), who has proposed reconstituting the old-age pension part of social security by repealing the payroll tax and substituting compulsory purchases of social insurance bonds. The proceeds of bond sales would be used to

finance current benefits, and the rate of return to bond holders would
be adjusted to the rate of growth of the economy or the interest rate on
long-term treasury bonds, whichever was higher. Although the purchase
of a minimum level of protection would be compulsory under this proposal, individuals would be allowed to substitute private insurance coverage for an equal value of social insurance bonds.[5]

Income Redistribution.   A third rationale for social insurance rests
upon its capacity to redistribute income within and between retirement
cohorts. The contention is that since the elderly are at high risk of being
poor, it is appropriate to transfer income from the working population
to the elderly by means of social security benefits. Viscusi and Zeckhauser
(1977) flatly assert that "transferring resources to the elderly is social
security's dominant accomplishment" (p. 50). Manser (1981) notes that
intergenerational redistribution in social security can be justified on the
grounds that later generations are expected to be better off than previous
ones (cf. Morgan, 1978). Ozawa (1976), responding to the objection there
are more efficient means available for giving support to the elderly poor,
stresses the comparative advantage in the "magnitude of distributive
impact" of social security over public assistance programs and argues
that redistribution is an essential purpose of the system:

> [A] 100 percent share of a peanut is still a peanut, but a 50 percent share of an
> elephant is half an elephant. The amount of aggregate benefits that goes to the
> lowest income class is a function not only of the degree of economic efficiency but
> also of the total amount of outlay (p. 213).

Of the rationales for social insurance, income redistribution has generated the most controversy, with strong criticisms of its role within the
current social security system coming from both ends of the ideological
spectrum. Right-wing critics have objected to any redistributional purpose in social security on grounds of equity, economic efficiency, and
morality (Ferrara, 1980; Weaver, 1982). Leftist critics have approached
the issue from the opposite direction, questioning the sincerity of social
security's redistributional goal, given the regressive nature of the payroll
tax, the meager benefits paid to low-wage earners, and what these leftist
critics regard as the program's covert social control functions.[6] Koeppel
(1976) characterizes social security as "inadequate and unfair, with workers and the poor carrying a disproportionate share of the burden of the
elderly." In a similar vein, Cates (1983) charges social security with "insuring inequality" through its embodiment of conservative social insurance principles and its role in blocking effective reform of public
assistance programs for the elderly. Finally, O'Connor (1973) succinctly
states the neo-Marxist analysis of the program as follows:

The basic purpose of social security is widely misunderstood.... Although social security contributes to social and political stability by conservatizing unemployed [*sic*] and retired workers, the primary purpose of the system is to create a sense of economic security within the ranks of employed workers (especially workers in the monopoly sector).... *Seen in this way, social insurance is not primarily insurance for workers, but a kind of insurance for capitalists and corporations* (p. 138. Emphasis in original).

D. Related Intergenerational Issues

While not counted among the conventional rationales for social insurance, a number of issues concerning the relationship between the generations have been raised as possible justifications for the present social security system. The first is the "compact between the generations" argument—the idea that each working generation supports the retired population with the expectation of receiving similar support upon retirement. Break (1977, 1981), for example, argues that since the insurance analogy no longer serves as an accurate description of social security, the program can only be rationalized as a compact between the generations, based on the simple economic logic that parents have children whom they expect to support them when they retire. Pogue and Sgontz (1977) elaborate this argument and cast it in the terms of a rational response to market uncertainties: money spent on childrens' education is conceived of as investment in human capital, which yields the parents a higher rate of return than a comparable investment in physical capital; a strong parental commitment to education thus encourages a strong filial commitment to support social security.

Other economists have objected to the concept of the intergenerational compact or do not appeal to it explicitly as a rationale for social security, although their analyses lead to essentially the same result. In the place of an intergenerational compact, they offer the idea of *entitlement* to benefits. Morgan (1977, 1978) forcefully argues the case in favor of the right of the retired generation to benefits on the grounds that the consumption foregone by people during their working lives to fund the social security system facilitates the increase in living standards enjoyed by all of society. In its purest form, this analysis approximates the insurance analogy (and at times Morgan seems to be arguing for a pure insurance interpretation of social security), but one significant difference lies in the emphasis it places on the collective contributions and benefits of the cohort rather than of the individual. Morgan distinguishes this presumed earned right to a benefit from intergenerational transfers on the basis that all generational cohorts (except the first few) are entitled to receive their contributions *plus interest* when they retire. The only redistribution that occurs is within generations in the form of disability benefits, survivors' benefits, and the implicit subsidy from those who die early to those who live a long time (Morgan, 1978). Musgrave (1981) makes a similar point about the right of retired workers to receive benefits, arguing that the essential nature of social security is "one of contribution and entitlement, not of redistribution" (pp. 119–120).

Finally, there is the issue of pay-as-you-go financing of social insurance, which has been a key point in the debate over intergenerational transfers in social security. Building on the work of Samuelson (1958), Aaron (1966) describes the social insurance "paradox" in which accumulating reserves results in a decrease in real net lifetime receipts compared with a pay-as-you-go financing.[7] However, Aaron does not appear to see this potential advantage as a rationale per se for the current social security system, noting that even in the absence of any net increase in welfare, an unfunded system may be justified on alternate grounds of market imperfections or income redistribution goals.

Among the many critics of the intergenerational compact and pay-as-you-go financing, Friedman's (1972) comparison of social security to a "chain letter" figures prominently. Friedman argues that by funding benefits out of current taxes the system pushes spending ahead of explicit taxes, producing deficits that must be financed by future generations. Rosen (1977) notes that Friedman's analogy to a chain letter may be appropriate, but it is incomplete. Chain letters must end ultimately, but if society survives there will always be future generations to tax. Rosen further argues that "the implicit rate of return on prior tax payments is sustained by a growing taxable base, whatever its source" (p. 93). In another analysis of intergenerational transfers, Browning (1973) similarly points out that while social insurance is, in a meaningful sense, debt financed, the problem of shifting costs to the "terminal generation" is hypothetical, occurring in the far-distant future when, perhaps, scarcity may no longer even be a problem and when taxes will harm no one.

III.   DEBATE OVER ECONOMIC EFFECTS

Another important ingredient of the recent debate over social security concerns the effects of the program on the economy. The three areas that have been the focus of greatest attention are: (1) effects on savings and capital accumulation; (2) effects on labor supply; and (3) the net impact on income redistribution. Below we shall briefly review these questions before turning to the discussion of the theoretical foundations underlying economic behavior in social security.

A. Effects on Savings

For two decades the debate among economists over the impact of social security on savings behavior has presented a curious case of "now you see it, now you don't." What has been seen, or not seen, is any consistent and significant negative impact that many economists presume social security must have on rates of savings. The empirical evidence has piled up, but no definitive answers have been forthcoming; a proliferation of studies using different methodologies and analytical frameworks have reached divergent conclusions, ranging from a small positive impact of social security on savings to large negative effects. While we can do little more than scratch the surface here, it is nevertheless useful to identify where and how these disputes have arisen.

Munnell (1974a) notes that traditionally there have been two popular but irreconcilable arguments concerning the effect of social security on household savings. The first, based on the life-cycle model used in the conventional neoclassical analysis of savings, assumes that families arrange their economic affairs to maximize total utility over their entire lifetimes, that savings are set aside solely to provide for consumption after retirement, and, furthermore, that both working and retirement phases are of a fixed and predictable duration (see Break, 1981). Social security, since it accomplishes the savings function by way of the "contribution and entitlement" mechanism, should thus act to reduce discretionary savings via a *wealth replacement* effect. The second argument predicts exactly the opposite outcome, an increase in savings, due to the fact that social security stimulates awareness of the need to save for retirement (a *recognition* effect) as well as encouraging additional savings as individuals approach retirement (Katona, 1965; Cagan, 1965).

This apparent theoretical stalemate has been the focal point of intense debate and empirical study over the past decade. Having identified the antinomy in existing theories, Munnell (1974a) concludes that social security has exerted dual effects on savings that have tended to offset one another and have accounted for the relative stability of the savings rate over time; in another study, Munnell (1974b) concludes that the net negative impact of social security on savings is small, in the range of 5 percent. Subsequently, Martin Feldstein emerged as the intellectual standard bearer for this side of the debate, producing a series of studies in which he argues for a large negative effect on savings (Feldstein, 1974, 1976a, 1976b, 1977, 1979a, 1979b; Feldstein and Pellechio, 1979). Feldstein reaches this conclusion based on an extended life-cycle model in which social security shows a substantial "asset substitution" effect, displacing private savings and resulting in a reduction of stock of private wealth on the order of 40 percent (Feldstein, 1977). During the 1970s other studies appeared that were consistent with Feldstein's general position that social security significantly reduced savings and capital formation (Boskin and Robinson, 1980; Kotlikoff, 1979a, 1979b).

Opposing arguments have come from two sources, the first relying on a different set of variables to explain savings behavior and the second using Feldstein's very own data to obtain a dramatically different conclusion. Barro (1974, 1978) has proposed a modification of the life-cycle model of savings behavior to include voluntary transfers between the generations. He hypothesizes that parents wishing to make bequests to their children will increase savings under conditions of pay-as-you-go pension financing in order to counteract the higher tax burdens imposed on the younger generation; conversely, he makes the argument that under social security, direct support of elderly parents by children is replaced by indirect support through the public pension program, again with no net decrease in savings. Darby (1979) provides some confirmation of the notion that bequests have a greater influence on savings behavior than does asset accumulation for retirement.

The most interesting challenge to the large negative savings effect thesis comes from the work of two research economists from the Social Security Administration, Leimer and Lesnoy (1980). Using Feldstein's own data, they obtained results that indicated no significant negative impact on savings. Further checking uncovered an error in Feldstein's computer program that accounted for the discrepancy, thus apparently negating Feldstein's original conclusion. In response, Feldstein (1980) quickly published an updated and revised version of the first study that, even without the help of a programming error, found a strong negative impact on personal savings.

To observers sitting on the sidelines, little can be gained from following the zigzag course of the savings debate, except perhaps a sense of bewilderment at the sheer magnitude of the range of estimated effects. The consensus among economists who are not confirmed adherents of either side of the debate is that the question remains open, and that empirical studies published to date need to be interpreted with caution. Break (1981), for example, characterizes the conclusions emerging from "work being done at the frontiers of economic research" as "fragile and tentative" (p. 74).[8]

B. Effects on Labor-Force Participation

Less controversial and better documented is social security's effect in reducing levels of labor-force participation among the elderly. The arguments on this point are quite simple: by providing benefits upon retirement, social security induces the elderly to withdraw from the labor force; and by placing a heavy implicit tax on earned income via the "retirement test," it discourages the elderly from working. Neither of these assertions is seriously open to question, nor can there be any doubt that rates of labor-force participation among the elderly have fallen sharply throughout this century and continue to decrease (see Achenbaum, 1978). What disagreement there is concerns the magnitude of the impact on labor-force participation and its significance for productivity in an advanced industrial economy.

Early studies of retirement behavior, based on a survey interview methodology and conducted by the Social Security Administration between 1941 and 1951 found that only a very small fraction (on the order of 3 to 6 percent) of retirees retired voluntarily in order to enjoy leisure (Campbell and Campbell, 1976). Subsequent surveys done in the 1960s found that the rate of voluntary retirement seemed to be on the rise, accounting for about 10 to nearly 20 percent of all male retirements both at age 65 and ages 62 to 65 (Palmore, 1964; Reno, 1971). In the overwhelming majority of cases, these early studies identified poor health, reaching compulsory retirement age, or declining work opportunities as the cause of retirement. Obviously, these factors are only tangentially related to the availability of retirement benefits, and the implication was that the potential impact of social security as an inducement to retirement was negligible.

More recent studies using methodologies other than surveys have challenged this conclusion. Based on analysis of labor-force participation statistical series, Campbell and Campbell (1976) suggest that sharp declines in the participation rate are linked to several aspects of social security: the eligibility for full benefits at age 65, the availability of early retirement benefits introduced for women in 1956 and for men in 1961, and the shift to part-time employment of workers subject to the retirement test. Analysis of the Survey Research Center (Michigan) income dynamics panel by Boskin (1977) provides supporting evidence. He concludes that "recent increases in social security benefits and coverage, combined with the earnings test, are a significant contributor to the rapid decline of the labor-force participation of the elderly" (p. 19). In various studies using a different methodology to analyze the 1973 Current Population Survey-Internal Revenue Service-Social Security Administration exact-match file, Pellechio (1978a, 1978b, 1979) reaches a similar conclusion for males aged 60 to 70 who were eligible for social security retirement benefits but were not covered by other public pension plans.

The implications of a reduction in the labor supply are not clear. Some contemporary economists have identified this negative impact as a problem and see the falling labor-force participation of the elderly as a serious loss in aggregate productivity. But removing older workers from the labor force was, in fact, one of the ancillary goals of the program in the 1930s, when high unemployment meant that there was a large surplus of labor and little demand for their services. Although unemployment rates in recent years have never approached levels of the Depression era, they have not been low in absolute terms for over a decade. This has led other economists to conclude that the negative effect of social security on the labor supply is not a serious problem at all, and in some respects—for example, supporting employers' preferences for younger workers—it may even be beneficial.

C. Effects on Income Redistribution

Although social security benefits are progressively weighted, the payroll tax is known to be one of the most regressive of all taxes (Brittain, 1972). And because the benefit structure and the payroll-tax burden have changed frequently over the program's history, the net redistributive impact of social security has not been easy to ascertain. Despite recurrent challenges from both the ideological left and right, conventional wisdom in economics and public policy has portrayed social security as a fundamentally egalitarian and progressive program. The evidence supporting this conclusion comes from the program's redistributive impact via intergenerational transfers. Since retirees are likely on average to have lower incomes than workers, the cross-sectional net effect of payroll taxes and social security benefits has been regarded as progressive. Plotnick and Skidmore (1975), for example, found that in the early 1970s social security lifted more people out of poverty than any other program.

The argument based on the progressiveness of intergenerational transfers begs the more important question of whether social security acts *over time* to redistribute income from the more affluent to the less affluent segments of the population. Liberal supporters of social security have typically acted on the assumption that it does, that the program's progressive elements outweigh and eventually overtake its regressive ones, and that social security effects a net downward redistribution of income to low-wage earners.

Numerous impediments stand in the way of assessing social security's overall redistributive impact, and a complete model must take into account not only the relative balance between the regressiveness of the payroll tax and the progressiveness of the benefit structure but also differences in the length of working lives, life expectancy and age-specific mortality, interaction between payroll taxes and income taxes, dual-income households, and a host of other factors influencing the "fairness" of the system across different segments of the population (Campbell,

1977). This is no easy task, and although no study to date has attempted to weigh the simultaneous impact of all these variables on income redistribution in social security, there are a few efforts worth noting. Ozawa (1976) cites the relative insensitivity of social security benefits to family size and large differences in life expectancy across racial groups as significant constraints on progressivity. She concludes that "it may well be that income redistribution is taking place in the opposite direction from what is generally believed" (p. 219). Aaron (1977) reports the results of a simulation study examining the impact of age of entry into the labor force, earning profiles, and mortality rates on the OAI segment of social security, in which he found that differential mortality rates *fully offset* the progressivity of the social security benefit formula. Aaron concludes that if social security's goal is downward redistribution of income, reforms are needed to bring its actual effects in line with this goal, either by increasing the progressivity of the benefit formula or by replacing the flat-rate payroll tax by a graduated tax.

IV. PUBLIC OPINION AND ECONOMIC RATIONALITY

Because of the central role it accords behavioral assumptions of rational choice and utility maximization, mainstream economics has had more than a little difficulty coming to terms with the widespread and seemingly uncritical support social security has received from the American public. As economic policy, social security has proved an easy target for attack on the grounds of its relative inefficiency as a tool of income maintenance. Narrowing in on social security's ambiguous objectives and complicated—even obscure—relationship between taxes paid and benefits received, critics have been able to build cogent and consistent indictments of the program's structure of costs and benefits, incentives and disincentives. In contrast, the defense of social security in conventional economic terms has tended to be vague on important questions of theory, such as accounting for individual motivation to work and save, and it has been hampered by use of the analogy to private insurance. Given their natural bias toward the economics of private goods and market transactions, mainstream economists have generally found it easier to suggest why social security should not exist, at least not in the form that it does, than to say why it should.

And yet the irony is that critics of social security have had little success in explaining the most important empirical result of all: the simple fact that the program has survived, even flourished politically, for so long with its ambiguities and apparent contradictions intact. During the past decade, social security has weathered several well-publicized financing crises—including more than a few premature announcements of its imminent bankruptcy—without suffering mass disaffection. The financial problems of the trust funds aside, the prospects for social security enduring more or less in its present form appear quite good (Tomasson, 1983).[9] How are we to account for this apparent paradox? Are conventional economic assumptions about behavior wrong, or is the broad appeal of social security merely symptomatic of mass economic irrationality? The answer to these questions can be found, I think, in how we conceive of rational economic behavior in the context of social policy. The first step is to understand how the public perceives social security.

A. Public Opinion, Preferences, and Information

More than any other social program, the old-age pension part of social security has managed to overcome the strong resistance Americans have often shown toward government intervention in social and economic affairs. Surveys from the 1930s and 1940s reveal that a remarkably high degree of public acceptance of social security was present from the very start. From 1935 to 1945, levels of approval ranged from 68 percent to 97 percent of national sample surveys (Schiltz, 1970), with the variations mostly accounted for by differing formats and wording of items contained in various surveys. Nor was initial public acceptance of the program passive: fully 81 percent of the sample in a 1941 survey expressed the willingness to pay an *additional* 3 percent tax on income to finance pension benefits (Schiltz, 1970).

Surveys done in the late 1940s and the 1950s confirmed the findings of earlier studies, while also revealing a broad base of support for extending coverage to ever-wider segments of the population. A 1961 Survey Research Center (Michigan) poll found that the public ranked "help for older people" as the number one priority for government spending, with 70 percent of the sample favoring increased spending in this area, compared with 54 percent supporting increased spending for hospital and medical benefits, and only 29 percent in favor of more money for unemployment benefits (Schiltz, 1970).[10]

During the 1970s, despite a great deal of unfavorable publicity arising from the depletion of the OASI Trust Fund, there were no indications of any wavering in traditional patterns of public support. In 1977, well after the initial disclosure of the trust fund's problems and in the middle of a heated congressional debate about social security reform, a Harris survey found virtually unanimous opposition among the public to cutting social security: 87 percent said that a one-third reduction in spending for the program would be a "very serious loss," while another 9 percent saw this action as a "serious loss" (Coughlin, 1980).

While the meaning of opinion-survey evidence is always open to question—and no more so than when selected findings are applied to complex policy issues—the cumulative weight of evidence from these and other opinion surveys points to a strong and enduring public preference for social security. To be sure, I am using the term *preference* here in a way that will arouse skepticism on the part of economists who view the free market as the only circumstance in which individual preferences can be ascertained. Of course, assessing preferences in this latter sense is impossible at present, since individual choices in social security are limited by mandatory participation in the program. Nor is it possible within the realm of public policy to generate direct information about the hierarchy of individual preferences, and indirect evidence is limited to comparing public-opinion survey data across different kinds of programs.

Still, working within the conventional framework of utility maximization, it would be reasonable to expect that individual attitudes toward the existing social security program would be shaped by patterns of differential costs and benefits to individuals. Those who stand to enjoy net economic benefits from the system would be expected to support the system, while those who believe that private-market alternatives will produce better returns on investment should oppose it. Although the logic of this simple explanatory model is reasonable, its usefulness in accounting for opinion-survey results is questionable. For one thing, levels of popular support have remained so high for so long that there has been little variance to explain. A second and potentially more vexing problem arises from the sheer complexity of determining actual costs and benefits in social security: over time these have shifted continuously as the program's coverage has expanded, benefit formulae have changed, and payroll taxes have increased. Indeed, given the widely ranging estimates of net tax and benefit effects offered by different economists, it would be difficult to predict even the hypothetical direction of the relationship between net social security costs and benefits on the one hand and attitudes on the other. Empirical results do not provide much help in solving this problem; while various surveys have found a slight negative relationship between income and education and support for social security, these patterns are nowhere near as pronounced as they are in attitudes toward other social programs, and, overall, the patterns reveal more consensus than cleavage (see Schiltz, 1980). In more ways than one, it seems that social security occupies a special place in public opinion.

One explanation—which is usually put forward as an objection—for the extraordinary breadth and longevity of social security's mass appeal identifies consumer ignorance as a source of economically "irrational" behavior. The most vocal critics of social security have long dismissed evidence of popular support as an artifact of deceptive advertising on the part of the Social Security Administration (Friedman, 1972). They have also argued that once the veils of confusion enveloping the program are lifted and its true nature stands revealed (i.e., principally as a mechanism to transfer income from one generation to another) taxpayers will then rise up and reject the current system (Ferrara, 1980; Weaver, 1982). A milder version of this argument holds that true attitudes toward social security are not yet known, because historical patterns of support were distorted by unrealistically low costs during the program's start-up phase. Up until the mid–1970s, apparent costs were kept low compared with benefits being paid; as the costs of financing social security have become painfully more apparent, "easy votes" in its favor have disappeared (Derthick, 1979b).[11]

This gap between the apparent benefits of government spending and perceived costs has been called the "fiscal illusion" (Lewis, 1982). On the surface, the fiscal illusion seems to offer a plausible explanation for the uncharacteristically generous attitude the public has shown toward social security, and it allows assumptions of utility maximization to be conveniently reconciled with the undifferentiated pattern of support observed in public-opinion surveys. The only problem with this argument is that it seems to be wrong—at least, it is not supported by recent empirical evidence. Surveys done over the past few years have found that the public is much better informed about social security than it was in the past, and that they continue to be in favor of more spending *despite a growing feeling that the payroll tax is too high* (Hart, 1979).[12] In social security, the fiscal illusion seems to have been turned upside down; awareness of costs, even to the point of arousing feelings that taxes are too high, has not diminished fundamental support for the program. It is important to note that there is no inherent contradiction or obvious irrationality in these attitudes; on the contrary, if the message of public opinion is to favor social security as a benefit program while objecting to the way in which it is financed, there are ample precedents to be found in current social security reforms proposed by many economists.

B. *Extended Conceptions of Rationality*

Instead of trying to force the question of rational choice in its conventional form, it is possible to attack the problem from a different angle, modifying the model to allow a wider variety of factors to come into play. In this way we can determine if better theoretical predictions can be obtained by altering a few behavioral assumptions, rather than rejecting the model or invoking the residual category of irrationality to explain empirical observations.[13] Specifically, I would like to suggest four ways to extend or modify the rational-choice model as it applies to social security: (1) extended self-interest, (2) enlightened self-interest, (3) compassion, and (4) commitment.

Extended Self-interest.   A minor but nontrivial extension of rational choice treats the welfare of families across generations, both actual and anticipated, as an influence on individual behavior in the present. Concerning social security, this extension of self-interest can be thought of in two ways. First, by providing a measure of income protection for the elderly, social security mitigates the financial burden falling directly on children (and perhaps other relatives) of retirees. Second, social security potentially serves to reduce feelings of guilt and resentment that might arise between elderly parents and their children in the absence of old-age pension benefits.[14] There is some empirical evidence to suggest that these factors play a part in shaping attitudes toward social security. An exploratory study by Goodwin and Tu (1975) found the perception that social security frees many younger people from having to support their aged parents to be strongly correlated with support for governmental sponsored old-age pensions.[15]

While requiring no fundamental revision of the assumptions of utility maximization, the extended self-interest model drives a thin wedge between the calculation of individual interests and support for social security. It forces us to confront the broader question of how financial expectations within families interact with the differential costs and benefits of government programs. At a minimum, this modification significantly complicates the question of how individuals define their economic interests in programs where direct costs must be weighed against benefits that may redound to individuals indirectly through the "extended" family.

Enlightened Self-interest.   Although difficult to pinpoint, the importance of attitudes and behavior that are not immediately driven by narrow self-interest should not be underestimated. Clearly, for society to function at even a minimal level, some accommodation must be reached between raw egoism and concern for the wider public good. The concept of enlightened self-interest is graphically illustrated in the obverse by Sen's (1977) caricature of a chance encounter between two Rational Economic Men, each bent on maximizing his individual utilities:

"Where is the railway station?" he asks me. "There," I say, pointing to the post office, "and would you please post this letter for me on the way?" "Yes," he says, determined to open the envelope and check whether it contains something valuable (p. 332).

Of course, most people in most circumstances do not behave in this way, and that is precisely the point of Sen's little parable. Under some conditions cooperation among individuals is preferable to each person rigidly pursuing his or her own selfish interests.[16]

It is worth considering that the popular support for social security can be at least partly explained by a similar dynamic: individuals who are not immediate beneficiaries of the program may believe that it serves a worthwhile purpose and that in its absence the common good would suffer—the "common good" here referring to benefits that are so widely dispersed across the population that they flow to any one individual only in the most indirect way. For example, Janowitz (1976) suggests that social security and other programs of the welfare state serve broadly integrative functions that reduce conflict and alienation throughout society.[17] On a more specific level, research by Armour and Coughlin (1982) into industrial conflict found that increases in the level of government spending for social welfare among a sample of industrialized societies were associated with decreases in labor unrest.

Compassion. Compassion (or sympathy) is usually excluded from economic models of behavior.[18] However, a substantial body of evidence, both empirical and impressionistic in nature, suggests that perceptions of need and concern about the plight of the disadvantaged are touchstones of public opinion on social security and other social welfare programs (Coughlin, 1980). Efforts to establish and, once established, expand the coverage of OAI and health care programs under social security have consistently highlighted the problem of poverty among the elderly. Even where extreme material deprivation is not specifically at issue, the elderly, as a group, seem to be regarded as intrinsically deserving of special consideration (for example, extra personal exemptions from income tax). Of all the explanations for social security's extraordinary popular appeal, the fact that the program is perceived as benefiting a deserving clientele seems to be the most persuasive (Coughlin, 1982; cf. Derthick, 1979b).

Commitment. Like compassion, commitment is a subjective condition that can have a profound influence on attitudes and behavior (Sen, 1977).[19] It is, after all, commitment that makes for heroes and religious martyrs, and that, in a more mundane fashion, provides the glue that holds human societies together.

It is commitment to values and belief systems that is of most interest to us here. Attitudes and opinions about social security do not exist in isolation from core values and beliefs around which mass ideologies are structured. Most Americans, like most mainstream economists, are deeply committed to the abstract principles of preserving individual initiative and minimum government, and unquestionably these values shape prevailing attitudes toward social security. Yet these and other traditional American values that emphasize hard work and individual responsibility must coexist with competing values that stress the right of individuals to a minimum standard of income, housing, nutrition, and health care. These values, which Marshall (1964) has termed the "social rights of citizenship," form a countervailing influence, a political context in which social welfare provisions above the minimum functional level required by modern economies can be justified. One major reason why social security has achieved such an impressive level of popular support is because it meshes with the public's commitment to the idea of "social rights" while at the same time it does not appear to contradict traditional values of work, savings, and differential reward.[20]

NOTES

1. Throughout this discussion the term *social security* refers to the old-age and survivors insurance program (OASI) under the Social Security Act of 1935 and subsequent amendments. This usage does not necessarily exclude disability insurance and Medicare, to the extent that these programs also fall under the Social Security Act and are funded by payroll taxes.

2. Initial disclosure of financing shortfalls involved only the OASI Trust Fund. More recently, financing problems in the Health Insurance (Medicare) Trust Fund have appeared and have also received widespread publicity.

3. Elsewhere Browning notes that only 15 percent of retirees cited disability as the reason for not working (see Ferrara, 1980, p. 284).

4. In the face of mounting problems with private pension schemes, in 1974 Congress passed the Employee Retirement Income Security Act (ERISA), which provides some protection against the arbitrary loss of benefits.

5. Browning (1973) presents a modification of this proposal that would allow social insurance bonds to be freely transferable. Individuals would still be forced to make an initial purchase of some minimum value but then would be free to sell their bonds or buy more, as they saw fit. Browning's rationale for this approach is to establish an efficient distribution that also generates information on individual preferences.

6. See Armour and Coughlin (1985) for a discussion of "broad" and "narrow" social control functions of social security.

7. This result occurs when the sum of the rates of growth of per capita wages and of population exceeds the rate of interest, and when the rate of interest equals the marginal rate of time preference and the marginal rate of transformation of present into future goods.

8. Cf. Stein (1980). Break adds the wry note that "one reaction to these developments will undoubtedly be increased skepticism about the use of econometric studies as a guide for government policy making" (p. 74).

9. It should be noted that the U.S. social security program is hardly an anomaly in this respect. Extensive government provisions for old-age and disability benefits are part of the welfare state in all industrialized societies. See Coughlin (1980) for a discussion of public-opinion survey research in eight industrial societies.

10. Cantril (1981) cites more recent survey data indicating that these sentiments have

not changed. Among federal government spending programs, help for the elderly was ranked second in importance out of 24 programs presented to respondents.

11. Derthick (1979b) also observes that "the financial deficit is not the only deficit in social security. There has also been a massive deficit in public understanding" (p. 105).

12. See Coughlin (1982) for a discussion of these data.

13. In the social sciences, the attempt to impose a predetermined, or *imputed*, model of rationality on attitudes and behavior invariably leaves a residual category consisting of outcomes the model cannot satisfactorily explain. Since all such models are reductive to one extent or another, there may be no general theoretical solution to the problem in economics or any other social science discipline. Political scientists and sociologists have pressed their own behavioral models into service and, no less than economists, have had to wrestle with glaring inconsistencies they encounter (see, e.g., Free and Cantril, 1968; Litwak, Hooyman, and Warren, 1973). In defense of such models it is usually argued that they serve a heuristic purpose and are acceptable if they can demonstrate sufficient predictive power. This has been precisely the defense of the rational-choice model in economics—that it predicts behavior without necessarily being an accurate description of how people actually behave (see Friedman, 1953). This rationale is fine as long as the model's predictions are reasonably good; when they are not, then the model needs to be abandoned or modified. Instead of imputing one set of rational motives to individuals, it is possible to proceed inductively, making few assumptions about the way in which people make sense of the world around them, outside of the assumption that they try to do so. This approach seeks to apprehend rationality as it actually occurs in the social world as seen through the eyes of the actors themselves; in this sense, I speak of *subjective* rationality. See Lewis (1982) for an informative discussion of the many facets of rationality in economic behavior.

14. Studies exploring in greater depth the psychological dynamics of intrafamilial financial expectations are needed to shed light on this hypothesis. Indirect evidence suggests that there are contradictions in these expectations. Divorce and geographical mobility have tended to weaken family ties, but in modern society the family remains, for better or worse, a "haven in a heartless world" (Lasch, 1977). Yet studies of household income reveal that when social security benefits go up, so does the number of old people living in poverty, the plausible explanation being that elderly parents use their little extra income to move out of their children's homes to set up their own households.

15. This argument is closely related to, and fully consistent with, studies by Barro (1974) and others discussed earlier that found intergenerational bequests to be a significant factor in savings behavior.

16. In an experimental setting, the Prisoner's Dilemma game similarly reflects the limits of individualistic rationality. See Sen (1977) for a discussion of this point.

17. In contrast, leftist critics of social security and other welfare policies view social security and other welfare programs primarily as a means of controlling mass insurrection among the poor (Piven and Cloward, 1971).

18. This exclusion seems to be based on the judgment that emotional states do not play a sufficiently important role in economic decisions to merit inclusion, since the existence of compassion and sympathy does not pose any inherent contradiction to utility maximization. For example, Sen (1977) notes that "pleased at others' pleasure and pained at others' pain ... one's own utility may thus be helped by sympathetic action" (p. 326).

19. Sen (1977) defines commitment as "a person choosing an act that he believes will yield a lower level of personal welfare to him than an alternative that is also available to him" (p. 327). As examples of commitment, Sen cites allegiance to class and community, and he argues that conceptually, such loyalties cannot be analyzed within the framework of utility maximization. On this last point I disagree: individuals who act according to their allegiances, either to social groups or to belief systems, may well be maximizing utilities that are intangible but no less important to their psychological satisfaction.

20. For further discussion of mass attitudes and beliefs, see Coughlin (1980, 1982); Litwak, Hooyman, and Warren (1973); and Huber and Form (1973). The general point here is that the study of social security should not be reduced solely to economic terms. For example, Smedley (1977) argues that social security "is not simply an economic institution," and that it "has developed out of the cultural, psychological, and sociological factors of our society" (p. 156). Harris and Marmor (1977) observe that the current emphasis economists place on the question of rates of return may be less helpful than it seems in understanding the equity of social security, because large intergroup variations in returns do not necessarily imply that the system is inequitable. Myles (1981) is critical of the use of market concepts to analyze the performance of social security, which is epitomized by some economists' preoccupation with the system's multitrillion-dollar "unfunded liabilities."

REFERENCES

Aaron, Henry, "The Social Insurance Paradox," *Canadian Journal of Economics and Political Science*, 32 (August 1966), 371–374.

Aaron, Henry, "Demographic Effects on the Equity of Social Security Benefits," in Martin Feldstein and Robert Inman, eds., *The Economics of Public Services*. London and Basingstoke: Macmillan Press, 1977, pp. 151–173.

Achenbaum, W. Andrew, *Old Age in the New Land*. Baltimore: Johns Hopkins University Press, 1978.

Armour, Philip K., and Richard M. Coughlin, "The Social Control Functions of Welfare Spending." Paper prepared for presentation at the Meetings of the Southwestern Social Sciences Association, San Antonio, Texas, March 1982.

Armour, Philip K., and Richard M. Coughlin, "Social Security and Social Control: Theory and Research in Communist and Capitalist Nations," *Social Science Quarterly*, 66 (December 1985), 770–788.

Barro, Robert J., "Are Government Bonds Net Wealth?" *Journal of Political Economy*, 82 (November–December 1974), 1095–1117.

Barro, Robert J., *The Impact of Social Security on Private Saving: Evidence from the U.S. Time Series*. Washington, DC: American Enterprise Institute, 1978.

Break, George F., "Social Security as a Tax," in Michael J. Boskin, ed., *The Crisis in Social Security*. San Francisco, CA: Institute for Contemporary Studies, 1977, pp. 107–124.

Break, George F., "The Economic Effects of the OASI Program," in Felicity Skidmore, ed., *Social Security Financing*. Cambridge, MA: MIT Press, 1981, pp. 45–80.

Brittain, John A., *The Payroll Tax for Social Security*. Washington, DC: Brookings, 1972.

Boskin, Michael J., "Social Security and Retirement Decisions," *Economic Inquiry*, 15 (January 1977), 1–24.

Boskin, Michael J., and Marc Robinson, "Social Security and Private Savings: Analytical Issues, Econometric Evidence, and Policy Implications." Prepared for Special Study of Economic Change, U.S. Congress Joint Economic Committee, Department of Economics, Stanford University, and National Bureau of Economic Research, March 1980.

Brittain, John A., *The Payroll Tax for Social Security*. Washington, D.C.: Brookings Institution, 1972.

Browning, Edgar K., "Social Insurance and Intergenerational Transfers," *Journal of Law and Economics*, (October 1973), 215–237.

Buchanan, James M., "Social Insurance in a Growing Economy: A Proposal for Radical Reform," *National Tax Journal*, 21 (1968), 386–395.

Cagan, Phillip, *The Effect of Pension Plans on Aggregate Savings*. Washington, DC: National Bureau of Economic Research, 1965.

Campbell, Colin D., and Rosemary G. Campbell, "Conflicting Views on the Effect of Old-Age and Survivors Insurance on Retirement," *Economic Inquiry*, 14 (September 1976), 369–386.

Campbell, Rita Ricardo, "The Problems of Fairness," in Michael J. Boskin, ed., *The Crisis in Social Security*. San Francisco, CA: Institute for Contemporary Studies, 1977, pp. 125–146.

Cantril, Albert, "Comments," in Felicity Skidmore, ed., *Social Security Financing*. Cambridge, MA: MIT Press, 1981, pp. 274–277.

Cates, Jerry R., *Insuring Inequality*. Ann Arbor: University of Michigan Press, 1983.

Coughlin, Richard M., *Ideology, Public Opinion & Welfare Policy*. Berkeley: Institute of International Studies, University of California, 1980.

Coughlin, Richard M., "Payroll Taxes for Social Security in the United States: The Future of Fiscal and Social Policy Illusions," *Journal of Economic Psychology*, 2 (1982), 165–185.

Darby, Michael R., *The Effects of Social Security on Income and the Capital Stock*. Washington, DC: American Enterprise Institute, 1979.

Derthick, Martha, *Policymaking for Social Security*. Washington, DC: Brookings Institution, 1979a.

Derthick, Martha, "How Easy Votes on Social Security Came to an End," *Public Interest*, 54 (Winter 1979b), 94–105.

Diamond, P.A., "A Framework for Social Security Analysis," *Journal of Public Economics*, 8 (1977), 275–298.

Feldstein, Martin S., "Social Security, Induced Retirement, and Aggregate Capital Accumulation," *Journal of Political Economy*, 82 (September–October 1974), 905–926.

Feldstein, Martin S., "Social Security and Saving: The Extended Life Cycle Theory," *American Economic Review, Papers and Proceedings*, 66 (May 1976a), 77–86.

Feldstein, Martin S., "Social Security and the Distribution of Wealth," *Journal of the American Statistical Association*, 71 (December 1976b), 800–807.

Feldstein, Martin S., "Social Security," in Michael J. Boskin, ed., *The Crisis in Social Security*. San Francisco, CA: Institute for Contemporary Studies, 1977, pp. 17–24.

Feldstein, Martin S., "Social Security and Private Savings: Another Look," *Social Security Bulletin*, 42 (May 1979a), 36–39.

Feldstein, Martin S., "The Effect of Social Security on Saving." Working Paper 355. Washington, DC: National Bureau of Economic Research, May 1979b.

Feldstein, Martin S., "Social Security, Induced Retirement, and Aggregate Capital Accumulation: A Correction and Updating." Working Paper 579. Washington, DC: National Bureau of Economic Research, November 1980.

Feldstein, Martin S., and Anthony J. Pellechio, "Social Security and Household Wealth Accumulation: New Microeconometric Evidence," *Review of Economics and Statistics*, 61 (August 1979), 361–368.

Ferrara, Peter J., *Social Security: The Inherent Contradiction*. San Francisco, CA: Cato Institute, 1980.

Free, Lloyd A., and Hadley Cantril, *The Political Beliefs of Americans*. New York: Simon & Schuster, 1968.

Friedman, Milton, *Essays in Positive Economics*. Chicago, IL: University of Chicago Press, 1953.

Friedman, Milton, *Capitalism and Freedom*. Chicago, IL: University of Chicago Press, 1962.

Friedman, Milton, "Payroll Taxes, No; General Revenues, Yes," in Michael J. Boskin, ed., *The Crisis in Social Security*. San Francisco, CA: Institute for Contemporary Studies, 1977, pp. 25–30.

Friedman, Milton, "The Poor Man's Welfare Payment to the Middle Class," *The Washington Monthly*, (May 1972), 16.

Goodwin, Leonard, and Joseph Tu, "The Social Psychological Basis for Public Acceptance of the Social Security System," *American Psychologist*, (September 1975), 875–883.

Harris, Robert, and Theodore Marmor, "Comment on Palmer," in G.S. Tolley and Richard V. Burkhauser, eds., *Income Support Policies for the Aged*. Cambridge, MA: Ballinger, 1977, pp. 177–179.

Hart, Peter D., Research Associates, *A Nationwide Survey of Attitudes toward Social Security*. Mimeograph, 1979.

Huber Joan, and William Form, *Income and Ideology*. New York: Free Press, 1973.

Janowitz, Morris, *Social Control of the Welfare State*. New York: Elsevier, 1976.

Katona, George, *Private Pensions and Individual Savings*. Ann Arbor: University of Michigan, Survey Research Center, 1965.

Koeppel, Barbara, "How America's Elderly Get Short-Changed," *Los Angeles Times* (April 18, 1976).

Kotlikoff, Laurence J., "Social Security and Equilibrium Capital Intensity," *Quarterly Journal of Economics*, 93 (May 1979a), 233–253.

Kotlikoff, Laurence J., "Testing the Theory of Social Security and Life Cycle Accumulation," *American Economic Review*, 69 (June 1979b), 396–410.

Lasch, Christopher, *Haven in a Heartless World: The Family Besieged*. New York: Basic Books, 1977.

Leimer, Dean R., and Selig D. Lesnoy, "Social Security and Private Savings: A Reexamination of the Time Series Evidence Using Alternative Social Security Wealth Variables." Paper prepared for presentation at the Annual Meeting of the American Economic Association, Washington, DC, August 1980.

Lewis, Alan, *The Psychology of Taxation*. New York: St. Martin's, 1982.

Litwak, Eugene, Nanct Hooyman, and Donald Warren, "Ideological Complexity and Middle-American Rationality," *Public Opinion Quarterly*, 37 (Fall 1973), 317–332.

Lubove, Roy, *The Struggle for Social Security, 1900–1935*. Cambridge, MA: Harvard University Press, 1968.

Manser, Marilyn E., "Historical and Political Issues in Social Security Financing," in Felicity Skidmore, ed., *Social Security Financing*. Cambridge, MA: MIT Press, 1981, pp. 21–44.

Marshall, T.H., *Class, Citizenship, and Social Development*. Garden City, NY: Doubleday, 1964.

Morgan, James N., "An Economic Theory of the Social Security System and Its Relation to Fiscal Policy," in G.S. Tolley and Richard V. Burkhauser, eds., *Income Support Policies for the Aged*. Cambridge, MA: Ballinger, 1977, pp. 107–126.

Morgan, James N., "Myth, Reality, Equity, and the Social Security System," *Challenge*, (March–April 1978), 59–61.

Munnell, Alicia H., *The Effect of Social Security on Individual Saving*. Cambridge, MA: Ballinger, 1974a.

Munnell, Alicia H., "The Impact of Social Security on Personal Savings," *National Tax Journal*, 27 (December 1974b), 553–567.

Munnell, Alicia H., *The Future of Social Security*, Washington, DC: Brookings Institution, 1977.

Musgrave, Richard A., "A Reappraisal of Social Security Financing," in Felicity Skidmore, ed., *Social Security Financing*. Cambridge, MA: MIT Press, 1981, pp. 89–128.

Myles, John, "The Trillion Dollar Misunderstanding," *Working Papers*, (July–August 1981), 23–31.

O'Connor, James, *The Fiscal Crisis of the State*. New York: St. Martin's Press, 1973.

Ozawa, Martha N., "Income Redistribution and Social Security," *Social Service Review*, 50 (June 1976), 209–235.

Palmore, E., "Retirement Patterns Among Aged Men: Findings of the 1963 Survey of the Aged," *Social Security Bulletin*, 27 (August 1964), 3–10.

Parsons, Donald O., and Douglas R. Munro, "Intergenerational Transfers in Social Security," in Michael J. Boskin, ed., *The Crisis in Social Security*. San Francisco, CA: Institute for Contemporary Studies, 1977, pp. 41–64.

Pechman, Joseph A., Henry J. Aaron, and Michael K. Taussig, *Social Security: Perspectives for Reform*. Washington, DC: Brookings Institution, 1968.

Pellechio, Anthony J., "The Effect of Social Security on Retirement." Working Paper 260. Washington, DC: National Bureau of Economic Research, July 1978a.

Pellechio, Anthony J., "The Social Security Earnings Test, Labor Supply Distortions, and Foregone Payroll Tax Revenue." Working Paper 272. Washington, DC: National Bureau of Economic Research, August 1978b.

Pellechio, Anthony J., "Social Security Financing and Retirement Behavior," *American Economic Review: Papers and Proceedings*, 69 (May 1979), 284–287.

Piven, Frances Fox, and Richard Cloward, *Regulating the Poor*. New York: Random House, 1971.

Plotnick, Robert D., and Felicity Skidmore, *Progress Against Poverty: A Review of the 1964–74 Decade*. New York: Academic Press, 1975.

Pogue, Thomas F., and L.G. Sgontz, "Social Security and Investment in Human Capital," *National Tax Journal*, 30 (June 1977), 157–169.

Reno, V., "Why Men Stop Working at or Before Age 65: Findings from the Survey of New Beneficiaries," *Social Security Bulletin*, 34 (June 1971), 3–17.

Rosen, Sherwin, "Social Security and the Economy," in Michael J. Boskin, ed., *The Crisis in Social Security*. San Francisco, CA: Institute for Contemporary Studies, 1977, pp. 87–106.

Samuelson, Paul A., "An Exact Consumption-Loan Model of Interest with or without the Social Contrivance of Money," *Journal of Political Economy*, 66 (December 1958), 467–482.

Schiltz, Michael E., "Public Attitudes toward Social Security 1935–1965." Research Report No. 33. Washington, DC: U.S. Department of Health, Education, and Welfare, Social Security Administration, Office of Research and Statistics, 1970.

Schulz, James H., *The Economics of Aging*. Belmont, CA: Wadsworth, 1980.

Shore, Warren, *Social Security: The Fraud in Your Future*. New York: Macmillan, 1975.

Sen, Amartya K., "Rational Fools: A Critique of the Behavioral Foundations of Economic Theory," *Philosophy and Public Affairs*, 6 (Fall 1976–Summer 1977), 317–344.

Smedley, Lawrence T., "Comment on Laffer and Ranson," in G.S. Tolley and Richard V. Burkhauser, eds., *Income Support Policies for the Aged*. Cambridge, MA: Ballinger, 1977, pp. 151–156.

Stein, Bruno, *Social Security and Pensions in Transition*. New York: The Free Press, 1980.

Thompson, Gayle B., "Pension Coverage and Benefits, 1972: Findings from the Retirement History Study," *Social Security Bulletin*, 41 (February 1978), 3–17.

Tomasson, Richard F., "Old-age Pensions under Social Security: Past and Future," *American Behavioral Scientist*, 26 (July-August 1983), 699–723.

Viscusi, W. Kip, and Richard J. Zeckhauser, "The Role of Social Security in Income Maintenance," in Michael J. Boskin, ed., *The Crisis in Social Security*. San Francisco, CA: Institute for Contemporary Studies, 1977, pp. 41–64.

U.S. Department of Health and Human Services, Social Security Administration, Office of Research and Statistics, *Social Security Bulletin, Annual Statistical Supplement*. Washington, DC: U.S. Government Printing Office, 1983.

Weaver, Carolyn L., *The Crisis in Social Security*. Durham, NC: Duke Press Policy Studies, 1982.

PART III

GROWTH AND DEVELOPMENT

INTRODUCTION TO PART III:

GROWTH AND DEVELOPMENT

Mainstream economists operate within a relatively circumscribed paradigm. The behavioral goal is to optimize profit. The means at hand are, by and large, some subset of the generalized factors of production: land, labor, capital, and entrepreneurship. A rational and well-informed single individual acting as a firm combines these means so as always to achieve that end. In contrast to this picture of the world, this part presents three papers that take a broader view of the same subject.

Spechler addresses the problems of sluggish economic growth and falling productivity that began for the Western nations in 1966 and has persisted to the present time. As he illustrates clearly, a large and varied literature has attempted to find common causes for the slowdown. Economic factors such as higher energy costs and resulting obsolescence, lower savings and investment rates, regulation, unions, and the reallocation of labor give partial explanations but leave significant portions of the declines unexplained. Failing to find satisfaction in his own backyard, Spechler explores less conventional explanations, among them Marxist, German historical, institutionalist and the behavioral theories of Simon and the Carnegie school, Katona and the survey approach, McClelland, and a large number of industrial relations and labor management relations experts. Two of his sentences about worker satisfaction sum up his conclusions on the entire topic: "Which side of the coin can be explained by worker satisfaction? It is clearly a complex matter."

161

Strumpel is a long-time colleague of Katona. The method he employs is a survey of attitudes and values in West Germany and Israel. The hypothesis is that different levels of material well-being in the two countries have created different value structures toward work, possessions, social justice, personal worth, and so on, and that these different values will color not only performance but perception of the country's economic and social climate as well. His findings have enormous significance for the political and economic well-being of the countries involved and of the world, if they can be generalized and are not specific to the times and societies involved in the study.

Green's paper dwells on the unique orientation anthropologists bring to the consideration of economic matters. Conventional economic analysis proceeds along what in anthropological terms are called formalist lines. The economy is characterized by rational, maximizing choice behavior, economics is a quantitative science, and economic activities are quite apart from other intrinsic qualities of the culture in question. Green is more sympathetic to perceiving anthropological economics in "substantive" terms, where economics is understood in the context of the religion, power structure, and kin relationships of the culture. Here, it is recognized that instead of a market form of exchange, conventions of reciprocity and redistribution may control. Instead of maximization, the goal of the economy may be survival.

Awareness of the possibility of cultural diversity is one thing. Appreciation of its many faces is another. There is a tendency in economics to treat the departure from full rationality as an aberration that must be explained—one that needs alternate hypotheses. Green's article reminds us that, indeed, full rationality and utility maximizing may be the behavioral aberration.

SOCIAL INFLUENCES ON GROWTH AND PRODUCTIVITY IN THE WEST, 1965–1984

Martin C. Spechler

I. INTRODUCTION: THE PROBLEM STATED

The long postwar boom is over—an unparalleled expansion that lasted from before the Korean War until the mid–1960s in most of the advanced countries of the West. From 1966 on, the universal expansion slackened noticeably, and the deceleration became quite uncomfortable in the period 1973 to 1974. From 1960 to 1973, real growth in the gross national product (GNP) was 5.1 percent annually for the Organization for Economic Cooperation and Development (OECD) countries—4 percent for the United States alone. Then from 1974 to 1981, the rates for both the OECD countries and the United States fell to 2.7 percent. Among sectors of the economy, manufacturing fell most in its rate of growth, especially in Western Europe.

Productivity slackened even more than output. The private American economy had less than half the productivity improvement in the years after 1966 than the 3.2 percent it had enjoyed from 1947 to 1966. According to the Bureau of Labor Statistics, hourly productivity in the nonfarm business sector of the United States actually fell between 1973 and 1975 and again from 1977 to 1980. Continental Western Europe felt the deceleration, too, though at somewhat higher growth rates (see Table 1).

Table 1. Annual Rates of Real Growth and Productivity Advance: United States and Western Europe, 1948–1981

| | Real Growth Rates of GDP (annual average) | | Growth of Labor Productivity | | | Growth of Labor Productivity in Manufacturing Value-Added | |
| | | | GDP Per Employee | | Output Per Hour* | | |
	OECD-Europe	United States	OECD-Europe	United States	United States	OECD-Europe	United States
1960–66	4.8%	4.9%	4.3%	3.1%	3.2% (1948–65)	5.0%	3.1%
1966–73	4.7	3.3	4.2	1.2	2.4 (1965–73)	5.5	2.9
1973–79	2.5	2.6	2.2	0.2	0.9 (1973–83)	2.8	0.9

*All workers, business sector only.

Sources: Economic Report of the President (1984, p. 266); OECD, Historical Statistics (various years).

In a longer perspective, American labor productivity growth was only 1.6 percent annually in the private domestic economy from 1889 to 1919 and only marginally higher up to World War II (Kendrick, 1961, p. 60). So the rates of the 1970s do, in a sense, mark a return to long-term normalcy. Perhaps the unprecedented advance in the years 1948 to 1966 in the United States and Western Europe is the exception meriting explanation.

This slowdown in growth and productivity certainly derived in some part from contractionary policies adopted by all Western governments in response to worsening inflation since the latter 1960s. Actual GNP fell short of productive potential. Recession no doubt accounted for the low productivity performance in the United States during the periods 1969–1970, 1974–1975, and 1977–1979. Balance-of-payments deficits and double-digit inflation incited by the first worldwide oil price rise in 1973–1974 forced restrictions on most OECD governments throughout the 1970s. Unlike the previous boom, world trade now fell more than domestic uses. Terms of trade and investment prospects worsened. As a result, capacity utilization in the late 1970s was lower than a decade earlier, particularly in steel, basic chemicals, shipbuilding, autos, and other manufacturing sectors. Unemployment rates roughly doubled.

In retrospect, though, we can see that insufficient aggregate demand cannot wholly explain the continually bad performance of Western economies. Adjusting for shortfalls of actual product caused by open unemployment indicates that the West's potential output (in aggregate, per-worker, or per-capita terms) would not have advanced as rapidly in the 1970s as it did from 1948 to 1966, even if expansionary monetary policy had been able to reduce unemployment to 3 or 4 percent (the OECD average for the years 1945 to 1970). Edward Denison (1979, 1980), for example, found that "irregular factors," mainly demand fluctuations, actually *improved* growth rates from 1973 to 1976 more than they had from 1948 to 1973! Besides, we need to know why democratic capitalist governments could no longer stimulate the private economy sufficiently to attain its full potential. Keynesian optimists, after all, had held that full employment would be consistent with price stability (Heller, 1964; Postan, 1967). Yet by 1968 experts began to doubt that full employment could be attained even with a certain degree of inflation.

Inflation has effects other than that of obstructing the approach to full capacity utilization. Especially when big and semirepressed, inflations are hard for private decision makers to anticipate. Relative price signals are obscured (Clark, 1982). Consequent mistakes in resource allocation may adversely affect aggregate supply, though this effect is uncertain and probably small, aside from hyperinflationary situations.[1] Inflation can also divert savings into durable consumer goods, speculative hoards of precious metals, and building. All of these will have a lower impact on future potential than would investment in equipment or social infrastructure. Inflation also reduces the "quality" of profits, because depreciation allowances are insufficient to replace the capital stock (Weintraub, 1981). Real tax rates rise, leaving less cash for financing investment. Since inflation has been accelerating in the West since the mid–1960s, it might have contributed to lower growth and productivity advance from that time.

Developments as of this writing do not reassure us that the period from 1973 to 1982 was only an interlude in export and investment-led growth reinforced by stabilizing macroeconomic policies. True, the average consumer inflation rates for the OECD countries are back to the 5 percent of the years 1970 to 1973, but the recovery in the United States and Western Europe seems unsustainable even if real oil prices continue to sag. Basic problems are unsolved. Budget deficits are rising nearly everywhere, causing excessive borrowing or inflation. Wage rigidity and regulation in continental Europe persist. Unruly international competition in manufactures encourages protectionism. Productivity growth in 1983–1985 has been considerably below previous cyclical recoveries.

II.   INADEQUACY OF NEOCLASSICAL EXPLANATIONS

Mainstream economists have not lacked for a neoclassical solution to why output and productivity have slowed in the West since 1973.[2] By standard accounts, rising oil prices in that year must have rendered much existing capital inefficient. Capital services of wasteful machines would be worth less, perhaps nothing at all. If capital inputs are measured by the cost of the stock available, the usual procedure, an underestimate of productivity would result. To put the matter a different way, unusually large (unmeasured) obsolescence of equipment resulted when a complementary input (energy) rose so in price during 1974 and 1979. Unmeasured obsolescence ought, of course, also to reduce *net* output, but usually a productivity slowdown of *gross* output is meant (Nadiri, 1970).

Most mainstream quantitative studies concede, however, that the OPEC energy-price increase cannot explain much of the productivity decline. Energy is not a large enough component of costs. According to Nordhaus (1980), the OPEC rise taken alone explains no more than 6 percent of the productivity and growth decline in the OECD countries overall and certainly less than that in the more self-reliant United States (see also Berndt, 1980; Norsworthy, Harper, and Kunze, 1979; Maddison, 1980).

A dissenting minority have found a larger effect of energy prices on labor productivity when labor is taken as highly substitutable in short-run equilibrium against energy and capital taken as complements (Hudson and Jorgenson, 1978). Bruno has found a considerable role for (imported) raw materials prices in the factor productivity decline (Bruno, 1982, 1984; Bruno and Sachs, 1985). It is also possible that the decline in productivity in mining and extraction has resulted from ore depletion and the incentive since 1973 to exploit existing sites more exhaustively and expensively.

While one cannot be certain, the present author is inclined to agree with a recent European report: "It is difficult to see how the rise in energy prices might have played a major role in the recent slowdown in productivity growth" (United Nations Economic Commission for Europe, 1983). Whatever effect raw materials prices may have had, they were hardly independent of the rapid growth in the West from 1948 to 1970. Without rising demand, OPEC and other raw materials' producers could not have raised prices so much.

Most neoclassical explanations ignore the growth and productivity slowdown that preceded the jump in energy and materials' prices and reduced investment. In the United States, the United Kingdom, West Germany, and France, growth during the 1966–1973 business cycle was lower than in the two previous cycles. Labor productivity—and even more clearly, total factor productivity—decelerated from the period 1965–1966 throughout the OECD area (Kendrick, 1980). It appears, moreover, that the productivity slowdown has continued since 1980, even while the real price of energy has fallen and investment recovered. We need to know why efficiency, technical progress, business profitability, and the other proximate influences on total factor productivity have weakened since the period from 1965 to 1966 and reduced the attractiveness of new investments, including those that workers themselves make to enhance their employability. Even technological advance can no longer be treated as exogenous (Stone, 1980).

A last difficulty with the energy-input price explanation is that the change in terms of trade of the OECD countries for the period 1971–1973 and again in 1979 should have reduced only the level of national income, not its subsequent growth rate, had social institutions recognized and adjusted promptly to the new external environment. Indeed, the very devaluation of existing capital ought to have raised the marginal efficiency of new investment. But policy response was tardy and ineffective, even among conservative countries like Japan, Switzerland, West Germany, and the United States. No country was willing to cut real wages directly—for instance, those of public employees—or to cut pensions and unemployment benefits, as they had in the early 1930s. Despite some union concessions and stagnant real wages, structural unemployment of labor persists. (The standardized average rate in 1983 is still 8 percent as compared with 3 percent in 1970 throughout the OECD). Massive underutilization of capital is supported by subsidies in nearly every country (Sachs, 1982).

Another neoclassical explanation points to declining saving and higher interest rates during the 1970s. Whether induced by the tax structure during inflation, the age structure, or otherwise, reduced saving would bring on a decline in the rate at which labor is outfitted with more and better equipment. Gross fixed capital formation in Western Europe grew at only 0.3 percent from 1973 to 1981, as compared with 5.6 percent annually from 1960 to 1973. The United States private economy had a like fall: from 5.4 percent to 0.4 percent in the two periods.

Lesser growth of business capital per worker apparently explains only a small share of the 1974–1979 slowdown, however, except for West German manufacturing, where real capital stock growth fell to 2.6 percent over 1973–1978 (United Nations Economic Commission for Europe, p. 51; Nordhaus, 1980; Brainard and Perry, 1981; cf. Norsworthy, Harper, and Kunze, 1979). Edward Denison (1980) estimates that the energy-price increase and the small decline in the growth of capital per worker do little *together* to explain why the residual went from +1.4 percent yearly during the period from 1948 to 1973 to −0.7 percent during the period 1973 to 1976 (cf. Kendrick, 1980). Still less of the prior slowdown from 1966 to 1973 can reasonably be assigned to this cause, since the rate of increase in capital available to workers in nonfarm businesses, particularly manufacturing, actually rose from the 1948 to 1966 average in many countries, including the United States.

But emphasis on available capital per employed worker, as in growth accounting or aggregate production function studies, may not tell the whole story. Both fixed capital *and* employment grew much more slowly in the West after 1973, particularly in manufacturing, the key sector for engendering technological change elsewhere in the economy. Because the employed labor force also failed to grow as before, labor productivity would not suffer from lack of capital directly, but embodied technology would not come into use as fast (Kendrick, 1976). The most persuasive evidence for the effect of low investment on productivity comes from an international cross-section: countries with a high net fixed capital formation also have had higher growth (see Figure 1).

In 1983, the President's Council of Economic Advisors stressed that an increase in national saving and investment would be one key policy lever to raise productivity (*Economic Report of the President*, 1983, pp. 83–84). The prescription may not follow though, if greater saving increases

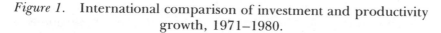

Figure 1. International comparison of investment and productivity growth, 1971–1980.

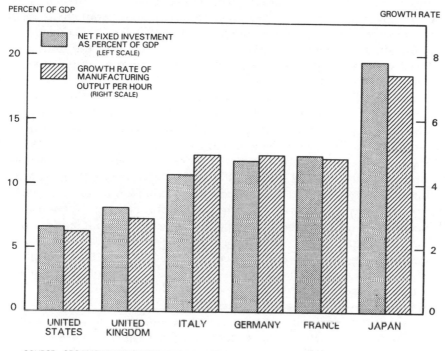

SOURCE: ORGANIZATION FOR ECONOMIC COOPERATION AND DEVELOPMENT.

the slack in the economy without increasing profitable investment opportunities.

But can we raise private saving and investment? Reduced taxes on corporate profits accruing to stockholders can have little effect on them. For some measures, corporate profits and personal income taxes are higher in faster-growing Europe than in the United States. Furthermore, since 1966 American marginal tax rates on corporate profits and capital gains have been lowered. Although inflation tends to raise the real incidence on equity finance, during the 1970s unexpected price increases made real rates on borrowed capital low or even negative.

Two other explanations often advanced for slower productivity involve the allocation of new workers. Investment in schooling had been an important element of growth earlier in the century; by the 1960s the phenomenon of diminishing returns may have set in sufficiently to offset continued gains in schooling per worker throughout the period (Freeman, 1976). Gains from the reallocation of underemployed farm and self-employed labor also may now have approached the point of exhaustion of their potential, at least as far as indigenous populations are concerned. By one account, reduced gains from this source may be responsible for two fifths of the deceleration in labor productivity from 1973 to 1978, as compared with the period from 1966 to 1973 (Kendrick, 1980). But the extended recession surely explains why the underemployed were not pulled into better jobs at the rate typical of the years between 1948 and 1973.

Demand shifts, likewise an exogenous development for mainstream economics, may have been away from sectors with high potential for technological progress to others where the productivity level and measured potential for productivity enhancement is less (Nordhaus, 1972). Jobs in service sectors absorb many women and young people, whose marginal productivity (as measured by their wage) is lower than average. Chinloy (1981) has found this the most important identifiable depressant of productivity growth rates during the 1970s. The entry of so-called secondary earners into the job market increases growth but tends to pull down output per worker or per worker hour, since the value of leisure, fulfillment, or experience is omitted from the GNP figures. But even Chinloy could not find that lower gains in "quality" per person employed contributed more than about 0.6 points to the annual slowdown after 1972, compared with the period from 1948 to 1972.

In the last twenty years, as more private goods have become available for consumption, citizens have demanded a cleaner environment in which to enjoy them. Compliance with environmental and safety standards has been costly, while the resulting benefits to society are left outside conventional GNP measures. Such investments in health and future amenity have risen, offsetting a part of the private economy's diminished investment share during the 1970s (*Economic Report of the President*, 1983). The adverse private impact of regulation on productivity and profits was certainly trivial until the mid–1970s[3] and thereafter cannot have been significant by all available studies (Bowles, Gordon, and Weisskopf, 1984, p. 422; Denison, 1980). Some industries, such as coal mining and electricity generation, may have had to bear disproportionate costs of safety though. More generally, there is no perceptible relation between the size of the public sector and relative growth rates.

Finally, while the growth and productivity slowdown is universal, faster-growing countries have suffered relatively more than the slower growing. Nevertheless, cross-national differences in manufacturing and overall productivity advance persist (see Figure 1). Japan and West Germany continue to grow faster than the United Kingdom and the United States, though the technology gap has already been closed. This puzzle too demands an answer beyond the usual analysis of diffusion, higher savings, and lower tax rates.

To summarize the weaknesses of mainstream explanations of the growth and productivity slowdown, we have seen they typically:

1. are insufficient quantitatively to explain the slowdown of 1973–1981.
2. ignore, for the most part, the beginnings of the slowdown from about 1966, particularly in the United States.
3. fail to explain the sources of lower investment and less technical progress.
4. do not pay attention to the mostly unsuccessful attempts by policy makers to adjust to a different environment.
5. do not account for the different degrees of slowdown seen among the Western countries.

The remainder of this survey article will therefore proceed to examine the alternative nonstandard paradigms that might be helpful in explaining growth and productivity issues. The next section mentions particular lines of empirical research that do contribute to our understanding of growth and productivity in the West. A concluding section attempts a tentative synthesis of findings so far.

III.   ALTERNATIVE PARADIGMS

At the most general level, what can nonstandard, particularly "social" or "behavioral," paradigms offer us? As generally recognized, the neoclassical paradigm pursues the intended or unintended consequences of changes in technology, information, tastes, or governmental policy instruments when rational individuals interact in the market. All else is measurement or commentary. Another discipline would be welcome if it could tell us why and when these constraints or data change. Then economics could be laid end to end with history, sociology, or political science—like rugs in mosque—to form a unified science without violating the canons of compartmentalization. Another kind of complementarity that auxiliary disciplines might exhibit would be to turn down explanations that economic theory must consider plausible (Leontief, 1966). Lately, more and more general theories, including uncertainty, temporary disequilibria, and expectation factors, have deprived abstract economics of the few unambiguous results it appeared to possess. Third, fraternal disciplines might provide nonarithmomorphic analysis for processes that, like the evolution of systems, cannot be seen as more or less. As Georgescu-Roegen (1966) taught, capitalism and like concepts overlap their dialectical opposites and may better suit the evolution of quality, just as a money measure suits the administrative problems of the practical economist. Proper description of an economic system, in the large or in the small, requires the notion of a pattern or structure whose elements are neither causally nor logically entailed by one another. When, for example, economists are called on to reform national income statistics to measure welfare better, this legitimate task cannot be addressed by positivist methods. Descriptive evaluation requires a conception of material welfare adequate to each epoch (Unger, 1975). The critical step of conceptualizing a period or process—for example, Rostow's (1960) "take-off"—must be judged as economic rhetoric (McCloskey, 1985).

If disciplinary interpenetration is to be more than a pious hope of bewildered enthusiasts, one cannot expect the concepts or procedures of today's academic houses to fit together like stones in a Herodian facade. Divergence of style has proceeded too long for that. Nevertheless, during this century there have flourished within economics four paradigms that did not exclude the social dimension or reduce all behavior to commercial or hedonistic rationality. Marxism, the German historical school, institutionalism, and behavioral economics all had consistent conceptual schemes in addition to being carriers of particular messages and teaching. Few readers will lack instruction in what Marx (or Veblen or Weber) taught as conclusions. Most now regard these figures and their followers as preachers of outmoded faiths at best, because so much of their message was wrong or primitively put. Yet, as methods that have survived their provenance, Marxism, Weberianism, institutionalism, and behavioral economics provide the only available escapes from the choice of (conscious) reductionism for the majority of economists or from eclecticism for the disgruntled few.

As a working paradigm, Marxism presents a stage theory of economic history in which progress—greater control over nature—accrues to ever broader classes—feudal lords, capitalists, eventually the proletariat. Ultimately human freedom from every kind of unnatural constraint will be possible. While many economic groups contend in every era, each stage is identified with growing polarization between the characteristic classes of the oppressors and the oppressed of that epoch. In the bourgeois age, for example, capitalists and proletarians are in conflict without reference to apprenticeship laws, Christian charity, or national boundaries.

Each stage works by laws not comparable with those of the next epoch. Because feudalism embraced forceful, legal, religious, and exchange means of extracting surplus product, it evinced a prolonged stability. Marxists deny such dynamic stability to capitalism because they are unimpressed by price mechanisms for clearing markets. Competing capitalists must, for security and enrichment, build capacity and reserves that will often be excessive from the point of view of profitability, leading to a crisis and greater centralization of ownership for the next round. Marxists deny an independent positive public role to the state, aside from transitional periods of a divided ruling class, such as that which existed in France between 1848 and 1849. So long as political power is subservient to special interests, palliatives like a progressive income tax and comprehensive education only delay or displace the class struggle; they never resolve it. The inability of modern states to deal with inflation without inflicting unemployment and displacement on the weak only proves this proposition. After the socialist revolution breaks out to counter the more and more apparent waste of productive forces, the working proletarians will, as a condition of their own freedom, operate the system by means of paid managers for the good of the entire community. With further education, this will bring on a noncoercive economic organization: full communism.

The Marxian stage analysis is broadly familiar, as are its revolutionary prescriptions, but can one identify a Marxian way of working that is independent of conclusions and universally understandable?

As a paradigm, Marxism fixes attention on people in social groups formed for production and realized in active struggle. Hedonistic individuals or abstract, statistically defined strata do not bring historic change. Rather, Marx and his followers rely upon class institutions such as unions, friendly societies, political parties, interlocking directorates, trusts, and similar organizations as antagonists in the saga of each age. The state, as "executive committee of the ruling class," may coordinate the suppression of unions or the mobilization of paupers for the factories. Less pervasive Marxist writings may resort to ill-defined accounts of how the capitalist "class" enforced factory acts to prevent individual employers from overexploiting the laboring class, or how "class" interests prevent humane spending to counter deflationary pressure (Marx, 1967, Chap. 10; Baran and Sweezy, 1966, Chap. 6).

The Marxian system is a paradigm no more capable of direct refutation or confirmation than is the neoclassical approach. This comes from its open texture; it invokes a condition of *ceteris paribus*. Like other paradigms, Marxism generates auxiliary hypotheses and insights that may be validated or refuted. The paradigm itself, however, is judged by its fruitfulness. Let us take an example: What permitted the formation of a modern labor force? Marx's most perceptive modern students stress the weakness of wage incentives, springing from increased productivity, for converting the preindustrial freeman and cottager into the wage laborer (Thompson, 1963; Marglin, 1974). The key problems were the control of surplus, which comprised the supervision of the length and quality of work and the transfer of the undiminished product to the capitalist. A recalcitrant work force could be recruited and tamed only by the legitimate use of force, often at the expense of debt peons, orphans, women, minors, and aliens. The establishment of the first factories apparently cannot be accounted for by mechanization; factory discipline seems to have been the crucial advantage over cottage industries. Control gives higher productivity or relative surplus value, but the objective is growth of profits.

Growth prospects in the contemporary world, according to Marxists, are dimmed by the class interests of monopoly capital. Marxists blame delayed innovation or smothered competition on those trusts, conglomerates, or financial institutions that stand to benefit materially by such control (Mandel, 1968, p. 504). The rich benefit greatly—but not, of course, exclusively—from tax programs, corporate "bailouts," acreage reduction, conservation, and even many welfare expenditures (Harrington, 1976, Chap. 12). These phenomena may restrict growth while serving profits. Imperialism may serve both, at least for a while.

Like the Marxists, the German historical school has concentrated on economic development and change, rather than on administrative problems. Gustav von Schmoller and his followers, especially Max Weber, tried to carry out two conflicting missions for economic history. On the one hand, one should give an idiographic account of the uniqueness of each epoch, as history never repeats itself in all its singularity. On the other hand, Weber particularly also wanted to give a causal rendering of why things turned out as they did and not otherwise. He approached causation through typical sequences and selected complexes observable in history. Consider hypothetically, Weber ruminated, what would have happened had the Greeks not emerged the victors at Marathon (Weber, 1949).

German historical writers from Weber to Eucken and Schumpeter have searched for an extra-economic force to move from stage to stage. Following Hegel, Weber's search was for the emerging logic in disorderly history—the rationalization of human behavior. Instrumentalism, which neoclassical economists see as the only ethos for behavior, Weber saw as only the most modern ethos that people may attach to their behavior. In his wide-ranging historical work, Weber began and ended with this question: What does rational capitalism require? Ironically, the answer was that to exploit to the full the material potential of the world, a nonrational source of inspiration and energy was essential. Otherwise, people aspire to honorific callings and consider themselves bound by stereotyped norms of conduct and achievement. Growth of productivity will hardly be possible in this old order. The required mental break could be triggered by ascetic sectarianism and the dread of damnation, as in Weber's Calvinist diaspora, or by persecuted minority status, as shown by immigrant Chinese, dissenters, Jews, or immigrant Japanese who settled in California (Landes, 1969; Hagen, 1970).

Working in the Weberian mode, Clifford Geertz (1963, 1968) has shown how national-religious idealism can lead to economic progress in a traditional environment. Shantri Muslims must save for the *hadj*, the expensive pilgrimage to Mecca, and thus organize their and others' work with a view to accumulation. To succeed, the rational capitalist must insulate his enterprise from the nepotism and particularistic demands characteristic of poor societies. Separate bookkeeping facilitates the maximization of returns on invested capital and symbolizes the division of enterprise from family. A dependable and impartial legal order, furthermore, encourages devotion to productive tasks, rather than to the ephemeral exploitation of market opportunities. For these reasons, incidentally, Weber suspected socialism would lead to political favoritism and artificial job tenure, both of which would detract from instrumental efficiency, whatever their ethical import. Where results are not measured, there patrimonialism will revive.

In the West, of course, Protestantism broke the traditional barriers to growth, at least according to Max Weber. The fact that historians have found no connection between Calvinism and capitalist enterprise in the Low Countries, France, Geneva, Scotland, and Hungary would not, it seems, have dissuaded Weber utterly from maintaining his view, since German historical thinking disbelieves in universal causes (Fischoff, 1968; Samuelsson, 1961). Rather, Weber interprets the causal significance of ecological correlations observed at a crucial time and place. More troubling, though, is Weber's use of eighteenth-century sermons to reveal the latent import of much earlier belief of sixteenth- or seventeenth-century capitalism.

In common with the German historical school, American institutionalists from Thorsten Veblen to J.K. Galbraith[4] generally did not hold out hope for significant causal generalizations about the historical process in all times and places. History depends too much on subjective elements for that. In Veblen's view, economics should account for evolutionary progress, "the result of heredity and experience in achieving ends." As anthropology illustrates, these ends have been numerous, but material gain or pure hedonism has perhaps not been as typical as the search for security and status (Polanyi, 1957). Predictably fair dealing makes market rationality possible.

Veblen interprets economic history as an ongoing conflict between the instincts leading to progress (the taste for workmanship, idle curiosity, parenthood) and the customs that sanction or forbid ways of dividing the yield from technique. Capitalism cannot be comprehended aside from customary privilege, since capital is primarily a claim of ownership, not invariably attached to physical goods. The particular forms evolved to express the forces of creativity and conservatism are not predetermined by the environment any more than new species are.

By focusing on the rules or institutions in any economy, Veblen gains a basis for criticism. Veblen's concept of use or function served him in exposing philistine or pecuniary values. Wealth is desired for display and invidious comparisons—hence its obviously unproductive employment in the hunt or in excessively fastidious housekeeping. As modern society becomes more anonymous and dispersed and its class lines blurred, "conspicuous consumption" displaces inadequately conspicuous leisure. The expensive handmade article is still valued over the functionally superior machine-made item that sells at a fraction of the price.

An important insight of the country boy Veblen was that urban people, pressed by status demands, have less "comfort" at home than do rural families of equal income. Rural folk also save more, as Brady and Friedman (1947) confirmed. More recently, it has been found that group influence is greatest for consumer goods like beer and cigarettes, which are consumed in social situations. Certain advertising messages derive power from the seeming desire of each of us to be instantly and favorably presentable to strangers.

Veblen's ideas have had many applications. A.S. Deaton (1976) has proposed explaining the disparity between budget cross-section income elasticities for clothing in Western Europe and the long-term behavior of expenditure shares by status considerations in the purchase of apparel. Long-term time series are "broadly consistent" with unitary elasticity, while short-term budget surveys show income elasticity of between one and two. Why? Deaton writes, "Richer consumers spend more on clothing not simply because they are rich but because it is expected of them, given their social position and place in the income distribution. Over time, each income group continues to spend the same proportion on clothing irrespective of changes in their absolute income. . . ." (p. 114). Similar considerations were invoked by Duesenberry (1949) to explain why a contemporary family with a certain income feels it is necessary to spend much more than a family of equivalent real income living in a previous time. With nearly everyone an urban employee in today's America, status seeking and the lack of community sumptuary standards can explain our low savings rates as compared with those of the more traditional Japanese, German, or Norwegian peoples. In Veblen's inimitable lexicon, pecuniary canons of taste erode accumulation and creativity, the sources of growth.

Pessimistic about societies, Veblen believed that businessmen would bring stagnation upon even the dynamic American economy of his time. As have nearly all institutionalists to date, Veblen stressed the drive for monopoly as an everyday business practice—it saves managerial time and effort if prices are held stable (Veblen, 1904, Chap. VI). Characteristic of oligopoly is "normal" profit, including a return on all past investments and acquired assets. Toward this convenient end customers and investors must be manipulated. Goods must be serviceable, yes, but chiefly they must be vendible. Much market research is directed toward what people may be persuaded to buy. Once a certain insulation from the market is achieved, not least by *not* charging the most one can or by raising prices only when labor contracts give the excuse, power is maintained by reputation.

Typically, modern society has conflicts among parties with ample discretion and power to fight or to settle; in such situations institutionalists like Commons or Galbraith have tried to identify the rules by which the sides habitually find a satisfactory solution without danger or endless bargaining. Knowledge of what has been considered fair and safe thus provides an incisive insight into economic policy results that mechanics cannot provide. For instance, oligopolistic competition is often carried on by incurring conventional costs for the sake of appearances. The equilibrium achieved is a "fair" one in the eyes of the oligopolists and tolerable to outsiders; greater precision requires investigation of each industry separately.

Veblen believed that his doctrine of conventional costs explained more than gilded banks and chauffeured poodles. For him, the accretion of nonfunctional costs can explain the decline of nations. "Related costs" and funded capital from an early technical stage, impose a penalty on a nation that takes the lead. As an enterprise will resist a new technique so long as expected average total costs using the new technology *and* amortizing past investments is not less than average variable costs with the older technology (see Ames and Rosenberg, 1963), business resists innovation, which would require writing down pecuniary assets and thus harm financial reputation. Examples of "related costs" offered by Veblen and others after him include England's small blast furnaces and small railway cars (suitable for railway overhead). Ascendant Germany, contrariwise, was laden with lighter conventional costs (Veblen, 1915).

J.K. Galbraith's writings have addressed how market power is used by large oligopolistic firms. For them, individual maximization is, in principle, ambiguous because of interactions; nor does competitive stress immediately compel obedience to the untutored demands of customers. Moreover, since directors are important to monitor corporate affairs and recourse to bank finance involving detailed scrutiny is infrequent, the habits and desires of the "technostructure"[5] become critical—short of a takeover, which, in any case, threatens only the medium-sized giants and that only in good stock-market years (Galbraith, 1967).

What will these unconstrained managers seek? Profits are indeed desirable; they objectively test the contribution of unrelated businesses and have a hallowed legitimacy. But growth increases prestige and pay and guarantees widespread promotions as well. Sales growth is, in Galbraith's opinion, a *clear* internal rule for success and may help in influencing government and assuring other outsiders of corporate capacity. In the many cases where technology permits standardizing or economies of scope, corporate size is practically unlimited, except for political considerations. On balance, recent evidence seems to indicate that, when a choice must be made, oligopolistic corporate managers do usually opt for growth over even long-term profits (Spechler, 1982).

Galbraith's institutional perspective has implications for pricing (Galbraith, 1945). Because the oligopolist group contemplates its world without end, it naturally prefers a long-term perspective that does not exploit the quick gain at the expense of comfortable security. Certain rules have evolved that offer a measure of immunity from threat. Prices are lower than otherwise and are changed infrequently, so that increased demand is normally met at the announced price[6] (Means, 1972; Stigler and Kindahl, 1973; Weiss, 1977). Customers are accommodated without bargaining and without surprises; potential competitors are presented no uncovered anatomy. Should there be a temporary shortage, intermediaries are not permitted to resell lest the reputation of established sellers for reasonable prices and quality be damaged. In the modulated rivalry with other oligopolists in many markets, each firm readily agrees to the lowest offered price and turns its attention to other production dimensions, where competition will be less unsettling.

What Galbraith seems to have in mind is a "disequilibrium" situation in which *the industry* sets a lower-than-feasible price for the amount it plans to sell (x') or, put another way, plans some spare capacity at posted prices (p'), which include generous, but historically normal, margins. Figure 2 highlights the influence of technology and planning on the oligopolistic group. Long-run average costs exhibit constant or perhaps slightly declining costs past a certain point, which most of the competitors have achieved, though in the short run, because of long-term contracts and production scheduling, costs would rise rapidly at amounts different from x'. For this reason, inventories absorb fluctuation. Short-run demand, D_s often from countervailing groups, is inflexible to price policy,

Figure 2. The normal oligopolistic industry in the planned sector.

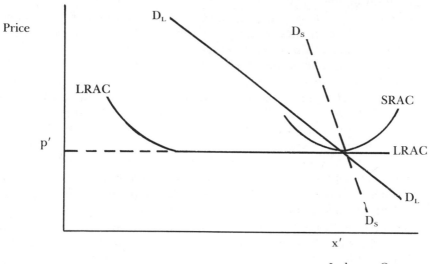

with marginal revenue from cuts being small or negative for the group as a whole. In this setting, the long-term returns to stable group arrangements are high.

It is this "irrational" disregard for (short-term) price policy that permits emphasis on quality and growth of output. By adopting fixed prices, the Quaker or the Javanese religious enthusiast emphasized technical virtuosity, reliability, and social rationality. Bureaucratic routine and the need for protection from rivalry fulfill this function in the welfare-corporate state. Whether the results are stagnation and manipulation—as Veblen and Galbraith feared—or expansion and free expression of engineering possibilities depends on the subjective choices of managers.

One behavioral school logically begins where institutionalism leaves off. Eschewing unbounded rationality, Herbert Simon, Richard Cyert, James March, and their co-workers (Simon and Stedry, 1969; Simon, 1966; Cyert, Dill, and March, 1958) provide a plausible general account and some specific examples to show that internal values and alignments will tell in decisions once corporations enjoy some slack or spare funds. Once a problem obtrudes, a firm normally proceeds according to an agenda of specific suggestions until it finds a "satisfactory" solution. The problem may be declining market share, inadequate capacity, new safety regulations, or something else. It is up to operational managers to propose and fight for a definite solution that will meet salient targets and objections. In the meantime, conventional rules of thumb keep the organization going.

One example of the empirical method used by this Carnegie school of behavorial economics, a study by Cyert and March, showed administrative pricing at the retail level. Absent major cost disruptions, department stores almost invariably set prices (95 percent of 197 prices checked) based on a 40 percent markup rounded to the nearest $.95 and did not reflect price elasticity of demand, as one would expect from neoclassical price theory.[7] Apparently management felt it did better with this convention than by computing the profit-maximizing levels in each case. Such microeconomic studies provide the background for macroeconomic theories of inflation based on cost markups.

The behavioral point of view, which is noncommittal about motivation, can generate refutable hypotheses about firm growth—for example, the so-called law of proportional growth (Simon and Bonini, 1958).

Another behavioral school of economics, whose mentor has been George Katona, traces economic actions to predispositions at the individual level (Strumpel, 1972). While applied most fruitfully to the prediction of short-run spending decisions, the paradigm devised by Katona and his associates also bears on the decision to enter or leave the work force, to move, or to gain an education (Barfield and Morgan, 1963; Katona, Strumpel, and Zahn, 1971). The desire for material acquisitions, for more savings, for security, or for a more exciting lifestyle can be correlated with a person's education, income, age, race, and cultural background. During the 1960s, for example, one study reported that college education was inducing more and more youngsters to reject traditional values and the business careers that embody them (Newcomb and Feldman, 1969).

David McClelland (1961) has traced a connection between the need for achievement, as measured in school books and other cultural artifacts, and subsequent economic growth in historical and contemporary underdeveloped societies.

Several of the works mentioned below owe their theoretical basis to the behavioral perspective—and also to institutional, Weberian, or Marxian perspectives.

IV. CURRENT NONSTANDARD METHODS

One of the best ways of understanding the growth slowdown is to see it as part of a long wave or cycle. According to some standard, historical, and Marxist writers, such recurrent and self-reversing fluctuations have characterized modern economic growth. That such long swings marked the industrialization phase of most northwest European countries and North America is beyond doubt (Kuznets, 1971, chap. 1). 18- to 25-year "Kuznets cycles" have been associated with family formation and building activity. Longer "Kondratieff" and shorter equipment and inventory cycles have also been identified (Schumpeter, 1939; van Duijn, 1983). Those economic historians, mostly Europeans, who believe in a Kondratieff long wave of 45 to 60 years relate them to major infrastructural investments like transportation networks.

Looking just at the United States in the twentieth century, real output growth has varied above and below its secular trend. The Dutch economist van Duijn (1983), for example, gives these subperiods:

1900–1929	3.4% per annum
1929–1948	2.3%
1948–1973	3.8%
1973–1980	2.4%

His dating indicates one and three-quarter cycles of half a century each. Others vary the specific dates. Writing in the mid–1920s, the Russian Kondratieff (1984) saw his last upswing from 1890–1906 to 1914–1920, with the 1920s representing for him the start of a downswing. Later upswings, employing only prices as basic materials, could be dated from 1933 to 1951 and again from 1972 (Rostow, 1980).

Most mainline economists see technological change as the exogenous force generating the pulsations of the long waves. According to Edwin Mansfield (1982; 1983, pp. 482–484), reduced patenting and innovation in pharmaceuticals, agricultural chemicals, and some other industries "suggest a slackening in the pace of innovation in the United States." Kendrick (1976) has developed a series on the *stock* of research and development (R&D) capital that shows a decline in its rate of growth by the early 1970s, and possibly earlier. American spending on R&D, as a percentage of the GNP, declined from a peak of 3 percent in 1964 to about 2.2 percent in 1978, mostly because of a decline in the number of expensive space programs (Mansfield et al., 1982, Chap. 6). Industry's financing of R&D also decelerated from 1960 to 1967. Basic research by all sources fell in real terms. On the other hand, Japanese and continental European R&D has remained steadier as a share of the GNP. (All have raised the share slightly since the late 1970s, with the United States still ahead.) One direct study of innovations (Boretsky, 1980) has shown a marked slowdown in major technological advances in the United States during the last decade—the only exceptions are several attempts to find substitutes for expensive fuels. Based on his long reading of the technical press as senior analyst in the U.S. Department of Commerce,

Boretsky judges that most postwar innovations are now contributing less to productivity than they once did, while the advances in genetic engineering will not come into wide use until the 1990s. Using econometric methods, Griliches (1980) also judges that slowed technical progress is a distinct possibility (see also van Duijn 1983, Chap. 11; Mensch, 1979, p. 130).

A downturn in innovation could be wholly exogenous, but various sources of evidence indicate that the rate of innovation may be sensitive to the defense budget, relative prices of research inputs, profitability, the attitudes toward long-term risk, long-term R&D spending, and the entry of small innovators (Kendrick, 1980; Mansfield, 1982; Loescher, 1984; Mandel, 1978). Reviving a theme of Kondratieff, Mensch considers that basic innovations have disproportionately come after a period of technical stagnation and social turbulence.

Keynesian authorities have not neglected the long run, despite Keynes's oft-quoted disinterest in it during the 1930s' crisis. Writing just before the boom of World War II, Alvin Hansen (1938, p. 314) noted that dominant industries were "extremely important" in expanding the productivity potential of the economy. But he feared that new innovations appearing at that time would not use *enough* capital, even if interest rates were to fall to minimal levels. Thus, for Keynesians like Hansen, the long wave reflects demand as much as supply. Fearing stagnation in the immediate future, Hansen wrote that communal spending would be crucial in reaching a new peak of prosperity in America by 1950. Incidentally, Hansen correctly predicted such a peak, but not for the right reason (p. 317).

A related point comes from W. W. Rostow (1964), long known for his emphasis on "leading sectors," like railroads, which supposedly attracted the investment needed to drive long expansions in American and British economic history. In his latest work (1980, 1983), Rostow downplays innovations as the stimulus for twentieth century expansions and revives the earlier idea of Kondratieff (and van Gelderen, 1913): long waves are stimulated by commodity prices. According to Rostow, energy and food bottlenecks and price increases increase investment to replace exhausted supplies (cf. Van Duijn 1983, p. 90). The relatively little attention Rostow (1960) gives to profit signals and optimizing adjustments— as well as his worldwide generalizations and famous "stages of economic growth"—does recall certain themes common to the German historical school.

An emphatically Marxian model of long waves has recently been revived by the Belgian writer Ernest Mandel (1978, 1980). Tracing his views to Kautsky, Parvus, Trotsky, and de Wolff, Mandel analyzes those fluctuations within the capitalist stage that are longer than the 10-year business cycle generated by renewal of fixed capital. Mandel's long waves will precede the secular breakdown of capitalism itself, which will come about by a worldwide proletarian revolution.

Marxists see profit (surplus) realization as the key determinant of investment and real output. Inventions occur during slumps—for example, during the 1880s and 1930s—when businessmen cannot avoid the disruptions the adoption of new inventions usually causes (Mensch, 1975, Chap. 4). The latest slump began in the West about 1966. Mandel adduces convincing evidence that in most capitalist countries profit rates were declining markedly by the mid- to late 1960s, in some instances earlier (Mandel, 1978, p. 25). It is recognized that before- and after-tax profit rates in the United States were declining between 1970 and 1973 (Nordhaus, 1973). Sautter (1978) dates the profit decline in Japan from 1970. Christian Goux (1978, p. 286) cites the same date for France. British profitability declined from the late 1960s, according to Glyn and Sutcliffe (1971, p. 66). Van der Zwan (van Duijn, 1983, p. 197) shows both before- and after-tax rates of return declining in the Netherlands from 1961 to 1965.

Declining profits are thoroughly expectable by Marxists because of overproduction in consumer-goods industries, the diffusion of previous innovations, and the inability of capitalist governments to coordinate the world market system abroad. More unpredictably, rising working-class consciousness prompted intolerable demands in the latter 1960s. The Marxian view is supported by official statistics showing falling capacity utilization throughout the West, rising wage and falling profit shares in national income, rising debt, and increasing numbers of strikes (Mazier, 1982, Fig. 2.5).

But what could revive the expansionary long wave? Mandel insists on extra-economic causes, which either increase relative surplus value and exploitation of the working class, reduce the value of capital, or allow a more rapid turnover of capital. Any of these can raise the profit rate for the duration of an expansion. To explain the expansionary long wave of 1948–1966 (which actually began in 1940 in the United States), Mandel adduces the defeat of fascism in Germany and the Cold War in the United States. Both events shook working-class confidence and unity. In the aftermath of World War II mass immigration of poor and powerless refugees depressed wages and raised growth and productivity in most of the advanced capitalist countries. The hegemony of the United States stabilized the world economy until about 1970. For Marxists, this hegemony can explain access to cheaper raw materials after the Korean War, low inflation, and profitable investment opportunities in the Third World (Mandel, 1978, p. 132; Weisskopf, 1981; Mazier, 1982).

Another Marxist interpretation of the "crisis" in Western European economies from the late 1960s on introduces the concept of a *régulation* within the capitalist order. Certain French writers (Mistral, Boyer; Mazier, 1982) have analyzed the "monopolistic *régulation*" of advanced capitalism designed to offset poorer profitability and overinvestment. This *régulation* includes inflexible prices; wages indexed to leading sectors; and a considerable role for taxes, wage supplements, and subsidies in easing the distribution of income and industrial crises. Several of the OECD countries, notably France, Italy, the Netherlands, and the United Kingdom, took action to preserve jobs in spite of market signals indicating a cut in manufacturing employment. Consequently, they suffered more inflation than did the United States and Switzerland, where workers were fired and immigrants repatriated. Sabel and Piore (1984) have tied the "*régulation* crisis" to the use of product-specific machines and semi-skilled workers to produce standardized goods, which can no longer be absorbed without massive aid to the Third World.

A recent "social" analysis of the situation in the United States, by Bowles, Gordon, and Weisskopf (1984), draws on a number of these neo-Marxist elements to explain the growth and productivity slowdown in the United States since about 1966. The central assertion of these authors is that the slowdown of 1966 to 1973 "created stresses and strains which the economy was unable to overcome [normally, by a recession] and thereby led to even more severe problems in subsequent years" (p. 31). In common with neo-Marxist writers, the authors cited threats to the "structures of domination" by U.S. corporate capitalism at home and abroad well before the oil-price shock of 1973–1974, which they attribute in considerable part to the machinations of large oil companies anyway. Thus the key component of the Bowles-Gordon-Weisskopf interpretation is that the profit decline and loss of control up to 1973 forced the authorities to engineer a "cold bath" recession to restore those "structures of domination," particularly to "cool off worker resistance" (p. 144).

The most original evidence adduced by Bowles, Gordon, and Weisskopf, and the most controversial, is that suggesting a breakdown of workplace control. After 1967, according to one series they have constructed, the cost of losing one's job fell (p. 89). Moreover, costs of supervision had risen; after 1966 manufacturing corporations were forced to reduce their supervisory staff relative to the number of operators. The wages of blacks and women gained after 1965 relative to those of white males. According to one index, the job accident rate was rising.[8] All this caused friction against "insistent corporate discipline." The results were more strikes, quits, absenteeism, and slowdowns—particularly in the coal-mining industry.

When these indirect indicators of lower work intensity were entered into a regression of hourly productivity in the American private economy, they explained 63 percent of the slowdown in the period of 1966 to 1973 as compared with productivity from 1948 to 1966. Another ingenious variable that seems to explain part of that early slowdown was a reduced failure rate of businesses, taken as a measure of "innovative pressure." As to the abrupt productivity deceleration from 1973 to 1979, Bowles, Gordon, and Weisskopf find reduced capital intensity and plant utilization account for much of the further drop in the rate of productivity advance.

Two kinds of criticism might be raised against the Bowles, Gordon, and Weisskopf analyses. First, the influence of social variables is theoretically unconstrained. If two variables move together statistically over a time interval, the variance explained can reach 100 percent, even if the economic importance or contribution of the explanatory variable is much less in reality. For example, strikes may reduce labor hours by only a percentage point or two, yet if they move with productivity, a regression will assign them considerable explanatory or predictive importance. True, strikes may indicate a deeper friction, causing additional loss of production, but that would need to be shown. Bowles, Gordon, and Weisskopf's proxy for work intensity may not itself explain most of the productivity slowdown during the period 1966 to 1973. By contrast, in growth-accounting or production-function analyses, the contribution of changes in labor quality are scaled by the share of labor in national income. Were Bowles, Gordon, and Weisskopf's facts entered into growth accounts, their explanatory power would be much less. Still, these researchers' methods are by far the most serious attempt to quantify what many—radicals and conservatives alike—felt was a breakdown in labor discipline in the late 1960s.

Second, one might quarrel with Bowles, Gordon, and Weisskopf's interpretation of their explanatory variables. Does a lower unemployment rate, part of their index of "lower work intensity," indicate that? Or could it also indicate that labor-market pressures were forcing employers to overcome their reluctance to hire blacks and women, even if they had to be trained and accommodated in a new and costly way? Similarly, could a reduced failure rate be interpreted as meaning that the "Salter-tail" of failing businesses was not being eliminated? As Dahmen (1982, p. 53) reminds us in connection with the parallel period in Swedish industry, firms that have been eliminated no longer weigh down the productivity statistics. Our interpretation is not simply a matter of taste; it is a matter of perspective and consistent supporting evidence. The surrounding historical case presented by Bowles, Gordon, and Weisskopf is so serious-minded and well-grounded in neo-Marxist theory that every open-minded researcher will want to examine it carefully. But other interpretative schemes are possible which incorporate the statistical associations they have established.

What I have called the institutionalist perspective above is not a research paradigm as coherent as the Marxist one. Several approaches deserve our attention, but all share the institutionalist concern for growth and productivity as the result of a creative impulse hindered by ceremonial, merely pecuniary, or power considerations. Akin to the behavioral school (Strumpel, 1972, p. 86), institutionalism considers the effective motivating principle of economic actors to be multifarious and variable.

There can be no doubt that on occasion and over time attitudes toward economic activity do change (Spechler, 1982b; Maital, 1982). Herbert Simon (1966) long ago showed that improvements in productivity without a change in technology could only be understood as the elimination of organizational slack (akin to Leibenstein's X-inefficiency). Wartime emergencies can motivate people to work harder. Over time though, it is often believed that people relax and shun work (McCracken et al., 1977, p. 156). A study by the Survey Research Center at the University of Michigan found that the numbers of paid leaves, vacations, and coffee breaks increased about 0.1 percent yearly in the 1970s. The net productivity effect of this trend cannot have been great, even if it were a new thing—a highly doubtful proposition.

For obvious reasons, work intensity is hardly ever measured over a long time for the same person on the same task. Even if it were, the impact of any variation in a changing dynamic economy would be tenuous. Clearly, production workers do work less intensively after a certain age, but not necessarily less productively, once experience, reliability, and responsibility are taken into account. Since the work force is constantly renewed with young or reentering workers, a work force of constant age structure would not on this account change its intensity of work.

Lacking direct measures of work intensity, many researchers have relied on measures of job satisfaction. These measures do not show enough credible variation to explain the productivity slowdown. According to a U.S. Department of Labor (1974) study, job satisfaction questionnaires show no secular trend: about 60 to 80 percent of American workers proclaim themselves satisfied, more or less, with their jobs, although more detailed questioning does show widespread sources of dissatisfaction with specific job characteristics or with pay. More instructive is the Michigan Quality of Employment Survey, which in 1969, 1972, and 1977 (Quinn and Staines, 1977) asked workers whether they felt they were asked to do "excessive amounts of work" or not. As shown in Table 2, adapted from Filer (1980, p. 121), many *fewer* in 1977 than in

Table 2.   Effort Component of Labor Supply

Response to the statement "I am not asked to do excessive amounts of work."

	Very True	Somewhat True	Not Too True	Not at All True
1969	43.1%	31.5%	14.8%	10.5%
1972	34.2	37.0	16.9	11.8
1977	27.9	38.6	19.2	14.3

Note: All entries are percentages of respondents.
   Collapsed Scales: (Very True = 4) (Somewhat True = 3) (Not Too True = 2) and (Not at
   All True = 1): Mean = 3.07 (1969), 2.93 (1972) and 2.80 (1977).
Source: Reproduced from Filer (1980, p. 121).

1969 (a 15.2 point difference) said it was "very true" that they were *not* asked to overwork. Some 3.8 per hundred *more* said it was "not at all true" that they were not being asked to do "excessive" amounts of work. From this "unmistakable increase in the proportion of workers who feel they are asked to do excessive amounts of work," Filer (p. 120) concludes:

> Either jobs have been getting harder with respect to the amount of work that they require of those who fill them, or else people are perceiving the jobs as having become harder (that is, the standard of effort that constitutes excessive amounts of work has fallen). If the amount of work people regard as being excessive has fallen, there is every reason to believe that they would be willing to put less effort into any given job, and therefore that output per man-hour of labor input would fall.

One might query the robustness of this evidence, since the table makes clear that considerably more of the respondents in 1977 chose the middle responses (57.8 versus 46.3 per hundred eight years before). This may reflect better personnel management, if we suppose that the optimal practice would be to have workers do, and be conscious of doing, a reasonable amount of work for the job. Egregious overmanning is reportedly down throughout American industry (Rees, 1980). With higher unemployment in 1977, one wonders too whether extreme responses might not have seemed a bit unguarded. In any event, we look forward to further data of this sort.

Occasional reports of declining job satisfaction need not betoken reduced productivity (cf. Vroom, 1969): the reverse is just as likely. Social psychologists have concluded that "there is no generalizable, functional, replicable link between work satisfaction and hard work" (Macarov, 1982, pp. 177–178). Only in direct-service tasks is there such a relationship, but such jobs have not been the source of the measured productivity decline that occurred in America and Western Europe from 1966 to 1982. Job satisfaction may follow from good performance, especially if it is praised and rewarded. Or both satisfaction and high productivity may be the result of superior management.

Joan Woodward has categorized a sample of Essex companies according to type of technology: unit, batch, or mass-production, or process types. Optimal management structure—and thus apparently also success—depends on the fit between supervisory hierarchy and technology. Personnel problems and production difficulties of different sorts characterize each technology. Both flow and unit technologies require better trained personnel; they both permit more autonomy and variety in job definition, and supervision is more "organic," as opposed to mechanical.

Such a framework throws light on recent experiments in job enlargement in the United States and Sweden. According to press reports, for example, the Volvo assembly plant at Kalman in Sweden invested 19 million kroner to install an "island," or team, assembly system for electrical, brake, wheel, and other systems involved in automobile production. Employees decide the pace and differentiation of tasks. Evidently high absenteeism, which afflicts mass-production plants in both countries, prompted this change, which reportedly resulted in higher profits and productivity as well as reduced turnover and no-shows. What emerges from first impressions of like experiments at General Foods' plant in Topeka, Kansas, the Saab Sodertalje engine works, and elsewhere is that recruitment of suitable employees and a rather radical shift in production and management techniques are required to make long-term use of job enlargement to the satisfaction of both employers and employees (Argyris, 1973). Undoubtably the high average income and educational level in the United States and Sweden and the good labor-relations tradition of the latter make these countries particularly fertile ground for experiments in workplace democracy.

Industrial social psychology has long pointed out the conditioned differences among workers with respect to the type of work they will accept (Vroom, 1969). For example, rural Protestants have been found to express more satisfaction with, and be absent less frequently from, jobs high in autonomy, responsibility, and variety; the reverse was the case for an urban Catholic group tested (Turner and Lawrence, 1965). Perhaps it is not so inexplicable that when American auto workers, long accustomed to the mechanical pacing and considerable dead time of the American assembly line, visited the site of the Swedish experiment, they were appalled at the speed of the work! In addition, line foremen, commonly rendered redundant by such enlargement and quality self-control, very often oppose them both. A consequence of all this is to throw doubt on the idea that, at the plant level, one can shift incrementally and smoothly from extrinsic (high-wage) rewards to intrinsic rewards (better conditions) or from high-quantity to high-quality work as market conditions indicate (*Work in America,* appendix; Hackman, 1975). The extreme case of the Soviet Union may again illustrate the point: the shift from an extremely taut, mechanistic environment with great reliance on specific premia for quantitative plan fulfillment to a new management style in order to achieve both higher quality and higher productivity has proved extremely difficult (Granick, 1975; Spechler, 1986).

David Granick (1972) has attempted to elucidate the relative progressiveness of various industrial economies by noting the career and internal control patterns typical of each country. Top French managers, for example, are preselected on graduation from certain elite schools. Because of the indoctrination there—together with government financing conditional on cooperation with the regime's goals, a high profits tax, and unions sensitive to distributional issues—Granick finds a great emphasis on growth at the expense of profitability. Lower-level technicians, neither involved in nor rewarded for corporate success, tend to devote themselves to technical virtuousity. Extreme decentralization, on the other hand, is characteristic of British firms. Granick is able to explain the low degree of economies of scale at the firm level by this feature, as compared with size-specific labor productivity in German industry. One of the drawbacks of Granick's approach, however, is the difficulty a less experienced and energetic observer than he may experience in trying to replicate his findings, which are drawn from numerous factory visits and interviews.

While it is logical to believe that commitment to the goals of the firm and job satisfaction may improve performance (Mowday, Porter, and Dubin, 1974; Mowday, Steers, and Porter, 1979), Janet Near (1984) has shown that American workers score higher on commitment and job satisfaction than a matched sample of about 3,500 respondents in seven industries in Japan. While Near did not measure productivity level or growth directly, overall Japanese productivity is lower than American but is rising much more rapidly. Which side of the coin can be explained by job satisfaction? It is clearly a complex matter.

Management styles are not strictly determined by the technical and market environment; they are capable of changing for the better or the worse. A persistent line of criticism, recently voiced by Hayes and Abernathy (1980) of the Harvard Business School, attributes the poor productivity performance of American industry—as compared with Japan—to the excessive concern among American managers for short-run financial results. Too few engineers or others who know production intimately rise to the highest positions here. Corporate executives devote too much time to finance, mergers, and the value of their securities (see Loescher, 1984, p. 6, for many references). A certain complacency about costs and quality continued in the United States through the late 1960s, until international competition began to be felt (McCracken et al., 1977, pp. 70–71; *Business Week*, Nov. 1, 1982, p. 66). The similarity of these complaints to Veblen's is obvious.

Managerial attention to short-term pecuniary results in the United States has perhaps been intensified by the practice of giving them annual bonuses, but being rewarded with shares, promotions, and pensions ought to have promoted a longer view, as well, among managers. Empirical evidence supporting the claim of greater shortsightedness by American (and European) managers during the late 1960s and early 1970s is, to say the least, rather sparse. Higher real interest rates since then would, of course, have justified a somewhat shorter view. Lower profits would have done the reverse.

One manifestation of farsightedness has been invoked to explain the productivity slowdown. It is the unwillingness of managers to adjust their experienced work forces to short-run output and planned output. As is well understood, short-run productivity functions indicate that year-to-year productivity varies directly with the rate of output growth. Industries with higher growth also usually display higher than average productivity gains (United Nations Economic Commission for Europe, 1983, p. 52). This results from the slowness of employment adjustment to output levels and the presence of overhead labor. When output falls, experienced and salaried help are hoarded because of the high cost of rehiring and retraining, possibly also because of "implicit contracts" for continuous employment. Moreover, in some situations—for example, in utilities—capacity is built ahead of demand. When demand fails to rise as expected, capital productivity falls sharply. By contrast, when demand rises faster than expected, learning by doing may be hastened and salaried workers may extend themselves temporarily. Average productivity will rise, as predicted by "Verdoorn's law."

Whether such short-run surprises can be built into a long-run explanation for the decline in productivity growth seems doubtful. One might imagine that the long-run rate could be raised by many year-to-year surprises of an expansive sort. But will businessmen not eventually learn? Are there no supply constraints? Indeed, some writers have used the argument of self-fulfilling prophecies and self-confirmed Keynesian policy optimism in order to explain the rapid growth during the years 1945 to 1964 (Postan, 1967; McCracken et al., 1977; Boltho, 1982, Chap. 1, p. 156). The use of facile psychology, like mirrors, allows people to see a thing and its opposite at the same time.

If management had to change in the late 1960s and early 1970s, often it did not change to the more cooperative, human-relations style some authorities had recommended (Lawler, 1977). Some industrial relations experts I have spoken with think management has become more confrontational. More demands have been made of the National Labor Relations Board to deauthorize union representatives than ever before (*The Economist*, Nov. 17, 1979, pp. 39–40). Today's workers have also begun to expect and demand more than their fathers and mothers did. A breakdown in necessary management-labor cooperation might have occurred too, because mutual notions about where the economy is headed and what rewards can be expected have broken down (Strumpel, 1980, p. 55). In Europe, union leaders may have seen no need or reward in further moderation. They could not afford to let management outbid them. Unions have already won a voice in plant closures and redundancies. The results of such new institutions are not yet very clear.

When they operate well, unions can moderate class conflict and contribute to greater productivity by negotiating and enforcing informal understandings or productivity deals, resolving local grievances, and cooperating in training (Brown and Medoff, 1978). One study found unionized plants had 20 to 30 percent higher productivity than nonunion plants in the same industries (Medoff and Freeman, 1983). What works in furniture, cement, and auto plants, however, may not work in coal mines in the United States (Connerton, Freeman, and Medoff, 1979; Clark, 1978). In the older areas of Great Britain, unions seem to have reduced productivity possibly because of uncontrollable jurisdictional disputes and political involvements (Caves, 1980). German unions seem to facilitate full exploitation of economics of scale in the automobile and perhaps other industries better than the British (Jones and Prais, 1979). Clearly, the ability of labor organizations to effect a jointly satisfactory "cooperative solution" in the labor-management game differs from country to country and from time to time.

One audacious attempt to cut through the complexities of microeconomic study is that of Mancur Olson (1982a, 1982b). Olson's earlier work dwelt on the difficulties of forming large organizations, because of freeriders. Now Olson conjectures that stable societies accumulate too many interest groups over time. Private interests collude against the public interest in growth, efficiency, and productivity—particularly if the private group is noninclusive. High monopolistic wage demands are a prominent example.

Olson may have a point, one reminiscent of Veblen. Superior German and Japanese productivity performance after World War II might be explained, at least in part, by the breakup of their cartels and monopolies and the weakening of their trade unions. The inclusiveness of Sweden's and Holland's wage bargaining may have helped their macroeconomic performance, at least when compared with the British record. Several economic historians have remarked about the convergence of the semi-developed and the most developed states in Europe. But this catching up might also be attributed to a "backlog of growth possibilities" (Maddison, 1979, 1980). The rich paid what Gerschenkron (1962, Chap. 1) called, echoing Veblen, "the penalty of taking the lead."

Reflecting on the effects of the American Civil War of the 1860s, Olson is also able to show statistically that newer or former Confederate states within the United States grew faster during the period 1965 to 1974. Why it took the Union states one hundred years to generate relatively more collusive interest groups is left unanswered, as Pryor (1983) shrewdly notes, and the former Confederate states hardly came out of the Civil War in the same way Germany and Japan emerged from World War II. Olson conjectures that social homogeneity and contact should increase the formation of vested interests, yet admittedly crude tests do not indicate that religiously and ethnically homogeneous nations have done better than more heterogeneous ones in growth and productivity since World War II (Pryor, 1983). Neither has the ruling Communist party—the ultimate inclusive group that excludes competitors by force of law—increased the productivity performance of Hungary, Poland, Czechoslovakia, and the Soviet Union.

Behavioral theories of the firm have been difficult to verify, since they seem to require arduous examination of privileged inside information. One researcher who has overcome the difficulties is M. J. Roberts (1975, 1981), who aims to explain how various public utilities have responded to demands of people or groups concerned with the environment by examining the strength of various internal factions in a number of companies.

Another long-established research program that owes something to behavioral insights is the work of Nelson and Winter (1973, 1974, 1981, 1982). They explain the spread and diffusion of new techniques and productivity throughout an industry without appealing to explicit maximizing behavior and marginal-cost pricing—behaviors not always found in reality. Plants innovate if profit is below target, but they can be wrong. When they are correct in their search for innovations, excess profits are reinvested and firm growth occurs. According to Nelson and Winter, the pattern generated by such satisficing decision rules in a changing environment can reproduce the pattern of aggregate productivity advance first noticed by Paul Douglas and Robert Solow (1957). Realistic size distributions are generated, one objective of Simon and Bonini (1958).

V. CONCLUSIONS

Can exposure to the four nonstandard paradigms, together with the useful findings of mainstream writers, give us any confidence about understanding the growth and productivity slowdown in the West? Certain elements do seem to be part of the picture, however variegated it must be until future years of data and further research sharpen the image.

1. The years between 1948 and 1966 were exceptionally good; nonrenewable sources of growth were exploited and therefore could not last. Among the factors that had to exhaust themselves were the end to the reallocation of labor and capital from low-productivity sectors like agriculture and retail proprietorships, the patience of unions, and the low sensitivity to inflation among the public. When inflation accelerated, governments depressed growth in order to restore stable conditions. Investment suffered in the meantime.

2. Growth proceeded in directions that further reduced measured advances in both growth and productivity. Less experienced workers had to be brought in and trained. People demanded more health, educational, and social services and a cleaner, safer environment. The often wasteful use of energy precipitated abrupt price increases in 1973 and 1979.

3. Political developments such as liberal American leadership and the liberalization of Western trade increased competition, but advances have not been so rapid in the last decade.

ACKNOWLEDGMENT

The author would like to dedicate this essay to two valued teachers and colleagues who encouraged it—Albert Hirschman and Richard Musgrave.

NOTES

1. In Israel, which can be considered a Western, or European, country and whose prolonged inflation was much more rapid than that of other Western nations, the effect has been estimated at a few percentage points of the GNP, based on the diversion of an extra 4 percent of the labor force to the private financial sector.

2. Theoretically, all output should be assignable in equilibrium to inputs properly measured, aside from economies of scale (Jorgenson and Griliches, 1967, 1972). In my opinion, their method merely shifts attention to why inputs become better (more productive).

3. OSHA was created in 1970; the Mine Enforcement Safety Administration, only in 1973; EPA came into being in 1970; the Consumer Product Safety Commission, in 1972. Enforcement has been irregular, to say the least.

4. Neither Galbraith nor Veblen would have accepted being labeled an institutionalist, preferring to define themselves as dissenters from the prevailing neoclassical orthodoxy.

5. Galbraith proceeds from the finding that about 85 percent of the top 200 American nonfinancial corporations are controlled by their managers (Galbraith, 1973, Chap. 9). He draws on data compiled by Robert Larner for 1963. A variety of close, Marxist studies by Zeitlin, Sweezy, and others have pared this figure down to 34 percent of *Fortune*'s top 500, a figure comparable to around half of Galbraith's, by invoking the use of bank proxies and the assumed power of 5- or 10-percent holdings in corporations of great size. As far as I am aware, no one has challenged the idea that there was a definite trend away from owner-managers, as established by Gardiner Means in 1929, who found that 44 percent of an analogous population of corporations was already in the hands of managers.

6. Means (1972) demonstrated that 50 concentrated manufacturing branches changed their posted prices relatively little during the 1957–1959 and 1960–62 recession in the United States, and price behavior in expansions also did not conform to classical expectations. Although the "administered-price" hypothesis wants better demarcation as to its proposed scope, the competing transactions cost notion to explain long-term contracts has had little empirical payoff thus far (Stigler and Kindahl, 1973; Weiss, 1977).

7. Cited in Baumol and Stewart, 1971. In a 1968 retest, Baumol and Stewart found the modal markup had increased to 45 percent, with the markup in nearly all stores falling between 40 and 45 percent.

8. This according to a series developed by Michele I. Naples under the supervision of David Gordon (1981). Statistics by the International Labor Organization on overall and fatal accident rates in industry and mining show a steady decline in all the main OECD countries, however (International Labor Organization, various years).

REFERENCES

Ames, E., and N. Rosenberg, "Changing Technological Leadership and Industrial Growth," *Economic Journal*, XXIII (March 1963), 13–31.

Argyris, C., "Personality and Organization Theory Revisited," *Administrative Science Quarterly* 18, no. 2 (June 1973), 141–167.

Baran, Paul and Paul Sweezy, *Monopoly Capital*. New York: Monthly Review Press, 1966.

Barfield, Richard, and James W. Morgan, *Early Retirement: The Decision and the Experience*. Ann Arbor, MI: Survey Research Center, Institute for Social Research, 1963.

Baumol, William and Stewart Maco, "On the Behavorial Theory of the Firm," in A. Wood and R. Marris, eds., *The Corporate Economy*. Cambridge, MA: Harvard University Press, 1971.

Bernabè, Franco, "The Labor Market and Unemployment," in A. Boltho, ed., *The European Economy, Growth and Crisis*. Oxford: Oxford University Press, 1982, pp. 159–188.

Berndt, E.R., "Energy Price Increases and the Productivity Slowdown in United States Manufacturing" in *Decline in Productivity Growth*. Boston: Federal Reserve Bank of Boston, 1980, pp. 60–89.

Boltho, Andrea, ed., *The European Economy. Growth and Crisis*. Oxford: Oxford University Press, 1982.

Boretsky, Michael, "The Role of Innovation," *Challenge*, 23, (November/December 1980), 9–15.

Bowles, Samuel, David Gordon, and Thomas E. Weisskopf, *Beyond the Waste Land*. New York: Anchor, 1984.

Boyer, R. and J. Mistral, *Accumulation, Inflation, Crises*. Paris: 1978.

Brady, D.S., and R. Friedman, "Savings and the Income Distribution," *Studies in Income and Wealth*, 10 (1947), pp. 247–265.

Brainard, William and George Perry, "Editor's Summary," *Brookings Paper on Economic Activity*, no. 1 (1981), vii–viii.

Brown, C., and J. Medoff, "Trade Unions in the Production Process," *Journal of Political Economy*, 86 (January 1978), 355–378.

Bruno, Michael, "Raw Materials, Profits, and the Productivity Slowdown," *Quarterly Journal of Economics*, XCIX (February 1984), 1–29.

Bruno, Michael, "World Shocks, Macroeconomic Response, and the Productivity Puzzle," in R.C.O. Matthews, ed., *Slower Growth in the Western World*. London: Heinemann, 1982, pp. 83–105.

Bruno, Michael, and Jeffrey Sachs, *Economics of Worldwide Stagnation*. Cambridge, MA: Harvard University Press, 1985.

Caves, Richard, and Lawrence Krause, eds., *Britain's Economic Performance*. Washington, D.C.: Brookings Institution, 1980.

Chinloy, Peter, *Labor Productivity*. Cambridge, MA: Abt Books, 1981.

Clark, Kim, "Unions and Productivity in the Cement Industry," Unpublished Ph.D. Dissertation, Harvard University, 1978.

Clark, Peter, "Inflation and Productivity Decline," *American Economic Review*, 72 (May 1982).

Connerton, M., R.B. Freeman, and J.L. Medoff, "Productivity and Industrial Relations: The Case of U.S. Bituminous Coal." Working Paper, National Bureau of Economic Research, December, 1979.

Cyert, R., W.R. Dill, and J.M. March, "Role of Expectations in Business Decision-Making," *Administrative Science Quarterly* 3 (1958), 307–340.

Dahmen, E., "A Neo-Schumpeterian Analysis of the Recent Industrial Development Crisis in Sweden," in C. Kindleberger and G. di Tella, eds., *Economics in the Long View: Essays in Honor of W.W. Rostow*. New York: New York University Press, 1982, pp. 48–62.

Data Resources, Inc., "The Macroeconomic Impact of Federal Pollution Control Programs: 1978 Assessment." Unpublished report, January 11, 1979.

Deaton, A.S., "The Structure of Demand, 1920–1970," in Carlo M. Cipolla, ed., *The Fontana Economic History of Europe*. New York: Collins, 1976, pp. 89–132.

Decline in Productivity Growth, The. Boston: Federal Reserve Bank of Boston, 1980.

Denison, Edward, *Accounting for Slower Economic Growth*. Washington, D.C.: Brookings Institution, 1979.

Denison, Edward, "Where Has Productivity Gone?" *Challenge* (November/December 1980).

Department of Commerce, *Long-Term Economic Growth*. Washington, D.C.: U.S. Government Printing Office, 1966.

Duesenberry, James S., *Income, Saving, and the Theory of Consumer Behavior*. Cambridge, MA: Harvard University Press, 1949.

Economic Report of the President. Washington, D.C.: U.S. Government Printing Office, 1983, 1984.

Eisenstadt, S.N., ed., *The Protestant Ethic and Modernization*. New York: Basic Books, 1968.

Filer, Randall K., "The Downturn in Productivity Growth: A New Look at its Nature and Causes," in S. Maital and N. Meltz, eds., *Lagging Productivity Growth*. Cambridge, MA: Ballinger, 1980, Chap. 4.

Fischoff, Ephraim, "The Protestant Ethic and the Spirit of Capitalism," in S.N. Eisenstadt, ed., *The Protestant Ethic and Modernization*. New York: Basic Books, 1968, pp. 67–86.

Freeman, Richard, *The Overeducated American*. New York: Academic Press, 1976.

Galbraith, J.K., *Economics and the Public Purpose*. Boston: Houghton-Mifflin, 1973.

Galbraith, J.K., *The New Industrial State*. Boston: Houghton-Mifflin, 1967.

Galbraith, J.K., *A Theory of Price Control*. Cambridge, MA: Harvard University Press, 1945.

Geertz, Clifford, "Religious Belief and Economic Behavior in a Central Javanese Town," in S.N. Eisenstadt, ed., *The Protestant Ethic and Modernization*. New York: Basic Books, 1968, pp. 309–332.

Geertz, Clifford, *Peddlars and Princes*. Chicago: University of Chicago Press, 1963.

Georgescu-Roegen, N., *Analytical Economics*. Cambridge, MA: Harvard University Press, 1966.

Gerschenkron, Alexander, *Economic Backwardness in Historical Perspective*. Cambridge, MA: Harvard University Press, 1962.

Glyn, Andrew and Bob Sutcliffe, *British Capitalism, Workers and the Profits Squeeze*. Harmondsworth: Penguin, 1971.

Goux, Christian, *Ruptures d'un Système Economique*. Paris: Reiffers, 1978.

Granick, David, *Enterprise Guidance in Eastern Europe, A Comparison of Four Socialist Economics*, Princeton, NJ: Princeton University Press, 1975.

Granick, David, *Managerial Comparisons of Four Developed Countries: France, Britain, United States and Russia*. Cambridge, MA: MIT Press, 1972.

Griliches, Zvi, "R and D and the Productivity Showdown," *American Economic Review*, 70, no. 2 (May 1980), 343–348.

Hackman, J. Richard, "Is Job Enrichment Just a Fad?" *Harvard Business Review*, 78 (September–October 1975), 129–138.

Hagen, Everett, "Internal Functioning of Capitalist Organizations," *Journal of Economic History* XXX, no. 1 (March 1970), 222–236.

Hansen, Alvin H., *Full Recovery or Stagnation?* New York: W.W. Norton, 1938.

Harrington, Michael, *The Twilight of Capitalism*. New York: Simon & Schuster, 1976.

Hayes, R.H., and W. Abernathy, "Managing Our Way to Economic Decline," *Harvard Business Review* (July–August 1980).

Heller, Walter, *New Dimensions in Political Economy*. Cambridge, MA: Harvard University Press, 1964.

Hudson, E.A. and D.W. Jorgenson, "Energy Prices and the U.S. Economy, 1972–76," *Data Resources U.S. Review*, (September 1978), 124–137.

International Labour Organization, *Yearbook of Labour Statistics*. New York: United Nations, various years.

Jones, D.T., and S.J. Prais, "Plant Size and Productivity in the Motor Industry: Some International Comparisons," *NIESR Bulletin*, (1980), 131–151.

Jorgenson, Dale W., and Z. Griliches, "The Explanation of Productivity Change," *Review of Economic Studies*, 34 (1967), 249–283.

Jorgenson, Dale W., and Z. Griliches, "Issues in Growth Accounting: A Reply to E.F. Denison," *Survey of Current Business*, 52 (1972), 65–94.

Katona, George, Burkhard Strumpel, and Ernest Zahn, *Aspirations and Affluence*. New York: McGraw-Hill, 1971.

Kendrick, John W., *The Formation and Stocks of Total Capital*. New York: National Bureau of Economic Research, 1976.

Kendrick, John W., ed., *International Comparisons of Productivity and Causes of the Slowdown*. Cambridge, MA: Ballinger, 1984.

Kendrick, John W., *Productivity Trends in the United States*. Princeton, NJ: Princeton University Press, 1961.

Kendrick, John W., "Productivity Trends in the United States," in S. Maital and N. Meltz, eds., *Lagging Productivity Growth*. Cambridge, MA: Ballinger, 1980, pp. 9–30.

Kindleberger, Charles and Guido di Tella, eds., *Economics in the Long View: Essays in Honor of W.W. Rostow*. New York: New York University Press, 1982, 3 vols.

Kondratieff, N.D., *The Long Wave Cycle*, translated by G. Daniels. New York: Richardson & Snyder, 1984.

Kuznets, Simon, *Economic Growth of Nations*. Cambridge, MA: Harvard University Press, 1971.

Landes, David, *The Unbound Prometheus*. Cambridge: Cambridge University Press, 1969.

Larner, Robert J., "Ownership and Control in the 200 Largest Nonfinancial Corporations, 1929 and 1963," *The American Economic Review*, 56 (1966), 777–787.

Lawler, E., III, "Reward Systems in Improving Life at Work," in J.R. Hackman and J.L. Shuttle, eds., *Improving Life at Work: Behavioral Science Approaches to Organizational Change*. Goodyear, 1977, pp. 204–205.

Leontief, W., *Essays on Economics*. New York: Oxford University Press, 1966.

Lindzey, Gardner, and Elliot Aronson, eds., *The Handbook of Social Psychology*, 2nd ed. Reading, MA: Addison-Wesley, 1969, 5 vols.

Loescher, Samuel, "Bureaucratic Measurement, Shuttling Stock Shares and Shortened Time Horizons; Implications for Economic Growth," *Quarterly Review of Economics and Business*, 1984.

McCloskey, Donald N., *The Rhetoric of Economics*. Madison, WI: University of Wisconsin Press, 1985.

Macarov, David, *Worker Productivity: Myths and Reality*. Beverly Hills, CA: Sage Publications, 1982.

McClelland, David, *The Achieving Society*. Princeton, NJ: Van Nostrand, 1961.

McCracken, Paul, et al., *Towards Full-Employment and Price Stability*. Paris: OECD, 1977.

Maddison, Angus, "Long-Run Dynamics of Productivity Growth," *Banca Nazionale del Lavoro Quarterly Review*, no. 128 (March 1979).

Maddison, Angus, "Western Economic Performance in the 1970s: A Perspective," *Banca Nazionale del Lavoro Quarterly Review*, (September 1980), 247–288.

Maital, Shlomo, and Noah Meltz, eds., *Lagging Productivity Growth*. Cambridge, MA: Ballinger, 1980.

Maital, Shlomo, and Noah Meltz, *Minds, Markets, and Money*. New York: Basic Books, 1982.

Mandel, Ernest, *Late Capitalism*. London: New Left Books, 1975.

Mandel, Ernest, *Long Waves of Capitalist Development*. Cambridge: Cambridge University Press, 1980.

Mandel, Ernest, *Marxist Economic Theory*. New York. Monthly Review Press, 1968.

Mandel, Ernest, *The Second Slump*, rev. ed. London: New Left Books, 1978.

Mansfield, Edwin, *Principles of Macroeconomics*, 4th ed. New York: Norton, 1983.

Mansfield, Edwin, "Research and Development, Productivity, and Inflation," *Science*, 209 (September 1980), 1091–1093.

Mansfield, Edwin, Anthony Romeo, Mark Schwartz, David Teece, Samuel Wagner, and Peter Brach, *Technology Transfer, Productivity, and Economic Policy*. New York: Norton, 1982.

Marshall, R.M., "Factors Influencing Changes in Productivity," in Charles Kindleberger and Guido di Tella, eds., *Economics in the Long View: Essays in Honor of W.W. Rostow*. New York: New York University Press, 1982, vol. III, pp. 83–109.

Marglin, S., "What Do Bosses Do?" *Review of Radical Political Economics*, 6, no. 2 (Summer 1974), 60–112.

Marx, Karl, *Capital*, vol. 1. New York: International Publishers, 1967.

Matthews, R.C.O., ed., *Slower Growth in the Western World*. London: Heinemann, 1982.

Mazier, Jacques, "Growth and Crisis—A Marxist Interpretation," in A. Botho, ed., *The European Economy: Growth in Crisis*, Oxford: Oxford University Press, 1982, pp. 38–71.

Means, Gardiner, "Administered Prices Revisited," *American Economic Review*, (June 1972), 292–306.

Medoff, James, and Richard Freeman, *What Do Unions Do?* New York: Basic Books, 1983.

Mensch, Gerhard, *Das technologische Patt*. Frankfurt-am-Main: 1975. Translated as *Stalemate in Technology, Innovations Overcome the Depression*. Cambridge, MA: Ballinger, 1979.

Mowday, R.T., L.W. Porter, and R. Dubin, "Unit Performance Situational Factors and

Employee Attitudes in Spatially Separated Work Units," *Organizational Behavior and Human Performance*, 12 (1974), 231–248.

Mowday, R.T., R.M. Steers, and L.W. Porter, "The Measurement of Organizational Commitment," *Journal of Vocational Behavior*, 14 (1979), 224–247.

Mueller, Dennis, ed., *The Political Economy of Growth*. New Haven, CT: Yale University Press, 1983.

Nadiri, H.I., "Some Approaches to the Theory and Measurement of Total Factor Productivity: A Survey," *Journal of Economic Literature*, VIII (December 1970) pp. 1137–77 [occasional paper].

Naples, Michele I., and Gordon, David, "The Industrial Accident Rate: Creating a Consistent Time Series." Institute for Labor Education and Research, December 1981.

Near, Janet, "Organizational Job Commitment and Job Characteristics: A Comparison of Japanese and American Workers." Mimeo, 1984.

Nelson, Richard, "Research on Productivity Growth and Productivity Differences: Dead Ends and New Departures," *Journal of Economic Literature*, XIX (September 1981), 1029–1064.

Nelson, Richard, and Sidney Winter, "Neo-classical vs. Evolutionary Theories of Economic Growth: Critique and Prospectus," *Economic Journal*, 84 (December 1974), 886–905.

Nelson, Richard, and Sidney Winter, "Toward an Evolutionary Theory of Economic Capabilities," *American Economic Review*, 63 (May 1973), 440–449.

Nelson, Richard, and Sidney Winter, *An Evolutionary Theory of Economic Change*. Cambridge, MA: Harvard University Press, 1982.

Newcomb, Theodore M., and Kenneth A. Feldman, *The Impact of College on Students*. San Francisco: Jossey-Bass, 1969.

Nordhaus, William D., "The Falling Share of Profit," *Brookings Papers on Economic Activity*, no. 1 (1974), 169–208.

Nordhaus, William D., "Oil and Economic Performance in Industrial Countries," *Brookings Papers on Economic Activity*, no. 2 (1980), 341–388.

Nordhaus, William D., "The Recent Productivity Slowdown," *Brookings Papers on Economic Activity*, no. 3 (1972), 493–536.

Norsworthy, J.R., H.J. Harper, and K. Kunze, "The Slowdown in Productivity Growth: Analysis of Some Contributing Factors," *Brookings Papers on Economic Activity*, no. 2 (1979), 387–421.

Olson, Mancur, "The Political Economics of Comparative Growth Rates," in Dennis Mueller, ed., *The Political Economy of Growth*. New Haven, CT: Yale University Press, 1983.

Olson, Mancur, *The Rise and Decline of Nations*. New Haven, CT: Yale University Press, 1982a.

Olson, Mancur, "Stagflation and the Political Economy of the Decline in Productivity," *American Economic Review*, 72 (May 1982b).

Perry, George, "Determinants of Wage Inflation around the World," *Brookings Papers on Economic Activity*, no. 2 (1975), 403–435.

Polanyi, Karl, *The Great Transformation*. Boston: Beacon Press, 1957.

Postan, Michael, *An Economic History of Western Europe 1945–64*. London: Methuen, 1967.

Pryor, Frederic L., "A Quasi-test of Olson's Hypothesis," in Dennis Mueller, ed., *The Political Economy of Growth*. New Haven, CT: Yale University Press, 1983, ch. 5.

Quinn, Robert P., and Graham L. Staines, *The 1977 Quality of Employment Survey*. Ann Arbor, MI: Institute for Social Research, 1977.

Rees, Albert, "On Interpreting Productivity Change," in S. Maital and N. Meltz, eds., *Lagging Productivity Growth*. Cambridge, MA: Ballinger, 1980, pp. 1–6.

Roberts, M.J., "An Evolutionary and Institutional View of the Behavior of Public and Private Companies," *American Economic Review*, 65, no. 2 (May 1975), 415–427.

Roberts, M.J. and J.S. Bluhm, *The Choices of Power: Utilities Face the Environmental Challenge.* Cambridge, MA: Harvard University Press, 1981.

Rostow, W.W., *The Stages of Economic Growth.* Cambridge: Cambridge University Press, 1960.

Rostow, W.W., "Leading Sectors and the Take-off," in W.W. Rostow, ed., *The Economics of Take-off into Sustained Growth.* London: Macmillan, 1964, pp. 1–21.

Rostow, W.W., "Technology and Unemployment in the Western World," *Challenge* (March/April 1983).

Rostow, W.W., *Why the Poor Get Richer and the Rich Slow Down.* London: Macmillan, 1980.

Sabel, Charles, and Michael Piore, *The Second Industrial Divide.* New York: Basic Books, 1984.

Sachs, Jeffrey, "Stabilization, Politics and the World Economy: Scope and Skepticism," *American Economic Review,* 72 (May 1982).

Samuelsson, Kurt, *Religion and Economic Action.* London: Heinemann, 1961.

Sautter, Christian, *Le Ralentissement de la Croissance au Japon et en France d'ici.* Paris: Ecole des Hautes Etudes en Sciences Sociales, Groupe d'Etudes et de Documentation sur le Japon Contemporain, 1978.

Schumpeter, Joseph A., *Business Cycles.* New York: McGraw-Hill, 1939, 2 vols.

Simon, H.A., "Theories of Decision-Making in Economics and Behavioral Science," *Surveys of Economic Theory,* vol. III. New York: St. Martin's, 1966, pp. 1–28.

Simon, H.A., and C.F. Bonini, "The Size Distribution of Business Firms," *American Economic Review,* 48 (September 1958), 607–617.

Simon, H.A., and Andrew C. Stedry, "Psychology and Economics," in G. Lindzey and E. Aronson, eds., *The Handbook of Social Psychology,* vol. IV. Reading, MA: Addison-Wesley, 1969, 269–314.

Solow, Robert, "Technical Change and the Aggregate Production Function," *Review of Economics and Statistics* 39 (1957), 312–320.

Spechler, Martin C., "Organization and Economic Behavior: An Interpretation of Recent Findings." *Weltwirtschaftliches Archiv,* 118, no. 2 (1982a), 366–380.

Spechler, Martin C., "Taste Variability Is Indisputable," *Forum for Social Economics* (Fall/Winter 1982b), 15–30.

Spechler, Martin C., "Quality in Soviet Industry." Mimeo, 1986.

Stigler, George, and James Kindahl, "Reply to Means," *American Economic Review* 63 (September 1973), 717–721.

Stone, Richard, "Whittling Away at the Residual: Some Thoughts on Denison's Growth Accounting," *Journal of Economic Literature,* XVIII (December 1980), 1539–1543.

Strumpel, Burkhard, "Economic Behavior and Economic Welfare: Models and Interdisciplinary Approaches," in B. Strumpel, J.N. Morgan, and E. Zahn, eds., *Human Behavior in Economic Affairs.* San Francisco: Jossey-Bass, 1972.

Strumpel, Burkhard, "The Role of Behavioral Research," in *The 1979 Founders Symposium-Institute for Social Research.* Ann Arbor, MI: Survey Research Center, 1980.

Thompson, E.P., *The Rise of the English Working Class.* New York: Vintage, 1963.

Turner, A.N., and P.R. Lawrence, *Industrial Jobs and the Worker: An Investigation of Response to Task Attributes.* Boston: Harvard Graduate School of Business Administration, Division of Research, 1965.

Unger, Roberto Mangabeira, *Knowledge and Politics.* New York: Free Press, 1975.

United Nations Economic Commission for Europe, *Economic Survey of Europe in 1983.*

U.S. Department of Labor, *Job Satisfaction: Is There a Trend?* Manpower Research Monograph No. 3. Washington, D.C., 1974.

van Duijn, J.J., *The Long Wave in Economic Life.* London: George Allen & Unwin, 1983.

van Gelderen, J. (J. Fedder), "Sprinvloed: beschouwingen over industrieele ontwikkeling en prijsbeweging," *De Nieuwe Tijd,* 18, (1913) pp. 253–277, 369–384, 445–464.

Veblen, Thorstein, *Imperial Germany and the Industrial Revolution*. New York: Macmillan, 1915.

Veblen, Thorstein, *The Theory of Business Enterprise*. New York: Scribner's. 1904.

Veblen, Thorstein, *The Theory of the Leisure Class*. New York: Scribner's, 1899.

Veblen, Thorstein, "Why Economics is Not an Evolutionary Science," *Quarterly Journal of Economics*, XII (July 1898). Reprinted in *Veblen on Marx, Race, Science and Economics*, New York: Capricorn, 1969, pp. 56–81.

Vroom, V.H., "Industrial Social Psychology," in G. Lindzey and E. Aronson, eds., *The Handbook of Social Psychology*. Reading, MA: Addison-Wesley, 1969, vol. V, pp. 196–268.

Weber, Max, *The Methodology of the Social Sciences*. New York: Free Press, 1949.

Weintraub, Sidney, *Our Stagflation Malaise*. Westport, CT: Quorum Books, 1981.

Weiss, L.M., "Reply to Means," *American Economic Review*, (September 1977), 610–620.

Weisskopf, Thomas, "The Current Economic Crisis in Historical Perspective," *Socialist Review* (May-June, 1981), 9–33.

Winter, Sidney G., "Satisfactory, Selection, and the Innovating Remnant," *Quarterly Journal of Economics* (May, 1971), 271.

Woodward, Joan, *Industrial Organization, Theory and Practice*. London: Oxford, 1963.

Work in America, Report of a Special Task Force to the Secretary of Health, Education, and Welfare. Cambridge, MA: MIT, n.d.

Zeitlin, M., "Corporate Ownership and Control: The Large Corporation and the Capitalist Class," *American Journal of Sociology*, 79, no. 5 (1974), 1073–1119.

THE CONTRIBUTION OF ANTHROPOLOGY TO ECONOMIC GROWTH AND DEVELOPMENT

Sebastian Green

I. INTRODUCTION

In 1981, there were 34 countries in the World Bank's low-income category in which the total output per person was less than $410 per annum. Apart from having low incomes, people in these countries also suffer low life expectancies, little education, and increasing population growth rates. Even if the somewhat optimistic economic growth rates forecast in the World Bank's "central case" (4.9 percent a year in low-income Asia and 3.3 percent in low-income Africa) are achieved, many African and Latin American countries will become poorer still for years to come.

While we know a fair amount about the technological and economic reasons for the low economic growth rates of the so-called less developed countries (LDCs), we know far less about the cultural and social factors that impinge upon the central goals of economic development. These comprise not only growth of output and productive capacity but also the alleviation of poverty through income redistribution and health, education, juridical, and other social reforms.

Following Schumacher (1973), it is widely recognized that high-tech, capital-intensive industries are right for countries with high capital/labor ratios and wrong for countries with reverse-type factor endowments. But we know relatively little about what types of educational system, what reforms to social and political institutions, and what changes to prevailing cultural values and beliefs are needed in order to enable sustained economic growth in LDCs. A key question in economic development concerns the reciprocal influence between cultural values and beliefs and a country's receptivity to internally and externally generated technological and economic changes. Importing Western cultural practices and institutions may be as inappropriate as importing capital-intensive technology.

II. ECONOMICS AND CULTURE

Although the pioneering work of Hoselitz, Prebisch, Myrdal, and others in the 1950s led to the realization that economic development cannot proceed without a profound social transformation (but not necessarily along Western lines), it is still true to say that the economist's model holds sway. The common view expressed in the early 1960s that the next few decades would bring the virtual disappearance of borderlines between economics, sociology, social psychology, anthropology, and political science has proved to be sadly misplaced. Theories of underdevelopment rely predominantly on economic analysis, stressing problems such as unequal exchange, deteriorating terms of trade, the introduction of inappropriate technology, and inadequate domestic returns/linkages from foreign investment. Moreover, the universal resort to planning as a guide to development has relied on, and indeed been justified by, economists' models of the imperfections in the market mechanism: structural rigidities in labor and capital markets and the existence of a subsistence economy characterized by production for use rather than exchange.

That culture or the ability of the people are important determinants of economic growth is perhaps recognized by economists, but their treatment of such factors appears to be almost universally disdainful. Reference to social conditions is often dragged in as an explanation of last resort. The advice of Epicurus, "Hoist sail, my dear boy, and steer clear of culture," explains the economist's reluctance to become embroiled in untidy social and political models (cf. Hicks and Redding, 1984).

Neoclassical economists concentrate mainly on quantitative relationships: the essence of their "mechanico descriptive" models is that they are reversible, that change is confined to quantity, and that the qualitative structure of the model is unaffected as quantities change within the limits set by the model (Georgescu-Roegen, 1975). Unless socioeconomic variables (or constraints) can be quantified, they must be relegated to the rejected sphere of *ceteris paribus*. That is perhaps the main reason economists are happier dealing with growth than with development and why it has taken so long to correct the assumption that increases in total output benefit the poor as well as the rich (the trickle-down effect). An appreciation of the historical importance of power relations and cultural values in determining how income is distributed in different countries would have alerted economists to the fact that "in most countries with low average incomes, even rapid growth does not benefit the poor very much, certainly not as much as the rich" (Roemer, 1981; p. 9).

III. THE ANTHROPOLOGICAL PERSPECTIVE

In contrast to the economist's preoccupation with quantifiable relationships, the anthropologist interested in development issues is concerned with the qualitative side of economic relationships. For example, assuming that economic growth occurs when there is a good fit between a country's internal resources and its external (partly enacted and partly given) environment, then just as this external environment is not confined to freewheeling economic markets but also includes intergovernmental, political, and social relations, so too the internal resources of a country are more than the aggregated, quantitative money value of land, labor, and capital.

Qualitative features such as cultural variation in entrepreneurial talent and leadership or differences in educational or religious systems directly affect economic growth, but economics does not concern itself with such matters. The importance of differences in social conditions on personal abilities was well demonstrated by David Morawetz in a 1980 World Bank Staff Working Paper on the clothing industry in Colombia. He argued that the 30- to 50-percent higher labor productivity in East Asia over Colombia was due to differences in the abilities of management at both top and middle levels and to cultural and social factors that affected worker identification with company goals; susceptibility to organization and discipline; protection against being fired; manual dexterity; and values about money, income, or duty being more salient than values about a relaxed, sociable work experience.

These are the sorts of issues that anthropologists look at in their studies of small-scale societies where the interrelationship between cultural, social, political, and economic forces constitutes the arena in which particular events are viewed. As Dalton (1971, p. 269) has pointed out, anthropologists rarely concentrate exclusively on economic matters, because "the *Gemeinschaft* structure of the small societies anthropologists study requires them to analyse kinship, religion, technology, ecology and polity, in order to say interesting things about economy."

For example, in countries where production is still organized through kin relations, or perhaps constrained by religious status systems as in the caste system in India, the introduction of factory labor is likely to bring about significant changes in family and other social structures. Conflict between traditional family or religious obligations and the requirements of the new order may slow down, or even curtail, the process of development. Where the domestic mode of production is widespread, we therefore require information on how and why individuals prefer, or are forced by prevailing values and beliefs to rely on, kinsmen for the production and internal and external distribution of output; how kin relations constrain or are affected by changes in the nature of production and distribution; how the domestic mode of production relates to ecology, technology, and production for exchange or for use just as much as we need quantitative measures of production, productive capacity, consumption, and income distribution.

A qualitative orientation leads anthropologists invariably to adopt a microfieldwork approach for their research and to prefer in-depth ethnographic descriptions to the normative analytic models of the economist. But the difficulty of generalizing from one-off case studies and the inherent dislike for normative analysis, have limited the usefulness of anthropology in making an effective contribution to development work. Anthropologists have been less concerned about promoting economic growth and development than understanding, say, the impact of economic changes such as innovation and diffusion, at the village level. This has led one writer to comment that:

> In keeping with their commitment to cultural diversity and relativity, anthropologists accepted the role of helping technicians and planners understand the uniqueness of each ethnic group's customs, perceptions and goals. This sustained the idea that the anthropologist's place is in the village and that his only contribution to development is to serve as interpreter in direct action programs (Hoben, 1982, p. 354).

Nevertheless, the insights of economic and applied anthropologists on the nature of socioeconomic activity at the village level do have analytic and policy implications for those involved in trying to promote economic growth and development. If, for example, behavioral differences among, say, poor farmers, are due to differences in status, education, or religion, then rural development programs may need to either change these behavioral factors or to bypass those individuals or groups who are likely to oppose the desired change. Despite the somewhat sinister overtones of social engineering and behavior modification, the anthropologist is well placed to recognize the likely behavioral resistance to externally imposed development initiatives and to suggest if, and how, such resistance can be overcome. At the same time, anthropologists have a role in highlighting and challenging ethnographic assumptions in development planning. In contrast to development economists who tend to be concerned with problems of national economic development and top-down, externally imposed growth initiatives, economic anthropologists focus on the situational factors (cultural, political, and geographic) that contextualize particular development initiatives and that may lead to an internally generated dynamic of growth and change—what Pitt (1975) and others have called development from below.

A particular problem area for economic development, one in which anthropologists have shown the importance of the cultural and institutional environment in people's choices, concerns the attitude of peasant farmers towards risk and uncertainty. It has been widely reported that farmers assess risk differently from the way it is assessed by development planners, not because of any intrinsic cognitive differences, but because of dufferent cultural circumstances leading to differences in risk preference. During the latter half of the 1970s, a major focus of inquiry for economic anthropoligists was the analysis of how (peasant) farmers in LDCs make choices about resource allocation. Most of these studies were positivist, focusing on understanding the uniqueness of each particular situation in terms of the customs, values, beliefs, perceptions, and goals of the key actors in any particular decision-making context.

In the next section, we consider some of the ideas in economic anthropology that hold relevance for a better understanding of the development process.

IV. ECONOMIC ANTHROPOLOGY: FORMALISM VERSUS SUBSTANTIVISM

Although the anthropological study of economic matters per se can be traced back at least five decades to the pioneering work of Malinowski in the 1930s and the works of Firth, Herskovitz, and Polanyi in the 1940s and 1950s, it was really the early 1960s that saw the crystallization of the subject as a specific theoretical subdiscipline within the broader field of social anthropology. The occasion was a debate over the relevance of economic concepts—such as price, investment, all-purpose money, maximization, and economizing—to subsistence economies, typically band, tribal, and peasant economies. While there are those who now argue that this debate was sterile, the implications of the debate still haunt current writers on economic anthropology and provide the intellectual backdrop for the subject.

The debate derived from the difficulty of fusing two distinct disciplines, anthropology and economics, into a composite subject. Walker (1942, p. 135) was one of the first writers to recognize the methodological conflict between the two subjects:

> It would appear that rather than ignorance being the reason why economists and anthropologists do not co-operate as well as is desirable, the cause is deeper, being a fundamentally different approach to the study of society. Anthropologists have focused on the community rather than the individual; they have used society as a system of mutually dependent elements and emphasised the influence of social forces on behaviour. The economist, on the other hand, derives the forms of economic behaviour from assumptions concerning man's original nature. He begins by considering how an isolated individual would dispose his resources and then assumes that the individual members of a social group behave in the same way.

While both schools of thought agreed that man's economic actions are dependent in part on the social fabric of society, the essence of the debate concerned the priority ascribed in resource-allocation decisions to, on the one hand, social (situational) factors and on the other hand to universal determinants of economic behavior. At the risk of caricaturing the conflicting viewpoints, they were as follows.

One school of thought, formalism, argued that social factors merely circumscribe and constrain economic behavior; they neither rule out choice nor determine economic behavior (see, for example, Le Clair, 1962, or the various contributions to Firth's ASA monograph, 1967). The formalists saw economic behavior as being determined by the interplay of personal self-interest and universal scarcity (wants greater than needs), which leads inexorably to a predilection for economizing and maximizing behavior. Moreover, this predilection is made meaningful because people are faced with real choices between alternative bundles of products which they can consume and resources which they can allocate. The formalists accepted that there are differences between types of economic systems, but regarded these as of degree rather than of kind (because of the universality of economizing). On this basis, they argued that the concepts and models of utilitarian microeconomics are applicable to all economies, for even if the market-exchange mechanism per se is absent, its functional equivalent is always in evidence. In its most extreme form, this orientation reduced the anthropological component of economics to no more than an occasional sleeping companion, rather than a fully fledged partner in a composite discipline.

An opposing view was provided by the substantivists under the lead of George Dalton who, following a line of argument initiated by the late Karl Polanyi, argued that there are fundamental differences between economies, such that the concepts of formal microeconomics are not universally relevant (see, for example, Dalton, 1969). Polanyi and Dalton rejected the formalist contention that because every society has an economy and because economy means economizing, therefore economizing (and maximizing) is a universal phenomenon. Instead they maintained that economy means material provisioning and that economizing is only one of a number of possible ways of dealing with the problem of resource allocation. Polanyi (1944), for example, saw primitive economy as an instituted process that is organized through social institutions such as kinship, marriage solemnities, age groups, secret societies, totemic associations, and public solemnities.

Following on from this view of economy, Polanyi and Dalton argued that in nonmarket economies, the interaction between the economic and other spheres of social life is so strong (Economy and society are embedded in each other [Dalton, 1971]) that it was inappropriate and misleading to apply formal economics (which presupposes an autonomous economic subsystem) to them. It was only in the case where the market-exchange principle separated out the economic from the social, by subordinating the substance of society itself to the laws of the market, that economy and economizing coincide.

In contrast to the formalist conception of economic rationality (personal self-interest and economizing), the substantivists invoked the notion of social rationality, and cultural adaptation within the constraint of survival. The two forms of rationality are quite different, as Sahlins (1969, p. 22) points out:

> The apparent identity between the formal rationality as economizing and the substantive rationality as adaptation is nevertheless misleading. Economizing is a strategy of the maximum, whereas adaptation is the achievement of a minimum.... Procedures of maximization, economizing, admit only one solution to any problem of resource allocation "the one best way." But survival is any way that works.

The substantivists distinguished among three types of transactional mode or patterns of integration for organizing resource allocation and income distribution in any economy: market exchange (the price mechanism), reciprocity (obligatory gift giving), and redistribution (obligatory transfer payments to central authority). Market exchange is fundamentally different from reciprocity and redistribution in that it separates out the economic sphere from the social, subjugating all economic activity to impersonal laws of supply and demand and the Weberian logic of economic rational action. Reciprocity and redistribution, however, are socioeconomic transactional modes that allow for the social, political, and cultural determination of economic action according to custom, rules, beliefs, and values on the one hand and the distribution of power on the other. It is important to stress the point that in those economies (or economic subsystems) where they predominate, socioeconomic transactional modes do not merely introduce social constraints into an otherwise predetermined pattern of economic motivation. Rather, they integrate culture into the basis of the economic decision-making process by internalizing the institutional framework of society into the psyche of economic man.

Our sympathy lies with the substantivists, notwithstanding their occasional tendency to reify culture as a determinant of economic action in non-market-oriented economies. While the formalists may be right to challenge the deterministic bias inherent in the substantivist orientation, they merely replace social determinism with economic determinism (the natural tendency of human beings) to "truck and barter"). In fact, the substantivist orientation allows a measure of voluntarism insofar as the prescriptive aspects of culture may be broad enough to allow a wide range of actual economic behavior. However, there is no reason to assume or even expect that consumers and producers in economies that are characterized by production for use or social exchange rather than production for market exchange will be free to choose one bundle of goods rather than another within the sole constraint of available purchasing power. In abstracting the individual out of his/her cultural milieu, the formalists have ignored the extent to which resource-allocation decisions are dependent on socioeconomic processes.

V. ECONOMIC ANTHROPOLOGY AND DEVELOPMENT

What is the relevance of all of this for economic development and growth? First, "primitive" economic organization exists in many parts of the world where nonmonetized production is a major source of income, where there is no all-purpose medium of exchange, where specialization and trade are weakly developed, and where technology is simple despite the skill with which natural resources are used. These economic communities exist in isolation from the commercialized sector of the economy, although economic development initiatives frequently impinge on and seek to end this isolation. The consequent interaction between primitive and market sectors poses special problems for the economist, who "although he is equipped to deal with the market sector, generally understands little of the primitive sector or how the two sectors interact" (Lockwood, 1971, p. 4).

Second, even in the market-integrated sector of LDCs there is economic exchange that is organized through socioeconomic transactional modes. No economy is organized exclusively by one pantransactionalist mode, and there is much to Marcel Mauss's (1954) point that the rules of reciprocity in primitive societies apply equally to our own society (see Green, 1976). The concepts of economic anthropology can shed light on the redistributive-, domestic-, and reciprocal-oriented subeconomies within LDCs and on the process of interaction with the market sector. In any development initiative that requires changes in the allocation of resources in LDCs it must first be determined whether the relevant resources are responsive to changes in market signals or whether they are organized through socioeconomic channels of allocation and distribution.

Third, market exchanges do not take place in a social vacuum. For example, a doctor treating a seriously ill patient would be castigated for charging a fee that reflected supply and demand at that point in time. "Do unto others as you would be done by them" is a powerful value constraining economic choices in our own culture and a value that derives from a socially based reciprocity. Similarly, in all cultures there are powerful values and beliefs that constrain the operation of market forces.

Fourth, brief mention must also be made of those anthropologists who have gone down a new path in search of a radical Marxist economic anthropology. We are unable to examine here the Marxist orientation, as it would take us beyond the bounds of economic anthropology into general theories of social and cultural change and the application of the concepts of historical materialism to primitive social formations. As John Taylor, reviewing E. Terray's book, *Marxism and Primitive Societies* (1972), points out: "Terray's work is not, therefore, anthropology; it is a theoretical analysis of primitive modes of production, which is part of a general theory of modes of production and their combinations."

We may note in passing that in recent years, Marxist anthropologists have become less interested in peasants who are exploited and for whom the only viable solution is revolution than in a study of how class interests emerge and are articulated in situations of economic change among rural peoples, and the relationships of local communities and institutions to the wider social and political context.

VI. GENERAL ANTHROPOLOGY AND DEVELOPMENT

Boundaries between the various subdisciplines within anthropology that deal with development issues are gradually disappearing. Apart from the traditional contribution of anthropology to the study of development in terms of providing the sorts of analytic frameworks discussed above and a vast body of informed ethnography on microdevelopment initiatives, anthropologists have in small number begun to work in the institutions that have both strategic and operational responsibility for fostering economic development within and across LDCs.

For example, the American Agency for International Development (AID) introduced a formal requirement for social soundness analysis in all projects in 1975, and the major part of such analysis has fallen to social anthropologists. Hoben (1982) has given an insider's review of the problems that anthropologists face in obtaining leverage for their analysis but concluded:

> Considerable progress was made in institutionalising the role of anthropologists in AID decision-making processes between 1976 and 1980. Requirements for social analysis have been broadened to cover all stages of policy program, and project design and development. The number of anthropologists working in the agency increased exponentially. There were, to be sure, many problems in the way anthropologists have been assigned to roles and tasks and with the way they have carried them out. Nevertheless, anthropologists working in AID have generally adapted their skills to the bureaucratic environment and have made a positive contribution to development assistance programs (p. 361).

The World Bank has also made limited use of professional anthropologists, mainly on a consultancy basis, for the appraisal of agricultural projects. Appreciation of the value of anthropological analysis led, in 1982, to the formal requirement that there be an anthropological analysis of all projects affecting people who are culturally, economically, socially, and politically marginal within their own native lands.

More generally though, anthropologists have a greater role to play than is at present the case, in the study of organizational behavior in international and local development agencies. Both the formulation and the implementation of development plans are parts of a behavioral process carried out by managers. As many studies of managerial behavior in industrialized market economies have shown, managerial action is often ruled by statuses, rituals, beliefs, values, and norms. The following tongue-in-cheek quotation from Graham Cleverley (1973, pp. 9–17) puts the case well:

> People are not rational. Nor are they susceptible to rational control systems. It is a truth that most management writers blindly ignore. Unfortunately, to ignore it is to ensure disaster. To base one's actions on what people ought to be like, rather than what they are like, is suicidal . . . for the manager, like the primitive tribesman, lives in a world of insecurity and fear, peopled with ill-understood forces. It is a world in which he is intensely vulnerable. And like the primitive tribesman, the manager is a human being. He will need to invent myths, to establish creeds, to cling to rituals, in the universal attempt to avoid the dark humanity of randomness and chance.

What passes for scientific analysis in development agencies is often no more than a "dressed-up" expression of personal or group vested interests. Development planning is as much an outcome of political, social, bureaucratic, and cognitive processes as it is a design of scientific specialists. Moreover, much research by management and organization theorists into decision making in organizations has shown that there are a whole host of simplifying procedures that people use when dealing with complex decisions. An evaluation of program formulation in development agencies requires an excursion beyond economics into the behavioral, social, and political factors underpinning the decision-making process (e.g., Lindblom, 1959; Quinn, 1978). While people working in development agencies are frequently aware of the limitations imposed by the cultures of the countries their programs are targeted at, these same people are frequently unaware of the way their own thinking is rooted in their own country or organizational culture. People bring their own intellectual baggage to bear on new problems, part of which has been conditioned by intrinsic cognitive limitations (Schwenk, 1984) and also by traditional or habitual ways of doing things: "the way we do things here." Because of the taken-for-granted nature of assumptions underpinning traditional ways of doing things, people are frequently unaware of their cultural blinkers or regard it a heresy to challenge them. This affects their ability to contemplate new options and new solutions. The anthropologist is, of course, no exception to this rule, but he or she is well placed to tease out these cultural assumptions and make them explicit.

Even when the formulation of development plans is conducted as a quasi-scientific exercise, it is generally agreed that implementation is a behavioral and administrative process. As Tolstoy put it in *War and Peace*, success in battles never depends on positions, orders, plans, or even numbers: a battle is won by people determined to win it. The most brilliant development plan is worse than useless if it cannot be implemented. In an excellent book on bureaucracy and the poor, Korten and Alfonso (1981, p. 2) write:

> Development programming in most developing countries is based on an organizational model which assumes that the major planning decisions will be made centrally, based on economic analyses made by highly trained technicians, resulting in project plans which will be implemented by subordinate agencies according to predetermined schedules and procedures.... The decisions are made by experts far removed from the people and their needs and implemented through structures intended to be more responsive to central direction than local reality.

A handful of anthropologists, along with some management specialists, have begun to suggest that there is a need for different kinds of bureaucratic organizations according to the specific cultural and institutional context of those who are the intended beneficiaries of development programs. However, much more work needs to be done in this area, and anthropologists have a greater role to play in the better management of development programs.

Of course, economic growth does not come about solely as the result of development programs. Much of the impetus for national growth and development in LDCs, as elsewhere, comes from the competitiveness of individual, domestic firms. In an era of increasing global competition, there is a growing need for firms to undergo strategic change in order that national competitiveness is not eroded by foreign competition. Our earlier remarks about the culturally biased, intellectual tunnel vision of development planners, apply equally to managers in business organizations. A key factor in improving business competitiveness and thereby enhancing national economic growth, is the ability of leaders, entrepreneurs and managers to create organization cultures which foster the development and implementation of competitive strategies. Culture is about shared webs of meaning (Geertz, 1975), and leadership is the management of these meanings and the shaping of interpretations. Entrepreneurs are not only the "creators of some of the more rational and tangible aspects of organizations such as structures and technologies but also as creators of symbols, ideologies, languages, beliefs, rituals and myths . . . " (Pettigrew, 1979, p. 574). Managers trying to accomplish strategic change in order to improve financial performance need to recognize that they are involved in a process of symbol manipulation wherein the need is to develop rituals which encourage innovation and change to improve competitive performance (see Trice and Beyer, 1984).

Anthropologists traditionally have been reluctant to compromise their academic purity by aiding in such social engineering, especially when it contributes to firm profitability. Nevertheless, a small but growing body of applied anthropology is emerging around the topic of corporate culture and firm performance (see, for example, Deal and Kennedy, 1982; Peters and Waterman, 1982; Davis, 1982). This is a welcome trend and one which has much to offer to micro and hence to macro economic growth.

To conclude, the comparative advantage of anthropologists lies in their methodological ability to expose the social and cultural aspects of economic activity wherever they occur, whether it be within organizations, within the market economy, or within those sectors of the economy that are integrated through reciprocity and redistribution.

REFERENCES

Cleverley, G., *Managers and Magic*. Harmondsworth: Penguin, 1973.
Dalton, G., *Economic Anthropology and Development*. New York: Basic Books, 1971.

Dalton, G., "Theoretical Issues in Economic Anthropology," *Current Anthropology*, 10 (February 1969).

Davis, S.M., "Transforming Organizations: The Key to Strategic Context," *Organizational Dynamics* (Winter 1982).

Deal, T. and A. Kennedy, *Corporate Culture: The Rites and Rituals of Corporate Life*. Reading, MA: Addison-Wesley, 1982.

Firth, R., *Themes in Economic Anthropology*, ASA6. London: Tavistock, 1967.

Geertz, C., *The Interpretation of Cultures*. Hutchinson, 1975.

Georgescu-Roegen, N., "Dynamic Models and Economic Growth," *World Development*, 11, nos. 11–12 (1975), 765–783.

Green, S., "The Scope and Information Requirements of Economic Anthropology," *International Social Science Journal*, XXVIII, no. 3 (1976).

Hicks, G., and S. Redding, "The Story of the East Asian Economic Miracle: Part One: Economic Theory Be Damned," *Euro Asian Business Review*, 2, no. 3 (1984).

Hoben, A., "Anthropologists and Development," *American Review of Anthropology*, 11 (1982), 349–375.

Korten, D., and F. Alfonso, eds., *Bureaucracy and the Poor: Closing the Gap*. Asian Institute of Management, 1981.

LeClair, E.E., Jr., "Economic Theory and Economic Anthropology," *American Anthropologist*, 64 (1962), 1179–1203.

Lindblom, C., "The Science of Muddling Through," *Public Administration Review*, (Spring 1959), 79–88.

Lockwood, B., *Samoan Village Economy*. Oxford: Oxford University Press, 1971.

Mauss, M., *The Gift*. Glencoe, IL: The Free Press, 1954.

Morawetz, D., *Twenty-five Years of Economic Development: 1950 to 1975*. New York: World Bank, 1977.

Morawetz, D., "Why the Emperor's New Clothes Are Not Made in Colombia." Working Paper, World Bank, 1980.

Peters, T. and R. Waterman, *In Search of Excellence: Lessons from America's Best Run Companies*. New York: Harper & Row, 1982.

Pettigrew, A., "On Studying Organizational Cultures," *Administrative Science Quarterly*, 24 (1979).

Pitt, D., ed., *Development from Below*. The Hague: Mouton, 1975.

Polanyi, K., *The Great Transformation*. New York: Rinehart, 1944.

Quinn, J.B., "Strategic Change: Logical Incrementalism," *Sloan Management Review*, (1978).

Roemer, S., *Cases in Economic Development*. Kent, England: Butterworths, 1981.

Sahlins, M., "Economic Anthropology and Anthropological Economics," *Social Science Information*, 8, no. 5 (1969), 13–33.

Schumacher, E., *Small Is Beautiful: Study of Economics As If People Mattered*. Bond and Briggs, 1983.

Schwenk, C., "Cognitive Simplification Processes in Strategic Decision-Making," *Strategic Management Journal*, 5 (1984).

Terray, E., *Marxism and Primitive Societies*. New York: Monthly Review Press, 1972.

Trice, R. and T. Beyer, "Studying Organizational Cultures Through Rites and Ceremonials," *Academy of Management Review*, 9, no. 4 (1984).

Walker, K.F., "The Study of Primitive Economics," *Oceania*, 13 (1942/3), 131–142.

COLLECTIVE VALUES
AND INVOLVEMENT IN
THE ECONOMY

Burkhard Strümpel and E. Yuchtman-Yaar

Since World War II Western democracies have witnessed two basic changes deeply affecting the economic situation of the common man: historically unprecedented increases in real income due to high growth in gross national product (GNP) and productivity in the wake of technological development, and the emergence of the welfare state, that is, the buildup of a considerable measure of economic security for the old, sick, and disabled. Affluence and economic security tend to cast doubt upon the general validity of two venerable propositions. The first is that the common man's economic behavior is ruled by survival needs, or at least by the overriding goal to increase his command over material resources. Second is that his political preferences and choices are dominated by his pocketbook, or economic self-interest.

With respect to the first proposition, it has been demonstrated that economic affluence and security provide the mass of consumers with discretion or latitude, allowing them to speed up or delay consumer investments (housing, automobiles, household appliances), thus making for aggregate changes in business activity (Katona, 1952). Beyond income allocation, these changes have opened up choices in the realm of labor-force participation. In many cultures, for example, married women going out to work has become an economically and socially accepted—but not prescribed—course of action. A similar measure of latitude has developed for early retirement or delayed entrance into the labor market

215

for students in institutions of higher learning (Katona, Strümpel, and Zahn, 1970).

To the extent that affluence prevails, the second proposition has been contested, the argument being that individual material concerns may have become less dominant while collective and/or nonmaterial goals such as protecting the environment, participation in decision making, social status, and "self-actualization"—all of which are not clearly related to command over material resources—may have increased in importance (Hirsch, 1976; Inglehart, 1977).

This perspective, to which could be added Daniel Bell's (1975) vision of a capitalist industrial economy whose very success undermines the motivation by which it was generated or Ezra Mishanks' skepticism of the capacity of late industrial societies to convert wealth into well-being, presents a challenge to behavioral economics to take up afresh the question of preferences, goals, and values. Do mass publics in affluent societies tend to dissociate themselves from the ethics and lifestyles of the industrial system of growth, to reduce their identification with the "official" economy based on monetarization, centralization, and division of labor?

I. VALUES IN BEHAVIORAL ECONOMICS

There is a whole range of psychological variables shaping economic behavior. We group these variables into two categories: preferences or values ("what people want"), and perceptions and expectations ("to what extent people think they will be able to achieve their goals"). Another group of psychological predispositions shaping economic action, namely, achievement orientation (widely known through the work of David McClelland and John W. Atkinson), contains elements of both. Closest to the economist's heart is the concept of expectations: If "tastes," or "preferences," are assumed to be the same over time, and if the "terms of trade" (i.e., the economic opportunities) do not change, then expectations (i.e., the subjective probability of success in reaching one's goals) should explain behavioral changes and ensuing aggregate trends. However, there are important analytical objectives in economics that require us to question the assumption commonplace among economists that tastes, preferences, or values do remain the same over time. Long-term behavioral changes, intercultural comparisons of behavior, and the microanalysis of subgroups of a population all require the consideration of what differences there may be and what changes may occur in people's tastes or values.

Different problems require different theoretical approaches. Katona's approach to explaining cyclical fluctuations in spending on consumer durables is intriguing in its simplicity and realism. Spending for consumer durables is, to a large extent, postponable and thus "discretionary." Its timing is subject to "waves of sentiment" that precede changing levels in buying activity. Sentiment expresses people's "willingness to buy" as measured by their expectations and perceptions of their economic status and future; of the present state of, and the outlook for, the national economy; and of prices and buying conditions for consumer goods. Willingness to buy transforms a larger or smaller proportion of disposable liquid or potentially liquid assets of the household ("ability to buy") into purchases.

Willingness to buy, strictly speaking, deals only with the distribution of purchases over time. When will people do whatever they desire to do anyway? The variable has been operationalized by George Katona purely as a cognitive phenomenon. People perceive the present, past, and future at one point in time as favorable, at another time as unfavorable. These variables clearly belong to the family of cognitive perceptions and expectations. The question then is, how can affective preferences, goals, or values be utilized in behavioral research?

Values are affective states formed long before the resultant behavior. They are relatively stable personality attributes, are generalized concepts, and are effective in several spheres of action. As Milton Rokeach (1970) says:

> While attitude and values are both widely assumed to be determinants of social behavior, value is a determinant of attitude as well as of behavior. If we further assume that a person possesses considerably fewer values than attitudes, then the value concept provides us with a more economical, analytical tool for describing and explaining similarities and differences between persons, groups, nations, and cultures.

A number of years ago, we adapted some of Rokeach's basic value categories to economic behavior. Two survey questions were developed for assessing people's goals and guiding principles in the economic sphere of their lives (Strümpel, 1976):

1. I would like you to tell me what you have found important in life. Would you please look at this card and tell me which of these is most important to *you* as a goal in *your* life, which comes next in importance, which is third, and so forth?

- A prosperous life (having a good income and being able to afford the "good" things in life)

- An important life (a life of achievement that brings me respect and recognition)
- A secure life (making certain that all basic needs and expenses are provided for)
- An exciting life (a stimulating, active life)

2.   Would you please look at this card and tell me which things on this list about a job (occupation) you would most prefer, which comes next, which is third, and so on?

- Income is steady
- Income is high
- There's no danger of being fired or unemployed
- Working hours are short
- Chances for advancement are good
- The work is important, gives feeling of accomplishment.

In a survey conducted in 1971 among American adults, the conservative value of "security" was widely acclaimed as most important (46 percent). A prosperous life was ranked first by the second largest number (30 percent), while "self-actualizing" (Maslow) values—an "important" or "exciting" life—were of prime importance to only 22 percent of the respondents. A prosperous life was most rarely selected by respondents with a college degree and by professionals (largely identical groups, of course). It was most frequently cited as the highest goal among such diverse groups as blacks and managerial workers. Conversely, images like "important" or "exciting life" held the greatest attraction for those who held college degrees (52 percent as against an average of only 17 percent at lower educational levels) and thus are largely group specific.

Clearly, characteristics such as income and age, which change continuously throughout one's lifetime, play a less important role in the prediction of values than such persistent subcultural affiliations as race and occupation. Thus goals or values may be expected to remain more stable than material aspirations—the latter, as we have seen, being related to income and age. However, as stable as values may be for any one individual, they still bear a close relationship to macrosocial dynamics. In other words, the frequency with which different values are expressed can be expected to change with societal trends like affluence, the educational revolution, changes in the role of blacks in society, or the substantial increase in the proportion of professional workers in the labor force. This fact points to the potential of using the concept of values as a variable for the analysis of medium- and long-term changes in economic behavior.

Two issues should be mentioned in summary fashion, since they are suggestive of the direction further research should take. Knowing about an individual's hierarchy of goals is not tantamount to knowing what behavior is deemed most suited to achieve the desired end. How does an individual perceive a particular action as affecting whatever goals he has? Furthermore, values or goals in life cannot be used to anticipate behavior without greater knowledge about people's perceptions of themselves. For instance, the goal or guiding principle of "a prosperous life" may have entirely different implications for a person who is or considers himself relatively well off than for one who is not or does not so consider himself. For the former, it may help to examine a conservative, defensive posture, identification with the status quo; for the latter it may make for a restless, active type of decision making in areas of work, career, and purchasing. Or a very strong preference for "work that is important, gives feeling of accomplishment" may activate one who is dissatisfied with his present job, as much as it may deactivate one who is satisfied. Finally and obviously, the same type of behavior may be the result of quite different values. For example, people may reduce their work load because of an increased dislike of work, an increased desire for leisure, or a decreased felt need for income. The list could be extended.

II. ECONOMIC MAN—ECONOMIC CITIZEN

There is precious little evidence on changes of economically relevant values over time. Ronald Inglehart (1977) has presented cross-national data suggesting the emergence of a postmaterialist set of societal value priorities (environmental protection, self-actualization, and participation in decision making) among younger people as opposed to a prevalence of defensive, "materialist" priorities (law and order, economic security, high income, fighting inflation) among older respondents. He identifies a particularly large generation gap in those countries that have experienced rapid increases in mass income. Inglehart interprets these findings by applying two hypotheses: a satiation hypothesis in the spirit of Maslow, Mishan, and F. Hirsch; and a socialization hypothesis about the process of goal formation within the life cycle. According to this hypothesis, values are formed early in life. For instance, the experience of rising affluence in later life tended to be less influential in shaping people's values and lifestyles than prosperity during childhood and adolescence.

The common thread of the two propositions presented above leads to the notion of *involvement*, meaning the extent to which the individual is active in and linked to the dominant economy in thought and action.

The choice of this term has been inspired by Albert O. Hirschman (1979), whose contributions have paid equal attention to people's private and public behavior. In a democratic, pluralist society mass publics are connected to the economy both as individual actors, that is, as workers and consumers, and as collective actors, that is, as voters or potential voters, as carriers of grass-root preferences, as media users, and as members or constituents of labor unions.

Involvement, then, can be defined and measured on two levels of individuals' reactions and orientations:

1. Preferred lifestyles of the "economic man," that is, the system of economically related values, cognitions, and behavioral predispositions that are directed toward a person's economic decisions and reactions: What are the rewards that have high priority for that person? How involved is he in his work, both quantitatively (actual and preferred working time) and qualitatively (identification with work, loyalty toward employer, etc.).

2. Orientations of the "economic citizen," that is, the system of values, cognitions, and predispositions that people hold with respect to the economy as a whole. How do people perceive the economy to function? What are their positions on important issues like distribution, employment policies, and protectionism? We expect the positions of economic citizens to be meaningfully related to the ensemble of their general political beliefs and values—those that are often loosely described as "right," "new left," and "old left."

In addition to taking into account the ideal type of the "involved" economic man and citizen, the typology that has guided our analytical work considers two positions that are at odds with all or some principles of the "official" economy. The first is an *instrumental* position related to the venerable "old left" position: growth and prospering business, yes, but conditionally, because the goal of distributional justice must be pursued even at the expense of business investment and growth. Hard work, yes, but it must be well paid. The second opposing view is the *fundamentalist* position identified with the "new left," or "green," opposition, which stems from the disapproval of virtually all the principles of the official economy mentioned above and, on the level of the economic citizen, from an equally basic disenchantment with such features of the modal worker's lifestyle as subordination to authority, monotony, and routine and a strict division between work and leisure. We call these three types the loyalist industrialist, the instrumental industrialist, and the postindustrialist, respectively.

1.   The *loyalist industrialist* views paid work and the accomplishments associated with it as inherent sources of rewards. Involvement in work is pervasive and tends to be unconditional. Neither pay nor working conditions, important as they may be to the person, are primary sources of variation of work commitment.

The basic theme of the *loyalist industrialist citizen* is that economic growth, productive investment, and technological progress are vital national goals and at the same time suitable strategies for overcoming the economic crisis. This outlook is likely to support such private business policies as tax incentives for productive investment or "tough" labor market and welfare policies—which are seen as strengthening this sector—even if they imply economic hardship for parts of the population.

2.   The *instrumental industrialist* views economic activity as an instrument for the attainment of material well-being. As long as economic gains are perceived as being contingent on individual performance, we would expect this type of person to be highly involved in the labor market, to conform to the roles of the employing organization, to be diligent, and to achieve high levels of performance.

The *instrumental industrialist citizen* tends to be critical toward the private sector. People of this type are largely concerned with a more egalitarian distribution of material resources. They support economic growth. However, they believe that the conflict between equity and efficiency, if it exists, should not be resolved at the expense of the former.

3.   *Postindustrialists*, unlike the other two types, are most prone to reducing their involvement in paid work, that is, their working time and involvement, if they can. To them, material gain does not have a high enough priority for its "extrinsic" rewards to inspire commitment to such work. They tend to set high standards for the "intrinsic" gratifications they wish to derive from work. These standards may be fulfilled by high-status occupations, but they are rarely met by the great majority of lower-status jobs. Therefore postindustrialists are likely to conform only grudgingly to the implicit roles and values of the advanced capitalist economy. Their involvement may shift to the nonwork sphere, which may absorb a large part of their activity: home production, do-it-yourself activity, or community work, for example.

Postindustrialist citizens would oppose the industrialist vision in both its productive and distributive variations. They would be critical of economic growth and of sophisticated, centralized labor-saving technology. Their concerns would center around what is customarily, albeit cursorily, described as "quality of life," including such considerations as protecting the social and physical environment, reducing centralization, and encouraging pluralism.

Pairing and juxtaposing the three types of economic people results in similarities and differences. The instrumental industrialist and the post-industrialist, for example, are similar in the negative sense: both attach conditions to their involvement in paid work. They differ, however, in that the advanced capitalist economy is better equipped to meet the conditions set by the instrumental industrialist than those set by the postindustrialist. Therefore the latter will be more likely to defect in thoughts and words, if not in deeds.

The confrontation between the three types of economic citizens produces different figurations of sociopolitical conflict. The conflict between the loyalist industrialist and the instrumental industrialist involves competition for valued material resources like income, low taxes, welfare disbursements, or public subsidies. The conflict between postindustrialism and both versions of industrialism has more to do with disagreement over the authority or legitimacy of the values themselves. While the persistent debate between the positions of growth and welfarism is more of the first type (production is good, but how should the product be allocated?), the more recent cleavage between industrial and postmaterialist positions is dominated by the controversy surrounding the very values by which modern economies are governed—growing production and rising productivity. The interesting—indeed, central—question regarding this typology is the relative frequency of the various combinations and the meaning of each combination for society.

III.   GERMANY AND ISRAEL—CONTRASTING PATTERNS OF INVOLVEMENT

Applying the above developed framework to two countries—West Germany and Israel—we propose that the different patterns of involvement are not purely idiosyncratic, that they are meaningfully related to structural characteristics, that is, the present and past economic experiences of a society. We consider the standing of both countries on two important "objective" dimensions, namely, welfare-state preponderance and average real income. We assume that where the welfare state is highly extended and perceived to be so by the public, "backlash" may be a likely reaction, particularly in times of stagnation, lackluster economic performance, and mismanaged public budgets. Where the level of mass income is high, the material satiation of the economic man and the postmaterial concerns of the economic citizen may be more prevalent than in a society with lower average income (Inglehart, 1977). From a structural point of view, Israel and Germany rank relatively high on the scale of welfare-state expendi-

Table 1. Personal Attitudes Toward Work

	Israel	Germany
Loyalist industrial	24%	11%
Instrumental industrial	59%	25%
Postindustrial	17%	59%
Missing/Don't know	——	5%
Total	100%	100%

*In answer to the question:

Here are four persons talking about work and why we work. Which of the four comes closest to what *you* think about work?

A. "Work is a business transaction. The more I get paid, the more I do: the less I get paid the less I do."

B. "I have a need to do the best I can regardless of pay."

C. "Working for a living is one of life's unpleasant necessities. I would not work if I didn't have to."

D. "I find my work interesting, but I don't let it interfere with the rest of my life."

The second alternative (B) indicates loyalist attitude, the first (A) represents instrumental attitude. The third and fourth (C and D) were combined as indicators of postindustrial attitude.

Source: International Survey on "Jobs in the 80's" Germany 1982, Israel 1982.

ture (Wilensky, 1976), but per capita GNP and average income levels are much higher in Germany.

These considerations lead us to expect systematic differences in the relative frequencies of the various types of economic men and economic citizens in the two countries. To the extent affluence breeds a certain measure of satiation with material goods, postindustrialists ought to be more frequent in the categories of both economic man and economic citizen. With regard to distributional conflict, affluence ought to have a tempering, moderating effect. Where there is less preoccupation with, and thus less severe competition for, material goods, backlash and blame attribution to marginal groups may be a less prevalent reaction of the economic citizen. Likewise, the instrumental industrialist's fundamental insistence on commensurate pay as a precondition for dedicated performance is bound to exacerbate conflict, because it implicitly repudiates needs as a criterion for distribution.

In contrast to German workers, who take their butter as well as their bread for granted, Israeli workers are still scrounging for the butter. We therefore anticipated a higher incidence of industrialists for Israel, both of the loyalist and the instrumental types, and a lower representation of postindustrialists than in Germany. This hypothesis extends to the realms of both the economic man and the economic citizen.

Evidence about the frame of mind of economic man in the two societies is provided in Tables 1 and 2. The frequency distributions in Table 1

Table 2. Commitment to Work*

	Israel				Germany			
	Total	Age			Total	Age		
		−29	37–54	55+		−29	30–54	55+
Fully committed	79%	75%	81%	71%	43%	32%	44%	58%
Not fully committed	18%	24%	16%	22%	40%	50%	39%	27%
Missing/Don't know	3%	1%	3%	7%	17%	19%	17%	15%
Total	100%	100%	100%	100%	100%	100%	100%	100%

*In answer to the question:
Here are two persons talking about their jobs.

A says: "I am fully committed to my work and often do more than I am required to do. My job is so important to me that I sacrifice a lot for it."

B says: "In my job I do what I am asked to do: Nobody can complain about me. But I don't see the point of extra exertions. After all, my job is not that important to me."

Which of the two says what you also tend to think, A or B?

Source: International Survey on "Jobs in the 80's" Germany 1982, Israel 1982.

indicate the respondents' first choices among four alternative approaches to work that correspond to our typology conceptually. Table 2 offers only two choices—the loyalist industrialist and the postindustrialist one.

Both tables make clear that the postindustrialist approach is much more widespread in Germany than in Israel. In Table 1, the most alienated respondents were added to the postindustrialist category; in Table 2 the category of "Missing/Don't know" seems to have attracted a large number of the most alienated respondents.

Another set of findings in relation to economic man is presented in Tables 3 and 4. The frequency distributions of Table 3 indicate preferences for investing more or less working time in relation to earnings. Willingness to work more hours in order to earn more money would be expected of instrumental-industrialists, whereas readiness to work less for less pay would be a more likely attitude among postindustrialists.

The findings in Table 3 reveal that the modal preference of Israelis and Germans is for the status quo; yet among those who opt for change, the disposition of Germans is more strongly for fewer working hours, with the Israelis being about equally divided between the two alternatives.

Table 4 deals with perceptions about the adequacy of manpower at the workplace. The answer may reflect actual workloads to a certain extent. Yet the relevance of this question for the typology of economic man stems from the assumption that a perceived shortage of workers is also an indicator of pressures felt at work. Such a reaction is expected more of the postindustrialist, who considers work a burden rather than

Table 3. Preferences for More or Less Working Time in Relation to Earnings

	Israel	Germany	
		1982*	*1968***
More working hours	12%	8%	40%
Same as now	74%	61%	54%
Less working hours	14%	27%	6%
Missing/Don't know	===	4%	===
Total	100%	100%	100%

*In answer to the question (1982):

  Is your present number of working hours what suits you best, or would you prefer longer or shorter working hours? We presume that payment would increase or decrease to a commensurate degree.

  A. Current weekly working hours okay.
  B. Longer weekly working hours better.
  C. Shorter weekly working hours better.
  D. Don't know.

**In answer to the question (1968):

  There are people who would prefer to work longer hours if they would be paid accordingly. Others would prefer to work fewer hours even if they earned less. How about you?

  A. Current weekly working hours okay.
  B. Longer weekly working hours better.
  C. Shorter weekly working hours better.
  D. Don't know.

Sources. International Survey on "Jobs in the 80's" Germany 1982, Israel 1982, Katone, Strümpel, and Zahn (1970, p. 221).

a rewarding activity. The figures presented in Table 4 tend to confirm the problematic relationship between many German workers and their work. While a significant minority (37 percent) of the German sample expressed a need for more workers, only 20 percent of the Israeli sample did so.

These results are consistent with our initial propositions regarding the prevalence of industrial versus postindustrial orientations. The industrial economic man clearly dominates the Israeli scene; in Germany there is a large measure of support for postindustrialist lifestyles, as expected. We now turn to empirical evidence concerning the economic citizen.

As a first step in the exploration of economic citizenship in Germany and Israel, we present in Table 5 respondents' evaluation of economic growth as good or bad. The frequency distributions of these evaluations show that the Israelis are practically unanimous in supporting the idea of growth, in contrast to a large minority of Germans who either have no clear position or disfavor this policy. The findings presented in Table 5 do not reveal the extent to which the advocacy of growth is motivated

Table 4. Perceived Adequacy of Manpower Size

	Israel*	Germany**
Need more workers	20%	37%
Just right	70%	54%
Need less workers	10%	4%
Missing/Don't know	—	5%
Total	100%	100%

*In answer to the question in Israel:
  Which of the following statements applies to your workplace?

  1. There is a shortage of workers in my workplace.
  2. The number of workers in my workplace is just right.
  3. There is a surplus of workers in my workplace.

**In answer to the question in Germany:
  How is it at your place of work: is there so much to do there that you actually would need more people, or do you think it would be unnecessary to have more employees?

  1. Yes, need more people.
  2. No, do not need more people.
  3. Don't know.

If answer to question in Germany is "No" or "Don't know":
At some places of work there are too many people employed so that at times there is nothing for them to do. How is it at your place of work? Are too many employed there, or wouldn't you say that?

  1. Yes, too many employed.
  2. No, not too many employed.
  3. Don't know.

Source: International Survey on "Jobs in the 80's" Germany 1982, Israel 1982.

by productive, distributive, or other concerns. Such information is provided, albeit indirectly, in Table 6. The percentages represent respondents' beliefs about the consequences that economic growth might have for distributional conflict (in Germany) and inequality (in Israel). The figures in Table 6 show that nearly identical proportions of Germans

Table 5. Attitudes Toward Economic Growth*

Economic Growth is:	Israel	Germany
Good	95%	60%
Bad	5%	10%
Don't know	——	30%
Total	100%	100%

*In answer to the question:
  On balance, do you think economic growth is good or bad?

Source: International Survey on "Jobs in the 80's" Germany 1982, Israel 1982.

Table 6. Consequences of Economic Growth

Economic Growth Has as a Consequence:

Israel*		Germany**	
More equality	15%	Social peace	42%
No change	46%	Don't know	20%
Less equality	39%	Social conflict	38%
Total	100%		100%

*In answer to the question in Israel:
Do you believe that as a result of economic growth the gap between the rich and the poor would increase, decrease, or stay the same?

1. Decrease
2. Increase
3. Stay the same

**In answer to the question in Germany:
Here are another two persons talking about economic growth.

E   says: "Additional economic growth could help avoid social strife, for the more that is produced, the bigger the pie that can be divided."

F   says: "I think that more economic growth will increase social strife, because people will then demand more and more, and their demands will increase faster than will the pie to be divided."

Which of the two persons do you agree with?

Source: International Survey on "Jobs in the 80's" Germany 1982, Israel 1989

and Israelis attribute negative results to economic growth (increased distributional conflict in Germany and more inequality in Israel; we assume inequality is viewed negatively by the large majority of Israelis). However, while a similar proportion of the respondents in Germany believe that growth would have positive effects (distributional peace), only a small minority of Israelis hold such a belief (more equality). Bearing in mind that about 95 percent of the Israelis support economic growth, as shown in Table 5, it seems safe to conclude that the materialistic attitude of the Israelis is oriented more to production than to distribution. They accept the undesirable distributional consequences of growth and consider them less important than the consequences for production. In contrast, many Germans take their concern over the distributional consequences of growth seriously enough to bring it into line with their general judgment about growth, which then becomes negative. Many of them do not accept growth at any price (e.g., at the price of making business richer and the poor poorer).

Table 7 exhibits the extent of support for or opposition to the unemployed when they are faced with the demand of either accepting available jobs or losing eligibility for unemployment benefits. A com-

Table 7.   Justified Requests of the Unemployed*

	Israel		Germany	
	Justified	*Unjustified*	*Justified*	*Unjustified*
Farther away from home	76%	24%	55%	45%
Less earning	62%	38%	48%	52%
Inconvenient working hours	74%	26%	61%	39%
Change of residence	38%	62%	26%	74%
Underutilization of skills	53%	47%	38%	62%
Worse working conditions	45%	55%	24%	76%
Temporary job	58%	42%	55%	45%
Vocational training	76%	24%	71%	29%

*Answers to the question:
  Which of the following is justified or unjustified to request of an unemployed person in order for
  him to accept a new job?

  1. That the job would be farther away from home than the previous job.
  2. That he would earn less than in the previous job.
  3. That the time schedule would be less convenient.
  4. That he would have to change his place of residence.
  5. That the job would require lower levels of skills and abilities than he possesses.
  6. That working conditions (pollution, noise, etc.) would be worse.
  7. That the job would be temporary.
  8. That the job would require vocational training.

Source: International Survey on "Jobs in the 80's" Germany 1982, Israel 1982.

parison between the Israeli and German attitudes reveals a consistent trend toward a "tougher" position by the Israelis; in fact, no single demand fails to get more approval from them. These results suggest again that the materialistic outlook in Israel is concerned more with production than with distribution.

Up to this point, our hypotheses about the effect of affluence and welfare-state preponderance on economic values, preferences, and priorities have dealt only with aggregate distributions of survey results for two societies. We have made no attempt so far—and will not do so in this paper—to empirically relate the dimension of the economic man to the dimension of the economic citizen through cross-section analysis. We will, however, present time-series evidence suggesting that German economic culture has indeed changed as affluence has increased, and that a "socialization effect" may be effecting this change, as reflected in an unusually large gap between an older, "loyalist" generation and a younger, "postindustrialist" generation. This evidence may be summarized as follows:

- "Which hours do you like best—the hours when you work or when you do not work—or do you like both?" The proportion of the

German working population opting for the second alternative, "When I do not work," has increased from 29 percent in 1962 to 38 percent in 1982 (unpublished data analyzed by Strümpel).

- The proportion of German adults describing themselves as "fully satisfied with their work" has diminished since the late 1960s (Figure 1), although the majority of workers have a relatively favorable opinion about recent changes in working conditions. Improved working conditions do not seem to be translated into satisfaction, as seemed to be the case up to the middle of the 1960s.
- Satisfaction with life generally, with income, and, on the behavioral level, with the rate of saving, appears to have increased during the last fifteen years. The apparent decline of satisfaction with work is the more startling (Figure 1).
- Preferences for shorter work hours (without commensurate reduction in pay) have dramatically increased since 1968 (Table 4). The number of workers expressing preferences for longer work hours has dwindled to a small minority. The age correlation of this variable has almost changed signs. In 1968, younger workers were more likely than older workers to desire longer work hours. In 1982, a relatively high proportion (31 percent) of younger workers (below 25 years) joined the highest age category (55 years and older) in their desire (30 percent) for shorter work hours, in comparison with only 23 percent of the age groups in between.
- The postindustrial response to the question eliciting the extent of job commitment is much more frequent among younger German workers than among older ones. No age correlation can be identified in Israel (Table 2).

IV. DISCUSSION

To what extent are values translated into preferences expressed in actual economic behavior? Preferences for involvement can only be translated into behavior contingent on prevailing constraints. Intervening constraints appear to be more powerful in the sphere of income acquisition than in the realm of income allocation. For instance, the full-time, 40-hour-a-week work schedule demanded of most able-bodied men and many women makes for the well-known disequilibrium between actual working time and time preferences.

While there are two million unemployed Germans, millions of full-time workers at given wage rates consider themselves to be overemployed. To the extent that preferences cannot be translated into actual

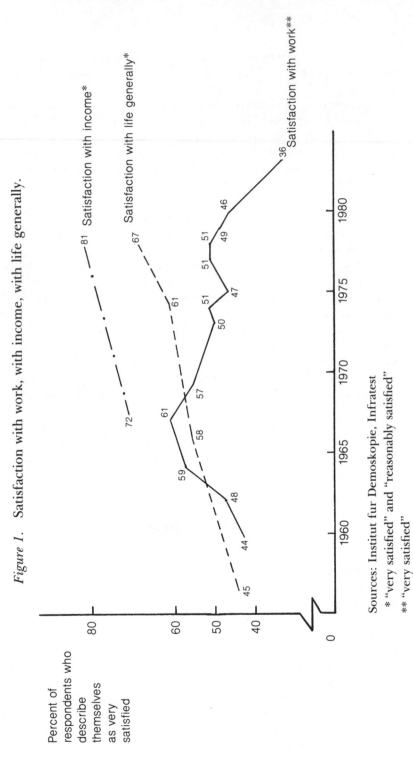

Figure 1. Satisfaction with work, with income, with life generally.

Percent of
respondents who
describe
themselves
as very
satisfied

Sources: Institut fur Demoskopie, Infratest
* "very satisfied" and "reasonably satisfied"
** "very satisfied"

choice, they become a liability for welfare, as expressed in felt well-being. The apparent decline in work satisfaction, contrasting with the apparent increase in satisfaction scores for income and life generally, is consistent with this interpretation.

The relationship between involvement and macroperformance may well be conditioned through a number of variables. First, business may be able to prevent the trend toward less involvement of the economic man from reaching the balance sheets. Rapid technological progress and demographic unemployment brought about by strong cohorts of people entering the labor force allow employers to hire workers least affected by the postindustrialist creed. Recent studies in German industry suggest that lifestyle and outward appearance, in addition to skill level and past work experience, have become very important criteria for deciding whom to hire (Hohn and Windolf, 1982). The key role of foreign workers (mainly Yugoslavs and Turks) in the German economy points in the same direction. The more one can supplant the most disappointed and alienated workers with machines or foreigners, the less the economy will be affected by hostile work attitudes.

Another question is raised by the trend toward satiation of the affluent German consumer and the effect this has on the industrial economy. Germans had already responded to affluence decades ago by voicing their desire to consolidate, to defend the status quo. Identified through an analysis of the 1960s (Katona, Strumpel, and Zahn, 1970), "enough is enough" proved to be one of the leitmotifs of German economic culture. Wage discipline was always popular. The common man often was satisfied with being granted compensation for inflation in the annual rounds of wage bargaining. For instance, during the years of reconstruction in the 1950s, unions were able to get away with wage contracts that remained far behind the increase in productivity.

There is evidence that Germany may be the most striking example of the transition to a postindustrial economic culture (Yankelovich et al., 1984). Nevertheless, the peculiar brand of "economic disarmament" encountered in that country, the reluctance to respond to opportunities for consumption and material gain, does not seem to have blocked economic growth. During the postwar boom, the German economy was able to compensate for a tight domestic labor market through the hiring of foreign workers, and for lagging consumer demand through a high export surplus. A similar explanation holds true today. Selective hiring practices, high demands on work effort on the job (albeit met grudgingly), labor-saving technology, and foreign workers—there is still a wide range of mechanisms that prevent the trend toward economic disarmament of parts of the German population from affecting the profits of Daimler-Benz or Siemens.

APPENDIX:
DATA DESCRIPTION

Israel

The Israeli sample for the data presented in Tables 1 through 4 consists of respondents who represent the adult Jewish population actively participating in the labor market (N = 965). The data for Tables 5 through 7 are based on a representative sample of the entire adult Jewish population (N = 1,722). In both samples all cases of missing data are omitted. Since the number of such cases per item is typically very small, their omission does not significantly affect the results.

Germany

The German sample for data from 1982 presented in Tables 1 through 4 consists of respondents who represent the adult German population (older than 16) actively participating in the labor market (N = 740). The data for Tables 5 through 7 are based on a representative sample of the entire adult German population (older than 16) (N = 1,166). In both samples all cases of missing data are included. The German sample from 1968 consists of 1,908 "heads of households," including those not participating in the labor force, representative of German households.

REFERENCES

Bell, D., "The Revolution of Rising Entitlements," *Fortune*, 91 (1975), 98–163.

Hirsch, F., *Social Limits to Growth*. Cambridge, MA: Harvard University Press, 1976.

Hirschman, A. O., *Shifting Involvements—Private Interest and Public Action*. Princeton, NJ: Princeton University Press, 1979.

Hirschman, A. O., *Exit, Voice, and Loyalty*. Cambridge, MA: Harvard University Press, 1973.

Hohn, H.-W., and P. Windolf, Arbeits Markt-chancen in der Krise. Frankfurt am Main: Campus, 1984.

Inglehart, R., *The Silent Revolution*. Princeton, NJ: Princeton University Press, 1977.

Katona, G., B. Strümpel, and E. Zahn, *Aspirations and Affluence*. New York: McGraw-Hill, 1970.

Rokeach, M., "A Theory of Organization and Change Within Value and Attitude Systems." Unpublished Manuscript, 1970.

Strümpel, B., *Economic Means for Human Needs*. Ann Arbor, MI: University of Michigan Press, 1976.

Wilensky, H., *The Welfare State and Equality: Structural and Ideological Roots of Public Expenditures*. Berkeley: University of California Press, 1976.

Yankelovich, D., H. Zetterberg, B. Strümpel, and M. Shanks, *The World at Work*. New York: Octagon, 1985.

PART IV

BEHAVIORAL FINANCE

INTRODUCTION TO PART IV:
BEHAVIORAL FINANCE

When psychology and economics disagree, to which should we entrust our souls? It all depends. For aggregate prediction of the stock market's outcomes in terms of efficiency, economics seems to be holding its own. For micro-micro description of investors' behavior, psychology offers much richer and more accurate scenarios. In the long run, moreover, psychology will have the upper hand. As long as positivist models with simplistic assumptions predict well, they survive; when their predictions go astray—what remains of the theory? With behavioral models, the realism of the assumptions renders the theory less predictive or more contingent in its predictions, but the durability and the longevity of better descriptive models is unquestionably superior to positivists' "whimsical" models. This part presents two complementary papers that lay the groundwork for the future development of a behavioral model of investment behavior.

The first paper, by four psychologists—Schachter, Hood, Andreassen, and Gerin—presents an alternative explanation of deviations from the random-walk model of stock-market prices. Instead of appealing to market imperfections (i.e., economic explanations) the authors use psychological variables. At times people seem to behave in a particular way simply because others are doing so. This is the essence of "mob" psychology, and it is attributed to aggregate psychological dependency. This state of aggregate dependency seems to exist differentially as the market

235

rises, falls, or stays stable for a long period of time, and can be used (ingeniously) to explain deviations from fully rational behavior of stock prices. The authors clearly admit the deviations they found were not sufficiently large to yield profit after transaction costs, but the deviations are there in the data, in remarkable persistence, and they require an explanation—an explanation pure economic theory provides only on an ad hoc basis. Perhaps the most important contribution of the authors will be to convince financial economists to broaden the search for explanations by relaxing the assumption of omniscient rationality (noting that such rationality on the part of the marginal investor is still insufficient to eliminate all deviations).

The second paper, this time by three economists—Maital, Filer, and Simon—finds results similar to those anticipated by Schachter et al. using simulation—a relatively neglected tool in economic research. Where the random-walk theorists (predecessors of the rational-expectations theorists) posit that only information matters in market outcomes, Maital, Filer, and Simon point to six other sources of influence on individuals' behavior in the market. Economic theorists claim that the market arbitrages away any profit possibility presented as a result of these idiosyncratic, or subjective, factors. The authors suggest that while students of markets accept efficient-market theory, practitioners in markets "know" otherwise. We are reminded of the days when physicists claimed that it was physically impossible for a pitcher to make a baseball curve, yet everyone who had ever played the game knew that it did.

The simulation presented by the authors provides us with insights regarding operant conditioning, illusory correlation, locus of control, and other psychological forces influencing investors' behavior. The tendency to own portfolios of different risk content is shown to be related to considerations other than rate of return. The simulation is presented in detail so that it can be replicated by the readers. Indeed, the next step needed is a simulation in which the participants buy and sell stocks from their portfolios to each other, instead of reacting to a sequence of given prices. Any bidders?

AGGREGATE VARIABLES IN PSYCHOLOGY AND ECONOMICS:
DEPENDENCE AND THE STOCK MARKET

Stanley Schachter, Donald C. Hood,

Paul B. Andreassen and William Gerin

The single number that summarizes the daily sales of department stores may seem of primary interest to merchants, but it is also the kind of number that can be of compelling interest to social scientists. It is an aggregate number—the resultant of the buying behavior and decisions of an entire population. Though aggregate numbers and variables are virtually the substance of much of economics, they are not the kind of variables that have been of particular interest to psychologists—essentially still absorbed in a search for laws and regularities of individual behavior, with no systematic attempt to extrapolate research findings and relationships on the individual level to aggregate or collective behavior.

I. EFFECTS OF AGGREGATE VARIABLES ON DEPARTMENT STORE SALES

To illustrate what is meant by a *psychological aggregate variable*, we return to that single number—department store sales. The magnitude of this number is affected by many obvious variables. It would be no surprise, for example, to learn that such sales are inversely related to precipitation. The fact of rain or snow is inescapable and the species is homogeneous enough in its dislike of getting wet and cold to make it less likely that people will go out shopping when it rains. Can we, though, expect similar results with less obvious variables? To learn, we examined the hypothesis that the magnitude of this number, department store sales, is, in part, a function of fear. To the extent that a population shares a degree of fear or anxiety sufficient to make numbers of this population somewhat reluctant to leave home, department store sales should suffer. To test this guess we related daily sales in one of Manhattan's largest department stores to the number of stories concerned with violence on the front page of *The New York Times* for each day over the period February 3, 1975 to December 31, 1977.

A.   *News Reports of Violence as an Aggregate Variable*

Violence was defined as any incident in which someone was deliberately killed, harmed, or threatened by other humans. Stories coded as violent include murders, kidnappings, rapes, race riots, assassination attempts and the like. We assume that if a story about violence makes the front page of the *Times*, it will be splashed over the city's other newspapers and highlighted on news broadcasts. In effect, most of the city's population know what happened at almost the same time. Obviously, there will be diversity of reaction to the news, but it is certainly reasonable to suggest that a goodly portion of this population will simultaneously grow a little uneasy and, if they can manage, find reasons to stay home. In short, most of seven million people are just a little reluctant to get out of the house. Since one can't buy anything at Gimbel's or Macy's without getting to mid-Manhattan, store sales just might go down on days when the morning papers have made much of some violent episode.

The relevant data are presented in Figure 1, which plots average daily sales in one major Manhattan department store on days when the *Times* featured none, one, or two or more stories about violence on the front page. Since there is a substantial day-of-the-week effect for both department store sales and violence, the data are presented separately for each day of the week. Clearly, there is a marked relationship between violence and sales. On all days of the week, sales are greatest on days with no violence. For five of the six days of the week, sales follow exactly the predicted sequence, being greatest on days of no violence and least on days with two or more violent incidents. Computing separately for each day the p value of the difference between 0, 1, and 2+ days and using Stouffer's method (Stouffer et al., 1949) of combining probabilities, $p = .02$ for the difference between 0 and 1 story days and $p < .001$ for the difference between 0 and 2+ days.

The data are clear-cut but, as with any correlation, causal interpre-

Figure 1. Relation between department store sales and stories about violence in *The New York Times*.

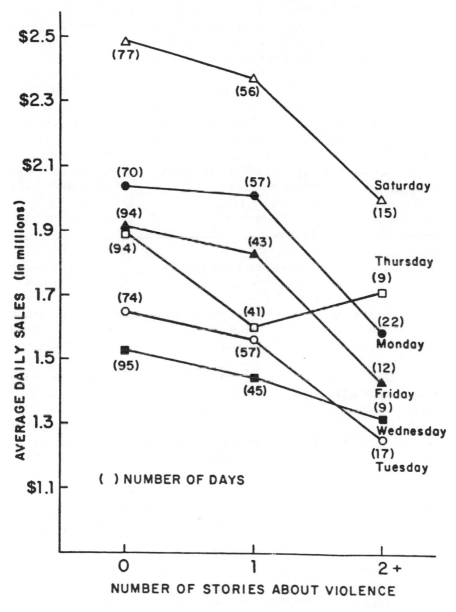

tation is ambiguous. Since the *Times* is a morning paper largely reporting events of the previous day, there is no possibility that decreasing sales could have caused violence, but there is always the possibility that some mediating variable is responsible for both effects. For example, during a heat wave, violence might increase and store sales simultaneously decrease, not because of community-wide fear but because of a natural reluctance to face the discomfort of the city's subways. Because of this we analytically controlled for possible effects of every plausible and semi-plausible mediating variable for which data were available. These include year, day of the week, season of the year, holidays, special sale days, and a variety of weather-related variables such as temperature, precipitation, and the like. None of these variables account for the relationship, and we are inclined to accept the interpretation that reports of violence in the mass media can create a community-wide state of uneasiness sufficient to affect department store sales.

Granting credibility to this interpretation, two facts are evident. First, the effect is not trivial. Gross sales decrease 6 percent on days when there is one story about violence on the front page and 19 percent when there are two or more such stories. Second, and the other side of the coin, even on days of multiple stories of violence, sales are still some 80 percent of sales on nonviolent days.

Effects of these magnitudes are probably typical of most aggregate variables. No matter how prominently stories of violence are featured in the mass media, undoubtedly some portion of the population is unaware of what has happened. Among those aware of the news, inevitably there will be a variety of reactions. Probably the most common response to such news will be some compound of uneasiness, despair, and melancholy sufficient to deter some unknown portion of the population thus affected from shopping. Undoubtedly, however, some people will be indifferent, and, following Brehm's (1966) notions of reactance, some may even be more likely to venture into the streets after news of violence than before. Granting the inevitability of a diversity of reaction, it does appear that for emotional reactions such as those engendered by news of violence, there can, within a population, be sufficient homogeneity to make a dent in a variable such as department store sales.

B.   *Aggregate Variables and the Stock Market*

Consider next another activity that, like shopping, can be treated in terms of aggregate variables—the stock market, an institution whose activity each day can also be summarized by numbers that are the resultant of the decisions and actions of hundreds of thousands of people. In essence, for each stock or, via indices such as the Standard & Poor's

Index, for the market as a whole, two numbers summarize the activities of this population—price (or price change) and the volume of sales.

II. EFFICIENT-MARKET THEORY

Of the staggering volume of research and theory devoted to these numbers, undoubtedly the dominant conceptual framework has been what is called the efficient-market theory. As Lorie and Hamilton (1973) describe the intellectual history of this theory, it was in good part designed to explain the apparent fact that successive daily price changes, like the path of a drunk wandering in a field, could best be described as a random walk; that is, from day to day, price changes are independent. This phenomenon has been studied extensively by Fama (1965a), Kendall (1953), Moore (1964) and many others, using data from a variety of markets. Using such techniques as runs tests and serial correlations, these investigators found that successive price changes were essentially random. What happened yesterday on the market had no systematic effect on what happened today or tomorrow.

The explanation that evolved for this phenomenon lay in the theory of market-making mechanisms called the efficient-market theory. This theory is superimposed on the familiar supply and demand model and presumes the following requirements for an efficient market. The marketplace proper must be characterized by:

a.   Full, rapid, and free information flow to all investors.
b.   Low transaction costs and continuous trading so that any investor can immediately act on a decision to buy or sell.

Of the investor, the efficient market theory requires that he or she be:

a.   A utility maximizer, that is, someone motivated to maximize profit.
b.   Rational; that is, within the limits of risk the individual is willing to assume, he or she is, given available information, capable of choosing the most effective way to maximize profit.

From this set of conditions it follows that the price of a stock adjusts to new information and is always the "proper" price, reflecting all relevant information. Given rational investors aware of and responsive to new information, it follows that any new information will immediately drive the price to its new proper level. An example will make clear why this should be so. Imagine that it is known with certainty that a stock valued at 10 today will be worth 15 two days hence. Obviously, this information will immediately move the price close to 15, for under the circumstances no rational person owning the stock will be willing to sell for less, nor would any rational person be willing to pay more.

People serve only one function in this schema. Driven by the profit motive, they are information processors who, according to a well-programmed set of rules, will, as an aggregate of interacting buyers and sellers, rapidly set the price most appropriate to the current state of information about a stock or commodity. Obviously, the assumptions about the rationality of the members of this aggregate are Utopian, and we doubt that even the most ardent champion of the efficient market theory would argue otherwise.[1] It is not our intention to argue the validity of these propositions but rather to examine how well this theory has worked and, where the data present problems for the theory, to suggest new variables and new ways of viewing the aggregate processes of the stock market.

III.   RANDOM-WALK HYPOTHESIS

We restrict our consideration to just one necessary consequence of the efficient market theory—successive changes in price are independent of one another and are best described as a random walk. This follows from the assertion that price, at any point in time, factors in all the known, relevant information. Price, then, is in static equilibrium and can change only if new information enters the system. By definition, new information is unpredictable; it is information that in no way has entered into determining the previous price. Since new information arrives randomly and unpredictably, it follows that today's price can have no systematic relationship to yesterday's price or to tomorrow's price. Therefore, daily price changes are independent of one another, and price movement will resemble a random walk.

Though there is much debate about the efficient market theory proper and about the conditions necessary for an efficient market, it is probably fair to say that there is agreement that a random walk accurately describes the pattern of successive price changes in the market. Indeed, texts (Samuelson, 1980), popularizations (Malkiel, 1973), and reviews of the theory (Lorie and Hamilton, 1973) tend to present the random walk as one of the basic facts of economics. And yet, even casual perusal of the research literature indicates that something is curiously awry. Though a random walk describes the movement of individual stocks on the New York Stock Exchange between 1957 and 1962 (Fama, 1965a), it is inadequate as a description of the movement of 54 individual stocks on the German stock exchange between 1968 and 1971 (Conrad and Jutt-ner, 1973) or of 51 stocks on the London exchange between 1968 and 1969 (Kemp and Reid, 1971). Though changes in the daily dollar rates of the German mark and the British pound are random, fluctuations in the Canadian dollar are not (Burt, Kaen, and Booth, 1977). Though the markets for wheat (Kendall, 1953), cotton (Kendall, 1953; Alexander, 1961) and, for some periods, cattle futures (Leuthold, 1972) appear at times to behave in a random fashion, the markets for corn, soybean futures (Stevenson and Bear, 1970), and, for some periods, cattle futures (Leuthold, 1972) distinctly do not. Rather than being a general description of market movement, the random-walk hypothesis appears adequate in some countries but not in others, for some periods of time but not for others, and for some commodities but not for others.

How does the efficient market theorist explain such failures of the random-walk hypothesis? In our reading, he attempts, nearly always, to identify some defect in the marketplace such as transaction costs, discontinuous trading, costs of information, price barriers and the like as possible explanations of these discrepancies. There is, however, an alternative. The investor is not quite the creature the economist hypothesizes. As well as the rational being of the economist's creation, the investor is also a social creature influenced as much by the opinions and actions of others as by his own assessment of hard economic facts. To illustrate this point, we examine the prices of the stock of the South Sea Company from 1711 to 1720.

A. Was the South Sea Bubble a Random Walk?

The South Sea Company was the villain of the colossal scam known as the South Sea Bubble—one of the genre of financial manias such as the Dutch tulip bulb craze and the Mississippi scheme, which are featured chapters in books such as Mackay's *Extraordinary Popular Delusions and the Madness of Crowds* (1841). The company was created in 1711 by an act of Parliament, as a means of coping with England's £9,000,000 of floating debt. It involved a scheme whereby the holders of government short-term obligations could, if they wished, exchange these various debt instruments for stock in the South Sea Company. The government granted the company an annuity of £558,678, which permitted the payment of 5 percent interest on the stock. As an inducement to investors, the company was granted a monopoly on England's trade to the South Seas—meaning the Spanish ports in South America. Since for much of the time between 1711 and 1720, England and Spain were either at war or in a state of chronic hostility, this monopoly was at best a chimera. Nevertheless the scheme aroused considerable interest, there was a large-scale exchange of government debt for stock, and over the course of this period various new offerings of stock in the South Sea Company met an enthusiastic reception from the speculators and investors of the time.

As an active trading enterprise, the company met with no particular success. Though an occasional ship was permitted to sail to Spanish ports, over the nine-year period under consideration the closest the company came to any meaningful business activity was in 1713 when Spain granted England and the company the Asiento, a contract to provide 4,800 slaves annually to the colonies of Spain. The slave trade was something of a shambles, and the company made little profit from the effort.

Throughout this period the price of the stock of the South Sea Company moved within a narrow range of the £100-a-share issuing price until January, 1720, when the company entered into a bidding war with the Bank of England for the privilege of assuming most of the national debt of England. It was a wild battle, and thanks to a grotesque combination of bribery and political machination, Parliament awarded the contract to the South Sea Company at the beginning of February, 1720. From that moment, all hell broke loose on Exchange Alley, and the stock rose from £128 a share on January 1, 1720, to £1,000 a share at the end of June, 1720. This was the peak, and from then on the price fell disastrously to £160 on December 24, 1720, when the books on the stock were closed for a 3-month period.

The average monthly prices of the stock over this entire time period and into 1723 are presented in Figure 2. These prices are culled from the financial section of *The Daily Courant*, a newspaper of the time. The daily prices for the period of speculative mania are presented in Figure 3 in which the uppermost curve plots the South Sea Company's stock price from January 21, 1720, the day the company's plan to take over the national debt was first presented to the House of Commons, until December 24, 1720, the day the books were closed.

To test this body of data for randomness, we follow the logic of Fama (1965a), who employed serial correlations and the runs test to demonstrate that the movement of stocks on the New York Stock Exchange from 1957 to 1962 resembled a random walk. The results of these analyses of South Sea Company stock prices are presented in Table 1, which compares the period from January 21, 1720, to December 24, 1720, the time of speculative mania and disaster, with the period from January 21, 1715, to December 24, 1715, a time which, according to historical sources (Carswell, 1960; Sperling, 1962), was uneventful.

It is evident that in 1720 the movement of this stock departed from a random walk. There are 29.1 percent fewer runs than would be expected by chance, and the serial correlation is +.27. Both figures are

Figure 2.   South Sea Company stock prices from 1713 to 1723.

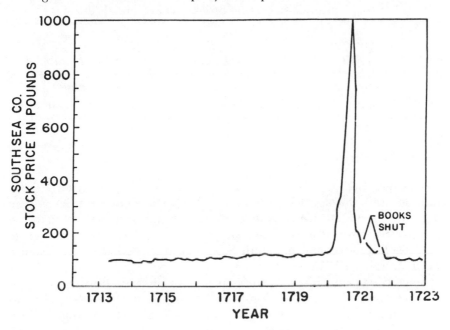

Figure 3.   Stock prices of the four companies listed in the
Daily Courant during 1720.

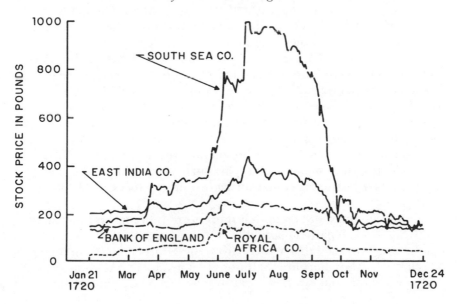

Table 1. Serial Correlations and Run Deviations in the Daily Price
of South Sea Company Stock in 1715 and 1720

Time Period	Serial Correlation	Runs (Deviation from Chance Expectations)
1715 (uneventful)	+.16**	−8.7%*
1720 (speculative mania)	+.27***	−29.1%***

*p < .05
**p = .01
***p < .001

significant, with p < .001. In 1715, the market also departed from a
random walk but at a more modest, though still significant, level. The
departure from chance runs in 1720 was significantly greater than the
comparable figure for 1715, at better than the .01 level of confidence.
Clearly, the movement of South Sea stock departed modestly from a
random walk in 1715, markedly in 1720.

Since the machinations of the South Sea Company during 1720, involving wholesale graft, stock manipulation, the spreading of false rumors, and the like, may represent an all-time high even of Anglo-Saxon
knavery, one may well feel that the movements of this particular stock
can hardly be considered an adequate test of the random walk hypothesis. We present, therefore, in Figure 3, data on the movement of all
the other stocks that were listed in the *Daily Courant*—the Bank of England, the East India Company, and the Royal Africa Company. It can
be seen that the four stocks did move in concert. They rose, peaked,
and declined at much the same time.

Table 2 presents the Pearson correlation coefficients of the average
daily prices of these four stocks, one to the other, over the January 21–
December 24 period in 1720 and for comparison in 1715. It is evident
that the prices of these four stocks were intercorrelated to an astonishing
degree during the hectic 1720 period and considerably less so during
the relatively tranquil year, 1715. Clearly, the movement of South Sea
stock during 1720 was not an idiosyncratic event. Whatever forces account for the movement of this particular stock, they were having a
similar, albeit less exaggerated, effect on other stocks available at the
time.

There is no question, then, that there were times when the course of
South Sea stock departed markedly from a random walk and times when
it at least approached this model. Given these facts one has an interpre-
tive choice—either there are conditions that make a market systematically
more or less random, or these are random events. Just as with Malkiel's

Table 2. Intercorrelations of Prices of Stocks Listed in the *Daily Courant* During 1715 and 1720

	1720		
	Bank of England	East India Company	Royal Africa Company
South Sea Company	.94	.96	.97
Bank of England		.90	.92
East India Company			.92

	1715		
	Bank of England	East India Company	Royal Africa Company
South Sea Company	.67	.91	.37
Bank of England		.58	.57
East India Company			.41

(1973) coin-tossing students, every now and then one must, just by chance, get a departure from randomness. Whenever, for example, over the course of time a market resembles that in Figure 2, whether or not one opts for randomness depends upon which portion of the curve one chooses to analyze. If, as we have done, one analyzes the curve for the 1720 period, chances are good that there will be long runs and that one will conclude nonrandomness. If one analyzes the curve for the 1715 period, chances are good but by no means certain that it will approach a random walk.

One might conclude, then, that the behavior of South Sea stock in 1720 was a chance event and that by analyzing just this portion of the curve we virtually guarantee a conclusion of nonrandomness. Given (a) the close tie-in between historical events and the stock price in 1720 and (b) the extraordinarily high correlations among the stocks on the London Exchange at the time, we believe this would be a difficult position to defend and prefer to believe that this was a period when individuals were not rational in the economist's sense. Following the historians (Carswell, 1960; Sperling, 1962), the Bubble was a time of hysteria, when all common sense, let alone rationality, was abandoned by the aggregate of investors. Isaac Newton, who lost £20,000 in his speculations on the company's stock, is reported to have said of the event, "I can calculate the motions of the heavenly bodies, but not the madness of people." A conservative banker of the time, after resisting for years, finally subscribed to shares after they had risen from 100 to 500 pounds a share, with the comment, "When the rest of the world are mad, we must imitate them in some measure." Such quotations put flesh on the hypothesis that events such as the South Sea Bubble are characterized not so much by rational information processing as by social contagion. At such times, people seem, in part, to buy or sell simply because others are doing so—a state of psychological dependence and social influence and influence-ability likely to lead to the autocorrelations and excessive runs that characterize a statistically dependent, nonrandom market; for if people are doing as others are doing, it is almost inevitable that they will do so sequentially.

Was the Bubble, then, pathologically interesting, an illustration of just how freakish and extreme events must become before the random walk is violated? Or, strictly in a probabilistic sense, was the Bubble the kind of unlikely event that sooner or later will occur in a random world? Whichever is the case, the efficient-market–random-walk view of market movement would certainly lead us to expect that such deviation from chance is a rare and unusual event. To learn just how rare, we examine a 22-year period on the New York Stock Exchange for randomness.

IV. RANDOM AND NONRANDOM WALKS ON THE NEW YORK STOCK EXCHANGE

We start with the period from October 1, 1957, to September 28, 1962, on the New York Stock Exchange (NYSE). This is the period that Fama (1965a) analyzed in his classic demonstration of the random nature of stock market movement. Trading during this time is compared with trading on the NYSE from January 1, 1972, to December 30,1979—a period chosen originally for only one reason: we started work on this problem in 1980 and simply looked at the immediately available data.

Fama's conclusions about the random nature of the market were based on analyses of serial correlations and runs in the daily changes in prices of each of the 30 stocks composing the Dow Jones index. We selected randomly ten of these stocks and on the left side of Table 3 present serial correlations, with a one-day lag, of daily price changes for each of these stocks during Fama's period, 1957 to 1962, and similar correlations for these same stocks during the more recent 1972 to 1979 period. There is no question that, by this indicator, the market did tend to behave randomly from 1957 to 1962, for only three of these ten correlations are significant at the .05 level of confidence. There is no question that by this same indicator the market did *not* move randomly between 1972 and 1979, for nine of the ten correlations during this period are significant at considerably better than the .01 level. For each of these ten stocks the correlation was higher in the period from 1972 to 1979 than

Table 3. Daily Serial Correlations and Percent Deviations of Obtained From Chance Runs for Ten Stocks on the NYSE

Stock	Daily Serial Correlations		Percent Deviation of Obtained Runs From Chance	
	10/57–9/62	1/72–12/79	10/57–9/62	1/72–12/79
Allied Chemical	.017	.108***	−4.3	−6.9***
AT&T	−.039	.078***	−4.6	−3.9*
DuPont	.013	.071**	−3.3	−5.0*
Exxon (Standard Oil of N.J.)	.008	.159***	−2.3	−11.6***
General Foods	.061*	.067**	−3.2	−5.2**
Goodyear	−.123*	.054*	+1.3	−2.0
International Harvester	−.017	.122***	+1.0	−5.0**
Proctor & Gamble	.099*	.104***	−3.8	−6.6***
Standard Oil (California)	.025	.153***	−0.7	−9.1***
U.S. Steel	.040	.108***	−1.7	−5.9**
Mean	.008	.108	−2.2	−6.1

*p < .05
**p < .01
***p < .001

it was in the period from 1957 to 1962—an event that, by the binomial test, could occur by chance only twice in 1,000 times.[2]

As for runs, the two right-hand columns of Table 4 present percent deviation from the expected number of runs in each of these stocks for the two time periods. During Fama's period, 1957 to 1962, the obtained number of runs does not depart from chance expectations for any of these stocks. In marked contrast, between 1972 and 1979, there are significantly fewer than chance runs for nine of these ten stocks. There are fewer runs in the 1972 to 1979 period than in the 1957 to 1962 period for nine of these ten stocks—a difference significant at the .02 level of confidence.

On the basis of serial correlations and runs, there appears to be no question that the price movement of a variety of stocks approximated a random walk during the years 1957 to1962 but departed significantly from the demands of a random-walk model during the years 1972 to 1979. The effects in this later period are not large, and it is important to note this fact explicitly in order not to exaggerate the magnitude of the departure from a random walk. The correlations, though significant, are small. Just as with department store sales, where even multiple violence had a significant but not huge effect, so whatever is responsible for these deviations from chance has a significant but not huge effect.

To provide some basis for later speculation about what could account

Table 4.   Daily Serial Correlations and Percent Deviations of Obtained
              From Chance Runs for Ten Stocks on the NYSE

	Daily Serial Correlations		Percent Deviation of Obtained Runs From Chance	
Stock	10/62–1/66	2/66–12/71	10/62–1/66	2/66–12/71
Allied Chemical	−.10**	+.09***	+2.8	−2.4
AT&T	−.11**	+.12***	+3.5	−5.8**
DuPont	−.07*	+.11***	+0.3	−6.3**
Exxon	+.09*	+.16***	−8.6**	−11.1***
General Foods	−.07*	+.14***	+1.6	−9.1***
Goodyear	−.04	+.06*	+2.3	−7.0***
International Harvester	+.17***	+.10***	−7.9**	−2.2
Proctor & Gamble	−.04	+.11***	+0.1	−5.6***
Standard Oil (Calif.)	−.00	+.11***	−0.8	−8.7***
U.S. Steel	−.01	+.03	+0.6	−0.8
Mean	−.02	+.10	−0.6	−5.9

*p < .05
**p < .01
***p < .001

for the differences in market behavior during these two time periods, we review characteristics of the market during the past 30-odd years. Many of the changes over these years are well known. Volume of activity increased steadily over this period; daily price variability increased over this time; institutional activity and market share increased markedly. These are changes, particularly institutional involvement, with major consequences that in later papers we shall explore. For the moment, we focus on what is probably the most dramatic change over this time period—changes in the price level of the market as a whole. Figure 4 plots the course of the Dow Jones industrial average from 1940 to 1980. It is obvious that Fama's period, 1957 to 1962, was part of a long, continuous up market that ended abruptly in 1966, when in January the Dow reached a high above 1,000 for the first time. During the previous 16 years, the Dow had climbed steadily from around 180 to the high of January 1966. There were, of course, perturbations, but the trend was distinctly up, with new highs occurring regularly.

In marked contrast, the market from 1966 to 1979 gives flatly no indications of any predominant trend. The Dow averaged about 880 throughout this period, with frequent, often violent, shifts in direction. The Dow high of January 1966 was not surpassed until January 1973, seven years later. Between January 1966 and December 1979, the Dow traded between 1,067 and 570, reaching the 1,000 mark only three times.

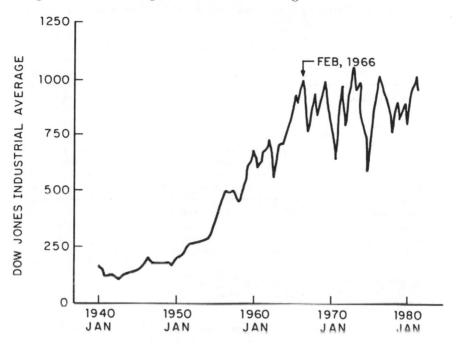

Figure 4. The Dow Jones Industrial Averages from 1940 to 1980.

Conceivably, the markedly different patterns of market activity during these two time periods may be associated with the fact that individual stocks between 1957 and 1962 did tend to move in a random fashion, while between 1972 and 1979 they did not. Before engaging in causal speculation, however, we note that the data plotted in Figure 4 suggest an independent test of the relationships already demonstrated. Fama's period of analysis ended in September 1962. At that time, the market took a brief sharp dip and then for three and a half years continued a climb almost uninterrupted by any marked deviations, from 536 on June 27, 1962, to 984 on January 31, 1966. In contrast, the market between January 1966 and December 1971 closely resembles the 1972–1979 period, during which, as we know, stocks did not behave randomly. Between 1966 and the end of 1971 there were numerous violent ups and downs and the market went nowhere, for the Dow was 976 on February 1, 1966, and 896 on December 31, 1971.

Table 4 presents the serial correlations and deviations from the expected number of runs for this sample of ten stocks during these two independent time periods. It is evident that the previous results have replicated exactly. For both serial correlations and runs, the market is random from 1962 to 1966 and nonrandom from 1966 to 1971.

Table 5. Serial Correlations and Percent Deviation of Obtained Runs From Chance of Various Indices of Market Behavior

Index	Serial Correlations		Significance of Differences
	Before 1/31/66	*After 1/31/66*	*(Before vs. After 1/66)*
Dow Jones Industrial	.09***	.21***	p < .001
S&P 500	.12***	.25***	p < .001
$(A - D)/(A + D)^{\dagger}$	.29***	.42***	p < .001

Index	Percent Deviation of Obtained Runs from Chance		Significance of Differences
	Before 1/31/66	*After 1/31/66*	*(Before vs. After 1/66)*
Dow Jones Industrial	− 10.5***	− 13.0***	n.s.
S&P 500	− 13.1***	− 17.5***	p = .10
$(A - D)/(A + D)^{\dagger}$	− 20.3***	− 29.0***	p < .01

*** = p < .001

$\dagger = \dfrac{\text{No. of stocks advancing} - \text{no. of stocks declining}}{\text{No. of stocks advancing} + \text{no. of stocks declining}}$

It is the case, then, that for the entire period from 1957 until the beginning of 1966, ten randomly selected Dow Jones stocks moved in a random fashion. From 1966 until the end of 1979, these same stocks moved in a significantly nonrandom, dependent pattern. Since these ten stocks are among the most prominent on the exchange, it is conceivable that they are not representative of the market as a whole during these times. We present, therefore, in Table 5, the serial correlations and deviations from expected numbers of runs of a variety of broader indices of market behavior for the time periods before and after the beginning of 1966. Four facts are evident:

1. For all indices, the magnitude of serial correlations and of deviation from chance runs are considerably greater than the means for these same measures of the ten individual stocks presented in Tables 3 and 4.
2. On all indices, both before and after February 1966, the movement of the market departs significantly from a random walk.
3. The more broadly based the index, the greater the departure from random expectations.
4. Finally, and central to present concerns, on all indices the departure from randomness is greater after February 1966 than before 1966.

The first two of these facts have been known since Kendall (1953) demonstrated that though the individual components of a market index may move in random fashion, the index itself may not. This fact is usually (Fama, 1965b) interpreted as due to infrequent trading; that is, there is a time lag between the last trade of the day of many individual securities and the market close. Presumably the positive autocorrelations of the indices are due to a tendency of such stocks to catch up to the market as a whole in the following day's trading.

Though this notion may, in part, explain the considerable magnitude of the effect for the broadly based indices that include large numbers of lightly traded stocks, it does seem a strained explanation of the fact that autocorrelations of the Dow Jones index are significantly greater than the autocorrelations of its component stocks—among the most heavily traded stocks on the exchange. An analysis of the trading times of the Dow Jones stocks on three recent trading days (April 13–15, 1982),[3] indicates that the final trade of the day for these 30 stocks was, on the average, made 3 minutes and 56 seconds before the market closed. Conceivably this minuscule lag might have an impact, but it does seem a remote possibility.

In any case, whether or not infrequent trading is the proper explanation of the fact that market indices are considerably less random than the individual components of the indices, this explanation cannot account for our central concern—the fact that, whether measured by indices or by individual stocks, the market after 1966 was considerably less random than it was between 1957 and 1966. Since the daily volume of trading between 1966 and 1979 was fourfold greater than it was between 1957 and 1966,[4] it is virtually inconceivable that infrequent trading can account for the fact of greater dependence and nonrandomness after 1966.

It does appear that for individual stocks and for various indices of general market activity, trading on the NYSE was significantly less random after 1966 than in the preceding nine years. Nonrandomness is not solely a property of lunatic events such as the South Sea Bubble, and the NYSE is one of a growing list of exchanges that at times moves randomly and at other, quite prolonged periods of time, distinctly does not. Any temptation to dismiss these findings as one more demonstration that a probabilistic model will, inevitably, manifest occasional departures from chance expectations must, it seems to us, be sharply tempered by the realization that Fama's (1965a) classic demonstration of the random walk is based on an analysis of four and a half years of data on price changes on the NYSE and that our demonstration of nonrandomness is based on almost 14 years of data on the same exchange.

These appear, then, to be solid facts. There are prolonged periods when price change on the market is independent from day to day and prolonged periods when the market demonstrates dependence, for yesterday's price change does, to some extent, predict today's price change. What are we to make of this? Is it possible to construct a coherent scheme that will allow us to understand when the market will or will not behave randomly? Can we impose a psychological formulation of dependence on the statistical fact of price dependence?

V.   SOME CAUSES AND CONSEQUENCES OF DEPENDENT AND INDEPENDENT MARKETS

The repeated demonstration that there are times when the market is nonrandom suggests that there is something more at work at such times than the classic price-setting mechanisms postulated by the efficient-market explanation of the random walk. Our attempts to understand the sources of nonrandomness in price change will be guided by one central assumption: the price of a stock is more than an objective, rationally determined number; it is an opinion, an aggregate opinion, the moment-to-moment resultant of the evaluation of the community of investors. As an opinion, stock price is subject to the same set of social pressures and cultural influences as any other opinion, such as the evaluation of a work of art, the preference for a political candidate, or the popularity and spread of a fad. The explicit recognition that price is a social fact will permit us to apply much of the research and theory of opinion formation and change to stock-market phenomena.

We turn first to the question of the fragility or vulnerability of an opinion. How likely is an opinion to change? As far as a stock goes, what conditions are likely to lead someone to reevaluate a stock enough to lead to a decision to buy or sell? Of the mélange of factors affecting such a decision, we shall consider a psychological dimension that has been called dependence (Schachter, 1951, 1959; Witkin, 1949)—which refers to the extent to which an individual relies on external sources such as the opinions and actions of others and relevant ephemeral daily events in forming and reappraising his or her own opinions.

There are, we suggest, two classes of variables that affect the degree of psychological dependence. First are purely situational variables—when circumstances change, when unexpected events occur, or when the individual is proven wrong (in the case of stocks, when the person is losing money), tendencies will arise to reevaluate opinions. Second are intrapersonal variables—people differ in the extent to which, situational variables held constant, they are dependent. For example, the more self-confident or expert a person is and the more reason that individual has to believe in his or her own opinions and abilities, the lower will be the vulnerability of his opinions to outside influences. This common-sense hypothesis is strongly supported by experiments such as that by Hochbaum (1954), which demonstrated that subjects who had experimentally been made to believe that they were particularly good at making certain kinds of judgements proved virtually invulnerable to social influence and group pressure in experimental situations where they were led to believe that their judgements differed from those of the group. In marked contrast, subjects who had been made to believe that they were not very good at making such judgements proved highly susceptible to influence. When faced with the fact that their judgements differed from those of other group members, the large majority of such subjects changed their opinions to conform to those of other group members. To the extent that such findings are generalized beyond this laboratory situation, one should anticipate that in any domain, those who are successful are likely to pursue their individual, idiosyncratic ways and, in that domain, will be relatively unaffected by outside opinions and events.

Given this framework, consider again the course of the stock prices plotted in Figure 4. To recapitulate: starting in mid–1949, the market began a remarkable 16-year upward climb, rising more than 600 percent by January 1966. There were, of course, perturbations and setbacks, but the overwhelming trend throughout this 16-year period was upward movement. January 1966 marked the end of this era, and from this time until 1980 the market was characterized by numerous violent short-term fluctuations but over the long term went nowhere for this period opened with the Dow at 980 and closed with the Dow below 900.

We suggest that these two prolonged and extraordinarily different periods of market activity may have had profoundly different effects on market participants. Men make markets, but markets, in turn, certainly make men. It is, at best, a minor insight to suggest that the fate of a person's investments can have a major impact on the mood, psyche, self-confidence, vulnerability to events and rumors, and resistance to change of the investor. Given the course of the market from 1950 to 1966, it was inevitable that, on the average, the investor made money—lots of money. Given what could be a 16-year history of repeated success, it seems reasonable to postulate a community of investors with a high degree of self-satisfaction, with little reason to shift tactics or opinions, and probably with relative invulnerability to the short-term effects of events in the world or the market. In effect, the market itself created a community of investors who resembled the consistently successful subjects in Hochbaum's (1954) experiment.

From February 1966 on, the market was a different affair. Obviously there were winners and losers throughout this later period, but on the whole, the average investor went nowhere. More importantly for present purposes, the fortunes of the average investor were buffeted like a boat in a storm, for throughout this period the market took numerous violent turns up and down. In short, there could be no real stability and no proven tactic. Things were in flux, and no hypothesis (other than that things were in flux) could prove correct for long. To make money virtually required accurately anticipating the opinions of others and correctly guessing the turn of the market. Since during this time investors were as often likely to be wrong as right and could have no firm bearing, it seems an intuitively sound guess that they may have been particularly vulnerable to the events of the time, the world, and the market itself.

Obviously there is no direct test of this speculative scenario, but this line of thought does have implications that allow us to examine some of the consequences of psychological dependence. For example, if it is correct that the pre-January 1966 market bred a community of psychologically independent investors with reason to be self-satisfied and set in their ways, it could be anticipated that pre–1966, investors as a whole would not only have been less influencible but would, as well, have been relatively insensitive to the events of the day. If, no matter what was going on in the world, the market tended in the long run to continue its upward drift, there was probably little reason to be much affected by daily happenings. If there is anything to this casual derivation, it should be anticipated that after 1966, an event with implications for the market would be more likely to stir investors to action than a comparable event before 1966. The effect of daily events on volume of trading should have been greater after January 1966 than before. In order to test this guess we examined the impact on volume of trading of events that seemed comparable whether they occurred before or after 1966—national elections and airline crashes.

VI. THE EFFECTS OF NATIONAL ELECTIONS ON TRADING ON THE NYSE

To evaluate the effect of elections on investment activity, we calculated the percentage change in the volume of shares traded on the NYSE from the day before Election Day to the day after. The data are presented in Table 6, where a comparison is made between elections during the pre- and post-1966 periods.

To increase the number of cases, the results of all presidential and interim elections from 1950 through 1982 are included. The market began its prolonged 16-year rise in 1949, peaked on January 30, 1966,

Table 6. The Effect of Elections on the Volume of Trading on the NYSE.

1950–1964				1966–1982			
Year	Presidential Candidates	Percent Change in Volume*	Percent Change in S&P Index**	Year	Presidential Candidates	Percent Change in Volume*	Percent Change in S&P Index**
1950	―――	−28.5	+1.31	1966	―――	+37.1	+0.81
1952	Eisenhower/Stevenson	+21.6	−0.28	1968	Nixon/Humphrey	+15.6	+0.16
1954		+50.8	+2.04	1970	―――	+28.6	+1.05
1956	Eisenhower/Stevenson	−6.4	−1.03	1972	Nixon/McGovern	+15.4	−0.55
1958	―――	+25.9	+0.91	1974		+87.8	+2.29
1960	Kennedy/Nixon	−2.5	+0.44	1976	Carter/Ford	+5.2	−1.14
1962		+6.0	+0.62	1978	―――	+15.2	−0.78
1964	Johnson/Goldwater	+6.5	0.00	1980	Reagan/Carter	+134.7	+1.77
				1982	―――	+86.3	+5.46
Mean		+9.2	+0.50	Mean		+47.3	+1.01
σ²			0.80	σ²			3.67

*No shares traded: $\dfrac{\text{Day after election} - \text{day before election}}{\text{Day before election}}$

**S&P Index: $\dfrac{\text{Day after election} - \text{day before election}}{\text{Day before election}}$

and from that time to 1982 persisted in a pattern of violent and jagged ups and downs.

It is evident that the market was far more responsive to elections after 1966, when trading on the first day after the election increased an average of 47.3 percent, than it was during the 1950–1964 period, when the average volume increase was only 9.2 percent (t = 2.2; p < .05).

As to stock prices, whether they went up or down depended, of course, on the particular election. However, this general line of speculation, as well as the demonstrated fact of volume differences, leads to the suspicion that price changes after 1966 should be more extreme than before 1966. Table 6 presents the percent change in the Standard and Poor's index from the day before to the day after each election. As demonstrated by the differences in variance, the variability of price change after 1966 is greater than before (F = 4.56; p < .05).

VII.   THE EFFECT OF AIRLINE CATASTROPHES ON TRADING

The "Disasters" section of the *World Almanac* for 1983 (pp. 749–750) lists all major aircraft accidents since 1937. As with elections, we analyzed the impact on the market of airline catastrophes occurring between 1950 and 1982 and compared the effect of airline catastrophes occurring before and after January 31, 1966. To be included in the analyses, (1) a crash had to occur on American soil; (2) it had to be reported on the front page of *The New York Times*; and (3) the airline and/or the aircraft manufacturer involved had to be listed on the NYSE, the American Stock Exchange, or the Over the Counter Exchange.

These criteria virtually guarantee that a considerable portion of the investment community would have been aware of the event and of the companies involved. To determine the impact of the incident on the market, we took the closing price and the volume of trading in shares of the companies involved on the day before the accident and compared them with averaged price and volume on the two days after the accident. We used the trading figures for the two days after the accident rather than those just for the first day after the event because there are good indications that for some of these stocks, trading was halted when the accident first became known. Since there is no way to learn how long trading was suspended, we based our analysis on combined first and second day (by which time trading would almost certainly have resumed) activity.

The effects of these catastrophes are presented in Table 7. The entries in the table are averaged volume and price relatives; that is, the change

Table 7. The Effects of Airline Catastrophes on Trading Volume and Prices of the Airline and Manufacturing Companies Involved

Time Period	N	Volume Relative	Price Relative		
			Range of Changes	Arithmatic Means	σ^2
1/50–1/66	9	+29.6%	−4.5 to + 0.4%	−1.48%	2.56
1/66–12/82	22	+166.7%	−10.9 to +11.4%	−0.90%	22.70
p value: pre- vs. post-1/66		< .05		n.s.	< .005

in volume and price of the stock involved is corrected for movement of the market as a whole. It is evident that aircraft catastrophes after January 30, 1966, had a far greater impact on trading volume than before 1966, for the volume after 1966 increased 167 percent, compared with only 29 percent after 1966. As to price, the data in the "Range of Change" column and the associated variance indicate that after 1966, when price went down, it went down drastically more than before 1966, and when for some perverse reason the price went up after an accident (as it does in 32 percent of the 31 cases), it went up far more after 1966 than before. It is clear that after January 1966 the market was far more responsive to events such as elections and catastrophes than it had been before that time.

Our speculation about the causes and consequences of variations in randomness in the movement of prices on the NYSE led to the demonstration that after 1966, when the market moved in a nonrandom fashion, it was more volatile and responsive to events such as elections and airline crashes than it had been before 1966, when the market tended to move randomly. We examine next the effects on investor behavior of events in the market itself, and we conduct a more fine-grained analysis of psychological dependence in the pre– and post–1966 markets.

VIII. RUNS AND TRADING VOLUME IN BULL AND BEAR MARKETS

The speculative psychological scenario designed to account for the differences in randomness of the pre– and post–1966 markets has undoubtedly created a somewhat monolithic impression—as if throughout these two periods the investment community was in a constant state either of psychological dependence or psychological independence. Obviously this is gross oversimplification. In any market, things change, new cir-

Table 8.   Characteristics of Bear, Bull, and Stable Markets
Before and After 1966

| | Number of Periods | Average Number of Trading Days per Period | Mean Dow Jones Index at: | | Average Daily Percent Change in Dow Index |
			Beginning of Period	End of Period	
			Before 1966*		
Bear	1	63	705	561	−0.32
Stable	3	200	603	593	−0.01
Bull	4	346	616	822	+0.11
			After 1966*		
Bear	5	189	955	743	−0.14
Stable	3	239	904	916	0.00
Bull	4	189	698	904	+0.17

*There were a total of 2,098 trading days in the pre-1966 period and 3,483 trading days in the post-1966 period.

cumstances arise, unanticipated events occur. At such times, it may be necessary to form new opinions or reevaluate old ones. When such is the case, dependence should increase and tendencies arise to gather information, talk things over, attend to the actions of others, and so on. The magnitude of such tendencies will depend, as suggested earlier, upon:

1.   the extent to which circumstances change and
2.   the extent to which one's opinion is proven incorrect or, in the case of the market, the amount of money one loses.

Given these conditions, to examine variability in psychological dependence within the pre– and post–66 markets requires the identification of intervals during which the course of the market changed markedly from the predominant trend of the time. To identify such intervals, bear, bull, and stable markets were selected by visual inspection of graphs of the monthly Dow Jones Industrial Average between 1957 and 1979. Three of the authors independently identified such periods, guided by the following criteria—for a minimum of three months the market was required to move fairly steadily in one direction with no sharp deviations from trend. The judges agreed in identifying 21 periods as bull, bear, or stable markets.[5] The characteristics of these periods are presented in Table 8. It is evident that a bear market was an extraordinarily rare event before 1966. The single bear market during this period lasted only 63 days, or 3.0 percent of the 2,098 trading days during this time. In addition, this pre–1966 bear was by far the most drastic of the entire 22 years, for the Dow Jones Index dropped an average of 0.32 percent per day as compared with an average 0.14 percent drop in the five post–1966 bear markets. Clearly, this pre–1966 bear market was, for this period, an exceedingly rare event during which the average investor, given the usual luck at the time, lost relatively huge amounts of money—precisely the circumstances that are hypothesized to lead to a community-wide increase in psychological dependence.

It is equally evident that bull markets were pretty much the way of the world before 1966, for two-thirds of all days during this time fell into periods categorized as bull. Given the conditions we have hypothesized will affect psychological dependence, it should follow from these facts that during the entire 22-year period under consideration, the investment community as an aggregate should have been maximally dependent during the pre–1966 bear period and minimally dependent during pre–1966 bull periods.

To test these guesses we examined the relationship of length of run to volume of trading during these periods. Our reasons for doing so follow. Possibly the most consequential information an investor can have is the knowledge of what other investors are doing and feeling. Obviously, the best aggregate index of these matters is the recent behavior of the market itself. If, for example, the market has been steadily falling, it is a reasonable inference that general investor sentiment is pessimistic. To the extent that a market has given indications of psychological dependence, such information should have observable consequences. As an example, consider the possible impact of down runs in psychologically dependent and independent markets. A down run is simply a sequence of days in which the market as a whole, as measured by the Dow, has decreased in price. It seems reasonable to suggest that such runs will be more strongly related to the volume of trading in psychologically dependent rather than independent markets. Either events and circumstances are such that they trigger a selling wave in a highly volatile and sensitive investment community, and/or in and of itself the knowledge that the market is falling triggers such an event. In either case, it could with reason be anticipated that the relationship of volume to length of run will be far stronger in the pre–1966 bear market than in post–1966 bear markets and weakest of all in pre–1966 bull markets.

The relevant data are presented in Figure 5, which compares the effects of down runs on volume during these three periods. To make up this figure, the NYSE volume on day n of a run was divided by the volume on the first day of the run. The logs of these ratios were averaged to yield the data plotted. The numbers in parentheses represent the number of indices averaged for each day of a run. Obviously, the number

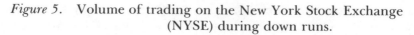

Figure 5.   Volume of trading on the New York Stock Exchange (NYSE) during down runs.

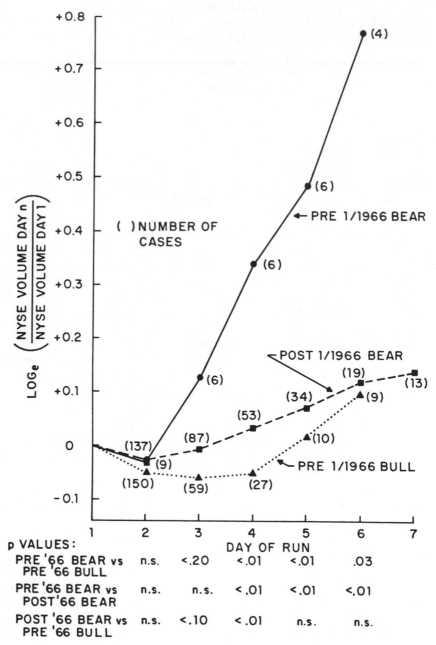

of cases decreases as the length of runs increases, for there are fewer long than short runs. These curves combine the data for all runs.[6] We note specifically that if the day of run is held constant, the mean indices for long runs are statistically indistinguishable from the indices of short runs—that is, the mean index for the third day of three-day runs, for example, is similar to the third-day mean of seven-day runs. Because of this, these curves combine the data of all runs of length two or greater in each of the periods.

It is clear in Figure 5 that, conforming to expectations, there is a dramatically stronger relationship between volume and length of run in the pre–1966 than in the post–1966 bear markets, and virtually no relationship at all in pre–1966 bull markets.

Turning next to up runs, that is, a succession of days in which the Dow Jones average increases, this same line of reasoning leads us to expect that the relationship between volume and length of run will be stronger in post–1966 bull markets than in pre–1966 bull markets.[7] The data are presented in Figure 6 and it is obvious that, again conforming to expectations, the volume-run length relationship is considerably stronger in post–1966 bull markets than in pre–1966 bulls.

These findings on volume and run length are one more indication that there are times when the market events of one day have no relationship to the market of the following day or days and the market is efficient. And there are times when this is distinctly not the case. By specifying the conditions that affect the degree of psychological dependence of the aggregate of investors (i.e., bull and bear periods in the pre– and post–1966 markets) we believe that we have specified some of the conditions and variables that affect the extent to which market movement describes a random walk.

IX. DISCUSSION

Let us review where we are and how we got there. The fact that there are times when the market is nonrandom suggests that at such times more is at work in determining price changes than the classical price-setting mechanisms hypothesized by the efficient-market explanation of the random walk. Our attempt to understand what "more is at work" is organized around the assumption that the price of a stock, as well as price changes, are to some extent matters of opinion. As such, stock prices should be vulnerable to the order of pressures that can affect any opinion. The hypothesis that an aggregate history of success and being correct will lead to stability of opinion and relative insensitivity to external events led to the well-supported expectation that after 1966, events such

Figure 6. Volume of trading on the New York Stock Exchange (NYSE) during up runs.

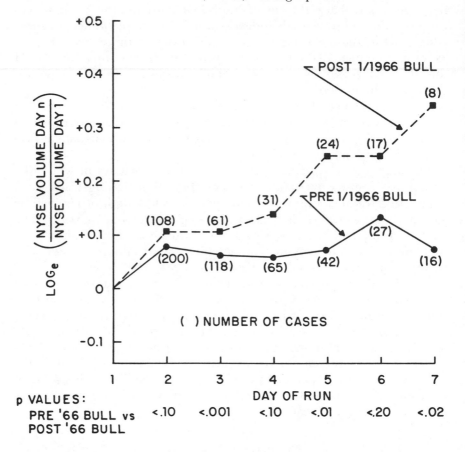

as elections and airline catastrophes would have a markedly greater effect on trading volume than before 1966. The hypothesis that new or changing circumstances as well as being proven wrong will result in increased psychological dependence led to a series of confirmed expectations on the differential relationship of volume of trading to run length in bull and bear markets before and after 1966.

Though such findings are consistent with this line of thought about opinions, we emphasize that we consider our attempt to derive psychological dependence from the changing characteristics of the market between 1957 and 1979 as little more than a speculative scenario—plausible but hardly proven. For the moment, we stress the facts—statistically dependent markets are associated with sensitivity to external events both in the world and in the market itself—facts that we relate to an aggregate or community-wide state of psychological dependence whatever its cause.

Returning to the efficient market theory, there is abundant evidence that markets are efficient in the sense that prices adjust quickly to new information and that no source of information can be consistently exploited to make profits abnormally greater than the costs of commissions. Deviations from a random walk are small even for events as extreme as the South Sea Bubble. However, though these deviations are small, they demand an explanation, for there are compelling reasons that they should not exist at all. Fama (1965a) argues that price changes should follow a random walk even if the marketplace contains inefficiencies, information arrives nonrandomly, and individuals differ in their assessment of prices; indeed, even if they differ in their ability to assess. His reason is simple. If information existed in a price series, someone would use it. Should a price deviate from its "proper" level, someone will take advantage of this fact to profit and, if that person's resources are sufficient, will, in the process, drive the price back to its proper level. Why, then, are there deviations? We have argued that the investor is a social creature as well as a rational utility maximizer. It is dependence on the opinions and actions of others that leads to deviations from a random walk and the competitive process described by Fama, which explains why such deviations are generally small.

Should the fact that deviations from a random walk are small, even in times of great psychological dependence, be taken as an indication that variables such as dependence play only a small part in the market process? As far as the random walk and what it reflects, obviously the answer is yes. As to other aspects of market behavior, we suggest that the explicit recognition that psychological variables other than rationality can have an impact on price and volume opens up realms of phenomena that, given the constrictions of existing market theory, have simply not been explored. The differences between the pre- and post–1966 markets as well as the differential relationships of volume to length of run in bull and bear markets are examples of such phenomena. In fact, the bull, bear, and stable market contexts seem almost classic settings for the examination of the impact of psychological aggregate variables. Bull and bear markets are dramatic events. Much as with the department store sales–reports of violence relationship, there is a community involved—in this case the aggregate of investors—whose members can be expected to react with sufficient homogeneity to lead to ordered relationships in a variety of domains. Since making money is gratifying and titillating and stimulates the juices, it requires no particular acumen to suppose that during a bull market, when for months on end the market is steadily rising, the aggregate of investors is excited, involved, eagerly reading the financial columns of the paper, and so on.

In depressing contrast, a bear market is a debilitating experience. Unless the investor has had the prescience to sell out early or is the kind of sophisticate with the guts to sell short or to fool with puts and calls, there is nothing he or she can do right, and day after day, month after month, the investor loses more and more money. Again, it requires little acumen to postulate a community of depressed, insecure, unstable investors.

Finally, in stable markets, for month after month nothing much happens. With trivial fluctuations, prices of most stocks remain, for a prolonged period, at much the same level. It is comfortable but slightly disappointing and certainly dull.

Given this picture of the aggregate states of mind that we suggest are characteristic of bull, bear, and stable markets, let us consider the relationship of volume of sales to day of the week in these three kinds of market. It is well known (Osborne, 1962) that the volume of trading on the stock market is lowest on Mondays and Fridays and heaviest in the middle of the week. The explanation of this pattern assuredly is banal. Anyone who has recovered from or prepared for the miscellaneous joys and pains of the weekend could predict such a result. Consider, though, the ways in which one might spend one's weekend during bull, bear, and stable markets. If the investor is depressed about or bored by the market, chances are good that that person will avoid thinking, reading, or talking about the market. If, on the other hand, the investor is exhilarated and excited by a rising market, it seems likely that he or she will be absorbed in the market, weekend or not.

Granting plausibility to this scenario, it could reasonably be anticipated that the relationship of volume of trading to day of the week will be weaker in bull than in either bear or stable markets. On the assumption that thinking and talking are goads to action, it should be expected that the Monday doldrums will be more characteristic of bear and stable markets than of bull markets. To check on this guess, we simply calculated separately for each week[8] of the 22-year period from October 1, 1957, to December 31, 1979, the ratio of sales on the NYSE for each day of the week to the volume of sales on the Monday of that week. The mean data are presented in Table 9, which compares bear, bull, and stable markets during this 22-year period. Obviously, the lower the number, the less the differential between Monday and the other days of the week. It is clear from the table that the day of the week has significantly less effect on volume of sales in bull markets than in either bear or stable markets.

We turn, finally, to the effect of tips or the recommendations of fi-

Table 9.   The Relationship of Day of Week to Volume of Trading on
the NYSE Between 1957 and 1979

Type of Market	Number of Weeks	$\dfrac{Vol\ Day\ n}{Vol\ Monday}$				
		Mon.	Tues.	Wed.	Thurs.	Fri.
Stable	195	1.00	1.125	1.156	1.121	1.082
Bull	369	1.00	1.046	1.085	1.084	1.046
Bear	171	1.00	1.110	1.132	1.150	1.106
p value:						
Bull vs. stable		——	< .001	< .001	< .05	< .10
Bull vs. bear		——	< .001	< .01	.001	.01
Bear vs. stable		——	n.s.	n.s.	n.s.	n.s.

nancial experts. Tips have, in fact, been an embarrassment to efficient market theory, for if price reflects all available information, the recommendation of an analyst or a columnist (which is usually based not on new information but on evaluation of widely available information) should have no impact on price. Tips do, however, have an effect even when published as secondhand research in the *Wall Street Journal,* and much of the research literature (Baker and Lehman, 1978; Lloyd-Davies and Canes, 1978; Low, 1982) has been concerned with attempting to explain away this effect. From our point of view, however, a tip or a recommendation to buy or sell is simply one more factor that affects an opinion. As such, it may or may not have an effect, depending on such variables as the status of the tipster and the receptivity of those who read or hear the recommendation.

Given our characterization of bull, bear, and stable periods we should, for example, anticipate that during bear periods the average investor, if he or she does not pull out of the market totally, should be particularly vulnerable to tips and to expert opinion. For months the investor has been steadily wrong and steadily losing money, conditions we hypothesized earlier should lead to psychological dependence. Compared with the situation during stable periods, when for month after month nothing much changes, it might be expected that buy-sell recommendations would have a substantial impact in bear markets. The effect of tips during bull markets, at least after January 1, 1966, are considerably more complex. Though in the aggregate the investor is certainly making money, a bull market is, after January 1, 1966, a relatively rare event and, therefore, we would assume an exciting one. Though the fact that he or she is making money should certainly make a cockier and less dependent investor, the excitement of the event may also make the person

Table 10.   The Effects of "Heard on the Street" Recommendations
on Stock Price

| Type of Market | N | Buy Recommendation, Residual Percent Price Change | |
		Day of Recommendation	Day after Recommendation
Stable	277	+0.8	+0.9
Bull	91	+1.4	+2.2
Bear	189	+1.2	+1.4
p value			
Bull vs. stable		< .02	< .001
Bear vs. stable		< .02	< .05
Bull vs. bear		n.s.	< .05

| Type of Market | N | Sell Recommendation, Residual Percent Price Change | |
		Day of Recommendation	Day after Recommendation
Stable	43	−2.2	−2.5
Bull	17	−2.1	−3.2
Bear	53	−4.7	−5.1
p value			
Bull vs. stable		n.s.	n.s.
Bear vs. stable		< .001	< .001
Bull vs. bear		< .01	< .01

a foolhardy one prone to take tips—like the poker player who, well ahead in the game, is prone to abandon a conservative strategy. All this is sheer guesswork obviously, so let us turn to the data.

To examine these hypotheses-guesses, we examined the impact of buy and sell recommendations of NYSE stocks in a daily column of the *Wall Street Journal* called "Heard on the Street" in all bear, bull, and stable markets (see Table 10) that fell between January 2, 1973, and December 31, 1979.[9] This column presents the opinions of well-known stock analysts, fund managers, and the like. There is hemming and hawing in the column, but it does frequently come up with clear, unequivocal recommendations to buy or sell a particular stock. To be coded as a buy or sell recommendation we required that:

1.   The recommending firm or individual was mentioned by name rather than, for example, by "some analysts favor"
2.   There had to be an unequivocal action verb in the column, such

as "recommended purchase" or "said he would get out of" rather than such comments as "was favorably disposed toward"
3. If several opinions were presented, they had to be unanimous.

The data are presented in Table 10. To partial out the movement of the market as a whole we used Lloyd-Davies and Canes' (1978) adaptation of the market residual technique devised by Fama, Fisher, Jensen, and Roll (1969). In effect, the numbers in the table are the percent change in the recommended stock's price, corrected for movement of the market as a whole, on the day of and the day after publication of the recommendation.

We note first that for both days and in all markets, the column has an effect. Buy recommendations drive the price up and sell recommendations drive it down, and for every entry in the table the difference from zero percent change is significant at, at least, the .001 level of confidence. Turning to the effects of type of market, it is clear that, as compared with stable markets, a recommendation to buy or sell has a major effect in bear markets. Obviously, the aggregate of investors is far more likely to take the advice of experts during bear markets than during stable markets. Comparing bull and stable markets, a buy recommendation has a far stronger impact on price during bull than during stable markets, whereas there is no such effect for a sell recommendation. Just why this discrepancy is so, we leave for once to the reader's speculation rather than ours and note simply that for the period analyzed there appears to be no question that, on the whole, the effects of stock recommendations are consistent with the common-sense speculations associated with our use of psychological aggregate variables.

For now, more than enough data have been presented to make a point that long ago should have been integrated into economic and financial theory. After all, as Kenneth Arrow (1982) reminds us, "Keynes argued long ago, the value of a security depends in good measure on other peoples' opinions."

ACKNOWLEDGMENTS

The Sloan Foundation supported this work with a grant to explore psychological dimensions of economic theory. Leon Festinger, Stanley Heshka, Steven Ross, Tom Schelling, and James Scott read early versions of this manuscript. Some of them liked what they read and others did not, but they were all generous with their time and ideas. We are grateful to William Apple, Yoav Ganzach, Neil

Grunberg, Steven Reich, Michael Rennert, and Barry Whittle, who have worked on various aspects of the studies described.

NOTES

1.   Undoubtedly the most difficult assumption to accept is that all members of the set of investors are, in the economist's sense, rational. However, Fama (1965a; 1970) has convincingly argued that if only a subset of investors is rational and blessed with sufficient resources, the market will as assuredly be efficient as if the population of investors is rational.

2.   This may overstate the statistical significance of this difference slightly, since the prices of these ten stocks are not totally independent of each other. The average inter-correlation among these stocks is +.24 before 1966 and +.31 afterward, accounting for approximately 6 percent and 9 percent of the variance, respectively.

3.   These data were obtained from the *New York Stock Sales Publication*, published by Francis Emory Fitch, Inc., which since July 1968 has listed every stock transaction on the NYSE and the exact time at which each occurred.

4.   Though it would have been ideal to calculate the time of last trade of the day for the 30 Dow stocks for a sample of days during the pre–1966 period, we were unable to locate any source of such data for this period.

5.   Two of the judges agreed in identifying 21 periods, and the third judge identified 20 of these same 21 periods, overlooking one period that all three judges later agreed was a stable period. There was complete agreement about whether a period was to be labeled bull, bear, or stable. The major disagreements concerned the precise month in which a period began or ended. The judges never differed by more than one month, and any differences of this sort were settled by referring to the closing prices of the first days of the months in question. Finally, as a check on this procedure, for each period a correlation was calculated between the daily closing Dow average and sequentially the day of the period. On the basis of this check, one stable period with a correlation of −.71 was eliminated. For the remaining 20 periods, these correlations averaged +.95 in bull markets, −.94 in bear markets, and +.11 in stable markets. A table reporting the dates and characteristics of each of these 20 periods can be obtained by writing to the authors.

6.   With the exception of the final days of runs greater than length eight. There were simply too few such runs to yield meaningful data.

7.   We should also, of course, expect these relationships to be strongest of all in the pre–1966 bear market. Unfortunately, there were virtually no long up runs during this period and we are unable to make the comparisons.

8.   Weeks in which the market was closed for one or more days are not included in this analysis.

9.   Our earlier speculations about the pre– and post–January 1966 market would certainly lead to the expectation that such recommendations would have stronger effects after 1966 than before. Unfortunately, the "Heard on the Street" column did not start publication until November 6, 1967.

REFERENCES

Arrow, K. J., "Risk Perception in Psychology and Economics," *Economic Inquiry*, XX (January, 1982), 1–9.

Baker, H. K., and E. R. Lehman, "The Effects of Public Information on Stock Prices," *Atlanta Economic Review*, (July-August, 1978), 14–18.

Brehm, J. W., *A Theory of Psychological Reactance*. New York: Academic Press, 1966.

Burt, J., F. R. Kaen, and G. G. Booth, "Foreign-exchange Market Efficiency under Flexible Exchange Rates," *Journal of Finance*, 32 (1977), 1325–1330.

Carswell, J., *The South Sea Bubble*. London: Cresset Press, 1960.

Conrad, K., and D. J. Juttner, "Recent Behavior of Stock Market Prices in Germany and the Random Walk Hypothesis," *Kyklos*, 26 (1973), 576–599.

Fama, E. F., "The Behavior of Stock-market Prices," *Journal of Business*, 38 (1965a), 34–105.

Fama, E. F., "Tomorrow in the New York Stock Exchange," *Journal of Business*, 38 (1965b), 285–299.

Fama, E. F., "Efficient Capital Markets: A Review of Theory and Empirical Work," *Journal of Finance*, 25 (1970), 383–433.

Fama, E., L. Fisher, M.C. Jensen, and R. Roll, "The Adjustment of Stock Prices to New Information," *International Economic Review*, 10 (February, 1969), 1–21.

Hochbaum, G. M., "The Relation Between Group Members' Self-confidence and their Reaction to Group Pressures to Uniformity," *American Sociological Review*, 19 (1954), 678–688.

Kemp, A. G., and G. C. Reid, "The Random Walk Hypothesis and the Recent Behavior of Equity Prices in Britain," *Economica*, 38 (1971), 28–51.

Kendall, M. G., "The Analysis of Economic Time Series, Part I: Prices," *Journal of the Royal Statistical Association*, 96, no. 1 (1953), 11–25.

Leuthold, R. M., "Random Walk and Price Trends: Live Cattle Futures Market," *Journal of Finance*, 27 (1972), 879–889.

Lloyd-Davies, P., and M. Canes, "Stock Prices and the Publication of Second-hand Information," *Journal of Business*, 51 (1978), 43–56.

Lorie, J. H., and M. T. Hamilton, *The Stock Market: Theories and Evidence*. Homewood, IL: Richard D. Irwin, Inc., 1973.

Low, R. J., "Stock Market Returns and the Publication of Security Analyst Recommendations." Unpublished master's thesis, Massachusetts Institute of Technology, The Sloan School of Management, 1982.

Mackay, C. *Extraordinary Popular Delusions and the Madness of Crowds*. London: Richard Bentley, 1841.

Malkiel, B. G., *A Random Walk down Wall Street*. New York: W. W. Norton, 1973.

Moore, A. B., "Some Characteristics of Changes in Common Stock Prices," in P.H. Cootner, ed., *The Random Character of Stock Market Prices*. Cambridge, MA: MIT Press, 1964, pp. 139–161.

Osborne, M. F. M., "Periodic Structure in the Brownian Motion of Stock Prices," *Operations Research*, 10 (1962), 345–379.

Samuelson, P. A., *Economics*, 11th ed. New York: McGraw-Hill, 1980.

Schachter, S., "Deviation, Rejection, and Communication," *Journal of Abnormal and Social Psychology*, 46 (1951), 190–207.

Schachter, S., *The Psychology of Affiliation*. Stanford, CA: Stanford University Press, 1959.

Sperling, J. G., *The South Sea Company: An Historical Essay and Bibliographical Finding List*. Boston: Baker Library, Harvard Graduate School of Business Administration, 1962.

Stevenson, R. A., and R. M. Bear, "Commodity Futures: Trends or Random Walks?" *Journal of Finance*, 25 (1970), 65–81.

Stouffer, S. A., E. A. Suchman, L. C. DeVinney, S. A. Star, and R. M. Williams, Jr., *The American Soldier, Vol. I. Adjustment During Army Life*. Princeton, NJ: Princeton University Press, 1949.

Witkin, H. A., "Importance of Individual Differences in Perception," *Journal of Personality*, 18 (1949), 145–170.
The World Almanac and Book of Facts 1983. New York: Newspaper Enterprise Association, 1983.

WHAT DO PEOPLE BRING TO THE STOCK MARKET (BESIDES MONEY)?
THE ECONOMIC PSYCHOLOGY OF STOCK MARKET BEHAVIOR

Shlomo Maital, Randall Filer and Julian Simon

I. INTRODUCTION

What people do depends on who they are, what they know and feel, what other people do, the structure of the choices they face, and how they perceive that structure. In other words, the choice behavior of an individual is determined by six factors: personality, cognition, affect, social interaction, circumstance, and perception. In the context of investment behavior, for instance, a person's decision to buy, sell, or hold particular stocks or bonds depends on: (a) personality traits related to risk propensity; (b) knowledge of investment theory and market behavior; (c) emotional forces; (d) what other investors are buying and selling; (e) the rate of return and systematic risk associated with each asset; and (f) the individual's *perception* of the market, the assets traded in it, and the behavior or intentions of other traders.

As with many types of choice behavior, the *economic* theory of financial markets and the *psychological* theory are at odds. The economic theory places strong emphasis on one of the above six factors, circumstance. There are at least three reasons for this. First, some individual differences in preferences and tastes may be brought to convergence by arbitrage and market forces.[1] Second, some personality traits, like risk aversion, are revealed in market behavior and prices, hence are best

273

observed indirectly, through individual stock portfolios, rather than directly, by questionnaire or interview. Finally, to the extent that perceptions and reality diverge, the resulting error may result in financial loss; the economic logic of markets is particularly hostile to such irrationality, except as a temporary, negligible aberration.[2] The economic model therefore posits that individual differences either disappear or find full expression in actual market behavior, thus obviating the need for "micro-micro" direct measurement.

In contrast, the small but growing body of literature on the psychology of investment behavior strongly emphasizes the role of psychological variables associated with individuals and with small- and large-group interactions. Large segments of the psychological literature—including cognitive psychology, learning theory, definition and measurement of personality traits, and social psychology—are now being applied to the understanding of financial markets.

In perhaps no other branch of economics is there a wider chasm between, to paraphrase G. B. Shaw's phrase, those who do and those who teach, than in the theory of financial markets. The economic theory of capital markets, expressed in college courses and scholarly books and articles, is built on the concept of efficient markets. This concept posits that asset prices accurately reflect information embodied in (a) the past history of such prices; (b) public sources; and (c) accessible, though costly, private sources. In the words of a leading corporate finance textbook, "The concept of an efficient market is astonishingly simple and remarkably well-supported by the facts" (Brealey and Myers, 1981, p. 273). In contrast, brokers and analysts are keenly aware of the powerful influence of psychological and emotional forces in financial markets. Perhaps the strongest case for this view is made by David N. Dreman (1977; 1979). His "VIP" theory states that the price of a security is a function of actual value (V), the interpretation of information (I), and the investor's current psychological state (P). "Incorrect interpretation of information and emotional factors can carry price far away from actual worth," Dreman argued (1977, p. 253). As one investment analyst—chosen by *Institutional Investor* as a 1983 "All-American" stock selector—told us, "My whole approach to analyzing the stock market is psychological. Emotions are simply stronger than reason, people do not change, and people make markets."[3]

The substantive objective of this paper is first, to review, compare, and contrast the economic and psychological models of investment behavior; second, to outline a rudimentary model synthesizing the two approaches; and third, to present the results of a game simulation of stock-market behavior aimed at exploring individual and aggregate choices in the face of random stock prices. We also have the methodological objective of illustrating just one among many uses of what seems to be an unusually promising research device that can produce fruitful results in a wide variety of research contexts. It has the enormous advantage that its very construction makes it impossible in principle for respondents to detect any "real" information in the stimuli, which cannot be asserted authoritatively for any actual price series, no matter how presented.

II.   THE ECONOMICS OF ASSET PRICING

The economic theory of financial markets contends—with important exceptions in the literature—that for a given information set, the intrinsic value of an asset fluctuates randomly. The so-called random walk theory was born when two types of research—theoretical and empirical—zeroed in on the same idea. In papers by Moore (1962), Granger and Morgenstern (1963), and Fama (1965), the authors claimed to demonstrate empirically that stock movements are random. At the same time, two major theory papers by Samuelson (1965b) and Mandelbrot (1966) proved that if (a) information-gathering is cheap, (b) buying and selling are costless, and (c) everyone *interprets* information in the same way, then stock market prices are martingales, and changes in prices of stocks behave as random walks. The implication of the efficient-market theory is, in Cootner's words (1964), that "prices have no memory, and yesterday has nothing to do with tomorrow." It follows that careful study of the *history* of a given stock's price is, for a profit-seeking investor, pointless.

Modern portfolio theory builds on the work of Markowitz (1971) and Tobin (1958). They showed how a rational investor can reduce financial risk by spreading it over a number of different stocks or assets. Markets dominated by such rational investors will establish a "price" for undertaking risk, measured by the higher rate of return needed to compensate investors for it. Building on the Tobin-Markowitz portfolio theory, Sharpe (1964) and Lintner (1965) constructed the capital asset-pricing model approach (CAPM). Their message was simple. Define the systematic risk associated with some financial asset as the sensitivity of that asset's rate of return to fluctuations in the entire market. Measure this risk as the ratio: σ_{im}/σ^2_m, where the numerator is the covariance between asset i's rate of return and the market portfolio m (e.g., Dow Jones 30-stock basket) rate of return, and the denominator is the variance of the market portfolio rate of return. Call this parameter beta. Then the risk premium (i.e., higher rate of return) commanded by an asset will be directly proportional to its beta.

According to the CAPM approach, the "riskiness" of an individual portfolio is simply the weighted average of each participating stock's beta, with weights determined by the stock's value in proportion to the value of the whole portfolio. Individual investors therefore reveal their risk preference by means of their portfolios. No individual differences in risk-rate of return trade-offs—the extra return a person demands in exchange for accepting more systematic risk—can persist, according to this theory, because arbitrage will eliminate them and move every investor onto a uniform marketwide risk-return curve. (The logic of how market forces smooth out individual differences is the same as that in note 1.)

III. DEPARTURES FROM EFFICIENCY

Brealey and Myers (1981), citing Roberts, define three different levels of market efficiency:

- Level one: Prices reflect all the information contained in the historical record of past prices (weak-form efficiency).
- Level two: Prices reflect, fully and accurately, both past prices and current *public* information (semistrong form).
- Level three: Prices reflect *all* information, public or private (strong form.

The alleged efficiency of financial markets at all levels has come under both theoretical and empirical assault. We first examine an interesting logical difficulty noted by Grossman and Stiglitz (1980). They suggest that the following three propositions—efficient markets, competitive markets, and costly information—cannot all be true. "Because information is costly," they note, "prices cannot perfectly reflect the information which is available, since if it did, those who spent resources to obtain it would receive no compensation" (p. 405). One interpretation of their result is that the efficiency of financial markets rests crucially on a sufficient number of investors who do not believe in it and hence are willing to spend resources to collect information.[4]

Perhaps fortuitously for the efficient-market theory, there is no lack of empirical studies that give heart to the disbelieving infidels and assault strong-form efficiency. Research has shown a continued, systematic relation between asset prices and the day of the week, month of the year, published news, expert opinion, price-earnings ratio, and presidential elections. (Efficient-market proponents accept some of this evidence but often note that the weakness of the relations and brokers' commissions prevent people from using knowledge of them to make money). We shall now review a small part of this evidence.

Overreaction: An *Institutional Investor* "All-American" analyst told us:

> There's an old saying on Wall Street about "fear and greed" motivating investors. My personal observation is that the stock market overreacts continually because of these psychological forces. When stocks are declining in a bear market and by any objective, fundamental technique are "undervalued," more times than not they get "cheaper." In bull markets, stocks that get "overvalued" fundamentally tend to go a lot higher before they turn down.[5]

De Bondt and Thaler (1984) studied the period from January 1931 to December 1982. They assigned firms to "winners" and "losers" categories, depending on stock-price behavior over a two-year period. Stocks that were "winners" in previous periods did significantly less well than the market in subsequent periods. The authors found that "over the last decade . . . the overreaction effect is particularly impressive. For that period, the top 35 stocks earn on average almost 40 percent less than is predicted by the simple (capital asset-pricing model)."

An article in *Institutional Investor* (1983) asks, "Who Spotted Last Year's Hottest Stocks?" The answer: "Analysts who called the shots in many of the Big Board's best performers had to forget they were duds in the past. Four of 1982's top 10 performing stocks—Chrysler Corp., Vendo Co., Winnebago Industries, and Federal National Mortgage Association—were among 1981's worst performers."[6]

Price-earning effect: Stocks with low price-earning ratios outperform the market (Dreman, 1977; Nicholson, 1968). Dreman cites results for the period 1967–1976, showing that "the lowest P/E stocks would have performed nearly seven times better than the highest P/E's" (1977, p. 292).

Month-of-the-year effect: Rozeff and Kinney (1976) found that in the United States, stock returns for January are substantially greater than returns for the other 11 months. Gultekin and Gultekin (1983) found that for a group of 17 capital markets around the world, 13 of them "have seasonality in stock return distributions."

Day-of-the-week effect: Osborne (1962) observed that trading volume on the stock market is highest in the middle of the week and lowest on Mondays and Fridays. Cross (1973) found stock prices rise on Fridays and fall on Mondays. Schachter and Hood (1984) found that this day-of-the-week effect is much more pronounced in bear markets and stable markets than it is in bull markets, on the grounds that "if one is depressed about or bored by the market, chances are good that one will avoid thinking, reading or talking about the market" (after or just before a weekend).

Biased interest rates: Modigliana and Cohn (1979) have offered a psychological explanation for the fact that common stocks were "systematically undervalued by 50 percent" in the 1970s. Under rapid inflation, they argued, investors capitalized equity earnings at a rate close to the nominal (inflation-inclusive) interest rate, rather than at the correct, inflation-corrected real rate. This error, they argued, would tend to correct itself during periods when inflation, and nominal rates of interest, fell rapidly—a prophecy fulfilled in the bull market of August 1982.

Excess volatility: Shiller (1981) has shown that stock prices are too volatile to be explained by "rational market" forces such as changes in dividends or real changes in the investor discount rate, and hence he questions the efficient-market theory. Copeland (1983), however, challenges Shiller's findings.

IV.   THE PSYCHOLOGY OF INVESTMENT BEHAVIOR

The economic logic of portfolio choice leads inexorably to the consideration of the behavioral implications of such choice. Applying psychology to economics in this area has been undertaken in at least half a dozen different directions.

1.   *Behavioral measures of risk aversion*:   Kogan and Wallace (1964) developed an operational measure of attitudes toward undertaking risk. A natural test of the Tobin–Markowitz portfolio theory, and also of the Sharpe–Lintner CAPM model, would be to determine whether independent, behavioral measures of risk aversion are in fact closely correlated with individual portfolio risk. Such research breaks the empty tautology of economics' revealed-preference principle, which asserts that people want what they choose and choose what they want (Samuelson, 1965a).

2.   *Subjective perception of risk*:   Statistically, risky assets are modeled as rates of return with a probability distribution, such that each rate of return has some objective probability attached to it. What is the relation between the way such probabilities are perceived (i.e., subjective probabilities) and the actual, objective probabilities? Work by Kahneman and Tversky (1979) and Kahneman, Slovic, and Tversky (1981) reveals a wide variety of fallacies, biases and plain errors in the mental processes that translate objective odds into subjective ones.

3.   *Attitudes toward randomness*:   Suppose we accept, for now, the evidence of randomly fluctuating stock prices as objective fact. How accurately do people perceive this reality? The idea of an aleatoric

(random) world, or stock market, is not appealing at all to those persons who feel that the world is subject to their direct control. When quantified, this aspect of personality should in theory be an important determinant of the extent and nature of individuals' behavior in financial markets.

The personality variable of "internal–external locus of control," developed by Rotter and associates and stemming from the social-learning approach to behavior, provides a useful operational measure of perceived control. In Rotter's (1966) words:

> If a person perceives a reinforcement as contingent upon his own behavior, then the occurrence of either a positive or negative reinforcement will strengthen or weaken potential for that behavior to recur in the same or similar situation. If he sees the reinforcement as being outside his own control or not contingent, that is, depending upon chance, fate, powerful others, or unpredictable, then the preceding behavior is less likely to be strengthened or weakened.

Based on work by James and Phares, Rotter developed a 29-item questionnaire (including six filler items), designed to measure the extent to which individuals believe they exert control over outcomes and events (internal locus of control) or are shaped, manipulated, and influenced by forces outside their own control (external locus of control) (see the appendix). Persons with high internal locus of control should, for instance, attach much greater significance to their past successes or failures in investments by attributing profits and losses to cause and effect, than persons with low internal locus of control, who see stock prices as random and hence not amenable to any systematic profit-laden investment strategy.[7]

4. *Risky shift*: In 1961, research by Stoner revealed that, contrary to common belief, a decision taken by a group of people will probably be *riskier* than decisions made by the individuals who comprise the group. This phenomenon became known as the "risky shift" and suggests that social interaction leads people to espouse more risky behavior than they would choose if they were acting entirely on their own. Psychologists now are doubtful about the veracity of the risky shift. Whatever the case, it is beyond doubt that financial behavior is in part a social phenomenon; the manner by which people pass information to one another and both receive and impart opinions and influence is an important ingredient in the understanding of financial markets.

5. *Machiavellianism*: Machiavelli wrote about how the Prince could and should manipulate his subjects. The personality trait known as Machiavellianism refers to an individual's belief in the extent to which others are amenable to such manipulation. A widely used scale for measuring this trait asks people to state whether a series of statements (for instance: "Barnum was probably right when he said that there's a sucker born

every minute") are closest, or most opposite, to their feelings. Rotstein (1982) found significant correlation between this trait and the riskiness of investment portfolios that subjects held. (See also Christie and Seis, 1970; Rim, 1966.)

6. *Dependency effect*:   The state of psychological dependence is one in which individuals believe that they are not very good at making judgments and hence alter their opinions to conform to group opinion. Such persons are more affected by the opinions and behaviors of others. Schachter and Hood (1984) argue that in the prolonged bull market of 1950 to 1966, there was a "16-year history of repeated success and reinforcement," making investors invulnerable to social influence or short-term events. This results in little stock volatility. In contrast, after 1967, when the market was an "unpredictable mess," investors acted erratically as rumors, tips, and guesses spread rapidly.[8] Schachter and Hood cite statistical evidence for this proposition.

Modern telecommunications and computer technology may exacerbate this type of volatility. A *New York Times* article by Michael Blumstein (1984) vividly described the effects of a speech by Paul Volcker, chairman of the Federal Reserve, saying that the economy looked very strong, which was interpreted by Wall Street to mean that interest rates would be driven higher. The report appeared at 9:30 A.M. on the Dow Jones news service ticker. Within the hour, treasury bonds plunged, and the Dow-Jones industrial stock average fell 11.51 points. "We hit bids," a trader told Blumstein (meaning traders sold for whatever price buyers were willing to pay). "When the statement came over the tape, they just went and hit the bids indiscriminately." As Blumstein noted:

> When a statement such as Mr. Volcker's crosses the tape, professional traders react not so much to what is said as to how they expect other people to react. The result is a scrambling to get half a step ahead of the crowd, and a snowballing that amplifies the market impact of news events.

"It used to take three weeks to react to the news," another trader said. "Now they react within seconds. Everyone's got access to all this news."

A psychological explanation of the sea change that has occurred in financial markets since 1968 rests on the distinction between classical (Pavlovian) conditioning and operant (Skinnerian) conditioning. Suppose that in the placid, pre–1968 markets, the stimulus of favorable profit prospects is met by the response of buying stocks, a response then reinforced by price rise and capital gains. Then strong, random shocks are introduced into the market, coupled with a new uncertainty about economic causality. Now the conditioning process may resemble that of Skinner's (1948) pigeon rather than Pavlov's dog. In a classic experiment,

Skinner gave pigeons food at brief, *random* intervals. This led to "superstitions." Whatever behavior the pigeon was doing before it was given food was reinforced by the food (say, blinking). So it blinked harder. Chances were that a food reward would be given again. This further strengthened the pigeon's belief in the efficacy of blinking. (A familiar behavioral law says that intermittent reinforcement is more powerful than never-fail reinforcement). Skinner created a whole cageful of erratically behaving pigeons, each of them persuaded that their hopping, bobbing, or blinking behavior was the reason they were getting food— even though no causal link between behavior and food existed at all. The parallel with a stock market filled with chartists, contrarians, hunch players, and the like, all of whose actions are reinforced from time to time and who are supremely confident their method works, is clear. Operant conditioning—the process of learning that some response to a stimulus and the consequences of that response are linked together—is a helpful basis for understanding seemingly irrational behavior in uncertain markets.

From time to time, markets change from a collection of individuals, each pursuing some idiosyncratic strategy, into a mob bent on one goal: buying more and more of the asset whose price is shooting skyward. This is known as a speculative bubble and has fascinated economists and psychologists alike. William James once said that "often enough, our faith beforehand in an uncertified result is the only thing that makes the result come true." Suppose no one believes there is a link between sunspots and stock prices. But suppose each individual thinks that every other individual believes there is such a link. The appearance of sunspots should lead each individual to buy stocks, on the grounds that other people will. Such behavior will be quite rational. As Keynes pointed out, there is nothing more disastrous than a "rational" investment strategy in an irrational market. Several recent papers have explored the speculative-bubble equilibria (Blanchard and Watson, 1982; Tirole, 1982; Cass and Shell, 1983). Such behavior may be termed *superrational*, since it involves discovering not *objective* cause and effect, but *perceived* cause and effect. Since people act on their perceptions, which may differ from reality, shrewd investors try to guess what the prevailing perceptions are, in the same way that Keynes' rational gameplayer tried to pick beauty-queen contestants he thought other players would pick, rather than the one he thought was objectively most attractive.[9]

V. AN ECLECTIC MODEL

An eclectic model of economic behavior posits that what people do or choose depends on what people have (income, wealth), what they

Figure 1.   A schematic view of rational and nonrational behavior
in financial markets.

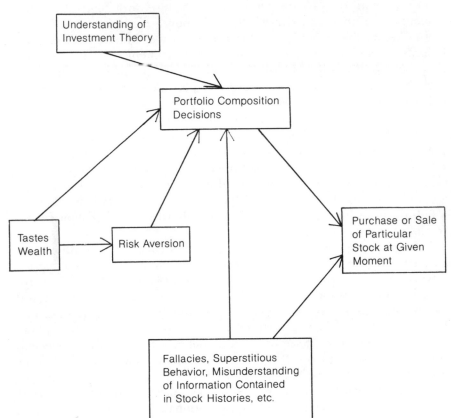

know (cognition), and what they perceive and feel (personality) (Maital, 1982; Maital and Maital, 1984a). As applied to financial markets, the model implies that an individual's portfolio decisions and purchase or sale of individual stocks will depend on his or her income and wealth, preferences and tastes, knowledge of investment principles, attitudes toward risk, and a wide range of variables related to personality (superstition, past experience, etc.).[10] This theory is portrayed graphically in Figure 1. The theory has both economic and psychological components.

The economic component posits that financial behavior depends on an individual's understanding of investment principles, which, in turn, are built on the two variables that determine an asset's intrinsic value: its rate of return and riskiness, and that individual's income and wealth.

Together, these two aspects determine an individual demand schedule for a stock or bond. The psychological component posits that individuals differ widely in the manner in which they perceive reality and in the way they act upon that perception. Among the psychological variables that should influence financial behavior are: subjective aversion to or affinity for risk; perception of a cause-and-effect relation between stock-market success and investment behavior; cognitive processes that govern information gathering and processing; susceptibility to advice and the opinions of others; and a belief in superstitions.

How should this model best be tested? We choose to observe directly a game simulation of stock-market behavior and attempt to link investment behavior to socioeconomic and psychological variables.

In 1972, Paul Slovic suggested in *The Journal of Finance* the hypothesis that "if we provide a stream of random price changes to intelligent but naive subjects, say undergraduate students in a finance course, they might discover in these random sequences some of the same rules that we see accepted by chartists or other analysts." Slovic describes the phenomenon of "illusory correlation," in which faulty prior expectations lead to wrong observations and inferences, even under "ideal conditions," and posits the existence of "illusory correlation" in financial analysis. And as far back as 1965, Simon had used simulated prices in unpublished experiments. McInish (1980) and Harstad and Marrese (1981) have employed our method in earlier related work.

We presented such a series of random price changes to undergraduates enrolled in a corporate finance course, as a game simulation of the stock market. Results of this simulation yielded a number of interesting findings regarding the psychology of behavior toward risk.

Game simulations have been used successfully to study many kinds of economic behavior, by Chamberlin (1962); Siegel and Fouraker (1960); Smith (1978); Shubik (1969); Edney (1979); Friedland, Maital, and Rutenberg (1978) and closest to the work presented here, Friedman, Harrison, and Salmon (1984). Brealey and Hodges (1973, 1975) gave subjects a five-year history of monthly stock prices for 50 stocks, along with a table of analysts' predictions and estimates of betas. According to Brealey and Hodges, games possess the "drawback of artificiality" but have the "advantage of being reproducible." Artificiality is mitigated in a well-conceived experiment by substitution of the desire to excel for realistic profits or losses. More important, the ally of artificiality is "controllability"; while actual stock prices may at times depart from randomness, use of randomly generated stock histories ensures that the histories contain no useful information. We investigated how people interpret various market signals and respond to them when such signals in fact bear no useful information.

VI.   A GAME SIMULATION OF STOCK-MARKET BEHAVIOR

Subjects: Our subjects were 87 undergraduate members of a corporate finance class at a university in the eastern United States. The experiment was conducted in the second half of the spring semester, after students had been exposed to "efficient-market" theory.

Design and Procedure: Several days prior to the game simulation, each subject was given a description of the game, a 36-week price history of seven common stocks (labelled alpha, beta, etc.), and three questionnaires. They were not told that the stock-price histories were fabricated.

The three questionnaires sought information on: (a) background—the subject's age, sex, grades, work experience, assets, religion, and parents' income; (b) risk aversion, as measured by the subject's selection of chance bets; and (c) the subject's locus of control (Rotter's scale). Materials given to participants are shown in the appendix.

Our measure of risk aversion was adapted from the scale devised by Kogan and Wallace (1964). Subjects were given six different pairs of chance bets. For each pair, they were asked to select one bet that they preferred. Every bet had an expected value of zero. Bets differed in the magnitude of individual gains and losses and in the probabilities attached to each gain or loss. Risk aversion was measured by the subject's choice of bets with odds closest to 50/50 (i.e., with the smallest variance of win-lose probabilities). A score of one was given to risk-averse choices, zero otherwise. The variable AVERS was defined as the sum of scores on five of the six questions (one pair of choices was between bets with identical odds).

For locus of control we used Rotter's 29-item questionnaire (see appendix). Six of the items were "fillers." We did a principle-components analysis of the 23 remaining questions. In the first principal component, only questions 13 (related to the efficacy of planning) and 15 (related to belief in luck) had factor loadings of substantial magnitude. We defined the variable CONTROL as the weighted average of z-scores for these two questions for each participant, with weights equal to factor loadings. A high score on CONTROL indicated internal control feelings.[11] Subjects were instructed:

> We want to find out how well people can buy and sell stocks for the maximum profit, using only information about the price movements of the stocks.... Your task is to buy, sell, or hold stocks and cash in such a way as to come out with the most money at the end of the experiment.... You will have $10,000 in cash to start.

One percent commission was charged on the value of each stock purchase and sale. Holding cash was permitted, and 5 percent interest per annum was paid on cash balances.

Each participant was given a form on which to write his or her portfolio decision for a given "round," or "week," of the game. After each subject made his or her portfolio decision for that week and handed in the form, the experimenters announced the prices for each of the seven stocks prevailing at the end of that week. Subjects were then asked to make another set of portfolio decisions. Six "weeks" of the game were completed. The game took one hour of class time to run. Short selling (sale of more stock than the subject held) and borrowing money was not permitted. Subjects were asked not to communicate with one another.

The 36-week price "histories" given to subjects a week before the game, as well as the stock prices for the six "weeks" of the game itself, are shown in Table 1A in the appendix. Note that stock prices during the game are predetermined and are not influenced by demand and supply of the participants.

VII. EMPIRICAL RESULTS

All game simulations assume that subjects believe the game's outcomes are of importance and have the same sort of meaning as the real thing. We believe the consistency of our results—some of which have been replicated—support this assumption. For a variety of groups, and over a number of years, subjects have said that they enjoyed playing the game, resisted its termination, and had strong involvement in their own outcomes.

Our results fall into three groups: "nonrationality," price-expectation formation, and risk aversion.

A. Economic "Nonrationality"

Given that the rational strategy when asset prices fluctuate randomly is buy-and-hold, or hold cash when it earns interest, we hypothesized that such behavior would be common. It was not. Table 2 shows the week-by-week distributions of the proportion of portfolios held in cash. Consistently, less than half of all participants held more than 10 percent of the portfolios in cash. One could explain this behavior by assuming that subjects believe the long-run return to stocks exceeds 5 percent, or that subjects have a game-utility function that values, not average success, but extreme success only ("winning"). However, in another small experiment by Harstad and Marrese (1981), where subjects received

Table 2.   Proportion of Portfolio Held in Cash: Distribution
by "Week"

Proportion of Portfolio Held in Cash (in percent)	Number of Persons Holding That Proportion:					
	Week 1	Week 2	Week 3	Week 4	Week 5	Week 6
0–10	53	60	53	47	56	57
11–20	12	11	11	9	7	12
21–30	8	5	9	11	6	4
31–40	2	2	1	3	3	2
41–50	3	3	7	9	6	4
51–60	2	1	0	2	2	3
61–70	2	2	3	2	3	1
71–80	2	1	0	0	0	0
81–90	0	0	0	0	1	0
91–100	3	2	3	4	3	4
	87	87	87	87	87	87

amounts proportional to their experimental portfolio value, no subjects at all held cash.

Though announced stock prices carry no real information, participants continued throughout the six weeks of the game to buy and sell actively in response to price changes. The distribution of the number of different stocks bought and sold week by week is shown in Table 3. The data indicate that for any given week (except for the first, when participants assembed their first portfolio), between a third and a half of the subjects neither bought nor sold stock. Few of them, however, sat out more than two or three "weeks" consecutively, and only 12 of the 87 participants practiced a firm "buy-and-hold" strategy. Out of 14

Table 3.   Number of Different Stocks Bought or Sold: Distribution
by "Week"

Number of Different Stocks	Number of Persons Who Bought or Sold That Number of Stocks					
	Week 1	Week 2	Week 3	Week 4	Week 5	Week 6
None	3	38	26	38	46	32
One	9	19	16	21	23	20
Two	20	26	35	19	14	23
Three	26	4	8	8	4	9
Four	17	0	2	1	0	3
Five	8	0	0	0	0	0
Six	1	0	0	0	0	0
Seven	3	0	0	0	0	0
	87	87	87	87	87	87

Table 4.   Number of Different Stocks Held: Distribution by "Week"

Number of Different Stocks Held	Number of Persons Holding That Number of Stocks					
	Week 1	Week 2	Week 3	Week 4	Week 5	Week 6
None	3	2	3	4	3	4
One	9	6	9	10	12	16
Two	20	18	14	16	17	22
Three	26	28	26	21	21	17
Four	17	20	19	20	18	14
Five	8	7	10	8	8	7
Six	1	2	5	6	6	5
Seven	3	4	1	2	2	2
	87	87	87	87	87	87

women subjects, three, or 21 percent, pursued buy-and-hold. Of the 73 men, only seven (nine percent) followed a buy-and-hold strategy. The more conservative behavior of women is a finding we shall document in greater detail later.

One of the hallowed principles of investment is "diversification of risk." When risk is purely random, as in our simulation, it cannot be diversified away. In real financial markets, however, *systematic* risk can be reduced by holding sufficient different stocks so that fluctuations in rates of return are offsetting. In our experiment, between two-thirds and three-quarters of our subjects chose to hold from two to four different stocks. The governing constraint here seemed to be informational and computational—how many different stocks subjects could think about at one time—rather than economic (see Table 4).

Despite the randomness of price movements, we could detect in the data clear market movements and the development of a consensus about "favorites" and "losers." Table 5 gives the proportion of the total "market" portfolio held in each of the seven stocks, week by week, along with measures of the riskiness of each stock. Initially, participants divided their $10,000 more or less evenly among the seven stocks, with a slight preference for Epsilon (we speculate this was because Epsilon had the highest absolute price per share, giving it the aura of a blue chip). In week 1, the price of Gamma slumped quite sharply and recovered only slightly in week 2. The market seemed to develop a consensus in week 3 that Gamma was seriously underpriced. Holdings of Gamma rose to one-third of total share holdings in that week, from only one-seventh in week 2. In week 3 the price of Gamma rose once again. When this was disclosed, there was a sell-off; subjects thought it had peaked. In week 5, the price of Gamma fell to an all-time low; in the final round of play, investors raised their holdings of Gamma to 40 percent of total share

Table 5.   Composition of Total Market Portfolio by "Week"

Stock	Standard Deviation of Weekly Price Change (in percent)	Beta	Proportion of Total Market Porfolio Held in Each Stock, by "Week"*					
			Week 1	Week 2	Week 3	Week 4	Week 5	Week 6
Alpha	2.8	0.41	0.085	0.090	0.074	0.069	0.071	0.039
Beta	6.0	0.23	0.104	0.112	0.116	0.109	0.107	0.088
Gamma	8.5	0.41	0.095	0.135	0.269	0.223	0.249	0.356
Delta	3.0	0.08	0.060	0.059	0.057	0.063	0.070	0.074
Epsilon	5.4	0.39	0.210	0.188	0.074	0.051	0.044	0.063
Zeta	2.3	−0.07	0.160	0.171	0.162	0.161	0.163	0.130
Eta	6.5	0.57	0.118	0.127	0.122	0.139	0.135	0.109
			0.832	0.882	0.874	0.815	0.839	0.859

*Note: The difference between 1.0 and the sum of the proportions held in each stock is the fraction of total portfolios held in cash.

holdings. Alas! Many stout hearted game-players were crushed; the malevolent random-number generator drove Gamma even lower that week, and the intrepid investors' portfolios took a bath.

Table 5 hints at the presence of "gambler's fallacy": the belief that consecutive events are causally related, though they are in fact random and independent (such as tosses of a coin). We thus looked for the presence of gambler's fallacy in examining how expectations regarding prices and price changes were formed.

Note, too, that there is no evidence in Table 5 of subjects shunning high-risk stocks. The most popular and least popular stocks, as of week 6, had the same beta value.

B.   Price-expectation Formation

Subjects presumably bought stock on the expectation that its price would rise. One way, therefore, to infer price expectations is by checking whether purchase of stock followed, in some systematic manner, previous price changes. The zero-order correlation coefficient between stock purchases and the prior week's price *level* was virtually zero (-0.04). But the correlation coefficient between stock purchases and the prior week's *change* in the stock's price was substantially greater: -0.10. We therefore regressed net purchases of stock (gross purchases minus sales) Y on both the prior week's price *level* X_1 and price *change* X_2 (standard errors are in brackets):

$$Y = 0.065\ X_1 - 66.87\ X_2 , R^2 = 0.01$$
$$[0.035] \qquad [12.36]$$

Table 6. Relations Between Downtick (Uptick) Purchases and Past
Downtick (Uptick) Success By Week

	Correlation Coefficients Between	
	Total Downtick Purchases and Past Downtick Success[1]	Total Uptick Purchases and Past Uptick Success[2]
Week 2	-0.06	***
Week 3	0.01	-0.29**
Week 4	-0.03	-0.20*
Week 5	0.03	0.02
Week 6	0.12	-0.20*

Notes:
   *Significant at 0.05.
  **Significant at 0.01
***Not meaningful; there were no successful uptick purchases in week 1.
   [1]A downtick purchase is one where a stock is purchased in week t, after the price of the stock has
   fallen in period $t - 1$ ($p_{t-1} < p_{t-2}$). Total downtick purchases refers to the total number of stock
   purchases that fulfill this condition. Past downtick *success* is the mber of previous downtick purchases,
   where the price in the following period *rose* ($p_{t+1} > p_t$).
   [2]An uptick purchase is one where a stock is purchased in week t, after the price of the stock has
   risen in period $t - 1$ ($p_{t-1} > p_{t-2}$). Total uptick purchases refers to the total number of stock
   purchases that fulfill this condition. Past uptick *success* is the number of previous uptick purchases,
   where the price of the stock in the following period rose ($p_{t+1} > p_t$).

The negative and statistically significant coefficient of X_2 suggests a belief
in the law of averages, or in "What comes up must come down."

One cannot in fact "learn" anything from a series of random numbers.
But that need not prevent the perception of learning. We searched for
such a learning process, after observing the evidence of gambler's fallacy,
by examining whether stock purchases made after "upticks" and "downticks" (rises and falls in price, respectively) were "successful" or "unsuccessful" (followed by a rise or fall in stock price, respectively). We then
tested to see whether these "successful" and unsuccessful" outcomes
influenced subsequent purchases and sales. A successful experience with
buying after upticks could reinforce such behavior and encourage "learning," thus creating a superstition in much the same way that Skinner's
pigeons, offered food randomly, persisted in whatever behavior they
were engaged in when the food happened to arrive.

Table 6 shows the week-by-week correlation between a previous downtick "success" (purchase of a stock after a fall in price and the subsequent
rise in the stock's price) and the extent of downtick purchases. None of
the correlations are statistically significant. Similar calculations, however,
for the relation between uptick success and total uptick stock purchases
do reveal a statistically significant, *negative* relation for weeks 3, 4, and
6. This is consistent with the following interpretation: You can make

money on an uptrend, but uptrends are followed by downswings, so be careful to bail out in time. The more money you made on past upswings, the more likely it is you will soon see a downswing.[12] This is a kind of "asymmetric" gambler's fallacy, because it does not seem to work when applied to downticks. In other words, our subjects appeared to believe that consecutively rising prices led them to expect an imminent fall but consecutively falling prices did not lead them to anticipate an imminent rise. The exception to this generalization was the purchase and sale of stock Gamma described earlier, where the price went to a historically unprecedented low.

C. Risk Aversion

To test the posited relation between portfolio risk on the one hand and risk aversion and locus of control on the other, we regressed the variance of each individual's portfolio on: AVERS (Kogan–Wallich risk aversion), CONTROL (Rotter's internal-external scale), the sex of the subject, "background" variables, and a constant for each of the six "weeks" and for the average portfolio risk over those six weeks. Results of these multiple regressions are shown in Table 7.

For the six-week average, and for two of the individual six weeks, AVERS is negative and statistically significant at $p < 0.05$; for two additional weeks, statistically significant at $p < 0.10$. Our hypothesis that greater portfolio risk is associated with less subjective risk aversion is therefore not rejected.

Similarly, with the exception of week 6, all coefficients of CONTROL (a measure of belief in "internal" control) were significant at $p < 0.10$; the overall regression for average risk and three of the five remaining regressions had the CONTROL coefficient significant at $p < 0.05$. The results tend to support our theory that those who believe they control their own fate are more likely to undertake risk and that locus of control is an additional dimension of subjective risk perception and risk aversion.

Samuel Johnson once said that a crowd of men acts like a single woman. In our experiment, a group of women in fact acted more like a single cool-headed, rational man. The 14 women subjects bought significantly less risky portfolios than their 73 male counterparts and were only half as active in trading as were the men (measured by commission payments). Moreover, as a group the women ended up with an average profit of $228, compared with an average $91 loss for the men.

The background variables—AUTO, STOCK, grades—were not consistently significant. Where they were significant, possession of a car was associated with less portfolio risk, as was GPA (a higher grade-point average), the latter indicating perhaps that material on random walks was better assimilated and understood. On the other hand, possession of stock (STOCK) and, in one regression, a summer job (SJOB) were positively associated with risk.

D. Replications

McInish (1980) replicated our game simulation, with several modifications, among 90 senior undergraduate business majors at the University of Delaware. There were 83 usable responses. McInish used the entire 23-item locus-of-control scale, rather than a principal component. In place of the chance-bet questions, he used a composite measure of risk aversion based on three Kogan and Wallich (1964) scenarios. Each scenario describes a potential real-life situation in which one has an opportunity to gain a favorable outcome (for instance, by taking a better job). Then the participant is asked to indicate the lowest odds of a successful outcome, from a low of zero in 10 to a high of 10 in 10, that he would consider acceptable. There are thus 11 possible choices, with a score of 11 representing the most conservative choice. The natural logarithms of scores on each of the three scenarios were added to obtain a measure of risk aversion. As a measure of portfolio risk, McInish used beta, a measure of systematic risk. The figure representing total commissions paid was used as a measure of investment activity.

McInish found, in a multiple regression with portfolio risk as the dependent variable, that "we confirm the FMS finding that there is a tendency for risk averse individuals to choose less risky portfolios"; he reports significant coefficients for "locus of control" and Kogan-Wallach risk aversion. He also found that older persons chose significantly less risky portfolios, and, in contrast to FMS, women chose more risky portfolios ("though not significantly more").

In the regression with commissions as the dependent variable, McInish found that "individuals who believe that they can control their environment have considerably more portfolio activity than those who believe they cannot" and that "women have considerably less portfolio activity," confirming findings reported above.

For his master's dissertation, Rotstein (1982) conducted a similar game among Israeli students, with the important addition that participants' *actual* investment portfolios were elicited and correlated with game portfolios. (The simulation itself was run individually by the experimenter with each subject, rather than in a group).

Rotstein found significant positive correlations between: (a) actual portfolio risk and risk in the game ($r = 0.65$); (b) actual turnover velocity of subjects' portfolios and turnover of the game portfolio ($r = 0.64$); (c) significant positive correlation between Machiavellianism and actual

Table 7. Portfolio Risk Regressed on Risk Aversion and Personal Characteristics For Weeks 1 through 6 and on Average (N = 87)*

Dependent Variable:[1] Portfolio Risk Explanatory Variables[2]	Portfolio Decision On						
	Week 1	Week 2	Week 3	Week 4	Week 5	Week 6	Average Over 6 Weeks
AVERS	-0.624*** (0.390)	-0.464 (0.421)	-1.11** (0.494)	-0.600*** (0.406)	-0.834** (0.450)	-2.71** (0.556)	-1.00** (0.344)
CONTROL	3.70** (1.83)	4.16** (1.97)	3.59*** (2.36)	3.98** (1.91)	3.49** (2.12)	—	2.82** (1.62)
SEX	-3.09** (1.27)	-3.23** (1.37)	-4.10** (1.61)	-2.90** (1.32)	-3.92** (1.45)	-6.46** (1.78)	-3.99** (1.12)
Other	n.s.	AUTO -2.80** (1.08)	STOCK 3.03** (1.27)	STOCK 2.55** (1.06) GPA -0.023** (0.011) SJOB 2.91** (1.34)	STOCK 3.33** (1.16) GPA -0.031** (0.012) AUTO -3.12** (1.17)	n.s.	GPA -0.018** (0.008) STOCK 2.34** (0.886)
CONSTANT	7.19	7.26	8.96	6.52	12.59		9.92
$\bar{R}^2$	0.12	0.15	0.12	0.14	0.26	0.27	0.25

Notes:
*Standard errors in brackets.
**Significant at p ≤ 0.05.
***Significant at p ≤ 0.10.
n.s. = Not significant at p < 0.05 (two-tailed).
In week 6, CONTROL did not enter estimating equation with any discernible effect.
Definitions of Variables:
[1]Dependent Variable: Risk, defined as:

$$\text{var(portfolio return)} = \sum_i a_i^2 \text{ var}(x_i) + \sum_i^i \sum_j^j a_i a_j \text{ cov}(x_i, x_j)$$

Where x_i is return on stock i and a_i is the proportion of portfolio held in that stock.

[2]Explanatory Variables:

AVERS: risk aversion; sum of scores on Kogan-Wallich chance-bet questionnaire.

CONTROL: Rotter locus-of-control questionnaire; first principal component extracted from factor analysis of responses to 23 questions; a high score indicates "internal" feeling of control.

SEX: dummy variable; female = 1, male = 0.

GPA: grade-point average.

SJOB: dummy variable; worked full time previous summer = 1; otherwise, 0.

STOCK: dummy variable; owns stocks now = 1; otherwise, 0.

AUTO dummy variable; owns automobile now = 1; otherwise, 0.

portfolio risk and between Machiavellianism and actual turnover velocity. Rotstein found evidence of "gambler's fallacy": there was a statistically significant tendency for subjects to sell stocks after their price had risen in the previous period, and to buy stocks after their price had fallen in the previous period, in the game simulation.

APPENDIX

Included in this appendix are the materials for the game simulation. The items are listed below.

1. Common-stock prices: mean, standard deviation, trend, beta, for weekly changes in price over a 36-week price "history" (Table 1A).
2. Stock-price histories for prior 36 weeks and six weeks of simulation.
3. Instructions to Subjects.
4. Background Information Questionnaire.
5. Chance Bets Questionnaire.
6. Internal-External Locus-of-Control Scale.
7. Sample Purchase/Sale Order Form.

Table 1A. Common Stock Prices: Mean, Standard Deviation, Trend, Beta of Weekly Changes in Price, Over a 36-Week Price "History"

| | *Weekly Percent Change in Price* | | | |
Stock	Mean	Standard Deviation	Trend[1]	Beta[2]
Alpha	-0.2	2.8	-0.4	0.41
Beta	0.2	6.0	0.6	0.23
Gamma	0.4	8.5	1.0	0.41
Delta	-0.01	3.0	-0.3	0.08
Epsilon	-0.4	5.4	0.0	0.39
Zeta	0.7	2.3	0.8	-0.07
Eta	-1.0	6.5	-0.7	0.57

Notes:
[1]Found from regression:
LOG (stock price$_t$) = Constant + TREND * t
[2]Found from regression:
Percent change in price$_j$ = Constant + beta * DOW$_j$

where j indexes the stock and DOW$_j$ is the average percent change in the prices of all stocks *except* stock j for a given week. Only the coefficient for alpha was statistically significant at 0.05.

Stock-Price Histories for Prior 36 Weeks and 6 Weeks of Simulation

WEEK	*ALPHA*	*BETA*	*GAMMA*	*DELTA*	*EPSILON*	*ZETA*	*ETA*
1	20 ½	19 ½	50	64 ⅜	88 ¼	18 ¼	32 ⅝
2	21	19 ⅝	50 ⅛	65 ⅞	85 ⅜	18	30 ¼
3	21 ⅜	19 ⅛	43 ⅞	65 ⅞	89 ¾	18 ¼	29 ⅞
4	21 ⅞	19 ⅜	44 ⅝	69 ⅝	84 ¼	18 ¼	32
5	22 ½	20 ⅝	42 ⅞	70 ¾	77 ⅞	18 ½	34 ¼
6	22 ⅞	22 ¼	42 ¼	69 ⅜	80 ¼	19 ⅜	32 ⅞
7	23 ⅝	22 ⅝	49 ⅛	67	78 ½	19 ⅝	30 ¾
8	23	22 ½	47 ⅞	66 ⅞	73 ⅝	19 ⅝	28
9	23 ¼	21 ¾	52 ⅞	67 ⅜	70 ⅝	18 ⅞	29
10	21 ⅞	19 ⅛	46 ½	66 ⅛	67 ⅜	19 ⅜	26
11	22 ½	20 ¼	45 ⅞	68 ⅝	63	19 ¼	26 ½
12	21 ⅜	18 ¾	47 ¾	66 ⅞	63 ½	19 ⅞	26 ¼
13	20 ¾	19 ¾	44 ½	63 ⅝	64 ⅜	20 ½	25 ¼
14	20 ⅛	22	41 ¼	62 ⅜	63 ⅞	20 ½	24 ⅞
15	19 ½	21 ¾	42 ½	63 ⅜	70	20	24 ½
16	19 ½	23 ½	46 ⅜	62 ⅜	69 ½	20 ⅛	22 ⅝
17	19 ⅝	24 ⅛	52 ⅞	60	76	20 ⅛	23 ⅜
18	19 ¼	26 ⅜	52 ⅜	57	76 ⅜	20 ⅝	25
19	19 ⅞	27 ⅜	56 ½	56 ⅞	78 ½	19 ¾	26
20	20 ¼	27 ½	62 ⅞	59 ⅜	83 ½	20 ⅜	26 ⅞
21	20 ½	27 ⅛	52 ¾	60 ⅝	85 ¼	20 ⅛	25 ½
22	20 ⅜	25 ⅝	52 ¼	63 ⅜	85 ¼	20 ½	23 ¾
23	19 ½	28	51	65 ⅛	90 ⅛	21 ⅝	22 ¾
24	19 ⅞	26 ⅝	55 ⅜	65 ¼	89 ⅛	22 ⅛	23 ⅜
25	19 ⅞	25 ⅞	53 ¼	64 ⅜	81 ¾	21 ⅝	23
26	19 ⅜	26	48 ½	63 ¼	79 ¾	21 ⅝	23 ¾
27	19 ½	24 ⅜	55	61	67 ¼	22 ¼	21 ¼
28	19 ½	22 ¾	63	59 ⅞	65 ⅝	22 ½	25
29	19 ¼	25	60	60 ⅛	73	23 ⅜	25 ½
30	20	24 ⅞	57 ⅝	56 ⅞	73 ¼	23 ¼	29 ⅜
31	19 ¾	22	62	59 ⅛	76 ⅞	23 ⅝	27 ⅞
32	19 ¼	21 ¾	68 ¼	59 ¾	77 ⅜	22 ⅞	27 ½
33	19 ½	22 ⅞	60 ¼	62 ⅛	72 ⅝	23	26 ⅜
34	20 ¼	22 ⅞	61 ¾	65 ¼	77 ⅜	23 ½	24 ¾
35	20 ⅝	22 ⅝	61	64 ⅛	77	23 ¼	25 ⅜
36	19 ¼	21	57 ¼	64 ⅛	78	23 ⅝	23 ⅛
	(Game Simulation—Price Revealed After Purchase/Sale Decision)						
1	20 ⅞	23 ¼	46 ⅜	65 ⅜	83 ⅜	24 ⅛	24 ⅝
2	21 ¼	23 ⅝	48 ⅛	66 ⅝	95 ¼	24 ½	23 ⅝
3	21 ⅝	24 ⅝	56 ½	65	91 ¼	25	25 ½
4	21 ⅞	24 ⅝	45 ½	63 ½	89 ⅜	24	25 ⅜
5	21 ⅛	24 ⅝	38 ¾	61 ⅞	96 ⅞	23 ¾	27
6	21 ¼	24 ¼	37 ⅛	60	104	23 ¾	25 ⅞

INSTRUCTIONS TO SUBJECTS

Thank you for agreeing to take part in an experimental stock-market research study. We want to find out how well people can buy and sell stocks for the maximum profit, using only information about the price movements of the stocks. Everything in this experiment is exactly as it is in a real buying and selling situation, except that the month and year the data cover are not revealed, so that you do not know whether the market as a whole is going up, down, or sideways. We tell you only that the period of research data is sometime during the last eleven years. And, of course, you do not use real money.

Your task is to buy, sell, or hold stocks and cash in such a way as to come out with the most money at the end of the experiment.

First, look at the stock-price history sheet. It shows recent information on the seven stocks which you can buy or sell. These stocks were chosen so that none had stock splits, stock dividends, or other unrevealed changes. We have included the cash dividends in the price itself, as if all dividends were immediately reinvested, so you can ignore price changes due to dividends being paid out.

The prices you see are closing prices on the dates given. The dates themselves have been adjusted for Saturdays, Sundays, and holidays so you cannot tell which year it was from the dates.

You will have $10,000 in cash to start with. You may buy stocks with any part of that sum that you wish, and you can hold any part of it in cash for as long as you like. *But you may not borrow money at any time.* You will earn interest at 5 percent per annum on any cash balance. Credit for interest will be given week by week, though it will not be calculated until after you have completed the experiment. (Interest on $10,000 over ten weeks of the experiment would be about $100). To simplify the bookkeeping there will be a flat 1 percent charge on each transaction for brokerage and taxes, no matter whether you buy or sell one share or a hundred.

You should keep a running record of your financial position on the current financial position sheet. *Do your best to avoid errors in arithmetic.*

After you have had time to place your first orders for your purchases and sales on the purchase/sale order form, this form will be collected.

Then, closing prices for the next Friday will be shown you, and you can consider your investment position. Again, indicate your purchase and sale orders on the purchase/sale order form for week 2, and hand the form in.

This process will be repeated for several weekly periods. At the end of the experiment, you can total up your assets in stocks and cash and determine how well you did.

You will only be playing against the stock market, of course, and none of you is affected by what anyone else does. Also, none of your transactions can be big enough to affect the market price.

To repeat, you do not know whether you are in a period of a rising or a falling stock market. The prices of a handful of stocks, such as those on the stock-price history sheet, would be a very unreliable index to how the market as a whole is doing, and whether you are in a bull or bear market. Just try to make as much money as you can by smart investing.

Good luck!

BACKGROUND INFORMATION

Subject's Number _____

Age _____ Sex _____ Grade-Point Average _____

Are you currently working at a paying part-time term job? _____

Did you work full time last summer? _____

During the past two years, have you at any time owned stocks, bonds, mutual funds, or other securities? _____

Do you have a savings account? _____

Do you own an automobile? _____

Do you now own any stocks? _____

What is your religious persuasion? _____

In what city did you grow up? _____ In what state? _____

Is your father's income:
    Less than $20,000 a year _____
    Between $20,000 and $40,000 _____
    More than $40,000 _____

CHANCE BETS QUESTIONNAIRE

Below you are shown pairs of dice bets that vary in terms of the chances of winning and losing and the amounts of money that can be won or lost. *For each pair*, please choose the bet that you would prefer to play. Indicate your decision by making a check in the box under the bet that you would prefer to play. Consider each pair separately—do not let your decision in one case influence your decision in another.

The chances of winning and losing are written as fractions. Thus, 1/4 means 1 chance in 4, 1/2 means 1 chance in 2, etc.

1. ☐   1/9 to win $1.20   vs.   ☐   1/2 to win $0.60
        8/9 to lose $0.15   1/2 to win $0.60

2. ☐   3/4 to win $0.10   vs.   ☐   1/9 to win $4.80
        1/4 to lose $0.30   8/9 to lose $0.60

3. ☐   1/9 to win $1.20   vs.   ☐   1/9 to win $4.80
        8/9 to lose $0.15   8/9 to lose $0.60

4. ☐   1/4 to lose $0.90   vs.   ☐   1/2 to win $0.30
        3/4 to win $0.30   1/2 to win $0.30

5. ☐   1/4 to win $1.80   vs.   ☐   1/9 to win $4.80
        3/4 to lose $0.60   8/9 to lose $0.60

6. ☐   1/9 to win $1.20   vs.   ☐   1/4 to win $1.80
        8/9 to win $0.15   3/4 to lose $0.60

INTERNAL-EXTERNAL LOCUS-OF-CONTROL SCALE

This is a questionnaire to find out the way in which certain important events in our society affect different people. Each item consists of a pair of alternatives lettered a or b. Please select the one statement of each pair (*and only one*) which you more strongly believe to be the case as far as you're concerned. Be sure to select the one you actually *believe* to be more true, rather than the one you think you should choose or the one you would like to be true. This is a measure of personal belief. Obviously, there are no right or wrong answers.

Your answers to the items on this questionnaire are to be recorded on a separate answer sheet.

The items themselves follow these instructions. Please answer these items carefully, but do not spend too much time on any one item. Be sure to find an answer for *every* choice. Find the number of the item on the answer sheet and put a check mark beside the statement, either a or b, which you believe is more true.

In some instances, you may find that you believe both statements or neither one. In such cases, be sure to select the *one* you most strongly believe to be the case as far as you're concerned. Also, try to respond to each item *independently* when making your choice; do not be influenced by your previous choices.

* 1. a) Children get into trouble because their parents punish them too much.
   b) The trouble with most children nowadays is that their parents are too easy with them.

2. a) Many of the unhappy things in people's lives are partly due to bad luck.
   b) People's misfortunes result from the mistakes they make.

3. a) One of the major reasons why we have wars is because people don't take enough interest in politics.
   b) There will always be wars, no matter how hard people try to prevent them.

4. a) In the long run, people get the respect they deserve in this world.
   b) Unfortunately, an individual's worth often passes unrecognized, no matter how hard he tries.

5. a) The idea that teachers are unfair to students is nonsense.
   b) Most students don't realize the extent to which their grades are influenced by accidental happenings.

6. a) Without the right breaks one cannot be an effective leader.
   b) Capable people who fail to become leaders have not taken advantage of their opportunities.

7. a) No matter how hard you try, some people just don't like you.
   b) People who can't get others to like them don't understand how to get along with others.

* 8. a) Heredity plays the major role in determining one's personality.
   b) It is one's experiences in life which determine what one is like.

9. a) I have often found that what is going to happen will happen.
   b) Trusting to fate has never turned out as well for me as making a decision to take a definite course of action.

10. a) In the case of a well-prepared student, there is rarely if ever such a thing as an unfair test.
    b) Many times exam questions tend to be so unrelated to course work that studying is really useless.

11. a) Becoming a success is a matter of hard work; luck has little or nothing to do with it.
    b) Getting a good job depends mainly on being in the right place at the right time.

12. a) The average citizen can have an influence in government decisions.
    b) This world is run by the few people in power, and there is not much the little guy can do about it.

13. a) When I make plans, I am almost certain that I can make them work.
    b) It is not always wise to plan too far ahead, because many things turn out to be a matter of good or bad fortune anyhow.

*14. a) There are certain people who are just no good.
     b) There is some good in everybody.

15. a) In my case, getting what I want has little or nothing to do with luck.
    b) Many times we might just as well decide what to do by flipping a coin.

16. a) Who gets to be the boss often depends on who was lucky enough to be in the right place first.
    b) Getting people to do the right thing depends upon ability; luck has little or nothing to do with it.

17. a) As far as world affairs are concerned, most of us are the victims of forces we can neither understand nor control.
    b) By taking an active part in political and social affairs, the people can control world events.

18. a) Most people don't realize the extent to which their lives are controlled by accidental happenings.
    b) There really is no such thing as "luck."

*19. a) One should always be willing to admit mistakes.
     b) It is usually best to cover up one's mistakes.

20. a) It is hard to know whether or not a person really likes you.
    b) How many friends you have depends on how nice a person you are.

21. a) In the long run the bad things that happen to us are balanced by the good ones.
    b) Most misfortunes are the result of lack of ability, ignorance, laziness, or all three.

22. a) With enough effort we can wipe out political corruption.
    b) It is difficult for people to have much control over the things politicians do in office.

23. a) Sometimes I can't understand how teachers arrive at the grades they give.
    b) There is a direct connection between how hard I study and the grades I get.

*24. a) A good leader expects people to decide for themselves what they should do.
    b) A good leader makes it clear to everybody what their jobs are.

25. a) Many times I feel that I have little influence over the things that happen to me.
    b) It is impossible for me to believe that chance or luck plays an important role in my life.

26. a) People are lonely because they don't try to be friendly.
    b) There's not much use in trying too hard to please people; if they like you, they like you.

*27. a) There is too much emphasis on athletics in high school.
    b) Team sports are an excellent way to build character.

28. a) What happens to me is my own doing.
    b) Sometimes I feel that I don't have enough control over the direction my life is taking.

29. a) Most of the time I can't understand why politicians behave the way they do.
    b) In the long run the people are responsible for bad government on a national as well as a local level.

---

*Filler

Source: Julian B. Rotter, "Generalized Expectancies for Internal Versus External Control of Reinforcement," in Julian B. Rotter, June E. Chance, and E. Jerry Phares, eds., *Applications of a Social Learning Theory of Personality* (New York: Holt, Rinehart & Winston, 1972), pp. 260–295.

WEEK 37
PURCHASE/SALE ORDER

Subject Number: _____

Purchase:

_____ shares of _____ at _____

_____ shares of _____ at _____

_____ shares of _____ at _____

_____ shares of _____ at _____

_____ shares of _____ at _____

_____ shares of _____ at _____

_____ shares of _____ at _____

Sell:

_____ shares of _____ at _____

_____ shares of _____ at _____

_____ shares of _____ at _____

_____ shares of _____ at _____

_____ shares of _____ at _____

_____ shares of _____ at _____

_____ shares of _____ at _____

ACKNOWLEDGMENTS

Partial support for preparation of this paper was provided to the second author by: Technion Vice-President's Fund, Ford Foundation (through the Israel Foundations Trustees), the Social Science Research Council, and the Sloan Grant for Applied Microeconomic Research, Princeton University. For helpful comments and criticism, we wish to thank (and absolve) Richard Spies, Burton Malkiel, and Jonas Prager. An earlier version of this paper was presented at the European Finance Association meeting, Jerusalem, September 1982 and earlier analyses of data developed with this method were presented to the Brown Bag Lunch at the University of Illinois College of Commerce, May, 1965.

NOTES

1. For example, let two investors, Al and Ben, have different subjective rates of time preference—10 percent for Al, 5 percent for Ben. In a smoothly working capital market, Al will borrow from Ben. Such loans increase Al's current consumption, thus reducing his subjective interest rate, and lower Ben's current consumption, raising his. This process will continue until their rates of time preference are equal; economic reasoning claims that if the rates do not equalize, individual utility is not maximal. See Maital (1982: Chapter 3), and Fisher (1907, 1911).

2. Persistent differences between perceptions and reality imply, claim Barro and Fischer (1976, p. 163), the need for "a theory of systematic mistakes"; the concept of systematic mistakes, they claim, is virtually a contradiction in terms.

3. Personal communication.

4. Mishkin (1981) has shown that not all participants in a market need to be rational in order for the market to be efficient; in some cases, it is sufficient for a single market participant to possess full information and act upon it in order for market prices to reflect that information accurately.

5. Personal communication.

6. Cf. a typical *Wall Street Journal* headline (Monday, August 13, 1984): "Year's Worst Performing Stocks Rebound to Lead the August Rally."

Market overreaction to news has been well known for decades. A little pamphlet published in 1917 (Guyon) and a favorite with Wall Street brokers cautions, in a section titled "The Menace of News": "If tomorrow morning's newspapers should announce the death of the President or the failure of the great corner house or the complete destruction of Gary, Indiana, it is more than likely that stocks sold on the news would bring the lowest prices of the day, for the very good reason that each seller would be competing with thousands of other sellers who would have learned the news at the same time.... From a speculative standpoint it is better to be deaf and blind than to permit your market operations to be influenced by what you hear and read." (See the section below on dependency.)

7. The empirical evidence linking locus of control and risk-taking is not clear-cut. McInish (1982) found that "externals chose more risky portfolios," while McInish (1980), in a replication of the game simulation described in the appendix, found that "*internals* chose more than externals." Higbee and Streufert (1969) found that internals (were) less risky than externals in "economic risk." In a military context, Higbee (1972) found that internals made quantitatively *more* military decisions; however, the proportion of those decisions that were risky did not differ significantly between internals and externals.

8. Famous studies by Asch (1948) and Hochbaum (1954) have demonstrated empirically the close link between "group members' self-confidence and their reaction to group pressures to uniformity."

9. " 'Sell Flash' Causes 27-Point Drop in Dow Jones Index," read a headline some

years ago. A single investment advisor, Joseph Granville, had advised subscribers to his market letter to sell immediately. The following day, the market was swamped with sell orders. A majority of investors may have disputed Granville's prediction of a market drop but enough of them felt that *others* believed Granville to generate a self-fulfilling prophecy.

10.   For studies linking personality and market behavior, see Baker (1971) and Lupfer (1970); Bart (1978) and Bart and Masse (1981) show how investors differ in degrees of optimism and in expectations. See also Gilad, Kaish, and Loeb (1985) and Gilad, Loeb and Kaish (1984) for a different, more specific eclectic theory of behavior.

11.   CONTROL was computed by means of factor analysis, a statistical method useful for grouping a large number of intercorrelated variables into a much smaller number of "factors." The first step involves calculation of a correlation matrix, giving correlation coefficients for each variable and all other variables. The factor-analysis algorithm then determines one or more linear combinations of the variables—known as underlying factors—that are in some sense best correlated with those variables. Correlations between variables and factors are known as factor loadings. These factor loadings are used in the following manner. If variable x has a 0.01 correlation with factor 1 and a 0.69 correlation with factor 2, then it is said to be most heavily loaded on factor 2. Variables that are in fact heavily loaded on factor 2 together define the nature of that factor. Factor analysis also generates a useful summary statistic: the fraction of the "general variance" in the set of variables accounted for by each separate factor, and all the factors taken together.

To compute CONTROL, three principal components were extracted from responses to 23 of the 29-item questionnaire (six items were fillers) by factor analysis (Varimax rotation). The first factor accounted for 54 percent of the common variance. Loadings were high on only two items, 13 and 15. Item 13 asked subjects to choose between (a) and (b):

(a)   When I make plans, I am almost certain that I can make them work.
(b)   It is not always wise to plan too far ahead because many things turn out to be a matter of good or bad fortune anyhow.

Item 15 required a choice between:

(a)   In my case, getting what I want has little or nothing to do with luck.
(b)   Many times we might just as well decide what to do by flipping a coin.

The variable we called CONTROL was defined as:

$$\text{CONTROL} = 0.19z_{13} + 0.43\ z_{15}$$

where the z's are z-scores of responses to questions 13 and 15, with the choice of item (a) scored as 1.0, otherwise, zero. Factor loadings on other items were less than 0.15.

12.   This is the precise opposite of the so-called technical view which contends that "if the price of a stock rose yesterday it is more likely to rise today" (Malkiel, 1975, p. 120).

REFERENCES

Asch, S. E., "The Doctrines of Suggestion, Prestige and Social Psychology," *Psychological Review*, 55 (1948), 150–77.
Baker, William G., "Personality Correlates of Stock Market Speculation," *Dissertation Abstracts International*, 31 (1971), 4376.
Barro, R. and S. Fischer, "Recent Developments in Monetary Theory," *Journal of Monetary Economics*, 2 (1976), 133–167.

Bart, J. T., "The nature of the Conflict between Transactors' Expectations of Capital Gain," *Journal of Finance*, 33 (1978), 1095–1107.

Bart, J. T., and I. J. Masse, "Divergence of Opinion and Risk," *Journal of Financial and Quantitative Analysis*, 16 (1981), 23–24.

Blanchard, O., and M. Watson, "Bubbles, Rational Expectations and Financial Markets." Working Paper, Harvard Institute for Economic Research, January 1982.

Blumstein, Michael, "Rapid Reactions on Wall St. Magnify Impact of News," *The New York Times*, (March 13, 1984), D1.

Brealey, R. A., and S. D. Hodges, "Portfolio Selection in a Dynamic and Uncertain World," *Financial Analysts Journal*, 29 (1973), 50–65.

Brealey, R. A., and S. D. Hodges, "Playing with Portfolios," *Journal of Finance*, 30 (1975).

Brealey, R. A., and S. Myers, *Principles of Corporate Finance*. New York: McGraw-Hill, 1981.

Cass, D., and K. Shell, "Do Sunspots Matter?" *Journal of Political Economy*, 91 (1983), 193–227.

Chamberlin, E. H., *The Theory of Monopolistic Competition*, 8th ed. Cambridge, MA: Harvard University Press, 1962.

Christie, R., and F. L. Seis, *Studies of Machiavellianism*. New York: Academic Press, 1970.

Cootner, P., ed., *The Random Character of Stock Prices*. Cambridge, MA: M.I.T. Press, 1964.

Copeland, B. L., Jr., "Do Stock Prices Move Too Much to be Justified by Subsequent Changes in Dividends? Comment," *American Economic Review*, 73 (1983), 234–235.

Cross, F., "The Behavior of Stock Prices on Fridays and Mondays," *Financial Analysts Journal*, 29 (1973), 67–69.

De Bondt, W., and R. Thaler, "Does the Stock Market Overreact to New Information?" Cornell University, Graduate School of Management, Ithaca, NY, 1984.

Dreman, D. N., *Psychology and the Stock Market*. New York: Amacom, 1977.

Dreman, D. N., *Contrarian Investment Strategy: The Psychology of Stock Market Success*. New York: Random House, 1979.

Edney, J., "The Nuts Game: A Concise Commons Dilemma Analog," *Environmental Psychology & Nonverbal Behavior*, 3 (1979), 252–254.

Fama, E., "The Behavior of Stock Market Prices," *Journal of Business*, (January 1965).

Fisher, I., *The Rate of Interest*. London: Macmillan, 1907.

Fisher, I., "The Impatience Theory of Interest," *Scientia*, 9 (1911), 380–401.

Friedland, N., S. Maital, and A. Rutenberg, "A Simulation Study of Income Tax Evasion," *Journal of Public Economics*, 10 (1978), 107–116.

Friedman, D., G. W. Harrison, and J. W. Salmon, "The Informational Efficiency of Experimental Asset Markets," *Journal of Political Economy*, 92 (1984).

Gilad, B., S. Kaish, and P. D. Loeb, "Cognitive Dissonance in Management Decision Making," *Journal of Behavioral Economics*, (Winter, 1985).

Gilad, B., P. D. Loeb, and S. Kaish, "The Analytics of the Nonadaptive Side of Rational Behavior," presented to the American Economics Association annual meeting, Dallas, Dec. 28–31, 1984.

Grossman, S., and J. E. Stiglitz, "On the Impossibility of Informationally Efficient Markets," *American Economic Review*, 70 (1980), 393–408.

Gultekin, M., and N. B. Gultekin, "Stock Market Seasonality: International Evidence." Working Paper #17–83, University of Pennsylvania, Wharton School, 1983.

Guyon, Don, *One-Way Pockets: The Book of Books on Wall Street Speculation*. Burlington, VT: Fraser Publishing Co., 1965. (Originally published by Capstone Publishing Co., New York, 1917).

Harstad, R. M., and Michael Marrese, "Implementation of Mechanism by Processes: Public Good Allocation Experiments," *Journal of Economic Behavior and Organization*, 2 (1981), 129–151.

Higbee, K. L., "Perceived Control and Military Riskiness," *Perceptual and Motor Skills*, 34 (1972), 95–100.

Higbee, K. L., and S. Streufert, "Perceived Control and Riskiness," *Psychonomic Science*, 17 (1969), 105–106.

Hochbaum, G., "The relation between Group Members' Self-confidence and the Reaction to Group Pressures to Uniformity," *American Sociological Review*, 19 (1954), 678–688.

Institutional Investor, "Who Spotted Last Year's Hottest Stocks?" (April 1983).

Kahneman, D., and A. Tversky, "Prospect Theory: An Analysis of Decision under Risk," *Econometrica*, 47 (1979), 263–291.

Kahneman, D., P. Slovic, and A. Tversky, *Judgment under Uncertainty: Heuristics and Biases*. New York: Cambridge University Press, 1981.

Kogan, N., and M. A. Wallace, *Risk Taking: A Study of in Cognition & Personality*. New York: Holt, Rinehart & Winston, 1964.

Lintner, J., "The Valuation and Risk Assets and the Selection of Risky Investments in Stock Portofolios and Capital Budgets," *Review of Economics & Statistics*, 47 (1965), 13–37.

Lupfer, M., "The Effects of Risk-taking Tendencies and Incentive Conditions on the Performance of Investment Groups," *Journal of Social Psychology*, 82 (1970), 135–36.

Maital, S., *Minds, Markets & Money: Psychological Foundations of Economic Behavior*. New York: Basic Books, 1982.

Maital, Shlomo, and Sharone L. Maital, *Economic Games People Play*. New York: Basic Books, 1984.

Maital, Sharone L., and Shlomo Maital, "Psychology & Economics," in Marc L. Bornstein, ed., *Psychology and its Allied Disciplines*. Hillsdale, NJ: Erlbaum, 1985 (3 volumes).

Malkiel, B., *A Random Walk Down Wall Street*, rev. ed. New York: Norton, 1975.

Mandelbrot, B., "Forecasts of Future Prices, Unbiased Markets, and Martingale Models," *Journal of Business: Security Prices, A Supplement*, 39 (1966), 242–255.

Markowitz, H., *Portfolio Selection: Efficient Diversification of Investments*. New Haven, CT: Yale University Press, 1971.

McInish, T. H., "A Game-Simulation of Stock Market Behavior: An Extension," *Simulation and Games*, 11 (1980), 477–484.

McInish, T. H., "Individual Investors and Risk-taking," *Journal of Economic Psychology*, 2 (1982), 125–136.

McInish, T. H., and R. K. Srivastav, "Ex-ante Expectations and Portfolio Selection," *The Financial Review*, 19 (1984), 84–96.

Mishkin, F., "Are Market Forecasts Rational?" *American Economic Review*, 71 (1981), 295–306.

Modigliani, F., and R. Cohn, "Inflation, Rational Valuation and the Market," *Financial Analysts Journal*, (March/April 1979), 24–44.

Nicholson, F., "Price Ratios in Relation to Investment Results," *Financial Analysts Journal*, (July–August 1968).

Osborne, M. F. M., "Periodic Structure in the Brownian Motion of Stock Prices," *Operations Research*, 10 (1962), 345–379.

Rim, Y., "Machiavellianism and Decisions Involving Risk," *British Journal of Social and Clinical Psychology*, 5 (1966), 30–36.

Rotstein, A., "Psychological Factors and Market Efficiency in a Stock Market Game and in Actual Investment." MSc. thesis, Faculty of Industrial Engineering & Management, Technion, Haifa, Israel, 1982.

Rotter, J., "Generalized Expectancies for Internal versus External Control of Reinforcement," *Psychological Monographs*, 80, 1 (1966).

Rotter, J., J. E. Chance, and E. R. Phares, *Applications of a Social Learning Theory*. New York: Holt Rinehart & Winston, 1972.

Rozeff, M. S., and W. R. Kinney, Jr., "Capital Market Seasonality: The Case of Stock Returns," *Journal of Financial Economics*, 3 (1976), 379–402.

Samuelson, P., *Foundations of Economic Analysis*. New York: Atheneum, 1965a.

Samuelson, P., "Proof That Properly Anticipated Prices Fluctuate Randomly," *Industrial Management Review*, 6 (1965b), 41–50.

Schachter, S., and D. Hood, "Psychological Aggregate Variables and the Stock Market," Presented to the First Annual Conference on Behavioral Economics, Society for Advancement of Behavioral Economics, Princeton, NJ, May 28–30, 1984.

Schachter, S., D. C. Hood, P. B. Andreassen, and W. Gerin, "Aggregate Variables in Psychology and Economics: Dependence & the Stock Market," in B. Gilad and S. Kaish, eds., *Handbook of Behavioral Economics*. Greenwich, CT: JAI Press, 1986.

Sharpe, W., "Capital Asset Prices: A Theory of Market Equilibrium under Conditions of Risk," *Journal of Finance*, 19 (1964), 425–442.

Shiller, R., "Do Stock Prices Move Too Much to be Justified by Subsequent Changes in Dividends?" *American Economic Review*, 71 (1981), 421–436.

Shubik, M., "A Note on a Simulated Stock Market," American Institute of Decision Sciences, (November 1969).

Siegel, S., and L. E. Fouraker, *Bargaining and Group Decision-making*. New York: McGraw-Hill, 1960.

Skinner, B. F., "Superstition in the Pigeon,"*Journal of Experimental Psychology*, 38 (1948), 168–172.

Slovic, P., "Psychological Study of Human Judgment: Implications for Investment Decision Making," *Journal of Finance*, 27 (1972), 779–799.

Smith, V., ed., *Research in Experimental Economics*. Greenwich, CT: JAI Press, 1978.

Stoner, J. A. F., "A Comparison of Individual and Group Decisions Involving Risk." Master's thesis, School of Industrial Management, M.I.T., 1961.

Tirole, J., "On the Possibility of Speculation under Rational Expectations," *Econometrica*, (September 1982).

Tobin, J., "Liquidity Preference as Behavior Toward Risk," *Review of Economic Studies*, (1958).

BIOGRAPHICAL SKETCHES OF THE CONTRIBUTORS

Paul B. Andreassen completed his doctoral work at Columbia University in 1983 and since then has been at Harvard University in the Department of Psychology. His current work on the stock market concerns the effects of price information on trading strategies, the causes and effects of news, and the detectability of non-randomness in price changes. His other research interests include consumer behavior, intrinsic motivation, and social categorization.

Richard M. Coughlin is Associate Professor and Chair of the Department of Sociology at the University of New Mexico. He received his B.A. from Harvard University and an M.A. and Ph.D. in sociology from the University of California at Berkeley. He has published articles in comparative social policy and economic psychology, and is the author of *Ideology, Public Opinion, and Welfare Policy*. His research interests include the welfare state, public opinion, social movements, and the impact of technology on society.

Randall K. Filer is Associate Professor of Economics at Hunter College of the City University of New York. He received his Ph.D. from Princeton University and taught at Brandeis University from 1978 to 1986. His research, focusing on earnings, includes published work on affective human capital, male-female wage differences, effort supply and the earnings of artists. Research currently in progress deals with occupational segregation and comparable worth, as well as the determinants of retirement age.

William Gerin is an Assistant Professor at Barnard College, Columbia University, in the Department of Psychology. His latest research investigates the effects of past trends on predictions about the future. He is particularly concerned with the effects of new information on trends.

Sebastian Green is a Research Fellow at the Centre for Business Strategy at the London Business School. He was formerly an Economic Advisor at the Price Commission and the National Consumer Council. He also taught at the University of the South Pacific in Fiji. His research interests relate to the application of economic anthropology to business practice in industrial economies, in particular, the relationship between corporate culture and business strategy.

Donald C. Hood has been a Professor in the Psychology Department of Columbia University since 1969, and Vice President for Arts and Sciences since 1982. He received his Ph.D. from Brown University in 1969. His primary interest is in basic visual mechanisms, including mechanisms of adaptation, color vision and retinal disease. He and Stanley Schachter have been collaborating on studies of the stock market since the mid-1970s.

F. Thomas Juster is Director of the Institute for Social Research and Professor of Economics at the University of Michigan. He received his B.S. in education from Rutgers University and his Ph.D. in economics from Columbia University. He is a senior advisor for the Brookings Panel on Economic Activity. He is the author of numerous chapters in *Time, Goods and Well-Being* (ISR Press, 1985), which he co-edited with Frank Stafford. His current research concerns the theory, measurement, and distribution of well-being. In addition, he has a chapter entitled "The Role of Microdata in the Production of Economic Knowledge," forthcoming in *Advances in Behavioral Economics* (Green and Kagel, eds.).

Stanley Kaish is Professor of Economics and Associate Dean for Management Studies at Rutgers University, Newark. He has a B.A. from Cornell University, an M.B.A. from Wharton, and a Ph.D. from New York University. He is co-founder and Chairman of the Board of Trustees of the Society for the Advancement of Behavioral Economics (SABE). He pursues his interest in business cycles as a Research Associate at the Center for International Business Cycle Research at Columbia University.

Philip A. Klein is Professor of Economics at the Pennsylvania State University and Research Associate at the Center for International Business Cycle Research at Columbia University. He has written extensively in the field of business cycles, most recently as co-author with Geoffrey H. Moore of *Monitoring Growth Cycles in Market-Oriented Countries* (1985). A past president of the Association for Evolutionary Economics, he has been writing in the field of institutional economics for more than thirty years. He is an Adjunct Scholar of the American Enterprise Institute and has been a consultant for the European Economic Community, the Organization for Economic Cooperation and Development, and the United Nations.

Howard Kunreuther is Professor of Decision Sciences and Public Policy and Management, as well as Director of the Wharton Risk and Decision Processes Center at the University of Pennsylvania. He has a B.A. from Bates College and a Ph.D. degree in economics from the Massachusetts Institute of Technology. His current research is concerned with the role of insurance compensation, incentive mechanisms, and regulation as policy tools for dealing with technological and natural hazards. He is author of numerous scientific papers concerned with risk and policy analysis, decision processes and protection against low-probability/high-consequence events, including *Insuring and Managing Risks: From Seveso to Bhopal and Beyond* (with Paul Kleindorfer) (Springer-Verlag, 1986).

Alan Lewis is a lecturer in Research Methods in the School of Humanities and Social Sciences at the University of Bath, England. His major publications include *The Psychology of Taxation* (1982) and, with A. Furnham, *The Economic Mind* (1986), both published by St. Martin's Press, New York. His major research interests are economic psychology and methodology in economics and psychology.

Shlomo Maital is Chairperson of the Economics Department at The Technion-Israel Institute of Technology. He is author of *Minds, Markets and Money* (Basic Books, 1982) and, with his wife Sharone, *Economic Games People Play* (Basic Books, 1984). His is a founder and board member of the Society for the Advancement of Behavioral Economics (SABE), a board member of the Israel Economics Association, and he organized an international conference on economics and psychology held in Israel in 1986. His research interests include all aspects of economic psychology.

John J. McGonagle, Jr., an attorney-at-law and economist, is Vice President of The Helicon Group, Ltd. in Allentown, Pennsylvania. He earned his B.A. in economics at Yale University, his J.D. at the University of Michigan Law School, his LL.M. in urban legal studies at the National Law Center of George Washington University, and his M.A. in business and applied economics at The Wharton School of the University of Pennsylvania. He is co-author of *Master Guide to Control of Corporations— With Checklists, Forms and Agreements* (Institute for Business Planning, Englewood Cliffs, 1985). He is currently co-authoring books on competitive intelligence and on disinformation. He is Vice President and a member of the Board of Trustees of the Society for the Advancement of Behavioral Economics (SABE). In addition, he served with President Reagan's Private Sector Survey on Cost Control (the Grace Commission).

Stanley Schachter is Robert Johnson Niven Professor of Social Psychology at Columbia University. He has worked extensively on problems in the areas of group psychology, addictive and appetitive behavior, and the psychological correlates of investment behavior.

Julian Simon teaches Business Administration at the University of Maryland in College Park. His main interest is the economics of population, currently with special attention to immigration. He has just finished a book on effort as an economic variable (forthcoming, Basil Blackwell).

Martin C. Spechler is Associate Professor of Economics and of West European Studies at Indiana University (Indianapolis and Bloomington campuses). A graduate of the interdisciplinary Social Studies program at Harvard University, he also holds M.A. and Ph.D. degrees in economics from Harvard University. He has taught at Harvard and the Hebrew University of Jerusalem. His research deals with Soviet economic history and West European political economy.

Burkhard Strümpel is a Professor of Economics at the Free University of Berlin and Director of the Center for the Socioeconomics of Work. He received his Ph.D. from the University of Cologne in 1962, and has taught economics at the University of Michigan.

Ephraim Yuchtman-Yaar is a Professor of Sociology and Dean of the School of the Social Sciences at the University of Tel Aviv. He holds a Ph.D. from the University of Michigan and he has taught there, as well as at Columbia University and the University of California, Riverside.